Advancing East Asian Regionalism

Since the 1997 crisis developments in East Asian regionalism have progressed rapidly. The end of the Asian miracle called into question not only the capacity of regional states to meet the needs of their peoples, but also challenged the viability of regional organisations, such as ASEAN, to adapt and respond to the changing circumstances. ASEAN and its three northern partners of China, Japan and South Korea recognised the urgent need to accelerate cooperation in response to the 1997 crisis and a host of other threats, as well as to maximise the opportunities arising from the growing interdependence of regional countries. Although there is much promise in this integration process, significant obstacles remain in its realisation.

Advancing East Asian Regionalism looks at the ways in which ASEAN has expanded since the crisis, particularly the creation of ASEAN+3, and evaluates the potential of East Asia to come together in a regional formation – one capable of representing the region as a whole while protecting the well-being of its peoples, markets and states. It couples case study material on regionalism, institutions, and sectoral cooperation, with theoretical debates on regionalisation, to push our understanding of East Asian regionalism forward. Providing up-to-date perspectives from regional policymakers, scholars and other experts actively involved in the issues of regionalism, this book will be essential reading to those studying Asian politics, regional studies and international relations.

Melissa G. Curley is a Lecturer in the School of Political Science and International Studies, University of Queensland.

Nicholas Thomas is a Research Assistant Professor and Coordinator of the China–ASEAN Project at the Centre of Asian Studies, University of Hong Kong.

Politics in Asia series
Formerly edited by Michael Leifer, London School of Economics

Advancing East Asian Regionalism

Edited by Melissa G. Curley and Nicholas Thomas

Routledge
Taylor & Francis Group

LONDON AND NEW YORK

First published 2007
by Routledge
2 Park Square, Milton Park, Abingdon, Oxon OX14 4RN

Simultaneously published in the USA and Canada
by Routledge
270 Madison Ave., New York, NY 10016

Routledge is an imprint of the Taylor & Francis Group, an informa business

Transferred to Digital Printing 2009

© 2007 Editorial selection, © Melissa G. Curley and Nicholas Thomas, ©
the contributors

Typeset in Baskerville by Taylor & Francis Books

British Library Cataloguing in Publication Data
A catalogue record for this book is available from the British Library

Library of Congress Cataloging in Publication Data
A catalog record for this title has been requested

ISBN10: 0–415–34909–5 (hbk)
ISBN10: 0–415–54687–7 (pbk
ISBN10: 0–203–02330–7 (ebk)

ISBN13: 978–0–415–34909–3 (hbk)
ISBN13: 978–0–415–54687–4 (pbk)
ISBN13: 978–0–203–02330–3 (ebk)

CONTENTS

ILLUSTRATIONS

Tables

LIST OF CONTRIBUTORS

Amitav Acharya is Deputy Director and Head of Research at the Institute of Defence and Strategic Studies, Nanyang Technological University, Singapore, where he also holds a professorship. His areas of specialisation include regionalism and multilateralism (a current focus being a study of international cooperation on counter-terrorism), Asian regional security and international relations theory.

Aileen San Pablo-Baviera is Professor and Dean of the Asian Center, University of the Philippines. She was a member of the East Asian Vision Group, and currently participates in the East Asian Studies Network and the Network of East Asian Think Tanks.

Shaun Breslin is Professor of Politics and International Studies at the University of Warwick, UK, and Honorary Professorial Fellow, Centre for European Studies, Renmin University, Beijing. He is also co-editor of *The Pacific Review*.

Jenina Joy Chavez is a Senior Associate with Focus on the Global South and heads its Philippines Programme. Her research and work focus include the role of international financial institutions in Asia, particularly the transition economies and in privatisation, the various forms of Asian regionalism, poverty, and trade and development policy.

Melissa G. Curley is a Lecturer in International Relations in the Department of Political Science and International Studies at the University of Queensland, Australia. Her research and teaching interests include NGO–state relations, non-traditional and human security, development and international relations, and the East Asian security environment.

Evelyn Goh is University Lecturer in International Relations at St Anne's College, University of Oxford. She is the author of *Constructing the US Rapprochement with China, 1961–1974: From Red Menace to Tacit Ally*, New York: Cambridge University Press, 2005; and she has also published on contemporary US foreign policy; US–China relations and Asia-Pacific security; Southeast Asian strategic relations with the US and China; and environmental security in East Asia.

Natasha Hamilton-Hart is an Assistant Professor in the Southeast Asian Studies Programme, National University of Singapore. She received her Ph.D. from Cornell University in 1999. Her research focuses on Southeast Asia and includes work on regional capital flows, corporate restructuring and administrative reform.

Shin-wha Lee is Professor and Chair of the Department of Political Science and International Relations, Korea University. Her previous positions include Special Advisor to the 'Rwandan Independent Inquiry' appointed by UN Secretary General Kofi Annan (1999) and Chair's Advisor of ASEAN+3 East Asian Vision Group (2000–2001). Currently, she also serves as the senior research fellow at Ilmin International Relations Institute, Korea University.

Hyun Myoung Jae recently received her Masters degree from the Department of Political Science and International Relations, Korea University. Her research interests include regional security issues and regionalism in Northeast Asia.

Miranda A. Schreurs is an Associate Professor in the Department of Government and Politics, University of Maryland, and specialises in environmental politics and policy making in Japan, East Asia, and Europe. She teaches courses on Japanese and East Asian politics, German and European politics, environmental policy and law, and qualitative research methodology.

Akihiko Tanaka is Professor of International Politics and is currently the Director of the Institute of Oriental Culture, University of Tokyo. Professor Tanaka's specialties include theories of international politics, contemporary international relations in East Asia, and issues in Japan–US relations.

Nicholas Thomas is a Research Assistant Professor and Coordinator of the China–ASEAN Project at the Centre of Asian Studies, University of Hong Kong. His current research interests and publications focus on East Asian regionalism and non-traditional security.

PREFACE

In 1999, the heads of government from the 10 Southeast Asian nations joined with the leaders of China, Japan and South Korea to explore ways to build cooperation and capacity throughout East Asia. This remarkable meeting drew together a number of different efforts by regional governments and began the process of exploring how they could be integrated into a cohesive whole. In less than a decade, the region has gone from acknowledging the need for better cooperation, to actively forging deeper ties across an ever increasing range of areas. While the efficacy of these ties is still being reviewed, they have served to crystallise a vision of an East Asian Community; one that unites Northeast Asia with Southeast Asia.

This book had its genesis in the Fifth China-ASEAN Roundtable on 'Regionalism and Community Building in East Asia', held in 2002 at the Centre of Asian Studies, University of Hong Kong. This series of Roundtables were designed to draw together scholars from regional research institutes in China and Southeast Asia to discuss issues of common scholarly concern, including economic, socio-cultural, and political and strategic developments in rapidly expanding China–Southeast Asian relations. The 2002 Roundtable adopted a broader perspective, one that reflected the dynamism present in region-building projects across the East Asian region, bringing together scholars and policy makers from think tanks as well as regional organisations.

Since then, the original Roundtable presenters have been joined by a number of other scholars with regional specialties in different areas, in an ongoing attempt to reflect the scope of the academic and policy debates on these issues now taking place. Over the last three years the authors have worked to understand and incorporate these changes into their respective chapters. With the East Asian Summit a reality, now is an appropriate time to present their analysis and try to understand what the implications are for the future of Asia.

Melissa G. Curley
Nicholas Thomas
July 2006
Hong Kong

ACKNOWLEDGEMENTS

This volume is the result of a long-running project that has explored various aspects of East Asian regionalism. The editors would like to thank all the participants of the Fifth China-ASEAN Roundtable for their intellectual input to the conference, which assisted in developing the book's thematic content, as well as those contributors who joined the project after the Roundtable.

Without the necessary funding the Roundtable as well as a number of subsequent events would not have been possible. The editors would like to extend a special note of thanks to the Japan Foundation Asia Center for their support of the Fifth Roundtable, as well as a number of other projects undertaken by the Centre of Asian Studies over the years.

Many thanks to Ms May Yip from the Centre of Asian Studies' administration staff for her invaluable assistance in preparing the manuscript for publication. The editors are also very grateful to Stephanie Rodgers and Helen Baker at RoutledgeCurzon for their editorial guidance and support.

ABBREVIATIONS

ABF	Asian Bond Fund
ABMI	Asian Bond Market Initiative
AFAS	ASEAN Framework Agreement on Services
ACT	ASEAN Consultation to Solve Trade and Investment Issues
ADB	Asian Development Bank
AEC	ASEAN Economic Community
AEC	Asian Environmental Conference
AEM	ASEAN Economic Ministers Meeting
AFSR	ASEAN Food Security Reserve
AFTA	ASEAN Free Trade Area
AIA	ASEAN Investment Area
AIC	ASEAN Industrial Cooperation scheme
AIDS	Acquired Immunodeficiency Syndrome
AIJV	ASEAN Industrial Joint Venture scheme
AIP	ASEAN Industrial Project
AMCA	ASEAN Ministers Responsible for Culture and Arts
AMF	Asian Monetary Fund
AMM	ASEAN Ministerial Meeting
APA	ASEAN People's Assembly
APEC	Asia–Pacific Economic Cooperation
ARCBC	ASEAN Regional Centre for Biodiversity Conservation
ARF	ASEAN Regional Forum
ASA	Association of Southeast Asia
ASC	ASEAN Security Community
ASCC	ASEAN Socio-Cultural Community
ASEAN	Association of Southeast Asian Nations
ASEAN+1	Association of Southeast Asian Nations + either China, Japan or South Korea
ASEAN+3	Association of Southeast Asian Nations + China, Japan and South Korea
ASEAN-4	Cambodia, Laos, Myanmar and Vietnam
ASEAN-6	Brunei Darussalam, Indonesia, Malaysia, the Philippines, Singapore and Thailand

ASEM	Asia–Europe Meeting
ASPAC	Asia–and Pacific Council
BBC	(ASEAN) Brand to Brand Complementation scheme
BIMP–EAGA	Brunei–Indonesia–Malaysia–Philippines East Asian Growth Area
BSA	Bilateral Swap Arrangement
CAFO	Conference of Asian Foundations and Organisations
CAFTA	China-ASEAN Free Trade Agreement
CBMs	Confidence-Building Measures
CECA	Closer Economic Cooperation Agreement
CEP	Comprehensive Economic Partnership
CEPT	Comprehensive Effective Preferential Tariff scheme
CER	Closer Economic Relationship (Australia and New Zealand)
CITES	Convention on International Trade in Endangered Species
CLMV	Cambodia, Laos, Myanmar and Vietnam
CMI	Chiang Mai Initiative
COBSEA	Coordinating Body on the Seas of East Asia
CSCA	Conference on Security and Cooperation in Asia
CSCAP	Council for Security Cooperation in the Asia–Pacific
CSCE	Conference on Security and Cooperation in Europe
CSOs	Civil Society Organisations
DPRK	Democratic People's Republic of Korea (North Korea)
DSM	Dispute Settlement Mechanism
EABC	East Asian Business Council
EAC	East Asian Community
EAEC	East Asian Economic Caucus
EAFTA	East Asian Free Trade Agreement
EASI	East Asia Strategic Initiative
EAEG	East Asia–Economic Group
EANET	Acid Deposition Monitoring Network in East Asia
EAS	East Asia Summit
EASG	East Asian Study Group
EAVG	East Asian Vision Group
ECOASIA	Environmental Congress for Asia and the Pacific
EHP	Early Harvest Programme
EMEAP	Executives' Meeting of East Asia–Pacific central banks
EU	European Union
EVSL	Early Voluntary Sectoral Liberalisation
FEALAC	Forum for East Asia and Latin America Cooperation
FTA	Free Trade Agreement
GATT	General Agreement on Tariffs and Trade
GDP	Gross Domestic Product
GEF	Global Environment Facility
GMS	Greater Mekong Subregion
GNP	Gross National Product

GONGO	Government–Organised Non–Governmental Organisation
GSP	Generalised System of Preferences
HLTF	High-level Task Force
HIV	Human Immunodeficiency Virus
ICSEA	Impacts Center Southeast Asia
IFAW	International Fund for Animal Welfare
IFI	International Financial Institution
IGBP	International Geosphere–Biosphere Programme
IMF	International Monetary Fund
IMO	International Maritime Organisation
INGO	International Non-Governmental Organisation
IUCN	World Conservation Union
JBIC	Japan Bank for International Cooperation
JCIE	Japan Centre of International Exchange
JSEPA	Japan–Singapore Economic Agreement for a New Age Partnership
LTP	Long-range Trans boundary Air Pollution
MAPHILINDO	MAlaya, the PHILippines, INDOnesia
Mercosur	Mercado Común del Sur [The Southern Cone Common Market (South America)]
MFA	Multifibre Arrangement
MFG	Manila Framework Group
MFN	Most Favoured Nation
MITI	Ministry of International Trade and Industry (Japan)
MOF	Ministry of Finance (Japan)
MRAs	Mutual Recognition Arrangements
MRM	Mutual Reassurance Measures
NAFTA	North American Free Trade Agreement
NATO	North Atlantic Treaty Organisation
NEACD	Northeast Asia Cooperation Dialogue
NEACEC	Northeast Asian Conference on Environmental Cooperation
NEASED	Northeast Asia Security Dialogue
NEASPEC	Northeast Asia–Subregional Programme on Environmental Cooperation
NEAT	Network of East Asian Think Tanks
NGO	Non-Governmental Organisation
NIEs	Newly Industralised Economies
NOAA	National Oceanographic and Atmospheric Association
NOWPAP	Northwest Pacific Action Plan
NPCSD	North Pacific Cooperative Security Dialogue
NTM	Non-Tariff Measures
OAS	Organisation of American States
ODA	Official Development Assistance
OSCE	Organisation for Security and Cooperation in Europe
PABSEC	Parliamentary Association of Black Sea Economic Cooperation

PAFTAD	Pacific Trade and Development Conference
PBEC	Pacific Basin Economic Council
PD	Preventive Diplomacy
PDSAP	Peace Disarmament Symbiosis in the Asia–Pacific
PECC	Pacific Economic Cooperation Conference
PEMSEA	Partnerships in Environmental Management for the Seas of East Asia
PMC	(ASEAN) Post–Ministerial Conference
PRC	Peoples Republic of China
QDR	Quadrennial Defence Review
ROK	Republic of Korea (South Korea)
RTIA	Regional Trade and Investment Area
RWESA	Rivers Watch East and Southeast
SADC	Southern African Development Community
SAP	Strategic Action Programme
SARS	Severe Acute Respiratory Syndrome
SCO	Shanghai Cooperation Organisation
SEACEN	Southeast Asian Central Banks
SEANWFZ	Southeast Asian Nuclear Weapon Free Zone
SEARIN	Southeast Asia Rivers Network
SEATO	Southeast Asian Treaty Organisation
SEAUEMA	Southeast Asia Urban Environmental Management Applications
SEPA	State Environmental Protection Agency
SIJORI	Singapore–Johor–Riau growth triangle
SME	Small and Medium-sized Enterprises
SOM	Senior Officials Meeting
START	SysTem for Analysis, Research, and Training
TAC	Treaty of Amity and Cooperation
TEMM	Trilateral Environmental Ministers Meeting
TRADP	Tumen River Area Development Programme
TRCOG	Trilateral Coordination and Overnight Group
UN	United Nations
UNDP	United Nations Development Programme
UNEP	United Nations Environment Programme
UNESCAP	United Nations Economic and Social Commission for Asia and the Pacific
UNESCO	United Nations Educational, Scientific and Cultural Organisation
UNU	United Nations University
WHO	World Health Organisation
WTO	World Trade Organisation

1 Advancing East Asian regionalism

An introduction

Melissa G. Curley and Nicholas Thomas

Introduction

In the post-1997 period there has been an explosion of region-building efforts across East Asia, most significantly within the grouping of Northeast and Southeast Asian countries known as ASEAN+3. As these countries have sought closer collaboration they have been presented with a singularly difficult challenge, namely how to integrate their disparate states with different needs, capacity levels and worldviews into a coherent whole. This challenge has been made more difficult by the dearth of models – outside that of the European Union – that might suggest appropriate strategies for member states to follow. Efforts to grapple with this problem have thus become a topic of intense interest for policy-makers and scholars alike.

Events surrounding the fallout from the 1997 Asian financial crisis spurred these countries into forging deeper linkages across an increasingly wide range of areas. Although these links were initially due to a desire to avoid a repetition of the 1997 Asian crisis, the lessons learnt, as well as the need to combat emergent new challenges, have seen East Asian states increasingly act in a more collective manner. Regional states now collaborate on areas as disparate as environmental concerns, public health threats, disaster relief and human resource development. The expanding ASEAN+3 dialogues in these and other areas are testimony to the commitment and resources being channelled into forging a more coherent grouping of East Asian states.

Yet, at the same time as they are working together, regional states remain divided by security concerns and historical animosities. Memories of Japanese military actions in World War II remain a major stumbling block to regional unity. China's strategic intentions towards the region are also dogged by controversy, despite the best efforts of PRC foreign ministry officials to present a benevolent face. In Southeast Asia, intra-regional tensions are also quite visible. Singapore's disputes with Malaysia over water supply and territory, historical and cultural stresses between Thailand and Cambodia, or the impact of illegal Indonesian migrant labourers in Malaysia, are but a few of the many issues that afflict regional diplomacy. All of this is compounded by the lack of a trusted state able to provide clear vision and leadership to mediate between different national interests and regional ambitions.

So where is the region going? How can it advance if it is also being held back? It is the aim of this book to attempt to capture and analyse the impact of these diverse pressures, particularly with respect to the efforts to build an East Asian Community (EAC). This introduction proceeds by first presenting the key themes and questions of the book. An outline of the evolution of an EAC is presented in the second section. This section reviews the process of regionalism and regional institutionalisation to date, in order to provide background and insight into the current opportunities and challenges and facing the development of an EAC. The 'three pillars' of a future EAC, covering security, economic and socio-cultural issues called for at the 2003 Bali Summit, are then examined in the third section. Regional cooperation and developments to date within each pillar are reviewed, before an assessment of the way forward is presented. It is intended that an understanding of these pressures will lead to an informed evaluation of the current community-building project as well as also provide directions for future scholarship.

Key Themes

The process of advancing East Asian regionalism is a complex undertaking. In 2003 the region's leaders announced their intent to create an EAC, supported by three pillars: a security pillar, an economic pillar and a socio-cultural pillar. This undertaking raised a set of three, interrelated questions: (1) Can we talk feasibly about the emergence of an 'East Asian Community'? (2) How sustainable are these institutional changes? (3) What will be the role of regional societies and their peoples in the process? If this process of East Asian regionalisation is to be understood then these questions need to be addressed, relative to the framework policy-makers are simultaneously attempting to construct.

Is an 'East Asian Community' emerging?

To begin to answer this question it is necessary to go back to 1999, when the region's leaders agreed to establish an eminent persons group, the East Asian Vision Group (EAVG), to find a collective way forward for the region. In their final report, 'Towards an East Asian Community', the members of the EAVG noted that they aimed to 'offer a common vision for East Asia that reflects the rapidly changing regional and global environment, as well as provide direction for future cooperation among East Asian nations'.[1] In other words, the report offered not only a final destination, an EAC, but recommendations as to how to get there.

Even before the EAVG had completed its work, another policy group – the East Asian Study Group (EASG) – was formed. Unlike the EAVG, this new group comprised senior officials who were tasked with making the earlier recommendations a reality. The EASG was less optimistic than its predecessor, focusing more on 'concrete measures' that could be implemented in the eventual build-up of regional integrative efforts, than on a grand vision of an EAC. However, within three years the 'grand vision' of an EAC was being called for by the region's policy-makers in a bid 'to consolidate and enhance the achievements of ASEAN as a dynamic, resilient cohesive regional association'.[2] At the conclusion of the 2003 Bali Summit, the member states of ASEAN+3 called for the establishment of an EAC. This remarkable policy shift, from the time of the EAVG report to the outcome from the Bali Summit, demonstrates the growing intent of East Asian states to develop a region-wide community.

Despite these efforts, an ongoing debate – that has largely stayed outside of the public realm – has taken place as to whether or not this new body takes the form of a community, bound together in a set of formal overlapping institutions with some pooling of sovereignty, or a community where a coalition of national interests come together to meet specific functional objectives in a regional context without a loss of sovereignty.[3] Although the 2003 decision to declare the body a community may have attempted to end this debate, it still remains to be seen whether new community-building endeavours will be deeper and more institutionalised than the region has seen in the past, or simply constitute another layer of meetings.

Even if such a community were to form, what shape would it take? In the next chapter Shaun Breslin addresses this question with respect to the theoretical debates on new regionalism, in general, and the impact of the EU model, in particular. As Breslin notes, an important consideration is that the EU is but one example of regionalisation and, in terms of its adherence to a highly formalised institutional structure, is the exception rather than the rule. Hence, while integration projects in East Asia have yielded certain commonalities with the EU – such as regional policy communities, deeper forms of regional functional cooperation, as well as the emergence of a cognitive region – the cumulative effect of the region's unique history, culture and social values will all act to mould the 'final' outcome.

Akihiko Tanaka continues this line of questioning in Chapter 3 through a historical narrative of the development of regional institutions in East Asia. Tanaka suggests that although the push to hold an East Asian Summit is a linear development from earlier region-building initiatives, it is an open-ended development focusing on functional cooperation rather than being driven by a singular vision. Part of the reason for this is that the process, post-1997, has been shaped by exogenous forces largely beyond the control of regional states. While the output from the EAVG and EASG reports may hold an endogenous key to taming these forces and allowing a regional vision to be articulated, Tanaka argues that the political leadership to do so still remains absent. Unless this leadership and vision emerges, the ability of the regional states to transform ASEAN+3 into something more substantive is questionable.

How sustainable are these institutional changes?

Even considering the current moves towards deeper integration, the question as to how much these changes will be able to contribute to the creation of a sustainable EAC must be considered. ASEAN has been repeatedly criticised for announcing plans that fail to be realised, while other institutions such as APEC and ASEM have invited criticism for lacking the capacity to achieve coherent, binding agreements on specific policy issues. Those who are broadly sympathetic to the view that intra-regional and trans-regional dialogue is necessary and beneficial in the long term appear to have more limited expectations of the 'concrete' outcomes that are achievable within their respective frameworks. The tension between the desire for concrete policy outcomes, versus recognition of the dialogues' own intangible value, is not easily reconciled and is discussed in a number of the following chapters.

One of the reasons for the lack of capacity, in both ASEAN and ASEAN+3, is the uneven commitment of East Asian states to regional-building projects. One such example of this can be seen in Northeast Asia, where there is a comparatively low level of indigenous regionalisation especially with respect to security concerns. This issue is explored in Chapter 4 by Shin-wha Lee and Hyun Myoung Jae. As they note, Northeast Asia has suffered from a legacy of mistrust stemming from both World War II activities and Cold War divisions, which have left it without any type of institutional mechanism for intra-regional collaboration. This is despite an increase in tensions between the Northeast Asian states since the 1990s. The authors argue that the creation of such a mechanism would help stabilise the subregion, even as other institutions such as the ASEAN Regional Forum continue their work.

Another important issue in the development of a sustainable regional community is the question of membership. If a community is to be formed then it implies a membership base sufficient to meet the aims of the regional organisation. This attempt to create such a community in East Asia – as in other parts of the world – has based its membership criteria in geographical terms. Yet, East Asia is a crossroads for many extra-regional interests. Other regional institutions and a number of non-East-Asian states have a longstanding involvement in regional affairs and organisations. Any attempt to create a community will need to take into account these extra-regional actors, but how such an open-region model will mesh with a closed-member community is yet to be fully articulated.

The role of such actors is a particular concern in terms of the regionalisation of security concerns. Evelyn Goh and Amitav Acharya in Chapter 5 are sceptical about the prospects of ASEAN+3's ability to supersede the institutional role currently being played by the ARF. They suggest that East Asian regionalism requires the central participation of the United States as it remains the key security player in the region. Given this, while the ARF may not be the only viable option for a regional security dialogue, in the absence of other alternatives, they argue that the ARF remains the reasonable choice in which to channel efforts into developing security regionalism.

Beyond the issue of capacity, the need for a community to create binding decision-making mechanisms, so as to ground its legitimacy at the regional level rather than remaining an amalgam of state interests, will challenge existing regional norms of non-interference and the maintenance of state sovereignty. The enduring commitment to these norms suggests that organisational development – from being an informal, consensus-driven 'talk shop' to something more institutionalised and binding – remains problematic in the prevailing political culture of East Asia.

In Chapter 6, Natasha Hamilton-Hart analyses the development of regional financial architecture and its relationship to the domestic policies of East Asian states. This chapter demonstrates how financial cooperation can bring clear benefits to regional states but that – despite these benefits – it is arguable whether such cooperation can spawn deeper integration in other areas. Hamilton-Hart notes that even though there is uneven domestic capacity to support deeper financial integration, the relative openness of many regional economies should provide the basis for common links to be forged across regional economies. However, while this cooperation should assist in the development of deeper integration in trade and monetary sectors, it is unlikely to have a significant impact on political or social regionalisation endeavours.

Nicholas Thomas explores the issue of institutional development further with respect to regional economic and financial policy in Chapter 7. Thomas reviews the development of regional economic and financial mechanisms within the ASEAN+3 zone since 1997. Particular attention is paid to the creation of regional economic trade and investment zones, such as the ASEAN Free Trade Area and the ASEAN Investment Area in the development of regional policy communities. This chapter also examines the challenges that accelerated economic regionalism will provoke, as well as its future potential to contribute to an EAC.

What will be the role of regional societies and their peoples?

If a regional community is to be forged then it has to go beyond the policy elites to include the peoples, societies and nations of East Asia. East Asian states have recognised that there can be greater efficiencies in cooperation, either in terms of resource allocation or in terms of outcomes. As such, it is reasonable to infer that there are further benefits to be derived from the inclusion of private sector corporations and civil society organisations in community-building initiatives.

Jenina Chavez in Chapter 8 provides a critical assessment of ASEAN's attempts at regional cooperation from 'below', particularly the role of subregional groups and the need to involve social organisations in the creation of a regional identity. This chapter looks at the different modes of regional cooperation practised in ASEAN and examines their contribution to the development of an ASEAN identity. It argues that ASEAN's preoccupation with trade and investment liberalisation limits the scope and possibility for deeper cooperation in other areas. Chavez draws upon the case of the Brunei–Indonesia–Malaysia–Philippines East Asian Growth Area (BIMP–EAGA) to highlight how a narrow focus on economic concerns constrains community building even among areas that supposedly have deeper cultural and historical roots. Ultimately Chavez argues that broader, socially driven engagement is crucial if ASEAN is to maximise both its potential and that held by larger East Asian region-building projects.

Of course, different states have different ways of engaging their private or social sectors. In some regional states – such as Japan, the Philippines, South Korea, or Thailand – there are well-established ties between the state, the private sector and civil society. In others – such as China, Laos, or Myanmar – there are relatively few such ties. Other states in the region tend to fall between these two groups in terms of non-state actors' participation. Given that the region is a reflection of its members' policies, the activities of these groups at the regional level will likewise be unevenly distributed.

In Chapter 9 Melissa Curley explores the potential emergence of a regional civil society in East Asia and the implications this has for the development of an EAC. This chapter addresses the extent to which a 'regional' civil society can be identified, or whether what is being witnessed are the efforts of domestic social organisations operating on a transnational level. This is an important question and one that has ramifications for virtually all other areas tied to the community-building effort. Curley notes that, despite the existence of quite inclusive and participatory regional civil society fora, the nature of civil organisations operating at the regional level is diverse, spanning a spectrum of actors that range from liberal-democratic groups with broad agendas, to often conservative government-organised non-governmental organisations whose agenda is closely linked to that of the state.

Nevertheless, since the inception of ASEAN+3, benefits from the participation of non-state actors operating at the regional level have already begun to flow. During repeated bouts of haze in Southeast Asia, environmental groups in different countries have worked together to develop regional strategies for combating the root causes. In early 2003, the involvement of civil society groups, universities and private laboratories was critical in stemming the SARS outbreak. In addition, coordination between civil society groups in the ASEAN+3 and ASEM countries is helping to build grassroots-based epistemic communities at the regional and pan-regional levels.

The development of regional cooperation on environmental issues is the subject of Chapter 10 by Miranda Schreurs. The author considers the impact development has had on the environment in many East Asian states as they have sought to modernise their economies and societies. The chapter also reviews factors which are now influencing them to work together to redress the balance by constructing regional mechanisms for transnational environmental cooperation. This chapter contrasts the efforts being undertaken in East Asia with those being developed in Europe, highlighting in particular the unwillingness of many East Asian states to submit to legally binding environmental accords. However, Schreurs suggests that one way for East Asia to overcome these challenges is through the involvement of international organisations and global treaty regimes, which would not only bolster the regional capacity to address environmental problems, but also allow states to participate in associated regulatory regimes without there being a direct tie to regional issues.

In advancing East Asian regionalisation there are any number of factors which suggest that an East Asian Community is unlikely, yet significant resources are being directed into programmes designed to foster deeper and wider integration between the ASEAN+3 states. In the concluding chapter Aileen Baviera proposes that despite these factors an EAC is still a viable option for regional states to pursue. Considering exogenous and endogenous issues, as well as the important questions of institutionalisation and identity, Baviera argues that with ASEAN as the main mechanism for regionalisation programmes, East Asian states have a venue through which to address their common concerns. In doing so, states can collaborate in a neutral space that serves to diminish historical tensions and cultural animosities while building confidence to seek greater cooperative benefits through mutual agreement of the norms and rules of community processes. Although this does not mean that the creation of an EAC is guaranteed, it suggests there is merit in exploring the idea further.

Evolution of an East Asian Community

Within the region, Southeast Asian countries have been the most active in forming associations. The goal of ASEAN was always to act as a representative body for all Southeast Asian states. In this respect ASEAN has always adhered to a regionally inclusive ideology, despite the divisiveness of geopolitics. The Northeast Asian countries were more restricted by Cold War divisions and historical legacies. It is therefore not surprising that many of the forerunners to ASEAN+3 were centred on Southeast Asian states.

There were three precursors to ASEAN in Southeast Asia. The Association of Southeast Asia (ASA) – comprising Malaya, the Philippines and Thailand – was established in 1961 to further economic and cultural cooperation between the three countries.

> Original proposals called for a common shipping line or shipping pool and joint development programs in the fields of industry, agriculture, education and health. Concrete results were direct railway communications between Malaya and Thailand and a number of immigration and customs agreements.[4]

However, the dispute over Sabah between Malaya and the Philippines flared up in late 1962 and essentially paralysed the grouping until 1966.[5] Progress towards developing closer ties began again in 1966 with a new set of projects. The following year Singapore and Indonesia were both invited to join the group. However, Indonesia expressed a preference for a new organisation for the five members. Originally called the Southeast Asian Association for Regional Cooperation, this new group was to become what is now known as the Association of Southeast Asian Nations.

At the same time as the ASA, Malaya and the Philippines joined with Indonesia to create MAPHILINDO in 1963.[6] Although regional events were to make this a short-lived grouping, it is notable for being the first regional association that Indonesia joined and the fact that a number of ASEAN principles –

particularly the commitment to consultation as well as the agreement not to use 'collective defence to serve the interests of any among the big powers' – were developed by MAPHILINDO.[7] The demise of the grouping (a result of the Philippines' dispute with Malaysia over Sabah as well as the Indonesian policy of *Konfrontasi*) still carries salutory lessons for ASEAN regarding the fragility of regional associations when sources of intra-regional tensions are not addressed.

The third organisation that preceded the formation of ASEAN was ASPAC – the Asia and Pacific Council. Unlike the two earlier groups, this organisation (formed in 1966) went beyond Southeast Asia to join Australia, Japan, South Korea, Taiwan with the Philippines and Thailand. Like the ASA and MAPHILINDO, ASPAC was designed to promote closer economic relations between its member states. However, it was also designed to act as an anti-communist alliance: 'ASPAC failed to become self-sustaining due to the refusal of other regional countries to become members and the shift in foreign policy away from Taiwan to recognising the People's Republic of China.'[8]

In each of these three cases, lessons learnt from both successes and failures fed into the formation of ASEAN, which became a reality on 8 August 1967.

Association of Southeast Asian Nations (ASEAN)

The establishment of ASEAN by Indonesia, Malaysia, the Philippines, Singapore, and Thailand was an attempt by like-minded states to stabilise the region, economically as well as in terms of national and regional security. As Malaysia's then Deputy Prime Minister Tun Abdul Razak stated, 'we are all conscious of our responsibility to shape our common destiny to prevent external intervention and interference'.[9]

If the first phase of ASEAN's development (1967–75) was fraught with uncertainties,[10] the second phase (1975–early 1990s) began to show the organisation's growing regional and international status. Internally, the Declaration of the ASEAN Concord (1976) and the signing of the Treaty of Amity and Cooperation (1976) provided the group with a much clearer sense of purpose and direction. The Agreement on ASEAN Preferential Trading Arrangements (1977) was another important step forward, creating the framework for the organisation to begin to realise its long-stated ambition of increased economic stability and security.[11] The establishment of the Secretariat and an accompanying structural reorganisation also served to further entrench the regional focus of the group.[12]

Externally, ASEAN's involvement in the Vietnam/Cambodia settlement process throughout the 1980s bolstered the group's international reputation, even as disagreements over the function of the group continued internally.[13] The need to develop common responses to particular issues also helped to strengthen intra-regional coordination mechanisms. As Narine wrote, 'as [ASEAN's] members discovered the benefits of being part of a larger organization it grew considerably as an institution. The habits of cooperation and consultation became an ingrained part of the ASEAN process.'[14]

During these two phases ASEAN member representatives and officials arguably developed a common set of norms and principles by which the organisation functioned. Collectively expressed as 'the ASEAN Way', these behavioural norms are based on the twinned Malay concepts of *musyawarah* and *muafakat* (dialogue and consensus), primarily within an informal, non-binding milieu.[15] They are reinforced by an adherence to the principle of non-interference in other states' affairs, premised on a commitment to state sovereignty. While the latter two points are pre-existing aspects of international law, they assume a far greater significance when employed by ASEAN, even as global norms and expectations surrounding these two points have changed.

As ASEAN has grown since the 1990s, it is important not to see these values and norms as static, but as evolving as the organisation developed new directions and interests. Since mid-1997, ASEAN states engaged in a debate over whether or not to reform the organisation's policy of non-intervention. This began in July 1997 with then Malaysian Deputy Prime Minister Anwar Ibrahim's call for a policy of 'constructive intervention', which would allow for closer ties between the newer, less economically developed states and their wealthier counterparts, as well as for the creation of more robust political and legal institutions and a concomitant development of civil society.[16] However, the onset of the Asian financial crisis highlighted the negative aspect of closer interdependence, where domestic problems in one country could – if left unchecked – spread to affect other regional states.

It was largely because of these pressures that 'constructive intervention' was superseded a year later by then Thai Foreign Minister Surin Pitsuwan's call for 'flexible engagement'. This proposal went well beyond earlier reform ideas to allow regional states to comment directly upon and collectively discuss issues in member countries where there was an identified interest to do so. As Surin Pitsuwan stated:

> [I]f domestic events in one member's territory impact adversely on another member's internal affairs, not to mention regional peace and prosperity, much can be said in favour of ASEAN members playing a more proactive role. Consequently, it is obvious that ASEAN countries have an overriding interest in the internal affairs of its fellow members and may, on occasion, find it necessary to 'recommend' a certain course of action on specific issues that affect us all, directly or indirectly.[17]

Although most of the other ASEAN foreign ministers did not support the concept of 'flexible engagement', it did lead to the notion of 'enhanced interaction' whereby member states could comment upon (but not directly intervene in) internal events in other ASEAN states. This new policy was soon tested with the arrest shortly thereafter of Anwar Ibrahim on charges of corruption. Malaysian responses to criticism from Indonesia and the Philippines, in particular, threatened to ferment the type of 'intraregional hostility . . . that ASEAN was created to prevent'.[18] While the tensions generated by Anwar Ibrahim's arrest gradually died down, the outbreak of violence in East Timor prompted a renewed questioning of ASEAN's non-interference policy.

The breakdown of law and order in East Timor in 1999 presented ASEAN with a particular challenge to its norm regime: namely, how far could the group and its individual members go in directly resolving the issue. One of the key lessons from the 1997 Asian crisis was that preventative cooperation – even in sensitive areas – produced more useful results. However, the violence in East Timor was more sensitive than any other problem ASEAN had so far confronted, primarily because it could have involved the intervention by ASEAN forces onto Indonesian territory. The precedent that such an action would have established was too confronting for many of the other, less developed countries to consider; especially Cambodia, which only joined the organisation four months prior to the violence erupting in East Timor.[19]

In the end it was left to the United Nations to lead the response to the violence and even though ASEAN states contributed to the international response it is a measure of the sensitivity of the issue that many of these delegations were limited to 'support personnel, medical, engineering security taskforces'.[20] In terms of changing institutional norms, what the East Timor case may signify is a willingness on the part of member states to defer more sensitive decisions to international bodies with the legitimate authority to enforce an outcome. If so, this decision may also indicate an awareness of the relative fragility of regional mechanisms and the need to proceed with caution rather than haste.

While it cannot be said that because of these challenges ASEAN has abandoned its principle of non-interference, it can be said that the acts which constitute non-interference have been progressively more narrowly defined, especially in the post-1999 period. This has allowed for closer policy coordination between regional states, while also allowing the states to continue to claim the ability to act independently. As ASEAN remains the core body for the advancement of East Asian regional architecture, the impact of this change in regional norms will be an important issue needing to be addressed.

Asia–Pacific Economic Cooperation (APEC)

The APEC group was formally proposed by Australia and held its first meeting in 1989 amid the uncertainties of the end of the Cold War. Although APEC began without a predefined agenda, the creation of an Asia–Pacific community – where free trade and investment between market economies with close economic links could flourish – was a common goal among the foundation members.[21] In its formation APEC drew upon the efforts of other groups such as the Pacific Basin Economic Council (PBEC) and the Pacific Economic Cooperation Council (PECC) as well as academic conferences such as the Pacific Trade and Development Conference (PAFTAD),[22] which continue to function alongside and intersect with its agenda.

APEC meetings were initially composed of trade and foreign ministers. The annual Leaders' Summit was introduced in 1993 when then US President Bill Clinton invited APEC leaders to the Seattle meeting. This precedent continued while annual meetings also gradually expanded to include other ministers with a trade or economic focus. APEC's membership has expanded gradually, though not without some dissatisfaction being expressed by existing members. Lincoln has argued that while APEC's expansion may have had a political logic, the lack of strong economic ties between the new members and East Asia diluted the focus on economic issues, such that reaching consensus on key areas became difficult, contributing further to the sense of institutional drift that began to set in around the time of the 1997 Asian crisis (see below).[23]

APEC's broad economic goal was to move towards 'open regionalism'. Members were to negotiate the reduction and elimination of barriers amongst themselves and then extend these benefits to other nations on a reciprocal basis.[24] Furthermore, the group would provide opportunities to facilitate trade and investment links. These goals were formally espoused in the 1994 Bogor Declaration, which committed member countries to strengthen the open multilateral trading system, enhance trade and liberalisation in the Asia–Pacific, and intensify Asia–Pacific development cooperation. The Declaration announced members' commitment to achieve the goal of free trade by 2010 for industrialised economies and developing economies by 2020.[25]

Dissatisfaction with APEC grew after the group's failure in 1997 to reach agreement over an early voluntary sectoral liberalisation programme. Japan, in particular, did not agree to the inclusion of fish and forestry products on the sector list, which, according to Lincoln, 'marked the end of activism in trying to accelerate trade liberalisation in APEC, which has led to a sense of drift in recent years'.[26] The events surrounding the 1997 Asian crisis, during which APEC was seen to do little to assist afflicted economies, and by the US preoccupation with the 'war on terror', have further exacerbated the perception that APEC's trade liberalisation agenda has floundered.[27] While Garnaut noted that APEC was not geared to play a major role in the financial crisis, he nevertheless argues 'it could have played a larger role in providing advice to the international organisations on recovery policy and strategy'.[28] The Leaders' Summit post-September 11 focused on global security issues, reflecting a US policy agenda, cementing the impression that APEC's free trade agenda has been lost.

Nevertheless, in broad terms, APEC can be seen as a success in a number of areas. The regular dialogues are recognised as beneficial to the region. While the industrialised economies have often complained of the slow nature of negotiations and that 'talk had triumphed over progress', the dialogue process is recognised as useful to government officials in developing economies by exposing officials to discussion on different issues. The Leaders' Summit is now seen as an important opportunity for member countries to gather together for bilateral talks to take place on the sidelines where they otherwise would not. Its failure to define the central concept of 'open regionalism' and the non-binding and voluntary process of negotiations are viewed as central reasons for the lack of progress on the free trade agenda.

However, APEC appears to have lost momentum alongside the rising interest in other regional groups – such as ASEAN+3 – that emerged following the 1997 crisis. The extent to which East Asian countries feel the need to 'solve their own problems' through such a mechanism, or indeed through dialogues and agreements such as the East Asian Summit or an East Asian Free Trade Agreement (EAFTA), can partly be attributed to the perception that APEC's agenda became too broad and was dominated by 'Western' interests. Indeed, it has been argued that discontent with APEC is a contributing factor for 'the emergence of narrower approaches to economic regionalism in Asia'.[29] While this may be the case, the continued engagement of APEC members in free trade initiatives beyond those within East Asia indicates that the group is still seen as retaining some degree of utility. The challenge will be how much utility it can maintain as increasing emphasis and resources are placed on the ASEAN+3 process.

ASEAN Regional Forum

The ASEAN Regional Forum (ARF) was established in July 1994 in response to a number of pressures for a consultative security mechanism in Asia. Its creation was in part a regional reaction to the end of the Cold War as well as a reflection of ASEAN's desire to continue its development of politico-security consultations following the successful outcome from the 1991 Paris Conference on Cambodia. Since the end of the Cold War there had been a number of calls for the creation of a regional security body. At the ASEAN Post-Ministerial Conference (PMC) in July 1990, then Australian Foreign Minister Gareth Evans suggested the formation of a Conference on Security and Cooperation in Asia (CSCA), 'along the lines of the Conference on Security and Cooperation in Europe (CSCE) established in Helsinki in 1975'.[30] This suggestion received support from non-Southeast Asian regional powers but was resisted by ASEAN members, wary of the implications for adopting the CSCE model, especially on the grounds that the CSCA might 'lead to a weakened Asian identity in the region and might force ASEAN to adopt European-style human rights, one of the central themes of the Helsinki Act'.[31] Nonetheless, the 1992 ASEAN Summit in Singapore called for the group to 'move towards a higher plane of political and economic cooperation to secure regional peace and prosperity'.[32]

While the first meeting of the ARF was a highly informal gathering primarily designed to 'make all the participants – especially China – "comfortable" with the process and the other states',[33] by the time of the second meeting, three workshops on confidence building, peacekeeping, and preventive diplomacy had been held between the ARF members and their dialogue partners, and a concept paper developing the structure of the Forum and the centrality of ASEAN and its related norms had been drafted.[34]

Importantly, the concept paper mapped out the evolution of the ARF, as its members developed their capacity to engage in regional security processes. This evolutionary process has three stages: 'Stage I: Promotion of Confidence-Building Measures [CBMs], Stage II: Development of Preventive Diplomacy [PD] Mechanisms, Stage III: Development of Conflict-Resolution Mechanisms'.[35] This gradual approach was adopted due to the perception that regional security processes were still quite 'young and fragile'.[36] Although these three stages of the ARF's development had support when the concept paper was first approved, realising their development has been problematic. As Caballero-Anthony observed, between the 1995 and 1997 meetings a plethora of CBMs emerged to support and strengthen the rationale and legitimacy of the ARF. However, attempts to move the Forum into the second stage have encountered resistance from some member countries concerned about the definition of preventive diplomacy and the reach of PD mechanisms into member states' affairs. Although the definitional question was resolved in March 1999, during a CSCAP Working Group meeting on CBMs on Preventive Diplomacy, its operationalisation still remains slow.[37]

Narine pointed out that the ARF is still a young organisation, with objectives designed to be realised over a longer term. Hence, it is difficult for the Forum to be 'fairly assessed for effectiveness and significance'.[38] Leifer also noted that the ARF was an 'embryonic, one-dimensional approach to regional security among states of considerable cultural and political diversity'.[39] However, it can equally be argued that in the period since its inception (1994–2005) a number of issue-based indicators have emerged from which a preliminary assessment can at least be made. An oft-cited successful indicator is the fact that since the creation of the ARF, there have been no major conflicts fought in East Asia. To a limited extent this is true. On the one hand, there has been no significant outbreak of interstate hostilities since the ARF was founded and, indeed, several former enemies (such as China and Vietnam) are now partners in developing CBMs. On the other hand, a technical state of war still exists on the Korean Peninsula and Japan and Russia are yet to reach a peace treaty from World War II, while other unresolved issues such as the sovereign control over the South China Sea and the China–Taiwan dispute still hold the potential to cause widespread region insecurity. So success here is relative.

One of the main negative indicators regarding the ARF is whether the pace of institutional reform will allow the Forum to develop as a regional security body, or if the relatively slow and uninstitutionalised nature of the ARF's evolution renders it less meaningful in a region where many new security challenges now threaten regional peace and prosperity. Issues such as the unresolved threat to regional stability generated by the repeated outbreaks of haze in Southeast Asia, the lack of a timely ARF response to the crisis in East Timor, or the absence of effective regional mechanisms to prevent narcotics trafficking and small-arms smuggling, could suggest a diminishing relevance. However, it is also necessary to consider that ARF members have addressed these issues via other international bodies as well as subregionally. In this latter area, the umbrella of the ARF acts as a venue to initiate, continue, or conclude negotiations becomes important.

To a certain extent both sets of indicators are dependent on assumptions relating to the appropriate role of the ARF in regional security affairs as well as the necessary speed of institutional change required for the ARF to remain relevant. The problem with either side of the debate is that there are no comparative models by which to compare the developments to date. Even where other security bodies do exist – such as the CSCE – the historical, economic, and cultural contexts of their security policy environment remain very different from that in the East Asian region. At the end of the day it is up to the members to validate the organisation by choosing to remain actively involved.

Given this, it is also possible to consider the success of the ARF in terms of its relevance to members' security needs. In other words, to what extent regional states are choosing to commit their resources to the ARF instead of other regional or international bodies. In taking the development of regional security forward – either via an evolved ARF or through the ASEAN Security Community (see below) – the question of how best to protect the regional community is one which the ARF will need to address.

Asia–Europe Meeting

The Asia–Europe Meeting (ASEM) dialogue represents another grouping that has played an important role in the development of an integrated East Asia. ASEM held its first summit meeting in Bangkok in March 1996 after France and Singapore made a proposal for an EU–Asia summit meeting in 1994. The rationale for ASEM followed the end of the Cold War on the premise that the relationship between the EU and Asia needed to be strengthened and modernised.[40] In an attempt not to duplicate the various bilateral and multilateral relationships that already existed between the founding members, ASEM was designed as an informal process involving dialogue, information sharing, and exchange of views, in principle on any aspect of common interest to the two regions. Its membership at the first summit included the then 10 members of the EU and 10 Asian countries: Brunei, China, Indonesia, Japan, South Korea, Malaysia, the Philippines, Singapore, Thailand, and Vietnam. This was the first time that Northeast Asian and Southeast Asian states had been brought together in a regional dialogue, beyond the then still limited activities of the ARF. This conjunction played an important role in building linkages between the two subregions, linkages that were later articulated as ASEAN+3.[41] In 2004 ASEM expanded its membership to include the 10 new EU member states as well as three Asian countries: Cambodia, Laos, and Myanmar. After this expansion, it seems likely that new membership will be put on hold until further consensus is reached within the group.

In keeping with the informal process – there is no Secretariat – rather the EU acts as the sole coordinator, with the Presidency and the ASEM Commission based on the Asian side on a rotational basis. ASEM has held five summits to date: Bangkok 1996; London 1998; Seoul 2000; Copenhagen 2002; and Hanoi 2004, with the sixth to be held in Finland in 2006. In addition to the biannual Leaders' Summit, ASEM has established a range of ministerial, senior officials, and other scheduled meetings and conferences to advance its agenda, while the Asia–Europe Business Forum gathers together the private and public sector to provide input to official ASEM dialogues and to exchange views. Three ASEM institutions and programmes have also been established: the Asia–Europe Foundation, the Trans-Eurasian Information Network project, and the ASEM Trust Fund, although there is also some discussion about the need to establish an ASEM Secretariat in the future.[42] One of ASEM's more significant documents is the 1999 Asia–Europe Vision Group report. The report's nine major and 22 other recommendations focused on ways to enhance cooperation in the three main pillar areas, as well as how to strengthen ASEM's dialogue and cooperation mechanisms.[43] Hence, in the space of nearly 10 years, ASEM has built up a considerable array of consultation and dialogue mechanisms, as well as conferences and other ad hoc programmes to further its mission.[44]

While there are many optimists about the value of ASEM's informal dialogue process to date, there are also detractors who question if there is much 'substance beneath the symbolism'. As Yeo Lay Hwee notes, what divides the supporter and detractors of ASEM is their expectation of what it can deliver, stemming from their interpretation of what ASEM is and should be.[45] ASEM has been criticised for being top-down and elitist, lacking the participation and engagement of civil society. It is not surprising that with such a broad agenda involving multiple dialogue partners, the ASEM process is at risk of becoming a problem in itself. The haphazard proliferation of activities, so-called 'forum fatigue', declining interest from parties involved, and wastage of resources are cited as challenges facing the ASEM framework of dialogue.[46] Related to these issues is the question of whether the ASEM process should become more institutionalised and formal in the future or whether sufficient common ground exists among members to move beyond its current informal structure. As Dent argued, the future of ASEM will depend on 'what its participants are willing to make of it', and for the purposes of our discussion, on the East Asian side, this will continue to change as domestic and regional political realities evolve.[47]

ASEAN+3

At the same time as ASEAN was beginning to move towards closer collaboration, it also reached north, inviting the heads of China, Japan, and South Korea to join a new regional arrangement known as ASEAN+3. The decision to invite the three countries stemmed from a number of overlapping issues. First, it was an evolution of a trend towards closer dialogues in the three Northeast Asian coun-tries that had its roots in the 1990's. Second, it was recognised that ASEAN's desire to secure itself against future crises could not be realised unless the Northeast Asian countries were included. This recognition arose during the 1997 Asian crisis, where it was clear that the region – both Southeast Asia and Northeast Asia – was interdependent, rather than two separate subregions.[48]

Third, it provided another vehicle for ASEAN to engage China in a non-confrontational dialogue.[49] Fourth, it was hoped that the ASEAN+3 model would give added impetus to the ASEAN–Japan relationship. The intertwining of the South Korean economy with its Southeast Asian counterparts, as evidenced by its exposure to the fallout from the 1997 Asian crisis, made it a logical third partner in this arrangement.

The development of ASEAN+3 has opened up new opportunities in the creation of an East Asian region. These opportunities are exemplified by the China–ASEAN and Japan–ASEAN FTA negotiations as well as South Korea's leading role in the EAVG process. ASEAN+3 has also acted as a catalyst for greater cooperation between the +3 countries. Initially such cooperation was limited to the leaderships of these countries. Within the ASEAN+3 arrangement, the dialogue has gradually expanded to encompass ministerial-level meetings, ranging from economic and finance ministers' meetings, through agriculture and forestry ministers' meetings, to tourism ministers' meetings. Outside of the ASEAN+3 dialogues, the +3 countries now hold a range of meetings to further cooperation. Such meetings range from +3 business councils, to +3 meetings of central bank heads, to coordinated research on information and communication technology.[50] Although as Chapter 4 shows, the impact of the meeting on +3 regionalisation is still arguable.

However, despite the emergence of ASEAN+3, thereby creating the possibility of a truly regional organisation being formed, many of the original problems associated with region building still exist. If anything, the inclusion of three new countries further complicates the process, given the political and economic power disparities between the countries of Southeast and Northeast Asia, as well as the expanded set of policy interests. Other issues, such as the strong protection of state sovereignty, are also prevalent in the three Northeast Asian countries, constituting yet another challenge for the region to move to a more integrated arrangement.

East Asian Summit

The inaugural East Asian Summit was held on 14 December 2005. While, at the time of writing, it is still unclear as to what role the EAS will play in region-building efforts, certain observations can be made as to its genesis and likely function. The EAS is the result of a joint lobbying effort led by Malaysia and China. For Malaysia the EAS appears to be closely tied to two earlier proposals: (1) the EAEC and (2) a push for Malaysia to host an ASEAN+3 Secretariat, both of which other members of ASEAN resisted. In these efforts, Malaysia has been trying to exert a greater presence over the shaping of an East Asian bloc. Particularly since the 1997 Asian crisis, China has gradually increased its presence in regional fora. Although its representatives are very quick to deny any leadership ambitions, it can be said that the ASEAN–China relationship is now the key axis in East Asian affairs, the one against which the ASEAN–Japan and ASEAN–South Korean relations are judged. For a number of years China has quietly but consistently lobbied for a more equal relationship with ASEAN. This is most clearly reflected in Chinese-language descriptions of ASEAN+1 and ASEAN+3, which are referred to as

10+1 and 10+3 respectively; diminishing the weight given to ASEAN and emphasising a relationship among a group of co-equal states. Hence, Malaysia and China were each seeking a vehicle through which their agendas could be realised. The 2003 call for an EAC made an accompanying EAS a possible option.

When it was first mooted there was concern that the EAS would be the EAEC in a modern form. This was particularly a concern of non-East-Asian states that had significant regional interests, although in the current arrangement this does not appear to be a valid concern. Rather the EAS will be a meeting of states which have all acceded to the ASEAN Treaty of Amity and Cooperation (TAC) and who are considered to have strong ties with the region. While this will include all 13 ASEAN+3 states, it will also mean that Australia, India, and New Zealand (but not Russia) are to be included. The incorporation of non-East-Asian states is also an indication that the more exclusive ambitions of Malaysia and China have been checked by other regional states, which highlights the earlier mentioned tension between 'open' and 'closed' models of regionalism. What this will mean for the creation of a regional organisation based on East Asian states is yet to be fully clarified.

Three pillars of East Asian regionalism

The stated intent of the region's leadership in calling for the development of three pillars is to support the development of an EAC. With the three pillars covering security, economic, and socio-cultural issues, it can be said that the creation of the EAC is the culmination of the political dialogues already being undertaken in the ASEAN+3 process. Other regional dialogues – such as the ARF, APEC, and ASEM – arguably support this core process as well as help to advance sector-specific objectives.

To a large extent the overarching political process is already in place. The challenge for the region is to unify and streamline the process so that it leads to the intended outcome. As this streamlining occurs, a key issue the region will have to address is how formalised the EAC will become. The outcome from the 2003 Bali Summit, with the call for an EAC, may have resolved the debate in favour of a more formalised arrangement, but this does not mean that the resulting regional architecture will resemble other, more developed regional organisations. Indeed the earlier opposition to the formalisation of the ASEAN+3 process indicates that reforms could be slow in being ratified. Nevertheless, the outcomes from the 2003 Bali Summit and the 2004 Vientiane Summit do mean that the majority of regional policy resources will be channelled into activities covered by one of the three pillars, which may allow the steps towards an EAC to be taken with relatively greater certainty than was the case previously.

The question that still confronts the region, however, is the issue of community membership. While the EAC is intended to involve the 13 states of East Asia, for each of the three pillars there are significant extra-regional interests that need to be considered. In economics, there are the negotiations and agreements that take place under the WTO as well as bilateral FTAs with non-Asian economies. In security matters, the role of the United States has a direct impact on regional stability. In cultural issues, transnational flows of information and ideas from other cultural communities and non-East-Asian societies compete on a daily basis with regional representations of identity and society. Thus, even as an EAC is being formed, extra-regional interests and pressures require it to look beyond its own narrow geographically based restrictions.[51] Although much of the rhetoric would argue for a closed region with a limited membership, the reality of member states' interests preclude such a scenario being fully realised. What is more likely is that, as the region coalesces, core and peripheral processes will develop in each of the pillars. If the EAC is to become a more institutionalised entity then one of the challenges it must face is the development of linkages between the core processes, so as to strengthen a central regional structure.

Each of the three pillars represents a core set of regional integration issues that are being addressed under the direction of the regional leadership. Although integration in each area was already underway before being linked to a particular pillar, there are still many issues to be resolved and quite complex challenges to overcome. A brief insight into each of these pillars is therefore essential to understand the integration project currently before the region and its peoples.

The ASEAN Security Community

The concept of an ASEAN Security Community (ASC) has been evolving since 1994, when the ARF was established. As noted earlier, there were other security communities in existence prior to the ARF, but it was the first organisation that drew East Asian states together with the major extra-regional security actors. The ASC is designed to expand the activities undertaken within the region under a security rubric. In this respect it represents a blueprint for a range of activities beyond those being promoted by the ARF.

Security communities exist in other regions and – along with economic issues – are common building blocks for the regional integration of states in other areas of shared interest. This is not surprising as it is the peaceful and stable nature of security communities that provides the conditions for other forms of cooperation to emerge. As Acharya has noted, security communities are typified by both the absence of war and the absence of any preparations for war between their members, in conjunction with collective actions and a subscription to a set of norms as well as a sense of identity.[52]

The role of extra-regional powers (particularly the United States, Australia, and India) in current security arrangements – at both the regional and state levels – highlights the problem of developing a regional security community limited by geographic concerns. As Buzan and Wæver have noted with respect to the role played by the United States, '[f]or better or worse, many of the East Asian states trust the United States more than they trust each other'.[53] In addition, the involvement of these extra-regional states often brings new issues onto the security agenda of other regional organisations. Examples of this can be seen in the response of APEC to the terrorist attacks of September 11, or in the way in which human rights are securitised in ASEM dialogues.

In advancing the ASC, policy-makers at the 2004 Vientiane Summit identified a large number of issues for development. These issues range from the long-called-for ASEAN extradition treaty allowing for the ARF to engage in preventative diplomacy efforts to develop the infrastructure and capacity for ASEAN to undertake humanitarian assistance missions and post-conflict development programmes.[34] Given that many of the issues either have been suggested for a number of years with minimal progress ('[r]esolving all outstanding issues to ensure early signing of the Nuclear Weapon States to the Protocol to the SEANWFZ Treaty') or represent unlikely policy priorities for some regional regimes (for example, the undertakings to strengthen 'democratic institutions and political participation' or to promote human rights), it is unclear how successful the ASC concept will be – a problem further compounded by the lack of concrete timetables for each of the initiatives to be enacted. Moreover, within the Vientiane ASEAN Security Community Plan of Action, there is little sense as to how all the different elements of the plan will relate to each other, nor is there any mention of a binding dispute resolution process. Finally, the realisation of these various goals will require a higher degree of coordination between member states, which will in turn necessitate the creation of a new set of values and principles 'that go beyond those already agreed upon'.[35] Failure to achieve this will hobble the ASC before it is operationalised.

While it would be possible to conclude that these limitations render the concept of an ASEAN Security Community redundant, it is noteworthy that the ASC Plan of Action does represent the most significant effort so far in the creation of a regional security order, one able to safeguard its members' interests while ensuring a peaceful and stable environment. Whether the security reality lives up to political rhetoric will be a key test in the creation of an EAC.

The ASEAN Economic Community

The mainstay of East Asian regionalism is the web of closer economic and commercial ties between the 13 states and markets. Without the underlying process of economic integration it is unlikely that a regional community would be a possibility. Although ASEAN had been encouraging closer trade and investment ties between its members since the first meeting of regional economic ministers in November 1975, this process has only begun to develop in concrete terms since January 1992 when the then six ASEAN states signed the Framework Agreement on Enhancing ASEAN Economic Cooperation, which was supported by the Agreement on the Comprehensive Effective Preferential Tariff (CEPT) scheme for the ASEAN Free Trade Area.

Despite this, it was not until the late 1990s when the region – spurred on by the 1997 Asian crisis, changes in the global economic structure, as well as economic and trade integration programmes in other regional blocs – began to make significant steps towards economic integration. An additional factor in this process was the modernisation of China and the proposal for a China–ASEAN Free Trade Agreement (CAFTA). A perceived lack of integration between the

ASEAN economies was seen as an impediment both to ASEAN collectively negotiating such an agreement, as well as to ASEAN products being able to compete with Chinese goods once the agreement was signed. These regional and global pressures have combined to promote the acceleration of economic integration across the East Asian region.

Nonetheless, the region remains starkly divided between wealthier and poorer states. Within ASEAN this divide can be easily seen in the GDP between the six older member states of the organisation and the four newer members. In 2003 the average per capita GDP in the ASEAN-6 was US$1,626 compared with US$356 in the ASEAN-4.[56] Once the three wealthier Northeast Asian states are included these economic disparities are only exacerbated further. Beyond the GDP measure there are also massive disparities in terms of size of national economies and the purchasing power of the currencies within those economies. Developing a regional infrastructure able to assist the poorer economies in meeting their populations' needs is one of the key challenges facing the creation of the economic community. A related challenge is that the poorer economies are also less integrated into regional and global economic and trade processes, which means that not only do they have fewer resources to devote to regional economic integration programmes, but also that they are less committed to such programmes.

Such disparities and challenges argue against the likelihood of an economic community being formed successfully in anything but the longer term.[57] However, regardless of such limitations, there are still significant resources being allocated to developing closer trade and investment links in addition to supporting endeavours in terms of creating policy networks between regional central banks and the finance bureaucracies as well as between regional market actors and policy-makers. During the 2004 Vientiane Summit regional leaders signed the Agreement for the Integration of Priority Sectors, designed to speed up integration in 11 core areas. These areas included 'electronics, e-ASEAN, healthcare, wood-based products, automotives, rubber-based products, textiles and apparels, agro-based products, fisheries, air travel and tourism'.[58] Even though the agreement was considered a significant contribution the to regional integration of trade and commercial activities, it must be noted that had the objectives of the AFTA and AIA been fully realised, there would be little need for an agreement of this type.

Outside of the summit dialogues, East Asian states are also engaged in advancing integration at the subregional level; either on a geographical basis (as is the case with the Greater Mekong Subregion (GMS) or the Brunei–Indonesia–Malaysia–Philippines East Asian Growth Area (BIMP–EAGA)) or on a sectoral level (as can be seen with the aviation agreements between Thailand, Singapore, and Brunei under ASEAN's '2+X' process). As economic integration remains the engine of East Asian regional-building endeavours, any slippage in this area has the potential to slow down broader integrative efforts.

The ASEAN Socio-Cultural Community

Of the three pillars, the institutionalisation of a social and cultural community will require the most development. There are a number of programmes within ASEAN for the development of Southeast Asian social and cultural exchanges going back almost to the inception of the organisation, but at the ASEAN+3 level such mechanisms are rudimentary at best. Within ASEAN the first social and cultural agreement – regarding cooperation in mass media and cultural activities – was signed in 1969. In contrast, it was not until 2003 that the first ASEAN Ministers Responsible for Culture and Arts (AMCA) met with their Northeast Asian counterparts (AMCA+3).[59] While this first meeting endeavoured to support cultural development and exchanges, it was not until the second meeting in 2005 that a more comprehensive regional programme began to emerge. At the second meeting of the AMCA+3, regional ministers and officials discussed the setting up of a regional taskforce on cultural heritage as well as a range of issues including the role of the +3 countries in the development of ASEAN small and medium-size cultural enterprises and public education programmes for the preservation of cultural heritage sites.[60]

At the ASEAN+1 level there are more concrete programmes in operation, although these are still limited in terms of community building. These programmes range from one-off events such as those contained in the ASEAN–Japan Year of Exchange (2003) to longer-term cultural exchanges such as the ASEAN–Japan Youth Friendship Programme or ASEAN-ROK Cultural Exchange Programme. In August 2005 China also signed a Memorandum of Understanding on Cultural Cooperation with ASEAN, the first such comprehensive cultural agreement between ASEAN and a +1 state.[61]

Integrating ASEAN, ASEAN+1, and ASEAN+3 social and cultural programmes into a single community will take time, not least because there is currently no vision as to what its aspects would look like. Although the ASEAN charter proposed at the 2005 summit, may provide a conduit for this vision to be realised. Despite this, there is still evidence of increasing interconnections between regional societies. Civil society organisations are increasing in number and scope within almost all countries. Regional CSOs also shadow the APEC and ASEM meetings, creating even broader regional and pan-regional links. Hence, although the region is still far from unified in terms of closer societal ties – with residual suspicions from historical and modern times still remaining – civil society organisations offer one avenue whereby these deeper transnational and regional ties could be forged.

Thus, the shape of the region from the point of view of its composite peoples and societies can be said to be very fluid. Until the decision to create a Socio-Cultural Community in 2003, there was little in the way of a coherent vision for a regional society from the policy elites. While the vision has now been articulated in the ASEAN Socio-Cultural Community Plan of Action promulgated at the 2004 Vientiane Summit through a list of 49 separate measures, there is still much that is still to be clarified, particularly with respect to desired outcomes and benchmarks.[62] Even as many of the 49 measures are already being implemented, the degree to which these measures can be extended beyond the 10 Southeast Asian states to include the three Northeast Asian partners in the creation of an EAC is questionable. While it remains to be seen how the ties being created across regional societies by civil society organisations and people-to-people interactions will mesh with the visions being promoted by regional policy-makers, it can be said that without broad-based popular recognition and support from the peoples of the region, any form of regional community in East Asia must surely fail.

Conclusion

To return to the central theme of this volume, the question as to whether or not the East Asian region is advancing towards a deeper form of regional community can, in part, be answered. From the preceding discussion, measures to evolve a more formal regional organisation, incorporating the 13 states of Southeast and Northeast Asia, have been clearly identified. These measures are born of the recognised need to protect member states' stability and security. In protecting their interests, the 13 states of ASEAN+3 have proposed the concept of an EAC, which will be supported by more integrated linkages across three key areas: security, economics as well as socio-cultural. On this basis alone, it would be tempting to conclude that East Asia is indeed advancing towards a more institutionalised regional community.

However, such a grand vision is not without its challenges – challenges that, if not addressed in a timely and comprehensive manner, call into question both the ability of the region to build a community as well as its underlying willingness to do so. These problems relate to: (1) wide disparities in the capacity of East Asian states to contribute to the community in a sustainable fashion; (2) an urgent need to address historical and contemporary tensions; (3) the role of extra-regional states and institutions in regional affairs; and (4) a still under-articulated regional identity.

The subsequent chapters in this volume explore the region's prospects as well as the challenges as it attempts to build an EAC – so as to understand where the region is going, what issues it must confront and resolve along the way, as well as the shape this emerging regional community may take. As East Asian states, markets, and communities seek to develop closer associations, it is hoped that this volume will inform the debates as they arise.

Notes

1   East Asian Vision Group, 'Letter of Transmittal', *Towards an East Asian Community*, 31 October 2001.
2   *Declaration of ASEAN II (Bali Concord II)*, Bali, 7 October 2003.
3   For more on this debate see: Nick Thomas, 'ASEAN+3: C/community building in East Asia?', *Journal of International and Area Studies*, 2001, vol. 8, no. 2, pp. 1–20.
4   Online. Available: http://www.rmaf.org.ph/Awardees/Biography/Biography ASEAN.htm.

5 Shaun Narine, *Explaining ASEAN: Regionalism in Southeast Asia*, Boulder, CO: Lynne Rienner, 2002, pp. 10–11.

6 MAPHILINDO stands for MAlaya, PHILippines, INDOnesia.

7 Gillian Goh, '"The ASEAN Way": Non-Intervention and ASEAN's role in Conflict Management', *Stanford Journal of East Asian Affairs*, 2003, vol. 3, no. 1, pp. 113–18.

8 Termsak Chalermpalanupap, 'ASEAN+3: An ASEAN Perspective', in James Chin and Nicholas Thomas (eds) *China and ASEAN: Changing Political and Strategic Ties*, Hong Kong: Centre of Asian Studies, 2005, p. 20.

9 As quoted in Roger Irvine, 'The Formative Years of ASEAN: 1967–75', in Alison Broinowski (ed.) *Understanding ASEAN*, London: Macmillan Press, 1982, quote on p. 16.

10 Most particularly the 1968 'Corregidor affair' when the Philippines was accused of training Muslim insurgents (on the island of Corregidor) for use on the island of Sabah, over which Malaysia and the Philippines contested sovereignty. However, this first phase also saw agreement of the *Declaration on a Zone of Peace, Freedom and Neutrality* (ZOPFAN) in 1971. Although this Declaration was more aspirational than absolute, it does stand out as an important achievement in consolidating a regional approach to security issues between the five states, despite their quite disparate conceptions of the strategic environment.

11 While it needs to be acknowledged that the PTA was the first of many ASEAN agreements where reality did not match the stated ambitions, it is cited here as an indicator of the willingness to advance the organisation's objectives.

12 For more on this second phase see: David Irvine, 'Making Haste Less Slowly: ASEAN from 1975', in Alison Broinowski (ed.) *Understanding ASEAN*, London: Macmillan Press, 1982, pp. 37–69.

13 For an excellent summary of Vietnam's involvement in Cambodia see: Gary Klintworth, *Vietnam's Intervention in Cambodia in International Law*, Canberra: Australian Government Printing Service, 1989.

14 Narine, 'Explaining ASEAN', p. 69.

15 It is useful to note that there are different spellings for these two concepts in the scholarly literature. However, the meanings always remain the same.

16 M. Rajaretnam, 'Principles in Crisis: The Need for New Directions', in Kao Kim Hourn (ed.) *ASEAN's Non-Interference Policy: principles under pressure?*, London: ASEAN Academic Press, 2000, pp. 37–50.

17 Surin Pitsuwan, 'Currency Turmoil in Asia: the strategic impact', *Remarks made at the Asia Pacific Roundtable*, Malaysia: Kuala Lumpur, 1 June 1998.

18 Narine, 'Explaining ASEAN', p. 169.

19 From Cambodia's accession to the Treaty of Amity and Cooperation and its subsequent membership of ASEAN, the organisation represented all 10 Southeast Asian states. Of the other four states, Brunei Darussalam joined in 1984, Vietnam in 1995, and Laos and Myanmar in 1997.

20 Mely Caballero-Anthony, *Regional Security in Southeast Asia: Beyond the ASEAN Way*, Singapore: ISEAS Publications, 2005, p. 215.

21 APEC's founding members included Australia, Brunei, Canada, Indonesia, Japan, South Korea, Malaysia, New Zealand, the Philippines, Singapore, Thailand, and the United States.

22 For a useful review of these institutions as well as the Asian Development Bank's relevance to East Asian regionalism, see Edward J. Lincoln, *East Asian Economic Regionalism*, Washington, DC: The Brookings Institution, 2004, pp. 114–39.

23 Ibid., p. 133.

24 Ibid., p. 129.

25 APEC Economic Leaders' Declaration of Common Resolve, Bogor, Indonesia, 15 November 1994, pp. 1–2. Online. Available : http://www.apec.org/apec/leaders_declarations/1994.downloadlinks.0001.LinkURL.Download.ver5.1.9.

26 Lincoln, *East Asian Economic Regionalism*, p. 130.
27 See Ross Garnaut, 'Introduction – APEC ideas and reality', in Ippei Yamazawa, *Asia Pacific Economic Cooperation (APEC). Challenges and tasks for the twenty-first century*, Pacific Trade and Development Conference Series, London: Routledge, 2000, pp. 1–18.
28 Ibid., p. 16
29 Ibid., p. 139.
30 Gareth Evans and Bruce Grant, *Australia's Foreign Relations in the World of the 1990s*, Melbourne: Melbourne University Press, 1992, p. 111.
31 Akiko Fukushima, *Multilateral Confidence Building Measures in Northeast Asia: Receding or Emerging?*. Online. Available : http://www.stimson.org/japan/pdf/fukushima.pdf.
32 See: *Singapore Declaration of 1992*, Singapore, 28 January 1992. Online. Available: http://www.aseansec.org/5120.htm. This call was preceded by two years of policy discussions within the ASEAN Institutes of Strategic and International Studies (ISIS) network. In 1991 the ISIS network issued a report.
33 Narine, 'Explaining ASEAN', p. 105.
34 Ibid.
35 *The ASEAN Regional Forum: A Concept Paper*, Bandar Seri Begawan, August 1995. Online. Available: http://www. aseansec.org/3826.htm.
36 Ibid.
37 Caballero-Anthony, 'Regional Security in Southeast Asia', pp. 128–43. CSCAP stands for Council for Security Cooperation in the Asia–Pacific and is the primary Track Two body for the ARF.
38 Narine, 'Explaining ASEAN', p. 106.
39 Michael Leifer, 'The ASEAN Regional Forum', *Adelphi Paper No. 302*, London: Oxford University Press, 1996, p. 59.
40 Introduction to the ASEM Process. Online. Available: http://europa.eu.int/comm/external_relations/asem/asem_process/index_process.htm.
41 The other main pan-regional body is FEALAC – the Forum for East Asia and Latin America Cooperation. FEALAC was inaugurated at the senior officials level in 1999. It was not until 2001 that the first ministerial meeting was held. For a good background to this initiative see: Zhang Jun, *Enhanced China-ASEAN Cooperation with the Framework of FEALAC*, China–ASEAN Occasional Paper Series, Hong Kong: Centre of Asian Studies, 2004. It is also worth noting that ASEAN has also begun to explore other pan-regional linkages with the Andean Community and the African Union, in 2000 and 2003 respectively.
42 *Chairman's Statement of the Fifth Asia–Europe Meeting*, Hanoi, 8–9 October 2004. Online. Available : http://europa.eu.int/comm/external_relations/asem/asem_summits/asem5/01_chair.pdf.
The Asia–Europe Vision Group also recommended the establishment of a 'lean but effective' Secretariat in 1999.
43 Asia–Europe Vision Group Report, Executive Summary. Online. Available: http://europa.eu.int/comm/external_relations/asean.
44 For a more in-depth discussion and critique of ASEM's activities and prospects for the future, see Wim Stokhof and Paul Van Der Velde (eds) *Asian-European Perspectives: Developing the ASEM Process*, Richmond, Surrey: Curzon Press, 2001.
45 Yeo Lay Hwee, 'ASEM: Looking Back, Looking Forward', *Contemporary Southeast Asia*, 2000, vol. 22, no. 1, p. 120.
46 Ibid.
47 Christopher M. Dent, 'ASEM and the "Cinderella Complex" of EU-East Asia Economic Relations', *Pacific Affairs*, 2001, vol. 74, no. 1, pp. 25–52.
48 The conceptualisation that ASEAN needed to engage the states to its north was already present in ASEAN policy circles prior to 1997, but the Asian crisis helped shift

the concept from dialogue to action more quickly than would have otherwise likely happened.

49 ASEAN had already engaged in discussions with China via the ASEAN Regional Forum. These discussions were instrumental in convincing the Chinese government of the benefits of multilateral engagement.

50 See for example: Shawn Donnan and Andrew Ward, 'China, Japan and Korea to widen co-operation', *Financial Times*, 7 October 2003.

51 A counter-approach that is also being used to support the creation of an East Asian Community argues that such an entity would allow regional states to resist pressure from extra-regional states and societies. This argument is predicated on a closed-region model for the EAC and more closely resembles the EAEC/EAEG model first suggested by Dr Mahathir, the former Prime Minister of Malaysia. However, the details in the Vientiane Action Programme indicate at least an awareness of the need to engage non-regional actors and interests even as the EAC develops. For further information see: *Vientiane Action Programme (VAP) 2004–2010*, Vientiane, November 2004.

52 Amitav Acharya, *Constructing a Security Community in Southeast Asia: ASEAN and the problem of regional order*, London: Routledge, 2001.

53 Barry Buzan and Ole Wæver, *Regions and Powers: The Structure of International Security*, Cambridge: Cambridge University Press, 2003, p. 176.

54 See the 'Annex', *ASEAN Security Community Plan of Action*, Vientiane, 29 November 2004.

55 Rodolfo Severino, 'Towards an ASEAN Security Community', *Trends in Southeast Asia Series No. 8*, Singapore: ISEAS, February 2004, p. 18.

56 ASEAN Secretariat, *ASEAN: Narrowing the Development Gap*, Jakarta, May 2005.

57 A good presentation of this argument is contained in: Lincoln, *East Asian Economic Regionalism*.

58 See: 'ASEAN Accelerates Integration of Priority Sectors', *ASEAN Secretariat Media Release*, Vientiane, 29 November 2004.

59 For information on this meeting and the preceding AMCA+3 Senior Officials Meeting see: 'ASEAN to set up Human Resource Development Committee', *Financial Times Information*, 14 October 2003; 'ASEAN Sec-General Thanks Malaysia's Effort to Organise AMCA Meetings', *Financial Times Information*, 14 October 2003.

60 See: *Chairperson's Press Statement of the Second Meeting of the ASEAN Ministers Responsible for Culture and Arts (AMCA) and the AMCA Plus Three*, Bangkok, 4 August 2005.

61 Ibid. For additional information see: 'China, ASEAN to expand cultural cooperation', *Xinhua*, 3 August 2005.

62 See *ASEAN Socio-Cultural Community Plan of Action*, Vientiane, 29 November 2004.

2 Theorising East Asian regionalism(s)

New regionalism and Asia's future(s)

Shaun Breslin

Introduction

Constructing a region is not an easy task. Consider a potential region containing states with vastly different levels of development, with different versions of domestic capitalism, different domestic political structures, different religions and belief systems: a region that has suffered from the expansionary military activities of one of its members and where memories of the war are still strong in the minds of many, with concerns about how to prevent the emergence of regional hegemons; a region where nations are divided with rival political regimes in an uneasy peace where the threat of conflict cannot be discounted; a region that is largely dependent on the presence of an external power, the United States, for the maintenance of security and largely dependent on that same external power for its economic fortunes; a region where there is little or no identification with belonging to that region amongst the general population.

While we might use this description to think of East Asia today, it can also be applied to the situation in Europe at the end of World War II. In the European case, the extent of the challenges noted above did not prevent the emergence of a regional order – a regional order that continues to evolve today, in terms of both membership and functions. As such, and on the most simple of levels, students of contemporary East Asian regionalism know that the current obstacles to regional formation *can* be overcome – but this does not mean that they necessarily *will* be overcome. Crucially, nor does it does not mean that even if these obstacles are overcome, then the regional organisation in East Asia will *necessarily* resemble the European Union or that East Asian regionalisation will emulate the European experience; it does not mean that Europe's present *will* be Asia's future.[1]

This chapter is divided into two main sections. The first traces the emergence of the so-called 'new-regionalism' literature in the mid-1990s and outlines some of its main characteristics as a precursor for further discussion in the second section. The section reviews the distinction between regionalism and regionalisation and their interrelationship; the role of non-state actors in these processes; the role and relationship between regionalisation, globalisation and capitalism in the new regionalism literature; new regionalism's understanding of multiple levels of regional governance; and the role and importance of 'regional identity' in the definition of what is – or what is not – a region. Finally, new regionalism and the security realm is discussed, noting that political–economic regions do not necessarily coincide despite formal integration.

In the second section two perspectives from the new regionalism literature are then applied to the case of East Asia, and particularly China's emerging role in the region. While it is obvious that China will focus on relations with close neighbours, it is important to recognise that its regional future may not only be solely with the rest of East Asia – but potentially also with the Russian Far East, Central Asia and Oceania. The task of defining the region, and the role of 'Asian Values', are considered alongside existing and future institutional experiments to form both a political and economic region, such as ASEAN, ASEM and ASEAN+3. The chapter then forwards a number of conclusions from using new regionalism perspectives to consider emerging East Asian regionalism and regionalisation.

Comparativism and the shadow of Europe

While it is not the focus of this chapter to compare processes of European and East Asian regionalism, it is useful to reflect briefly on the dangers of Eurocentricism and its implications for our understanding of contemporary regionalisation in East Asia. It is suggested that there are three – or perhaps three and a half – interrelated problems. The half problem is the question of temporal comparisons. There is little point in comparing regionalism in East Asia (or anywhere else) today with regionalism in Europe today as it is a comparison of two unlikes. Rather, the comparison should be made between East Asia today and Europe at a similar stage of the evolution of regionalism (though identifying when the similar stage was in Europe is an inherently difficult task).

The first more major point is that although the European experience is just one experience of region building, it is often elevated in importance above other experiences in the study of comparative regionalisms.[2] This does not always take place in an overt manner. For example, it is common to come across descriptions of loose and/or informal integration of ASEAN, Mercosur, SADC and elsewhere. At the risk of massively oversimplifying the nature of European integration,[3] if Europe is compared with any of the above examples, then the distinction between the formalised European structure and loose and informal structures elsewhere is indeed striking. But if all of the above were compared in a single study with Europe, then it could be concluded that it is Europe that is the exception from the dominant norm. Yet the question of why Europe has such formalised structures is asked much more rarely than why ASEAN *et al.* are characterised by loose, informal integration. Europe becomes *the* benchmark against which all other regional projects are judged.

Second, in some of the literature at least, Europe is not so much considered as *a* case, but as the *archetypal case* that creates the norm and an expectation that other cases will emulate.[4] The problem is not so much studying the processes that led to the creation of the European Union, but assuming that these processes are universal.

Third, the European experience has had a much greater impact on theory building than other regional projects. It is not surprising that 'integration theory' has drawn much and indeed most from the long-running and successful (in its own terms) experience of integration in Europe. Nevertheless, the experiences of other regional projects have, at times, been all but ignored in theory building. For example, Rosamond notes that 'neofunctionalism can be read at one level as a theory provoked entirely by the integrative activity among the original six member-states'.[5]

For Gamble and Payne,[6] the European example had resulted in a conception of integration that placed too great an emphasis on institutionalised arrangements and intergovernmental processes of region building. They argued that outside Europe, regional integration was largely occurring through the commercial activities of non-state actors, and often without the need for the creation of formal regional organisations. What was needed was a new look at regionalism built on a wider set of case studies to generate new theoretical understandings. Part of the answer was to consider the evolution of formal regional organisations away from the core heartlands of the global political economy, with Latin America and Africa providing fruitful arenas for research. But if anything, East Asia provided an even more productive case, encompassing the study of the introduction of new regional forms, the evolution of existing ones, competing conceptions of region, and increasing informal economic integration outside formal regional projects (and even between rival political regimes). It is not just that 'new regionalism' approaches can help us understand what is happening in East Asia, but also that the East Asian experience has helped inform those approaches themselves.

Towards a 'new regionalism' approach

The inability of existing integration theories to explain adequately the process of regional integration outside Europe led to the emergence of a new strand of literature in the mid-1990s. This literature is often grouped together under the broad heading of 'new regionalism' – though not all authors explicitly use the term to classify their work.[7]

The term 'new regionalism' had first been used in the urban studies literature to refer to subnational regional processes.[8] As far as the author is aware, the first person to use the term explicitly in the international relations literature was Hurrell,[9] although the wide use of the term owes much to the publications emerging from the UNU WIDER project on new regionalism.[10]

Some of this literature explicitly focuses on comparisons of non-EU regional projects and regionalism in non-core areas of the global political economy.[11] In general, the intention of this approach is not to ignore the European experience, but to add to it. Whilst some of the resulting theories and approaches have much in common with earlier theories and approaches, if for no other reason the 'new regionalism' was 'new' because most of the case studies it drew from were 'new' experiments in region building.

Characteristics of the 'new regionalism'

Given the now relatively large literature on new regionalism, it is difficult to construct a single understanding of what the approach actually stands for – or indeed, if it can be considered to represent a clear single coherent approach at all.[12] One of the key difficulties in trying to generalise is because there is no attempt to find a 'once and for all' explanation or theory. In this respect, it is not a theory but a framework – a framework which not only allows for diversity, but indeed emphasises the fact that there is no single answer; no single set of relationships; no single simple understanding. As Katzenstein argues, 'Because they often mediate between national and global effects, regional effects, as in the story of Goldilocks, are neither too hot, nor too cold, but just right.'[13]

This understanding draws the researcher into considering, particularly through comparative approaches, how different sets of relationships emerge with different balances of power between actors in different and specific historical, geographical, social and political contexts. So, although it is possible to attempt to draw out the main characteristics of the new regionalism approach, caveats about oversimplifying the debate and different interpretations within this broadly defined approach obviously apply. The following discussion of the main characteristics of the new regionalism literature serves as a precursor to the analysis of the East Asian context presented in the second section.

Regionalism and regionalisation – form and process

The distinction between regionalism and regionalisation is now broadly accepted in the literature. Regionalism is largely considered to refer to formalised regions with officially agreed membership and boundaries that emerge as a result of intergovernmental dialogues and treaties. While such formal regions will necessarily encompass some form of institutionalisation, there is no conception that a specific form/type/amount of institutionalisation is required to qualify as a 'proper' region. Rather, the interest is in what factors explain the wide variation in the institutional level of regions.[14]

While regionalism refers to the form, regionalisation refers to the processes by which societies and economies become integrated – particularly but not only in the economic sphere. Perhaps the best definition comes from Väyrynen, who argues that: 'The process of regionalisation fills the region with substance such as economic interdependence, institutional ties, political trust, and cultural belonging.'[15] Such regionalisation and economic integration in particular can occur without the creation of formal political regionalism. They are 'regions without prescribed or proscribed borders'[16] based on 'transnational flows and networks'[17] rather than cartography and political borders.[18] Here the example of economic integration in East Asia is particularly important, as regionalisation not only occurred in, despite the lack of 'commercial agreements . . . among East Asian countries prior to the mid-1990s',[19] but has also been relatively unhindered by, political conflicts between China and Japan and across the Taiwan Straits.

Clearly, regionalism and regionalisation are not necessarily mutually exclusive. Indeed, 'old regionalism' scholars saw the emergence of regionalism as a response to regionalisation. Neofunctionalists and neoliberal institutionalists share a conviction that as economic regionalisation occurs, states often move towards cooperation to find regional solutions to common problems. In other cases, there is the suggestion that regionalism creates regionalisation through the reduction of transaction costs in economic activity between member states,[20] and the creation of a form of regional identity.

However, not all regional projects have created regionalisation, and to a large extent, the success of a regional organisation depends on the extent to which regionalism is accompanied by regionalisation. For example, Manoli[21] has shown that although the Parliamentary Association of Black Sea Economic Cooperation (PABSEC)[22] has formally recognised boundaries, an institutionalised structure, and a permanent secretariat, the economies of member states are no more integrated than before the creation of PABSEC in 1993. The formal region is mapped on top of different processes of economic regionalisation that pull member states' economies more towards extra-regional economies (particularly the EU) than to each other. Bull notes a similar lack of real integration in Central America:

> Central American formal integration has not been followed by a more spontaneous regionalisation, understood as 'the growth of societal integration within a region and to the often undirected process of social and economic interaction'. In consequence, as the official integration process stalled, the regional project in Central America lost its dynamism.[23]

Thus, a key question for students of new regionalism is why regionalisation leads to regionalism or vice versa in some cases and not in others (with no assumption of convergence towards a single form) – explaining difference rather than predicting convergence remains at the heart of much of this work. There is certainly no reason to judge progress towards regionalism against a pre-existing conception of what a regional organisation should look like, or to deduce that there is no regional community in East Asia in the absence of a formal East Asian Regional Community. For the time being at least, there is a need to identify the regional specific issues that are to be addressed if we are to reach a 'tipping point' where sufficient regional elites accept the desirability of moving to a more formal relationship for it to become a reality (see Thomas in Chapter 7).[24]

Regional actors

The distinction between regionalism and regionalisation draws attention to whose interests are served by regional projects, and who are the main actors. It is obvious that intergovernmental agreements are signed by governments. When it comes to regionalisation, the focus of attention moves to the role of non-state actors, and particularly the investment and trade decisions of non-state economic actors. Economic integration, and possibly the formal regional projects that flow from such integration, are seen as largely driven by the market, rather than by states.

It is worth noting here that this does not mean that states and state actors are irrelevant as ineluctable market forces establish new spatial patterns of economic activity that cut across national political borders.[25] Non-state actors might drive regionalisation through investment and trade flows, but at the very least, states play an essential role in creating the environment in which non-state actors can pursue their interests. For example, taxes are not lowered (or removed) on their own and money can only be freely exchanged across national political borders if governments allow it (legally at least). Neither do ports, roads and railways build themselves. Although specifically commenting on globalisation rather than regionalisation, the findings of a German Bundestag report are germane here. The report concluded that the hard infrastructure that is so necessary for the physical transportation of goods is usually funded by governments rather than by the private sector and that: 'The growing worldwide integration of economies came not by any law of nature – it has been the result of active and deliberate policies.'[26]

National and local governments across the world have implemented numerous policy initiatives to facilitate increased transnational economic relationships – to open their national economic space and to encourage regionalisation. Indeed, Milner has correctly pointed to the importance of domestic politics in explaining the development (or not) of regionalism.[27] Solingen similarly emphasises the importance of domestic coalitions' regional preferences, arguing that the structure of the regional order will reflect either liberal–internationalist, statist–internationalist, or mixed forms of governance depending on the balance between economic cooperation and political accommodation on the one hand, and economic cooperation and conflict on the other.[28]

For Gamble and Payne, the new regionalism should be understood as a state strategy to respond simultaneously to national political pressures and the internationalised structure of the global political economy (and in particular, internationally mobile finance capital). Nevertheless, it is non-state economic actors that decide whether to respond or not, and where they are going to invest. As Mattli argues, allowing non-state actors to get on with economic activity is essential if economic regionalisation is going to occur (either as a precursor to, or as a result of, regionalism).[29]

Although somewhat critical of the emphasis on economic actors at the expense of other non-state actors, Shaw nevertheless argues that one of the key characteristics of new regionalism approaches is to move beyond the state and to consider:

> a trio of heterogeneous actors: not just states (& interstate global & regional institutions) but also economic structures (e.g. multinational corporations

(MNCs) & informal sectors) and civil societies from international non-governmental organisations (INGOs) to grass-roots movements. To be sure the balance among this trio varies between regions & issue-areas & over time but none of them can be excluded or overlooked in any ongoing relationship.[30]

In particular, the new regionalism scholars argue that the focus on intergovernmentalism and state actors that characterises the work of many in the realist tradition in international relations cannot hope to capture the different regional dynamics at play beneath (or perhaps beyond) the state level of interaction.

Furthermore, the financial and trade flows that Hurrell suggests 'are the most important driving forces for economic regionalisation'[31] are rarely simply confined to the region itself. For example, if a Taiwanese company sources components from a Malaysian supplier to produce goods in its factory in China, then we could argue that regional economic integration is taking place. But if the Taiwanese company is producing under contract for a company based in the United States, and exporting the finished good back to the United States or to Europe (as is often the case), then the regional relationship is conditioned by (or perhaps even dependent on) extra-regional relations. As such, rather than conceive of regionalisation and globalisation as contending forces, new regional approaches instead lead us towards a consideration of how the two interact.

Regionalisation, globalisation and capitalism

In his critique of mainstream European integration theories, Cocks took issue with what he perceived to be the historical basis of most studies. Starting from a Marxist perspective, Cocks argued that in many ways the distinction between state building and region building was artificial as both were essentially concerned with allowing capitalism to flourish, and legitimating the hegemony of the capitalist mode of production:

> I conceive successful political integration in Europe since the sixteenth century as a method of state-building at the national and international level. It has performed two critical state functions: provision of the political infrastructure for the expansion of productive forces in protocapitalist and capitalist societies; and an appropriate means for legitimating the power necessary to maintain the social relations integral to these societies.[32]

As the above discussion on actors perhaps indicates, many of the new regionalism scholars share Cocks's interest in the relationship between regional formation and capitalism. Whilst not necessarily sharing Cocks's Marxist ontology, the work of Marxian (and particularly Gramscian) scholars has been highly influential – not least amongst them, Robert Cox and his conceptions of world order.

Hurrell began his influential 1995 paper by citing Salvatore[33] and Friedberg,[34] who had both argued that protectionism built on regional trade blocs was the future of the world rather than globalisation. As will be discussed in more detail below, financial crises in Asia and Latin America in the late 1990s have resulted in considerations of the way in which regional cooperation/agreements can act as a bulwark against the worst excesses of unregulated global capitalism. But in general, rather than perceiving of globalisation and regionalism as contending forces, most scholars instead perceive them to be symbiotic in nature.[35]

On one level, regionalisation and globalisation are seen as largely driven by the same processes – what Oman refers to as 'the ongoing development . . . of post-Taylorist "flexible" approaches to the organisation of production within and between firms'[36] that have facilitated the ongoing de-territorialisation of production. In this respect, regionalisation can be perceived on one level as the localised manifestation of wider global processes. As Smart argues, capitalist practices are embedded in local structures, and certain contexts can generate new and vibrant variations upon the theme of capitalism. If nothing else, globalisation produces a considerably diverse set of local outcomes.[37] On another level, domestic policies relating to both regionalism and regionalisation are often shaped by globalisation – and in particular, the desire to participate in the global capitalist economy.

For Bowles, the hegemony of neoliberalism provides the key to understanding the growth of regional projects and processes, and in particular, the enthusiasm of developing states elites for such projects:

> By 1991 the purpose of forming a regional trading bloc was no longer premised on the need to be more independent of the global economy but rather seen as a measure to ensure continued participation in it. The fear of developing countries was no longer one of dependence on the global economy but rather was seen as a measure to ensure continued participation in it.[38]

In terms of regionalism, this is manifest in the desire of elites in many less developed states to join regional organisations that guarantee access to large markets, even if the quid pro quo for gaining membership is introducing domestic economic liberalisation.

On one level, this is evident in accepting the criteria required to join 'closed' regional projects such as the EU and NAFTA. On another, it is evident in those avowedly 'open' regional projects designed to promote neoliberalism and accelerate liberalisation where any liberalisation measures apply to all other economies, not just members – for example, APEC.[39] In short, regionalism is seen as 'a tool in the process of the internationalisation of the state, in which national political practices are adjusted to the exigencies of the global economy and the main source of state legitimacy becomes external actors and institutions'.[40]

'North–South' regions

The changing policy preference of elites in many developmental states has resulted in another key characteristic of new regionalism. The desire to gain access to lucrative markets in and investment from more developed states has resulted in what Hurrell considered to be one of the defining features of the new regionalism in practice – regionalism that cuts across the North–South divide.[41] The extension of the European Community to include the 'Southern' (or at least, relatively less developed) states of Spain, Portugal and Greece in the 1980s (not to mention the more recent expansion of the EU), the inclusion of Mexico in NAFTA, and the evolution of East Asian regionalisation have all created regional projects that tie (to varying degrees) economic peripheries to regional cores. For the less developed economies in the region, this can create an asymmetric dependence on their more developed neighbours – but a dependence that is not only tolerated, but actively promoted by state elites as the best way of generating economic growth. As Bernard and Ravenhill have argued, this idea of generating growth through an unequal relationship with the regional economy led to the creation of export processing and other special economic zones as a means by a number of East Asian states in the 1979s and 1980s.[42]

The post-Washington consensus consensus[43]

The above analysis points to regions as a conduit for the expansion of neoliberal economic policies built on a conception of the hegemony of neoliberalism in terms of both policy and ideology.[44] Whilst this understanding still holds true today, a new tone entered the emerging literature on new regionalisms in the late 1990s. The financial crises that hit, to greater or lesser extents, East Asia, Russia and Latin America led many policy-makers as well as academics to question the legitimacy, validity and efficacy of the post-Washington consensus.

The rethink did not entail a rejection of the neoliberal discourse – far from it. But the financial crises propelled a renewed emphasis on the agency of state and non-state actors in directing, managing, perhaps mitigating the impact of the specific types of global economic activity that dominated the 1990s.[45]

The idea that globalisation was not only inevitable but beneficial for development was challenged. Furthermore, the efficacy of the policy descriptions from the international financial institutions (IFIs) to deal with the crises also came into question. The idea that the crises could be overcome by more liberalisation – more globalisation – was resisted by those who thought that too much or too fast liberalisation had been a key cause of the crises in the first place.

Furthermore, the solutions promoted by the IFIs were considered by some to be politically loaded. As Western developed states both dominated the decision-making processes of the IFIs and largely shaped their ideological preferences, post-crises prescriptions were sometimes perceived as a means of enforcing 'proper' Anglo-American capitalism on states that had developed different forms of capitalism aimed at protecting domestic interests in one way or another.[46]

Despite the fact that neither ASEAN not APEC was able or prepared to offer regional solutions independent of those prescriptions offered by the IFIs, there nevertheless emerged in many parts of the world a desire to create regional alternatives to dependence on the Western-centric IFIs. The development of the ASEAN+3 process in East Asia is one such example which is explored further in the second section.

The idea of region as both a conduit for liberalisation and a mode of resisting liberalisation might appear to be contradictory. But what is being resisted is unfettered liberalisation (or globalisation), not the neoliberal project per se. As such, regions can be perceived as a mediating layer of governance between national and global economies[47] – what Wallace refers to as a 'filter for globalisation'.[48] As we shall see below, the move to create a region-wide system of currency swaps – the Chiang Mai Initiative (CMI) – is an example of how East Asian states are also cooperating to filter potentially negative impacts of globalisation at the regional level – albeit in a much looser institutional form than the EU.

Regionalism and multi-level governance

Despite the fact that the European regional project has been characterised by the evolution of a single European Union, Wallace argues that within the EU, there are different locations of governance and multiple layers and levels of integration.[49] On one level, individual member states remain crucial levels of governance, and had obstinately refused to wither away as some early theorists of integration theory had predicted. More importantly for this chapter, different levels and layers of integration between member states exist under the overarching umbrella of the EU. For example, even before the expansion of the EU from 15 to 25 in 2004, not all member states had joined the Schengen zone, and not all member states had adopted the single European currency. Moreover, the EU is not the only regional project in Europe. When it comes to security, you cannot simply map the European members of NATO on top of a map of EU member states and expect the two to coincide.

This understanding of multiple levels of regional governance provides yet another characteristic of the new regionalism literature. Here the 'new' approaches have something in common with understandings of regional integration that predate the 'old' analyses of European integration. In proposing a solution to the problems of the Tennessee Valley in the Great Depression, David Mitrany argued that form should follow function. For example, if the problem was electricity generation, then an authority should be established that only dealt with issues relating to electricity generation. If another problem was poverty alleviation amongst farmers, then a separate organisation should be established with jurisdiction over only germane issues. Each organisation should be functionally discrete with the membership and organisation of each differing and shaped by the specific function at hand.

Mitrany's approach was challenged on two grounds. First, how is it possible to separate out functionally discrete issues? How can you deal with poverty alleviation without considering land usage, environmental issues, fiscal regimes, and other issues – including in this case electricity generation? Far better to construct a single holistic organisation that can coordinate affairs over a wide range of interconnected issues than to create numerous functionally discrete organisations. Second, and very much related, even if functionally discrete organisations were established based on technical expertise in the first instance, their authority would inevitably spill over into other forms of authority and governance – just as the technological expertise in the functionally discrete European Coal and Steel Community eventually spilt over into the establishment of the EU.

As already noted, new regionalism scholars reject the necessary and inevitable spillover into an EU-style form of regional governance in all cases. Rather, and building on Coxian approaches to world order,[50] the real world of new regionalisms is characterised by multiple forms, layers and levels of integration. This is partly a result of different functional arrangements. Most obviously, the security region might differ widely from the broadly defined economic region. But so too might the region of production differ from the financial region generating different types of region with different memberships and different levels of institutionalisation. But it is also a result of different levels of 'region' – both writ small and writ large.

At the lower level, much of the real integration that is taking place between economies is not between the economies of two or more nation states.[51] Rather, it often occurs between subnational entities across national boundaries. Thus, for example, Tijuana becomes integrated with San Diego across the Mexico–US border to a much greater extent than the Mexican and US economies become integrated as a whole. Indeed, in the case of integration between parts of southern China and Hong Kong, it can be argued that parts of China are now more integrated with external economies than they are with the rest of the domestic Chinese economy. Whilst much of this microregional integration occurs without the creation of formal regional mechanisms (microregionalisation), there are many cases of formal microregionalism – for example, southern African development corridors and the ASEAN 'growth triangles'.

At the higher level, the coexistence of different forms of region at different levels has resulted in overlapping regional membership. For example, if APEC is conceived of as a regional organisation (and it is not clear that it should), then its wide geographic reach means that its member states are all simultaneously members of smaller, more discrete regional organisations. Even if APEC is discounted, then it can be seen that the concept of multiple regional memberships still holds true. For example, Malaysia is involved in ASEAN growth triangles, in ASEAN itself, in the fast track for the ASEAN Free Trade Area liberalisation (as opposed to the slower track for the new members), the ASEAN Regional Forum, ASEAN+3, the China–ASEAN Free Trade Agreement, the East Asia Economic Caucus, ASEM, APEC, the Asian Development Bank and the Colombo Plan.[52]

Regional identity

The majority of new regional studies is undertaken by scholars who work in the broadly defined field of international political economy. It is perhaps not surprising then that the majority of the work produced by these scholars is primarily concerned with economic dimensions of regionalism and regionalisation. However, despite the emphasis on economics, there is also a related focus on the importance of identity that draws from the work of social constructivists and the importance of imagined or cognitive regions.

There is a general agreement that the cohesion of a region in large part depends on a shared sense of regional identity – a shared belief that the members of a region have something in common that binds them together and marks them out as in some way different from non-members. Building on Adler's work (and his collaborations with Barnett),[53] the sources of regional identity are most often defined in cultural terms. Cultural affinity can emerge from shared histories, languages, religions and so on. But it is often constructed in opposition to an 'other' – be that a shared common security threat and the construction of imagined security communities, or a shared rejection of dominant values and norms. For example, for all that divides East Asian states, a shared rejection and in some places suspicion of dominant Western values and norms can provide a basis for agreeing on what is to be rejected. If Asian values are taken as a basis for a cognitive region, it is not built on 'what we are', but 'what we are not'.

New regionalism and the cognitive region come together when the shared common challenge is economic. This might also entail values – a rejection of the free market liberal form of capitalism championed by Western states both bilaterally and through the IFIs. Or it might entail a recognition that the national economy is not and cannot be isolated from what happens in other regional economies – as was the case in the Asian financial crisis.

What is not clear is when identity is important. Is a shared identity a necessary precursor for the creation of a region, or is it something that consolidates and holds the region together once it has been formed? Moreover, does a shared identity create the region, or does the region create identity? Nor is it clear who identity is important for. Does it matter that normal individual citizens do not have a sense of regional identity if finance ministers do and coordinate national economic policies accordingly, or investment managers do and structure their corporate strategies accordingly? If not, then a subsidiary question is whose region is it? As Chavez argues in her contribution to this volume, East Asian regionalism is highly elite driven: not only is there a 'shallow' popular identity, but also a considerable democratic deficit.

New regionalism, security and (old) international relations

In some respects, interest in new regionalism emerged from security debates. On one level, the end of the Cold War is the starting point for many scholars. For some scholars, the question was whether regional orders might fill the void and balance the power of the United States in a unipolar world after the collapse of the Soviet Union.[54] More generally, the shift from a bipolar geostrategic environment to a unipolar geoeconomic environment provided the context for the promotion of neoliberal globalisation (which has largely generated the renewed interest in regionalism). It also allowed regional projects to re-emerge in Africa, the Middle East and Southeast Asia relatively unhindered by superpower interference – particularly if they were regional projects that did not reject the neoliberal project.[55]

Having said that, perhaps the biggest and the most valid criticism of the new regionalism approach is its relative lack of attention to the security realm. As noted above, there is a relatively large literature in the related constructivist field considering the importance of identity and security – not least Acharya's work on East Asia[56] – and the fourth volume in the UNU/Wider project on new regionalism does contain contributions that fall firmly in the security field.[57] Indeed as is befitting the 'new' regionalism approach, often inspired by 'new' political economy, 'new' security issues and human security typically come to the fore in the literature.[58] In this respect, security is often closely related to developmental concerns when security is raised as an issue in new regionalism discourses.

The relative neglect of security issues and the relatively strong economic focus of new regional studies were in some ways a response to a perceived dominance of security discourses on regionalism within the international relations community.[59] But whilst the new regionalism school might have in part been originally inspired by perceived failings of realist ontologies and an overly strong focus on security, it is important to ensure that new approaches are not wholly depoliticised or 'de-securitised'.

For example, an overly strong focus on economics that ignores politico-security issues can lead to a rather unrealistic appraisal of potential regional trajectories. Whilst an analysis of economic interaction between China and Japan might point towards a shared regional future, considerations of the bilateral political relationship may well instead suggest conflict or, at the very least, that East Asian regionalism is a non-starter.[60] This divergence is even starker in the case of different types and/or levels of China's relationship with Taiwan. Conversely much of the international relations literature on East Asia (and also from East Asia) points to political obstacles to regional integration and often ignores the informal regional economic integration that already exists. If the international relations and new regionalisms literatures engage with each other (at least occasionally) then hopefully the potential pitfalls of omission of both can be avoided.

East Asia's regional futures: new regionalism and the role of China

Having established the basic characteristics of the broad church of new regionalism studies, the remainder of this chapter will now show how these approaches can provide a theoretical basis for understanding the dynamics of regional integration in East Asia. Other chapters in this volume consider individual issue areas in detail – for example, Hamilton-Hart on financial integration and Curley on civil society. The emphasis here is on how new regional approaches can help us think about China's position in, and impact on, East Asian regional processes. China has been chosen as the focus of attention because the policy preferences of Chinese elites are increasingly seen as being a key determinant of what will happen to regional projects in the future. In addition, China's emergence as an important international economic actor has already had a profound impact on investment and trade flows and patterns of regionalisation, and is unlikely to become less important any time soon.

Multiple forms of regional integration

The most obvious implication of applying new regional approaches to China and East Asian regionalism is that Europe does not have to be the only benchmark and model for what might be East Asia's future. Asking if East Asia might develop a regional organisation akin to the EU is an interesting question – but not the only question. And if the answer is 'no', then this does not mean that East Asia has no regional future.

What the European case does show is that the political/economic region and the security region do not have to coincide – or at least, do not yet fully coincide despite many years of formal integration in the EU. Further, whilst the new regionalisms literature largely leaves security studies to others, the disjuncture between security regions and other regional forms in East Asia is marked and likely to persist. It is particularly notable that of China's partners in the Shanghai Cooperation Organisation,[61] only Russia is usually discussed in wider analyses of East Asian regionalism – and even then only rarely and usually to explain why it is not being considered. Whilst this may be a concrete example of the disjuncture between security and other regions, it also leads us towards a number of other issues.

As China's elites increasingly define security in terms other than just guns, bombs and bullets, conceptions of what might form a security region will change. The issue of economic security will be dealt with in detail later in this chapter, and the focus will be on relations with other East Asian economies. Indeed, the majority of studies of China and regionalism focus on relationships with East Asian neighbours (for good reasons). But China's regional future does not just have to be with the rest of East Asia. For example, in addition to more traditional security concerns, the search for energy security concerns might also lead China towards regional cooperation with Central Asian neighbours.

Russia is China's regional partner not only in the SCO, but also in the Tumen River Area Development Programme (TRADP). Although little concrete regional integration has actually taken place in the TRADP for a number of reasons,[62] the project does remind us of two important points. First, China's neighbours are not all East Asian neighbours, and at least one of China's regional futures might be in a partnership with non-Asian states/economies. Second, it is not a matter of regional cooperation with East Asia or Central Asia. Individual states can be and are members of multiple, sometimes overlapping regional organisations, and there is no reason why China will not develop deeper regional cooperation with both Central and East Asian neighbours in the future, based on the different functional objectives of each region.

The TRADP is also a reminder that multiple regions can also exist at different levels. By this, consider the concept of microregionalism and the argument that regions do not have to encompass entire national entities working together. Though the TRADP has been largely unsuccessful in its own terms, it draws attention to the importance of different processes of microregional integration that tie (or attempt to tie) parts of China to other economies (or parts of national economies). So it is not just a question of considering multiple forms of region, but multiple forms at different levels and the way that they interact with each other.

Furthermore, it is necessary to think about how different forms of microregional integration interact with those parts of the national economy that are not participating in microregional processes. When regionalism and regionalisation are considered, it is inevitably in terms of integration. But if only parts of a national economy are becoming integrated into wider transnational networks of economic activity with weak linkages back to other parts of the domestic economy, then one of the consequences of regional economic integration might be national economic fragmentation.

Which region (or where is East Asia)?

As with the wider discussions of new regionalisms, the end of the Cold War marked a key turning point in analyses of East Asian regionalisms. For example, the transition from the geostrategic context of Cold War politics that spawned the creation of ASEAN to a geoeconomic context means that ASEAN has in many ways outlived its use – or its original use at least. With the incorporation of former enemies into ASEAN and a move towards economic cooperation with China (as well as South Korea and Japan), much of the original *raison d'être* for the organisation has gone to be replaced by new economic/development rationales.

ASEAN's search for a role as a mechanism of regional economic governance has borne some fruits but, as Webber argues, the failure of ASEAN as an organisation to act in any meaningful manner to the financial crises of 1997 exposed many of its institutional and political flaws.[63] Moreover, Webber also points to the inaction of APEC during the crisis, suggesting that both the 'small' and 'big' versions of regional governance failed to provide any form of effective governance when it was most needed. When US pressure stymied Japanese proposals to establish an Asian Monetary Fund in 1997, regional states were left with no regional solutions and instead had no option but to accept the type of solutions imposed by Western-dominated financial institutions.

Although the failure of ASEAN and APEC to find effective and/or accept-able solutions to the 1997 Asian crisis had much to do with political will and their institutional frameworks, there is also an extent to which they were the wrong size. In short, ASEAN was too small and APEC was too big. But recognising the limitations of existing organisations is quite a different thing from establishing an effective new replacement that is the right size and contains the necessary polit-ical will and institutions to act.

Defining a regional identity: Asian values?

On one level, it is difficult to identify what the limits of a regional organisation should be before it is created. Often, as was the case with Southeast Asia, accep-tance of what constitutes that region develops after the event. In the case of Southeast Asia, a broadly accepted definition of the parameters of the region emerged as a consequence of first colonisation, subsequently the command structure of military forces during World War II,[64] and more latterly, ASEAN. In other cases, definitions and understandings emerge as a result of outside influ-ences.

In the case of East Asia, the initiative to establish the Asia–Europe Meeting (ASEM) process necessitated Asia deciding where it was, and who was in it. And as Tanaka argues in the next chapter, it is easy to forget that ASEM was the first time that leaders from China, Japan and South Korea met together in a purely 'Asian' forum – a coming together that played an important role in laying the foundations for the ASEAN+3 process. The exclusion of the Australasian states from the Asia that participates in ASEM, against the expressed wishes of Australasian elites, was a sign of the rejection of the concept of the Pacific as a focus of region. The absence of the South Asian states, this time by choice rather than exclusion, resulted in an exclusionary definition of Asia for the purposes of ASEM with a membership that increasingly corresponds with conceptions of which states should become involved in establishing a collective regional economic governance – an issue that will be returned to later.

The rejection of Australasia from the ASEM process also draws attention to conceptions of values, belief systems and power. It was a decision based not just on geography, but also more importantly on conceptions of what Asia was not. On one level, Asia was not white. Perhaps more importantly, an Asian polity was not built on the precepts of individualism and liberal democracy and Asian economies were not built on the form of capitalisms that dominate in the Anglo-Saxon part of Pacific Asia. Much has been written about the concept of Asian values, and whether it simply provides an artificial justification for the mainte-nance of authoritarianism, but it is not the intention of this chapter to repeat them here. However, it is important to point to the widespread rejection of 'Western' values that many – and not just state elites – saw as a deliberate tool of Western hegemony even before 1997. To be sure there are many differences between the many different values in the region – not least the different values held by different groups in the region's multi-ethnic/religious states. But what binds the region together in the future might be a shared conception of alien belief systems and economic paradigms that regional elites collectively reject, rather than an agreed set of norms that they collectively agree on.

Defining a regional identity: the emergence of a financial region

Whilst cultural values might be important in shaping some form of regional identity, it is arguably in the economic realm that regional elites have developed a shared conception of what constitutes the region, and how regional cooperation can ensure national economic security. In particular, notwithstanding the original intentions of its architects, APEC has evolved into an organisation which, at best, does little to provide economic security for its East Asian members and, at worst, might be conceived as an organisation that prevents the formation of a real East Asian regional group.

The financial crises also confirmed for the Chinese leadership that what happens in the region has significant consequences for China, sparking new debates over the nature of 'economic security'.[65] Working together to head off potential crises at a regional level is increasingly seen as being in China's own self-interest – especially if such regional cooperation can mitigate the need to rely on the US-dominated global financial institutions in times of crisis. Furthermore, regional leaders are also increasingly accepting that any regional economic future will have to include China. A good example is China's participation in the CMI, which created a regional network of currency swap deals to act as a bulwark against global financial instability.

On a very simply level, the CMI suggests a growing recognition of how national economic fortunes cannot be isolated and insulated from what happens in the rest of the region. Moreover, it suggests a rejection of global solutions in favour of regional mechanisms for resolving (or heading off) regional crises. It also points towards a shared recognition of what the region actually is (and what is not part of the region) that has become quasi-formalised through the ASEAN+3 process (through which the CMI was arranged). While Taiwan remains absent due to the intergovernmental nature of ASEAN+3 discussions, it has evolved into a major forum for regional dialogue and consultation – and notwithstanding the persistence of APEC may become the major regional institution in the future.

Defining the region: a region of production?

Of course, ASEAN+3 is about more than just financial cooperation. The evolution of a region of production is also a key element in the evolution of China's participation in and cooperation with East Asian regional organisations, and led to the proposals to create a China–ASEAN Free Trade Agreement (CAFTA). First proposed at the Manila Summit in 1999, the CAFTA initiative took on a new impetus with the signing of the Framework Agreement on China–ASEAN Comprehensive Economic Cooperation at the Eighth ASEAN Summit Meeting in Cambodia in 2002. The CAFTA is conceived as a dual-speed process, with initial common tariff reduction to be completed by 2006, and a full free trade area in place by 2013.

On the face of it, the CAFTA is a key symbol of China's importance for the regional economy, as well as an important practical step in fostering closer economic integration. It is intended to act as a spur to intra-regional investment and to increase access to the Chinese market for ASEAN producers – though the other side of the same coin is a fear that it might also lead to a new influx of Chinese imports. But the CAFTA is in many ways a means to other ends, rather than just an end in itself. Stubbs notes that Japan was originally reluctant to join the ASEAN+3 process for fear of antagonising the United States:

> Although Japan was still reluctant to get involved, the Chinese government's agreement to take up ASEAN's invitation essentially forced Tokyo's hand. Beijing was interested in building on the economic ties that were developing with Southeast Asia and the Japanese government could not afford to let China gain an uncontested leadership position in the region.[66]

In a similar vein, the CAFTA might be seen as a means of trying to force the Japanese government's hand and promote a type of Asian regionalism akin to the EAEG. Indeed, Mahathir was explicit in his desire to see the CAFTA as a stepping-stone to a pan-Asian free trade area. Even if the CAFTA is a means to an end, it is also an important step towards China–ASEAN cooperation and regional economic integration in its own right.

A reality check

The above sections suggest that there are good reasons for thinking that the foundations are in place for closer regional relations in the future. This does not mean that the creation of a formal regional organisation with levels of institutionalisation akin to the EU is just around the corner. Indeed, as this chapter has hopefully shown, the expectation of an inevitable endgame is at best misguided and largely misleading. In addition, there is also strong evidence that points more towards disunity or at least continued confusion in regional formation, rather than towards an Asian community.

Hund is sceptical that there are any clear signs that ASEAN will move closer to China at all.[67] He argues that only Singapore and Thailand have embraced the free trade area with China – and this is nothing to do with regionalism. Rather, it reflects the general preferences of the Thai and Singaporean elites for trade liberalisation as shown by the free trade agreements that they have signed with states outside the region. In other regional states, the focus is less on cooperation with China, and more on how to resist the threat that China poses economically. Indeed, with China's rise resulting in investment and jobs being lost in a number of regional states, intra-regional conflict might be a more realistic scenario than cooperation.

Perhaps more important, the massive political barriers that stand in the way of a more formalised relationship cannot be overlooked – particularly, but not least, with respect to any relationship that goes beyond technical economic agreements. Dialogue between China and ASEAN can only proceed if the single biggest threat to regional security – China's relations with Taiwan – are not discussed at all. And with Chinese scholars who called for the creation of a 'normal' relationship with Japan branded as 'traitors' in officially sanctioned publications, the time does not yet appear right for historical grievances to be forgotten.

A still contested conception of region

Notwithstanding previous comments about the emerging consensus over what (or who) forms the region, this process is far from complete and what the region is (or should be) remains contested. For example, as Table 2.1 suggests, there is a correlation between those economies involved in both formal economic regionalism and informal economic regionalisation in East Asia. However, even though it only considers economic relations, as is indicated in the table, the correlation is not total, and there is still no definitive map of where the East Asian regional economy starts and ends.

In addition, wider conceptions of region remain alive in the form of the East Asian Summit (EAS). Unlike APEC, Russia, the United States and the other countries from the American continent are absent. But the inclusion of India, Australia and New Zealand means that ASEAN+3 is not the only regional game in town. It is not just that not everybody shares China's preference for an exclusive 'Asian Asia' region where troublesome concepts like democracy and human rights do not get in the way of economic cooperation. It is also that other regional states (notably, but not only, Japan) specifically want to stop China from achieving its regional objectives, and the 'big' region of the EAS is seen as an effective means of neutralising Chinese power. The EAS might well turn out to be not much more than a talking shop exactly because of its size and diversity and because of its geostrategic role in preventing Chinese hegemony. Nevertheless, it shows that different reasons for promoting conflicting conceptions of region are alive and well and remain a key determinant of whether a working regional organisation can ever be constructed.

Capitalism, regionalism and extra-regional actors

China's re-engagement with the global economy has played a key role in configuring both the regional economy as a whole and the individual economies of regional states. Investment that once might have gone to Thailand, Indonesia or Malaysia now largely takes advantage of the cheaper production costs in China instead. Rather than producing exports to the rest of the world, many regional economies are increasingly dependent on selling components and materials to China instead. But at the same time (and notwithstanding the oft-stated fears of dependence on China), the Chinese economy is itself largely dependent on investment from and trade with the rest of the region (particularly in the form of components from the region to produce exports).

The process of regionalisation of production is thus based on a complex web of relationships built on a hierarchy of asymmetric dependencies. It is a process that is driven by the investment and trade decisions of non-state economic actors, and the governmental policies put in place in regional states to facilitate private economic flows. As such, East Asian regionalisation can be conceived, in keeping with Cocks's analysis of Europeanisation,[68] as facilitating the expansion of capitalist productive forces built on the implicit acceptance of the hegemony of the neoliberal hegemonic project.

Crucially, this regionalisation is contingent on what happens outside the region, and a key issue for regional formation remains the pivotal role of extra-regional actors in promoting the regional economic interaction that regional initiatives are at least in part concerned with addressing. Without external demand, the formation of a region of production centred on manufacturing in China would have taken on a very different form and moved at a different pace. Further, despite what investment statistics in East Asia appear to demonstrate, the region remains heavily dependent on technology and crucially finance capital from outside the region to fund the regionalisation of manufacturing. As such, if the ASEAN+3 process does continue to evolve into a more formalised regional project, its success will depend on, first, its continued devolution of economic authority to non-state actors, and, second, its continued openness to extra-regional actors and the wider global economy.

Conclusion

In combination, the move towards currency swaps under the CMI, the creation of the CAFTA and the evolution of an informal region of production demonstrate the potentially contradictory relationship between globalisation and regionalisation. On one level, the region can be seen as a means of facilitating globalisation and neoliberal capitalism, whilst on another level, emerging regionalism can be seen as a means of providing a specifically regional means of providing economic security and a bulwark against uncontrolled global capital flows. And in this respect, the challenge of regional governance is no different from the challenges facing national governments – how to get the benefits of participation in the global economy without any of the potential damage.

Five main conclusions emerge from using new regionalism perspectives to consider the case of China and East Asia. First, the relationship between regionalism and regionalisation is exposed by an examination of East Asia. So too is the importance of non-state actors in promoting regional integration alongside the formal political initiatives of national governments. There may not be a formal East Asian Community, but actual economic integration is occurring, and new transna-

Table 2.1 Correlating regions and economies

ASEM	ASEAN+3	CMI*	Region of production**
Brunei	Brunei	–	–
	Cambodia	–	–
China	China	China^{JK}	China
Hong Kong	–	–	Hong Kong
Indonesia	Indonesia	Indonesia^{CJK}	Indonesia
Japan	Japan	Japan^{CK}	Japan
	Laos	–	–
Malaysia	Malaysia	Malaysia^{CJK}	Malaysia
	Myanmar	–	–
Philippines	Philippines	Philippines^{CJK}	Philippines
Singapore	Singapore	Singapore^{J}	Singapore
South Korea	South Korea	South Korea^{CJ}	South Korea
Taiwan	–	–	Taiwan
Thailand	Thailand	Thailand^{CHK}	Thailand
Vietnam	Vietnam	–	Vietnam

* Those arrangements signed by C(hina), J(apan) or K(orea) with ASEAN states or each other.
** This is a highly subjective classification that not all will agree with.

tional economic spaces are emerging that do not simply map on top of national political borders. Second, this regionalisation is contingent on extra-regional economic relations. East Asia's new regionalism is built on a widespread acceptance of neoliberal capitalism, and designed to facilitate the capitalist mode of production – albeit a mode of capitalism that needs to be regulated. Third, the best way of ensuring this regulation is increasingly seen to be the regional rather than the global level (even if what that region is or should be remains unclear). Fourth, regional governance is characterised by multiple forms of overlapping regions, including different levels of region from the micro through the meso to the macro.[69]

Finally, regional identity is important, and economic self-interest can create a shared regional identity at the elite level. Notwithstanding the potentially conflicting imperatives of globalising and regulating, there is a growing sense of regional identity in terms of what the region actually is. The consensus is far from complete, and competing regional projects persist. Arguably those who favour a wide conception of region in the form of the EAS do so for pragmatic strategic reasons. In some respects it is the fact that the EAS brings in extra-regional actors that can constrain Chinese power in the region that makes it an attractive option – though of course, this might mean that the imagined economic region never evolves into a formal political community.

Notes

1 See Richard Higgott, 'The International Political Economy of Regionalism: Europe and Asia Compared', in William Coleman and Geoffrey Underhill (eds) *Regionalism and Global Economic Integration: Europe, Asia, and the Americas*, London: Routledge, 1998.

2　I should perhaps add here that this is not the fault of 'Europeanists', but of those studying other areas that choose Europe as the main unit of comparison. Of course there are many more who (probably sensibly) eschew comparison and restrict their analyses to single cases. Though on a related issue, as Warleigh points out, 'With a few worthy exceptions, those involved in EU studies have barely made reference in their work to regional integration elsewhere.' Alex Warleigh, 'In Defence of Intra-disciplinarity: "European Studies", the "New Regionalism", and the Issue of Democratisation', *Cambridge Journal of International Relations*, 2004, vol. 17, no. 2, pp. 301–18.

3　Helen Wallace argues that the understanding of how Europe works is often informed by a study of formal processes which are heavily institutionalised, and ignores the many different levels and layers of more informal interaction. Helen Wallace, 'The Institutional Setting: Five Variations on a Theme', in Helen Wallace and William Wallace (eds) *Policy-Making in the European Union*, 4th edn, Oxford: Oxford University Press, 2000, pp. 3–37.

4　Bela Ballasa's highly influential work on economic integration is also relevant here. Ballasa established a model of integration that predicted a linear progression in formal cooperation between states from a free trade area to a customs union to a common market and finally to full economic union. The fact that Ballasa's model has more or less correlated with the transformation of the EEC to the EU has given force to his predictions – but whether it is an ineluctable process that defines all process of regional integration is an entirely different question. Bela Balassa, *The Theory of Economic Integration*, London: Allen and Unwin, 1961.

5　Ben Rosamond, *Theories of European Integration*, Basingstoke: Macmillan, 2000, p. 10.

6　Andrew Gamble and Anthony Payne (eds), *Regionalism and World Order*, Basingstoke: Macmillan, 1996.

7　In addition to the works explicitly cited elsewhere in this chapter, the analyses of new regionalisms draws from readings from the following sources. Alfredo Robles, *The Political Economy of Interregional Relations: ASEAN and the EU*, Aldershot: Ashgate, 2004; Edward Mansfield and Helen Milner (eds), *The Political Economy of Regionalism*, New York: Columbia University Press, 1997; Finn Laursen (ed.), *Comparative Regional Integration: Theoretical Perspectives*, Aldershot: Ashgate, 2003; Fredrik Soderbaum, *The Political Economy of Regionalism: The Case of Southern Africa*, Basingstoke: Palgrave, 2004; Fredrik Söderbaum and Ian Taylor (eds), *Regionalism and Uneven Development in Southern Africa: The Case of the Maputo Development Corridor*, Aldershot: Ashgate, 2003; Fredrik Söderbaum and Timothy Shaw (eds), *Theories of New Regionalism: A Palgrave Reader*, Basingstoke: Palgrave, 2003; J. Andrew Grant and Fredrik Söderbaum (eds), *The New Regionalism in Africa*, Aldershot: Ashgate, 2003; David Francis, *The Politics of Economic Regionalism: Sierra Leone in ECOWAS*, Aldershot: Ashgate, 2001; James Mittelman (ed.), *The Globalization Syndrome: Transformation and Resistance*, Princeton, NJ: Princeton University Press, 2000; Louise Fawcett and Andrew Hurrell (eds), *Regionalism in World Politics: Regional Organization and International Order*, Oxford: Oxford University Press, 1996; Meshack Khosa and Yvonne Muthien, *Regionalism in the New South Africa*, Aldershot: Ashgate, 1998; Michael Schulz, Fredrik Söderbaum and Joakim Ojendal (eds), *Regionalization in a Globalizing World*, London: Zed, 2001; Morten Boas, Marianne Marchand and Timothy Shaw, 'Special Issue: New Regionalisms in the New Millennium', *Third World Quarterly*, 1999, vol. 20, no. 5, pp. 897–1070; Nicola Phillips, 'Regionalist Governance in the New Political Economy of Development: "Relaunching" Mercosur', *Third World Quarterly*, 2001, vol. pp. 22, no. 4, pp. 565–83; Nicola Phillips, *The Southern Cone Model: The Political Economy of Regional Capitalist Development in Latin America*, London: Routledge, 2004; Peter Katzenstein, 'Introduction: Asian Regionalism in Comparative Perspective', in Peter Katzenstein and Takashi Shiraishi (eds) *Network Power: Japan and Asia*, Ithaca, NY: Cornell University Press, 1997, pp. 1–46; Sandra MacLean, Fahimul Quadir and Timothy

Shaw (eds), *Crises of Governance in Asia and Africa*, Aldershot: Ashgate, 2001; Stephen Calleya, *Navigating Regional Dynamics in the Post-Cold War World*, Aldershot: Dartmouth, 1997; Theodore Pelagidis and Harry Papasotiriou, 'Globalization or Regionalism? States, Markets, and the Structure of International Trade', *Review of International Studies*, 2002, vol. 28, no. 3, pp. 519–35; Tony Heron, *The New Political Economy of United States-Caribbean Relations: The Apparel Industry and the Politics of NAFTA Parity*, Aldershot: Ashgate, 2004.

 8 For two good critiques of this literature with an emphasis on the relationship between regionalism and globalisation, see Gordon MacLeod, 'New Regionalism Reconsidered: Globalization and the Remaking of Political Economic Space', *International Journal of Urban and Regional Research*, 2001, vol. 25, no. 4, pp. 804–29; Allen J. Scott and Michael Storper, 'Regions, Globalization, Development', *Regional Studies*, 2003, vol. 37, nos 6 and 7, pp. 579–93.

 9 Andrew Hurrell, 'Explaining the Resurgence of Regionalism in World Politics', Review of International Studies, 1995, vol. 21, no. 4, p. 332.

10 Björn Hettne, András Inotai and Osvaldo Sunkel (eds), *National Perspectives on the New Regionalism in the North*, Basingstoke: Macmillan, 2000; Björn Hettne, András Inotai and Osvaldo Sunkel (eds), *National Perspectives on the New Regionalism in the South*, Basingstoke: Macmillan, 2000; Björn Hettne, András Inotai and Osvaldo Sunkel (eds), *Comparing Regionalisms: Implications for Global Development*, Basingstoke: Palgrave, 2001; Björn Hettne, András Inotai and Osvaldo Sunkel (eds), *Globalism and the New Regionalism*, New York: St. Martin's Press, 1999; Björn Hettne, András Inotai and Osvaldo Sunkel (eds), *National Perspectives on the New Regionalism in the Third World*, Basingstoke: Macmillan, 2000; and Björn Hettne, András Inotai and Osvaldo Sunkel (eds), *The New Regionalism and the Future of Security and Development*, Basingstoke: Palgrave, 2000.

11 For example, Glenn Hook and Ian Kearns (eds), *Subregionalism and World Order*, Basingstoke: Macmillan, 1999.

12 And with all 'new' approaches, it does not take long before the new becomes the old which requires a new critique. See, for example, Kanishka Jayasuriya (ed.), *Governing the Asia Pacific: Beyond the 'New Regionalism'*, Basingstoke: Palgrave, 2004. However, I have incorporated the conception of 'regulatory regionalism' at the heart of this volume into my broad church of new regionalism approaches.

13 Peter Katzenstein, 'Regionalism in Asia', in Shaun Breslin *et al.* (eds) *New Regionalisms in the Global Political Economy: Theories and Cases*, London: Routledge, 2002, p. 104.

14 Hurrell, 'Explaining the Resurgence of Regionalism', p. 332.

15 Raimo Väyrynen, 'Regionalism: Old and New', *International Studies Review*, 2003, vol. 5, no. 1, pp. 25–51.

16 Ash Amin, 'Regions Unbound: Towards a New Politics and Place', *Geografiska Annaler B*, 2004, vol. 86, no. 1, p. 34.

17 Ibid., p. 31.

18 Although Castells is not considered to be a 'new regionalism' scholar, his understanding of how networks operate without and beyond physical spaces is also relevant here. Manuel Castells, *The Rise of the Network Society: The Information Age: Economy, Society, and Culture, Volume 1*, Oxford: Blackwell, 1996.

19 Edward Mansfield and Helen Milner, 'The New Wave of Regionalism', *International Organization*, 1999, vol. 53, no. 3, p. 598.

20 Indeed, one of the main issues addressed in the economics literature is the extent to which preferential regional trading arrangements lead to trade and financial diversion.

21 Panagiota Manoli, 'The Formation of Black Sea Economic Cooperation: A Case of Subregionalism', Ph.D. Thesis, University of Warwick, Department of Politics and International Studies, 2003.

22 Albania, Armenia, Azerbaijan, Bulgaria, Georgia, Greece, Moldova, Romania, the Russian Federation, Turkey and Ukraine.
23 Benedicte Bull, '"New Regionalism" in Central America', *Third World Quarterly*, 1999, vol. 20, no. 5, p. 958.
24 Martha Finnemore and Kathryn Sikkink, 'International Norm Dynamics and Political Change', *International Organization*, 1998, vol. 52, no. 4, p. 892.
25 Perhaps the most 'extreme' vision of a world where states have no power is Kenichi Ohmae, *The End of the Nation State: The Rise of Regional Economies*, New York: Free Press, 1996.
26 German Bundestag Study Commission (Select Committee), *Globalisation of the World Economy – Challenges and Responses*, 2001. Online. Available: http://www.bundestag.de/gremien/welt/welt_zwischenbericht/zwb003_vorw_einl_engl.pdf.
27 Helen Milner, 'International Theories of Cooperation among Nations: Strengths and Weaknesses', *World Politics*, 1992, vol. 44, no. 3, pp. 466–94.
28 Etel Solingen, 'Economic Liberalization, Political Coalitions, and Emerging Regional Order', in David Lake and Patrick Morgan (eds) *Regional Orders: Building Security in a New World*, University Park, PA: Pennsylvania State University Press, 1997; Etel Solingen, *Regional Orders at Century's Dawn: Global and Domestic Influences on Grand Strategy*, Princeton, NJ: Princeton University Press, 1998. This interpretation of Solingen's work is taken from Väyrynen, 2003, 'Regionalism: Old and New', p. 36.
29 Walter Mattli, *The Logic of Regional Integration: Europe and Beyond*, Cambridge: Cambridge University Press, 1999.
30 Tim Shaw, 'New Regionalisms in Africa in the New Millennium: Comparative Perspectives on Renaissance, Realisms and/or Regressions', *New Political Economy*, 2000, vol. 5, no. 3, p. 400.
31 Hurrell, 'Explaining the Resurgence of Regionalism', p. 334.
32 Peter Cocks, 'Towards a Marxist Theory of European Integration', *International Organization*, 1980, vol. 34, no. 1, p. 4.
33 Dominick Salvatore, 'Protectionism and World Welfare: Introduction', in Dominick Salvatore (ed.) *Protectionism and World Welfare*, Cambridge: Cambridge University Press, 1993, p. 10.
34 Aaron Friedberg, 'Ripe for Rivalry: Prospects for Peace in a Multipolar Asia', *International Security*, 1993/4, vol. 18, no. 3, pp. 5–53.
35 See James Mittelman, 'Rethinking the "New Regionalism" in the Context of Globalization', *Global Governance*, 1996, vol. 2, no. 2, pp. 189–214.
36 Charles Oman, 'Globalization, Regionalization, and Inequality', in Andrew Hurrell and Ngaire Woods (eds) *Inequality, Globalization and World Politics*, Oxford: Oxford University Press, 1999, p. 36.
37 Alan Smart, 'The Emergence of Local Capitalisms in China: Overseas Chinese Investment and Pattern of Development', in Si-Ming Li and Wing-Shing Tang (eds) *China's Regions, Polity, & Economy: A Study of Spatial Transformation in the Post-Reform Era*, Hong Kong: University of Hong Kong Press, 2000, p. 64.
38 Paul Bowles, 'ASEAN, AFTA and the "New Regionalism"', *Pacific Affairs*, 1997, vol. 70, no. 2, p. 225.
39 Jean Grugel, 'New Regionalism and Modes of Governance – Comparing US and EU Strategies in Latin America', *European Journal of International Relations*, vol. 10, no. 4, pp. 604–5.
40 Bull, 'New Regionalism', p. 959.
41 See also Jean Grugel and Wil Hout (eds), 'ASEAN, AFTA and the "New Regionalism", in *Regionalism Across the North South Divide*, London: Routledge, 1998, and Bowles, 'ASEAN, AFTA and the New Regionalism'.
42 Mitchell Bernard and John Ravenhill, 'Beyond Product Cycles and Flying Geese: Regionalization, Hierarchy, and the Industrialization of East Asia', *World Politics*, 1995, no. 47, pp. 171–209.

43 'If there is a consensus today about what strategies are most likely to promote the development of the poorest countries in the world, it is this: there is no consensus except that the Washington consensus did not provide the answer', Joseph Stiglitz, 'The Post Washington Consensus Consensus', Columbia University Initiative for Policy Dialogue Working Paper, 2004, p. 1.

44 Robert Cox, 'Civil Society at the Turn of the Millennium: Prospects for an Alternative', Review of International Studies, 1999, vol. 25, no. 1, p. 12.

45 Nicola Phillips, 'Governance after Financial Crisis: South American Perspectives on the Reformulation of Regionalism', in Shaun Breslin, Christopher Hughes, Nicola Phillips and Ben Rosamond (eds) *New Regionalisms in the Global Political Economy: Theories and Cases*, London: Routledge, 2002, p. 66.

46 Richard Higgott, 'The Asian Economic Crisis: A Study in the Politics of Resentment', *New Political Economy*, 1999, vol. 3, no. 3, pp. 333–56.

47 See Peter Katzenstein, 'Regionalism in Comparative Perspective', Cooperation and Conflict, 1996, vol. 31, no. 2, pp. 123–60; Robert Lawrence, Regionalism, Multilateralism and Deeper Integration, Washington, DC: Brookings Institution, 1996.

48 Helen Wallace, 'Europeanisation and Globalisation: Complementary or Contradictory Trends?', in Shaun Breslin, Christopher Hughes, Nicola Phillips and Ben Rosamond (eds) *New Regionalisms in the Global Political Economy: Theories and Cases*, London: Routledge, 2002, p. 149.

49 Ibid., pp. 144–5.

50 In particular, Chapters Six and Seven of Robert Cox with Timothy Sinclair, *Approaches to World Order*, Cambridge: Cambridge University Press, 1996.

51 See, for example, Shaun Breslin and Glenn Hook (eds), *Microregionalism and World Order*, Basingstoke: Palgrave, 2002; Markus Perkmann and Ngai-Ling Sum (eds), *Globalization, Regionalization and Cross-Border Regions*, Basingstoke: Palgrave, 2002; Myo Thant, Min Tang and Hiroshi Kakazu (eds), *Growth Triangles in Asia: A New Approach to Regional Economic Cooperation*, Oxford: Oxford University Press, 1994; James Scott, 'European and North American Contexts for Cross-border Regionalism', *Regional Studies: The Journal of the Regional Studies Association*, 1999, vol. 33, no. 7, pp. 605–17.

52 International (rather than regional) organisations such as the Commonwealth and the Group of 15 non-aligned states are not considered to be a regional organisation here.

53 For example, Emanuel Adler, 'Imagined (Security) Communities: Cognitive Regions in International Relations', *Millennium*, 1997, vol. 26, no. 2, pp. 249–77; Emanuel Adler and Michael Barnett (eds), *Security Communities*, Cambridge: Cambridge University Press, 1998.

54 For example, Richard Rosecrance and Peter Schott, 'Concerts and Regional Intervention', in David Lake and Patrick Morgan (eds) *Regional Orders: Building Security in a New World*, University Park, PA: Pennsylvania State University Press, 1997.

55 Väyrynen, 'Regionalism: Old and New', p. 28.

56 For example, Amitav Acharya, *Constructing a Security Community in Southeast Asia: ASEAN and the Problem of Regional Order*, London: Routledge, 2001; Amitav Acharya, *Regionalism and Multilateralism: Essays on Cooperative Security in the Asia Pacific*, 2nd edn, Singapore: Eastern Universities Press, 2003.

57 Hettne, *The New Regionalism and the Future of Security and Development*.

58 For example, James Hentz and Morten Bøås, *New and Critical Security and Regionalism Beyond the Nation State*, Aldershot: Ashgate, 2003.

59 Thanks to Richard Higgott for this point.

60 This sets an interesting challenge for those liberal theorists who might have expected economic integration to lead to stability and perhaps ultimately harmony.

61 Russia, Kazakhstan, Kyrgyzstan, Tajikistan and Uzbekistan.

62 For details, see Christopher Hughes, 'Tumen River Area Development Programme (TRADP): Frustrated Microregionalism as a Microcosm of Political Rivalries', in Shaun Breslin and Glenn Hook (eds) *Microregionalism and World Order*, Basingstoke:

Palgrave, 2002, pp. 115–43; Gilbert Rozman, 'Flawed Regionalism: Reconceptualizing Northeast Asia in the 1990s', *Pacific Review*, 1998, vol.11, no. 1, pp. 1–27; Shaun Breslin, 'Decentralisation, Globalisation and China's Partial Engagement with the Global Economy', *New Political Economy*, 2000, vol. 5, no. 2, pp. 205–26.

63 Douglas Webber, 'Two Funerals and a Wedding? The Ups and Downs of Regionalism in East Asia and Asia-Pacific after the Asian Crisis', *The Pacific Review*, 2001, vol. 14, no. 3, pp. 339–72.

64 Philip Charrier, 'ASEAN's Inheritance: the Regionalization of Southeast Asia, 1941–61', *The Pacific Review*, 2001, vol. 14, no. 3, pp. 313–38.

65 See Zha Daojiong, 'Chinese Considerations of "Economic Security"', *Journal of Chinese Political Science*, 1999, vol. 5, no. 1, pp. 69–87.

66 Richard Stubbs, 'ASEAN+3: Emerging East Asian Regionalism?', Asian Survey, 2002, vol. 42, no. 3, p. 443.

67 Markus Hund, 'ASEAN+3: Towards a New Age of Pan-East Asian Regionalism? A Skeptic's Appraisal', *The Pacific Review*, 2003, vol. 16, no. 3, pp. 383–417.

68 Cocks, 'Towards a Marxist Theory of European Integration'.

69 Linda Low, 'Multilateralism, Regionalism, Bilateral and Crossregional Free Trade Arrangements: All Paved with Good Intentions for ASEAN', *Asia Economic Journal*, 2003, vol. 17, no. 1, pp. 65–86.

3 The development of the ASEAN+3 framework

Akihiko Tanaka

Introduction

ASEAN+3 is now an established international institution in East Asia. It includes the leaders of the 10 Association of Southeast Asian Nations (ASEAN) member countries, as well as their Chinese, Japanese, and South Korean counterparts. Annual summits bring together these 13 leaders as well as a wide range of other officials. The summit held in Vientiane in November 2004 was the eighth such gathering. In addition to the leaders meeting, there are many other functional meetings including meetings of the regional foreign ministers, economic ministers, and finance ministers as well as many other meetings of representatives from lower levels of government. In addition, non-governmental policy networks such as the Network of East Asian Think Tanks (NEAT) are now being created to support the ASEAN+3 process. The further transformation of the ASEAN+3 Summit has now been realised, with the first East Asian Summit (EAS) taking place in Kuala Lumpur in December 2005.

There are many questions concerning East Asian regionalism that need to be asked if its advancement is to be understood. Looking to the past, it could be asked how was the ASEAN+3 framework born? Where did the idea come from? How does it relate to other international multilateral frameworks? To what extent did former Malaysian Prime Minister Dr Mahathir Mohamad's idea of an East Asia Economic Caucus (EAEC) affect the formation of ASEAN+3? How did the 1997 Asian crisis affect the development of ASEAN+3? What kind of influence do external powers such as the United States or the European Union have on the formation of East Asian institutions? In exploring these questions, a number of issues for the future development of East Asian regionalism become apparent, such as what are the major items on the policy agenda for ASEAN+3? Can it become a basis of a future East Asian Community? What are the major obstacles for its future development? While Breslin, in the preceding chapter, raised same of these questions from a theoretical presentation, this chapter will seek to advance the understanding of Breslin's conclusions by presenting an historical narrative of ASEAN+3's development, from which answers to these questions can be drawn.

To answer those questions, it is necessary to review the recent background to the emergence of ASEAN+3. This will enable a fuller understanding of the political and economic forces driving its evolution, especially in terms of the changes to regional power structures during the 1990s that allowed the process to be regularised. This chapter draws upon this analysis to make observations about both the evolution and future of ASEAN+3. Ultimately, the chapter concludes that ASEAN+3 has not yet proven its viability as a regional institution able to play a more substantive role beyond that of simply a 'talk shop'. Whether it crosses the gap that divides substantive institutions from talk shops depends on the willingness of the ASEAN+3 members seriously to implement the East Asian Vision Group's major recommendations, which was discussed in the first chapter.

Before ASEAN+3

Regional multilateralism grew very slowly in Asia. As was discussed earlier, while multilateral organisations such as the Southeast Asian Treaty Organisation (SEATO) and the Asian and Pacific Council (ASPAC) did exist prior to the creation of ASEAN+3, they were largely ineffective. The former was an unproductive military alliance created by the United States in the early days of the Cold War that lost its significance in the 1970s when the regional strategic environment changed drastically as a result of Sino-American rapprochement. This led to SEATO being disbanded in 1977. The Asian and Pacific Council, which was instigated by South Korea in 1966 as an anti-communist political forum, also lost its significance in the early 1970s and was disbanded in 1972.

More successful multilateral institutions in Asia were of the following three types. The first were specialised institutions such as the Asian Development Bank, established in 1966. The second were non-governmental or semi-governmental institutions such as the Pacific Basin Economic Council (PBEC) (established 1968) and the Pacific Economic Cooperation Conference (PECC) (established 1980). The third were regionally focused institutions such as ASEAN (established 1967). In all three cases, their cooperative structures, based upon trade and socio-economic development agendas, proved to be more sustainable than the earlier exclusionary, strategic endeavours.

As the following discussion reveals, ASEAN has emerged as the main focal point of multilateral engagements in East Asia. The first small step was taken when ASEAN invited the foreign ministers of its dialogue partners for a Post-Ministerial Conference (PMC) of the ASEAN Ministerial Meeting (AMM) in 1979. The ASEAN PMCs were the only occasions in which foreign ministers of major countries in the Asia Pacific could gather together to discuss political issues. However, they had their own limitations, namely that the issues discussed in the ASEAN PMCs were largely limited to those related to Southeast Asia, while major countries such as China, South Korea, and Vietnam were not involved in the process.

A major breakthrough for regional multilateralism was the creation of the Asia–Pacific Economic Cooperation (APEC) group in 1989. With the arrival of APEC, Asian and Pacific countries had, for the first time, an official, multilateral institution with a very inclusive membership structure. APEC's original members were the then ASEAN six member countries, as well as Australia, Canada, Japan, South Korea, New Zealand, and the United States. China, Hong Kong, and Taiwan joined APEC at the Seoul Meeting in 1991; Mexico and Papua New Guinea, at the Seattle Meeting in 1993; Chile, at Jakarta in 1994; and Russia, Vietnam, and Peru in 1998.

The creators of APEC conceived of it as a potential countermeasure against a 'Fortress Europe', which Asians as well as Americans had concerns about as they saw Europe moving towards a single European market. To the non-North-American members, it was also a hedge against a possible rise of protectionism in North America.[1] To prevent a self-fulfilling prophecy of reinforcing protectionist trends in Europe and North America, APEC did not attempt to develop any measures that might, in turn, be viewed as discriminatory. Hence, the catch-phrase of 'open regionalism' was used to express the institutional philosophy. As the GATT Uruguay Round was successfully concluded in 1994 and as the spectre of a 'Fortress Europe' receded, APEC focused on delivering more substantive goals. The goal of 'free trade' by the year 2010 for developed countries and 2020 for developing countries was agreed to during the Bogor Summit in 1994. This was followed up with an 'action agenda' in 1995 to realise the goal of 'free trade', with an action plan being agreed upon in 1996.[2]

In other words, the basic motives behind the creation of APEC as well as its substantive measures were economically and commercially focused. As its name indicated, it was conceived of as a multilateral framework for economic coopera-tion. (It was for this reason that Taiwan (under the name 'Chinese Taipei') and Hong Kong were able to join an otherwise state-based institution.) However, the work of APEC also held a high degree of political significance. A major innova-tion was the informal leaders meeting created at the initiative of President Clinton in 1993. The Seattle meeting of the APEC leaders was the first summit meeting in which the heads of government across the Asia–Pacific region partici-pated. However, APEC lost its dynamism when the initiative on Early Voluntary Sectoral Liberalisation (EVSL) failed in 1998, when the United States and Japan were unable to reach an agreement on specific sectors to be liberalised. Soon afterwards the United States shifted its attention to China's participation in the WTO, as a vehicle to promote open trade in the Asia–Pacific.

Another breakthrough for East Asian institutions was the formation of the ASEAN Regional Forum (ARF).[3] As its name suggests, the ARF is centred on the ASEAN countries that felt the need to create a security framework in which they could advance their own interests alongside the major powers in the region. It was also a necessary response to a variety of proposals for a regional multilat-eral security framework, such as the Australian call for a Conference on Security and Cooperation in Asia (CSCA)[4] or the Canadian concept of a North Pacific Security Forum. The establishment of the ARF was agreed in July 1993 at the

ASEAN PMC and the first ARF meeting took place in July in 1994. The original members were the six ASEAN countries, Vietnam, Laos, Japan, the United States, Canada, Australia, New Zealand, South Korea, China, Russia, Papua New Guinea, and a representative of the EU. The ARF now has 25 members: Cambodia joined in 1995; India and Myanmar in 1996; Mongolia in 1999; the Democratic People's Republic of Korea (DPRK) in 2000; Pakistan in 2004; and East Timor in 2005. Bangladesh is scheduled to become the 26th ARF member in 2006.

As was the case of APEC, the ARF started without any grand design, with its *raison d'être* only vaguely stated. Indeed, the first meeting was ridiculed by some as a mere 'talk shop'. Nonetheless, it was a measure as to how far the region had come that so many regional states – some of whom had recently been enemies – were able to discuss common strategic and security concerns. It was only in the second meeting in 1995 that more advanced objectives concerning a three-stage development of the organisation were agreed upon. The three stages encompassed a range of progressively more sensitive diplomatic and security initiatives, including: confidence-building measures, preventive diplomacy initiatives, and conflict resolution. The ARF members agreed that initial attention should be given to confidence-building measures. In order to promote these measures, the ARF members agreed to strengthen political–security dialogues, increase transparency by publishing documents on member states' defence policies, further promoting exchanges among the military, and encouraging the members to join the UN register of conventional weapons transfers.

While APEC and ARF represented the successful beginnings of multilateralism in the Asia–Pacific region, similar efforts focused on East Asia did not develop as quickly. An early but unsuccessful proposal was put forward by Malaysian Prime Minister Mahathir Mohamad in late 1990.[5] During a visit by Chinese Prime Minister Li Peng in December 1991, Prime Minister Mahathir suggested that, given the then stalled Uruguay Round negotiations, it was desirable to create an Asian common market comprising the six ASEAN countries as well as, China, Japan, South Korea, Hong Kong, Taiwan, and the Indochinese countries.[6] Prime Minister Li Peng responded rather cautiously, saying that it was impossible to determine the types and modality of cooperation because East Asian countries differed greatly in terms of economic systems as well as their stages of economic development.[7]

The proposal was an abrupt one, with little policy development being carried out, even by the Malaysians. Concrete components of the proposal only began to be worked out in January 1991.[8] Even as the content of the proposal was still being discussed, cautious views as well as criticism emerged. Japanese concerns revolved around the issue that such economic cooperation could accelerate protectionism.[9] Then Indonesian President Suharto supported the idea of the ASEAN states working together but 'warned against forming a trade bloc'.[10] US Ambassador to Japan, Michael Armacost, criticised the proposal, saying it would hinder the activities of APEC, which was then only two years old.[11]

Faced with these criticisms, Malaysia changed the name of the proposal from a trade bloc to an 'East Asian Economic Group' (EAEG) and began to emphasise that its proposal was consistent with GATT as well as APEC goals.[12] At the ASEAN Economic Ministers Meeting held at Kuala Lumpur in October 1991, Prime Minister Mahathir 'stressed the need to work together with the East Asian economies through the formation of the East Asian Economic Group (EAEG) which will be GATT-consistent, compatible with APEC, and not detrimental to ASEAN's cohesiveness'.[13] ASEAN economic ministers, trying to stay away from the bad connotation that EAEG had already created, decided to use 'Caucus' instead of 'Group', and such caucus was only to meet 'as and when the need arises'.[14] Hereafter, this proposal was referred to as the East Asian Economic Caucus (EAEC). Criticism, however, did not subside with a simple change in name. Then US Secretary of State, James Baker, when he visited Japan in November 1991, told Japanese Foreign Minister Michio Watanabe that the EAEC would draw a line in the Pacific, dividing Japan and the United States, and that the United States would not accept it.[15] Faced with such a strong US position against the EAEC, the Japanese Ministry of Foreign Affairs (MOFA) and Ministry of International Trade and Industry (MITI) began to take a cautious attitude towards the proposed group, though some officials who had long been unhappy with US negotiating practices in Japan–US economic relations remained sympathetic towards the original idea.

No new support for the EAEC emerged within ASEAN either. The ASEAN Summit, held in January 1992, discussed the issue but its Singapore Declaration of 1992 only stated that,

> [w]ith respect to an EAEC, ASEAN recognises that consultations on issues of common concern among East Asian economies, as and when the need arises, could contribute to expanding cooperation among the region's economies, and the promotion of an open and free global trading system,[16]

thus avoiding any concrete steps towards its realisation. The AMM held in the summer of 1992 decided not to make any commitment to the idea by asking the Joint Consultative Meeting (JCM) 'to study an appropriate modality that would complete the elaboration of the concept of EAEC'.[17] The JCM submitted its study to the AMM in the summer of 1993, suggesting that the ASEAN Economic Ministers Meeting (AEM) would be the appropriate body to consider the EAEC idea further. However, the AEM held in October 1993 only noted that consultations had been made and that the momentum of the progress should continue.[18]

However, in retrospect, a significant meeting took place at the time of the AMM and ARF in 1994. Foreign ministers of the ASEAN six member countries, China, Japan, and South Korea had lunch together on 25 July to discuss informally the possibility of the EAEC. Nothing of significance was agreed, partly because of Japanese Foreign Minister Yohei Kono's cautious attitude. However, informal or not, the meeting was significant from an historical perspective, as it was the first meeting of foreign ministers whose countries were to form the ASEAN+3 group. The EAEC idea did not proceed much thereafter. The Bangkok Declaration of the ASEAN Summit in 1995 had only one sentence referring to EAEC, saying that 'ASEAN shall continue with efforts to advance further the East Asian Economic Caucus (EAEC)',[19] without elaboration.

Even as the EAEC idea was stagnant, a new framework that might combine East Asian countries emerged out of the proposal of creating a dialogue between Europe and Asia, to be called the Asia–Europe Meeting (ASEM). During the early 1990s, concerns were raised in Western Europe that Europeans were slow in cultivating the necessary relations with a rapidly developing Asia. This led to a number of proposals in favour of expanding bilateral relations. One of the most prominent of these was the European Commission's 'New Asian Strategy', first promulgated in July 1994. European delegations discussed this proposal with their ASEAN counterparts at the EU–ASEAN Ministerial Meeting held at Karlsruhe in September 1994. A month later, in response to the European eagerness, the then Singaporean Prime Minister Goh Chok Tong proposed an Asia–Europe summit during a visit to France. In his address to the French Institute of Foreign Relations, Prime Minister Goh stated that is was time 'for Europe and East Asia to engage in a dialogue at the highest level to forge the third link in the tripolar world'.[20] Prime Minister Goh made a further statement on this topic at the 1995 World Economic Forum Meeting.[21] By that time, Goh had sounded out regional leaders about the idea and, according to Singaporean Foreign Minister S. Jayakumar, developed an 'ASEAN consensus on a Europe–Asia summit'.[22] The ASEAN's Senior Officials Meeting (SOM), held on 18 March 1995, discussed the ASEM idea and decided to hold its first summit in Thailand in the first half of 1996.[23] What was not yet clear was who would represent Asia. The other major issue was whether or not Australia and New Zealand would be included among the Asian participants.

As the ASEM participation issue was being debated in regional capitals, another proposal that might have some bearing on this issue was mooted – a Thai suggestion to hold an economic ministers meeting in Phuket. The Thai proposal assumed participation from ASEAN member states, China, Japan, and South Korea. As the proposed participants were identical with the EAEC members, Japan was reluctant to give full endorsement and suggested also including Australia and New Zealand, on the understanding that if Australia and New Zealand participated, Japan would also take part, otherwise it would not attend.[24] When Thailand notified Japan that ASEAN could not reach a consensus about Australia and New Zealand's participation, Japan decided not to participate in the Phuket meeting. As Japan's absence deprived the meeting of any significance, it was cancelled.[25]

The EU–ASEAN Senior Officials Meeting held in early May 1995 formally decided to hold a Europe–Asia Meeting, where the membership issue was further discussed. 'Sources said the initial group of Asian participants would include the six ASEAN countries and Vietnam (which will join the grouping in July), Japan,

China and South Korea, while the European side should be restricted to the current 15 EU countries.'[26] In addition to these countries, 'Hong Kong, Taiwan, Australia, New Zealand and India indicated that they want to be part of the inaugural meeting'.[27] Japan was the main advocate for the inclusion of Australia and New Zealand. It was reported that Japan sent a paper to Singapore, which chaired the preparatory meeting of ASEM, requesting the inclusion of Australia and New Zealand among the Asian participants. Singapore and Indonesia supported the Japanese idea but Malaysia objected, arguing that these two countries 'do not share our Asian values'.[28] Japanese Foreign Minister Yohei Kono also insisted, in an informal foreign ministers lunch attended by the ASEAN seven countries, China, Japan, and South Korea, that Australia and New Zealand be included in the Asian participants of ASEM. Malaysian Foreign Minister Abdullah Badawi strongly opposed Kono's proposal. In the end, diverging from its attitude to the Phuket Economic Ministers Meeting, Japan did not make the participation of Australia and New Zealand a precondition of its participation in ASEM.[29] With Japan's concession, Asian members of the ASEM were finalised and coincided largely with the supposed members of the EAEC.

Thereafter, Japan became less reluctant to the grouping of ASEAN, China, Japan, and South Korea. It was helped, on the one hand, by the fact that the Clinton presidency was more relaxed about Asian multilateral groupings than the earlier Bush administration. On the other hand, Japan, as a host of the 1995 Osaka APEC Summit, wanted to secure the participation of Prime Minister Mahathir. Hence, it could not afford to offend him.[30] Thus, on 19 November 1995, economic ministers of ASEAN countries, China, Japan, and South Korea who attended the APEC ministerial meetings held an informal lunch meeting to discuss preparations for ASEM. It is passingly ironic that the economic gathering that was not realised half a year earlier in Phuket due to Japanese intransigence was subsequently held in the Japanese city of Osaka.

In February 1996, further preparatory meetings for ASEM were held: the Foreign Ministers Meeting of the seven ASEAN countries as well as China, Japan, and South Korea, in Phuket on 2–3 February; and economic ministers of the same countries later that same month. On 29 February 1996, the heads of governments from these countries arrived at Bangkok to attend the ASEM Summit, before which they held a separate meeting. Although technically a preparatory meeting of the Asian members of ASEM, it was the first meeting of the heads of government in East Asia. Although the term EAEC was being phased out, the exact same grouping emerged as a subset of the new framework of ASEM. While the EAEC, as an attempt to carve out a subset of APEC members and designate it as an East Asian caucus, had failed, the same countries emerged through the Asian-side of the ASEM group.

However, this ASEM–Asian leaders meeting had more features than the original EAEC proposal suggested. As its name indicated, the EAEC was focused on economic affairs, whereas the ASEM was more comprehensive in its subject matter including political, social and cultural issues. The leaders of East Asia thus met for the first time in early 1996 for an occasion where Asians met

Europeans on an equal footing. Given the long history of colonisation and subjugation in the region, the Bangkok meeting was significant as an indication of Asia's potential role in global affairs. However, as the series of ASEM-related gatherings increased, what became apparent to the Asian side was that they lacked the same regional solidarity as did the European members, all of whom were members of the EU. 'East Asia' had been defined as an intersection of ASEM and APEC but it was simply an intersection without any specific features of its own.[31]

Birth of ASEAN+3

The first ASEAN+3 Summit was held in Kuala Lumpur on 15 December 1997. Although this meeting took place in the midst of the Asian financial crisis, it was not realised because of the crisis. The idea was hinted by Goh Chok Tong in his speech at the fifth ASEAN Summit in Bangkok; he suggested inviting China, Japan, and South Korea to an ASEAN informal summit without specifying exactly when. There was also a Malaysian idea to invite the three Northeast Asian countries to the informal summit of 1996. But these ideas did not materialise at the informal summit in Jakarta in December 1996.[32] The catalyst to realise these ideas came from a rather ironic direction, namely Japanese Prime Minister Ryutaro Hashimoto, on a visit to Southeast Asia in January 1997,[33] during which he enunciated the three pillars of Japan's new ASEAN policy (the Hashimoto Doctrine): closer and more frequent summit-level dialogues, multilateral cultural cooperation, and joint efforts to deal with global issues.[34] In order to realise closer dialogue among the leaders, at each stop on his itinerary Hashimoto proposed to hold a Japan–ASEAN Summit in conjunction with the ASEAN informal summit to be held in December 1997 and to regularise it.[35]

All ASEAN leaders who met with Hashimoto agreed to the proposal in principle, but were rather cautious as to the concrete planning of such a regularised Japan–ASEAN Summit. The main concern of ASEAN was that if the group had a special regular summit only with Japan it might risk offending other countries. As Lee Poh Ping argued, 'Japan is not the only big power operating in Southeast Asia. The other powers like China and the US may wonder why Japan should be the only country to have the regular summit with ASEAN and not China or US.'[36] Some in Southeast Asia might wonder if Hashimoto tried to use ASEAN as a counterweight against China, given the fairly tense Sino-Japanese relations after the Taiwan Straits crisis in March 1996, and the subsequent Hashimoto–Clinton Joint Declaration that was destined to strengthen US–Japan security ties in a more broader regional scope. Prime Minister Mahathir was reported to have said to Hashimoto that 'a policy of friendship is better than a policy of containment' towards China.[37] In any case, as an official of an ASEAN country said: 'The ASEAN way is the consensus way. Each ASEAN country will never give a categorical "yes" until they had met as a group to discuss the matter.'[38]

To the slight surprise of Prime Minister Hashimoto, the consensus that emerged in ASEAN was to invite not only Japan, but also China and South Korea to the ASEAN informal leaders meeting to be held in Kuala Lumpur in December, and hold three separate summits between ASEAN and the three Northeast Asian countries, as well as one joint summit between ASEAN leaders and the three Northeast Asian countries. Malaysia had discussed this idea among ASEAN members as early as February. Then, when Prime Minister Mahathir visited Japan in late March, he raised the option publicly.[39] A consensus on the matter was forged at an informal meeting of the ASEAN foreign ministers, which took place at the Non-Aligned Nations Foreign Ministers Meeting in New Delhi in early April,[40] with the formal decision being taken at the ASEAN Special Ministerial Meeting on 31 May 1997. The Hashimoto Doctrine, originally designed to regularise the ASEAN+Japan Summit, thus indirectly contributed to the establishment of the first ASEAN+3 Summit.

From the viewpoint of Dr Mahathir, Hashimoto's proposal provided a very good pretext to make a counter-offer towards realising a virtual form of the EAEC Summit, about which Japan might be regarded as the least enthusiastic. In any case, when ASEAN decided to invite Northeast Asian leaders to its summit, it did not anticipate that this meeting would be held in the midst of the Asian financial crisis. On the contrary, the atmosphere surrounding the special ministerial meeting was that of confidence and pride; a more important decision that this special AMM made was to accept the membership of Laos, Cambodia, and Myanmar. Though Cambodian membership was to be postponed due to its political turmoil in July, the expectation then was that seven ASEAN countries were about to become the ASEAN 10, and that a completed ASEAN would have its 30th anniversary summit in December, alongside the three main countries of Northeast Asia.[41]

While the foreign ministers were euphoric about the future of ASEAN, specialists in financial affairs were beginning to worry about the future of Asian economies. On 13 May 1997, an unprecedented sell-out of the Thai baht was launched and the Bank of Thailand (BOT) intervened in the foreign currency market with US$5 billion.[42] Despite these efforts, the market rate of the baht soared to as high as 26.35 to the dollar, as opposed to the official fixed rate of 25.86.[43] On the following day, the BOT and the central banks of Singapore, Malaysia, and Hong Kong made a joint intervention with as much as US$10 billion, successfully fending off a further speculative attack on the baht.[44] Although this restored some calm to the market, it was all undone on 2 July 1997, when the BOT announced its decision to float the baht. It plunged from 24.4 to the dollar on 1 July to 29.15 on 2 July. The Thai crisis triggered crises in other economies including Indonesia, the Philippines, and South Korea. The impact was not limited to the markets, but spread to affect the economic, social, and political sectors.

The initial response to the currency crises was to create a mechanism to assist the affected governments.[45] With respect to the baht crisis, an international conference for the rescue of the Thai currency was held in Tokyo on 11 August 1997. Apart from the main international organisations (IMF, World Bank, and

ADB), Japan, Indonesia, Malaysia, Singapore, Hong Kong, South Korea, Australia, and China all pledged contributions. Although the meeting did not prevent the further drop of the Thai baht, it symbolically indicated a sense of cooperation among regional countries.

Officials in the Japanese Ministry of Finance (MOF) were confident in achieving a cooperative scheme without the involvement of the United States and Europe, and went ahead to explore the possibility of creating a longstanding cooperative financial institution in East Asia. Based on the plan that MOF officials had already prepared internally in late 1996, they suggested launching a new Asian Monetary Fund (AMF) at the September 1997 IMF–World Bank Conference in Hong Kong. The basic idea was to create a US$100 billion fund from contributions from China, Hong Kong, Japan, Korea, Australia, Indonesia, Malaysia, Singapore, Thailand, and the Philippines.[46] The fact that this original plan did not include the United States, and assumed the AMF would enjoy a fair degree of independence from the IMF, angered the United States. It successfully lobbied the countries intending to contribute to the AMF and other countries including European countries to prevent Japan from hosting a meeting of finance ministers of the 10 supposed contributors of the AMF on the occasion of the IMF–World Bank Conference. As a result, the Japanese proposal to establish an AMF did not materialise.[47]

In contrast to the activities of their finance counterparts, regional diplomats were at a loss in the face of the rapidly unfolding financial crisis. Preparations for the ASEAN Summit and the first ASEAN+3 meetings proceeded but urgent necessities to cope with the crisis overshadowed the auspicious mood of the 30th anniversary summit of ASEAN, and for ASEAN leaders to welcome leaders of China, Japan, and South Korea. In the end, Indonesian President Suharto decided not to attend the summit because of illness and South Korean President Kim Young Sum sent Prime Minister Koh Kun because of the economic turmoil as well as the pending presidential elections. In terms of substance, while the ASEAN Summit itself could at least be proud of the publication of the 'ASEAN Vision 2020' document, the first ASEAN+3 Summit ended up being a typical 'talk-shop' meeting, with leaders stating their respective views without agreeing on any concrete measures. According to the Japanese Foreign Ministry, the major issues discussed during the summit were as follows:

> Views were expressed that there were no prospects of recovery for ASEAN economies and its economic difficulties would continue for the coming several years. Under these circumstances, ASEAN participants expressed their expectation about the role that Japan would play.
>
> On financial issues, it was confirmed that the implementation of the Manila Framework should be the priority. Some expressed concerns about the negative impact of IMF conditionality on economic activities.
>
> Regarding ASEM, the importance of the dialogues between Europe, which was accelerating its integration with the introduction of the Euro, and Asia, especially in economic issues, was confirmed.[48]

The first ASEAN+3 Summit, though disappointing in terms of its substantial achievement, was nevertheless historic. This was ostensibly the first meeting for the leaders of East Asian countries. From the viewpoint of Dr Mahathir, it was the first meeting of the virtual EAEC. The future of East Asian regionalism was, however, still very opaque. In response to Dr Mahathir's proposal to regularise the meeting, Chinese President Jiang Zemin and Japanese Prime Minister Rytaro Hashimoto responded cautiously, although both also offered support programmes to assist in the region's economic stability.[49]

The institutionalisation of ASEAN+3

The Asian financial crisis and its fallout over 1997 and 1998 saw turbulent political and social changes sweep in many regional countries. In Thailand, Prime Minister Chavalit Yongchaiyudh resigned in November 1997 and was replaced by Chuan Leekpai, leader of the Democratic Party. In South Korea, Kim Dae Jung, a newly elected President, had no alternative but to accept the stringent economic policy recommendations of the IMF. President Suharto's 32-year-long regime in Indonesia was brought to an end in the midst of riots in May 1998. In Japan, Prime Minister Hashimoto was forced to resign because of the defeat in the Upper House elections in July, which reflected the public dissatisfaction with the LDPs management of the economy. In Malaysia, Prime Minister Mahathir's power remained intact but the dismissal of Deputy Prime Minister Anwar Ibrahim in September 1998 indicated the existence of serious policy differences within the ruling elite.

It was against this backdrop that Vietnam, the host of the 1998 ASEAN Summit, announced on 3 August 1998 its invitation to the leaders of China, Japan, and South Korea again to attend a summit in December 1998.[50] In response to the invitation, China decided to send Vice President Hu Jintao. Japan was represented by Prime Minister Keizo Obuchi, and President Kim Dae Jung attended on behalf of South Korea. In contrast to the first ASEAN+3 Summit in 1997, the decision to hold a second ASEAN+3 Summit was clearly influenced by the necessity to cooperate in the wake of the economic crisis. ASEAN members and South Korea, in particular, needed an occasion to secure additional assistance from Japan. In fact, both China and Japan found in the ASEAN+3 Summit a useful occasion to demonstrate their importance in the regional and international arenas. China, whose own domestic economy largely avoided the impact of the financial crisis, behaved as a responsible international economic player by deciding not to devalue its currency. US President Clinton's later visit to China was an acknowledgement of China's increasing importance. By helping to realise a second ASEAN+3 Summit, China further solidified this image on the world stage.

Japan, on the other hand, was suffering from an acute sense of marginalisation in international society. It was shocking to many Japanese that the US President did not stop over in Japan when he made a nine-day tour of China. Worse still was the fact that President Clinton criticised Japan for its economic

mismanagement.[51] Many in Japan felt slighted by the leader of its most important ally. The age of 'Japan bashing' had, it was felt, been replaced first by that of
'Japan passing', and now 'Japan nothing'.[52] Obuchi, who was personally ridiculed
by international media and referred to as a 'cold pizza' when he became Prime
Minister in August 1998, nevertheless seemed determined to prove that Japan
could play an important role even under conditions of economic distress. The
New Miyazawa Initiative, disclosed in October 1998 and involving a US$30
billion aid package for Asian countries, was a concrete effort to prove this. The
ASEAN+3 Summit provided a timely occasion to explain this aid package, reinforcing Japan's importance to the rest of the world, in general, and to Asian
countries, in particular.

The second ASEAN+3 Summit in Hanoi on 16 December 1998 was a more
substantive meeting than the previous affair, with key policies being put forward by
the three Northeast Asian states. The focus of discussion centred on cooperation to
cope with the financial and economic crisis. Prime Minister Obuchi renewed
Japan's commitment to implement the New Miyazawa Initiative involving US$30
billion in financial support to countries affected by the financial crisis. Vice
President Hu Jintao proposed to hold a conference of deputy finance ministers and
vice governors of central banks to discuss financial affairs.[53] President Kim Dae
Jung proposed the establishment of an East Asian Vision Group (EAVG)
'composed of eminent intellectuals charged with the task of drawing up a vision
for mid-to-long-term cooperation in East Asia for the twenty-first century'.[54]
Meanwhile, the ASEAN countries 'expressed their high appreciation for the role of
and contribution by the three countries of the People's Republic of China, Japan
and the Republic of Korea in overcoming the economic and financial crisis
affecting the region'.[55]

The biggest decision that the meeting adopted was to regularise the
ASEAN+3 Summit. According to the press release, 'Summit meetings will now
be held between the Heads of State/Government of ASEAN and the People's
Republic of China, Japan and the Republic of Korea on the occasion of Formal
and Informal ASEAN Summits.'[56] This was the beginning of the institutionalisation of the ASEAN+3 framework. When the leaders of ASEAN+3 met for
the first time in 1997, it was an informal one-off gathering. Following the
second meeting, it was decided that a third meeting was to be held in the future.
Kim Dae Jung's proposal of establishing an advisory panel to discuss the future
vision of East Asia also secured the continued existence of the ASEAN+3
framework. Hu Jintao's proposal to set up a meeting of financial experts was
another important step towards institutionalising ASEAN+3. The same
grouping was recognised as a valid mechanism for collaborating in various functional areas including financial cooperation. The terms of reference of the
EAVG, finalised in late 1999, indicated that the EAVG's 'findings will be
submitted in writing to the ASEAN+3 Summit in 2001'.[57] Thus by the time the
third ASEAN+3 Summit was held in Manila in November 1999, it was already
commonly understood that ASEAN+3 summits would be held on an annual
basis.

Financial cooperation within the ASEAN+3 framework proceeded rapidly. The first meeting of deputy finance ministers and deputy governors of central banks of ASEAN+3 countries took place in Hanoi on 18 March 1999 and agreed to monitor the movements of short-term capital.[58] On 30 April 1999, the ASEAN+3 Finance Ministers Meeting was held in Manila, in which finance ministers agreed to cooperate on various economic measures.

Philippines President Estrada, as the host of the 1999 informal summit, became very active and vocal about the need to expand ASEAN+3 cooperation. When Estrada visited Japan in June 1999, he mentioned the long-term goal of creating an 'East Asian common currency'.[59] The Philippines Undersecretary of Foreign Affairs, Lauro L. Baja Jr, talked about the possibility of ASEAN+3 evolving into a new caucus to discuss political and security affairs,[60] while the Philippines Foreign Secretary, Domingo L. Siazon Jr, discussed the possibility of a future free trade area and common currency.[61] These ambitious ideas were premature. Being an embryonic institution, ASEAN+3 was not equipped with the necessary consultative mechanisms at the time to reach any consensus on such ambitious proposals. But, as Chapters 6 and 7 show, the ideas of a regional free trade area and a common currency are still on the regional agendas, albeit in medium and long-term timeframes.

What was achieved was more modest but still significant. The leaders who gathered in Manila on 27 November 1999 agreed to issue a 'Joint Statement on East Asia Cooperation', which said in part:

> Mindful of the challenges and opportunities in the new millennium, as well as the growing regional interdependence in the age of globalization and information, they agreed to promote dialogue and to deepen and consolidate collective efforts with a view to advancing mutual understanding, trust, good neighbourliness and friendly relations, peace, stability and prosperity in East Asia and the world.[62]

Although the leaders were not able to agree on concrete measures as President Estrada wanted, they agreed that the scope of cooperation within ASEAN+3 would be very comprehensive. The items to be included were: economic cooperation, monetary and financial cooperation, social and human resources development, scientific and technical development, cultural and information areas, development cooperation, political–security area, and transnational issues. They also agreed to hold an ASEAN+3 Foreign Ministers Meeting on the sidelines of the PMC.

Another important development in Manila was the informal breakfast attended by the leaders of China, Japan, and South Korea. Within the ASEAN+3 gathering, the '+3' component of three-way cooperation was much weaker than the corresponding ASEAN cooperation. In fact, there had never been a summit among the leaders of the three countries in Northeast Asia. At the initiative of Japan's Prime Minister Obuchi, the three leaders agreed to have a separate meeting of their own for the first time.

With the third meeting in Manila, ASEAN+3 clearly established a life of its own as a viable international institution in East Asia. It was determined that its summit would be held annually; it defined the scope of the group's activities as being very comprehensive; it created functional ministerial meetings; and it created an advisory panel to consider future directions.

The development of ASEAN+3: 2000 and beyond

The year 2000 saw rapid progress in financial cooperation within the ASEAN+3 framework. Deputy finance ministers and vice governors of central banks of ASEAN+3 met in Bandar Seri Begawan on 24 March and agreed to explore mechanisms of financial cooperation at a time of economic crisis. Based on such examination, the ASEAN+3 Finance Ministers Meeting held at Chiang Mai on 6 May 2000 agreed to create a system of 'currency swaps' among member states. Other functional fora were added to the ASEAN+3 framework: the Economic Ministers Meeting was held first in Yangon on 2 May 2000 and has been held annually since then. As Table 3.1 indicates, other areas such as labour, agriculture, tourism, energy, and the environment are also now being discussed at the ministerial level.

Annual summits, however, have continued to be the focal point for ASEAN+3 cooperation. At the 2000 Singapore Summit, a range of new ideas were raised such as the desirability of transforming the ASEAN+3 Summit into an East Asian Summit and desirable forms of free trade in the region. President Kim Dae Jung proposed the establishment of an East Asian Study Group (EASG) composed of government officials to 'explore practical ways and means to deepen and expand the existing cooperation' among ASEAN+3; it was tasked to 'assess the recommendations of the EAVG' and to 'explore the idea and implications of an East Asian Summit'.[63]

The EAVG presented its report to the ASEAN+3 Summit in November 2001 with the opening statement stating, 'We, the people of East Asia, aspire to create an East Asian community of peace, prosperity and progress based on the full development of all peoples in the region.'[64] The goals the EAVG agreed upon to create an East Asian community included:

> To prevent conflict and promote peace among the nations of East Asia;
> To promote trade, investment, finance and development in the region;
> To advance human security and well-being, in particular by facilitating regional efforts for environmental protection and good governance;
> To bolster common prosperity by enhancing cooperation in education and human resources development; and
> To foster the identity of an East Asian community by encouraging active exchanges and regular dialogues at both the governmental and non-governmental levels.[65]

The report, based on these goals, made 57 concrete recommendations including 22 major recommendations encompassing five areas of cooperation: economic, financial, political and security, environment and energy, and social, cultural, and education. The most noteworthy recommendations included:

> Establishment of the East Asian Free Trade Area (EAFTA) and liberalisation of trade well ahead of the APEC Bogor goal.
> Establishment of a self-help regional facility for financial cooperation.
> Adoption of a better exchange rate coordination mechanism consistent with both financial stability and economic development.
> Evolution of the annual summit meetings of ASEAN+3 into the East Asian Summit.

The EASG examined all EAVG recommendations and presented its report to the 2002 Phnom Penh Summit. This was the first substantive government-level policy agreement reached within the ASEAN+3 process. The EASG report positively assessed the EAVG report by saying; 'It provided East Asian countries with a good compass to show the right direction towards a bright future of East Asia.'[66] After examining all EAVG recommendations, the EASG concluded that 17 of them

Table 3.1 Scope of ASEAN+3 cooperation

Area	*Year of establishment*
Political and security	2000
Economic, trade, and investment	2000
Financial and monetary	2000
Agriculture, fishery, forestry	2001
Labour	2001
Environment	2002
Tourism	2002
Culture and arts	2003
Energy	2004
Health	2004
Information technology and communications	2004
Social welfare and development	2004
Transnational crime and counter -terrorism	2004
Science and technology (SOM only)	2001
Youth (SOM only)	2004

Source: ASEAN Annual Report 2003–4.

should be selected as 'short-term measures' to be implemented, and 9 of them should be selected as 'medium-term and long-term measures to require further studies'.[67] The EASG report was significant in the sense that the newly established framework of ASEAN+3 could agree at all concrete measures of joint action. However, it revealed its limitations too: the EASG virtually postponed its judgement on difficult issues by designating them as 'medium-term and long-term measures'. For example, the five recommendations of the EAVG listed above were all categorised as 'medium-term and long-term measures' that required further study. Nonetheless, although limited, the outcomes from the EASG report do show a willingness to move beyond talk into substantive policy actions.

While officials of the EASG deliberated over various measures in 2001 and 2002, the regional political momentum moved from Seoul and Tokyo to Beijing. President Kim Dae Jung's failure to improve the North–South relationship after a historic visit to Pyongyang in 2000 led to declining approval ratings in 2001 and compromised him during the 2002 presidential campaign. A series of leadership changes deprived Japan of opportunities to shape regional policies. Prime Minister Keizo Obuchi, who was a strong supporter of Japan's ties with ASEAN+3, was replaced by Yoshiro Mori after falling ill in April 2000. Mori, unable to improve his popularity, was forced to resign next spring and Junichiro Koizumi took office in April 2001. Koizumi, though immensely popular when he assumed the prime ministership, was slow to focus on developing an Asia policy. Rather his immediate task was to improve relations with the United States and to cooperate with it and the wider international community after the September 11 terrorist attacks.

In the meantime, China, which had long been reluctant and passive to any multilateral cooperative frameworks, began to take active initiatives to cultivate its relationship with ASEAN countries. Prime Minister Zhu Rongji, at the ASEAN–China Summit in November 2000, proposed to establish an FTA between China and ASEAN countries.[68] At the following summit in 2001, Zhu agreed with his ASEAN counterparts to conclude an FTA between ASEAN and China within 10 years. The led, at the 2002 ASEAN+China Summit, to China and ASEAN concluding a 'Framework Agreement of Comprehensive Economic Cooperation', which stipulated approaches and modalities to facilitate economic cooperation including an FTA. This agreement included a provision to realise trade liberalisation immediately in some sectors, known as the 'Early Harvest Programme'.[69] In 2003, China became the first dialogue partner of ASEAN to sign its Treaty of Amity and Cooperation. Since then China has continued to expand the scope and depth of its cooperation with ASEAN, with a new bilateral dispute resolution mechanism being agreed upon in 2004 and cooperation in disaster planning and relief operations being undertaken in 2005.[70]

Japan had long been reluctant to engage in any kind of bilateral FTAs, but seeing the emergence of increasing complex network of FTAs throughout the world, finally decided to start focusing seriously on the conclusion of an FTA agreement. The first country with which it did so was Singapore, which had few sensitive export products to Japan. The negotiations started in October 2000 and were concluded by January 2002 when Prime Minister Koizumi visited Singapore. In his policy speech there, Koizumi proposed to create a 'community that acts together and advances together'.[71] In the subsequent summit in Phnom Penh, ASEAN and Japan issued a 'Joint Declaration on the Comprehensive Economic Partnership' (CEP), and in the 2003 Summit, they concluded a 'Framework for Comprehensive Economic Partnership'. As building blocks to establish a Japan–ASEAN CEP, bilateral FTA negotiations were started in December 2003 between Japan and Thailand, between Japan and the Philippines, and between Japan and Malaysia. Japan and South Korea also agreed to start bilateral FTA negotiations in 2003. Since then Japan has also acceded to the Treaty of Amity and Cooperation (in 2004) but still remains far behind China in terms of other bilateral agreements, treaties, and memoranda with ASEAN.

These Chinese and Japanese efforts to forge their economic relationships with ASEAN countries were essentially China–ASEAN and Japan–ASEAN bilateral cooperative activities. The two powers in Northeast Asia have spent more energy since 2001 on improving their respective ties with ASEAN and did not take many stronger initiatives to promote wider East Asian cooperation. However, as the negotiations of their respective FTAs bring about concrete results, a more region-wide attempt will be put on the agenda. For example, one of the challenges in the immediate future will be when to start a Japan–China FTA, and once Japan and China start negotiating their FTA, East Asia will approach the stage of creating a region-wide FTA (or CEP). However, the success of such an endeavour is contingent upon China and Japan successfully resolving their various historical and contemporary differences. As events in mid-2005 clearly showed, whether it be with regards to visits to the Yasukuni Shrine or relating to bilateral cooperation in resource development, there is still a long way for both sides to go before they can work together in a constructive manner.[72]

Another item on the agenda for East Asian countries is the commencement of an East Asian Summit. The event, which was virtually put on the shelf after the proposal of EAVG, was revealed in 2005 when the first EAS was held. What impact the EAS will have on the equalisation and normalisation of all relations within the 13-member group is – as yet – unknown. However, with an emphasis being steadily placed on concrete results, the region's collective leadership will have to work hard to ensure that the EAS is seen as a viable success rather than a missed opportunity.

Conclusion

Based on the above narrative, several observations can be made. First, ASEAN+3 is not an institution that was intentionally designed by somebody for specific goals or visions in mind. It came into being with little forward planning. Visions as expressed in the EAVG were those created after the birth of ASEAN+3; they were the visions of an East Asian Community, not those of ASEAN+3. Despite appeasing rhetoric to the contrary, any list of the founding fathers of ASEAN+3 would have to include Dr Mahathir for his EAEC proposal. Without his persistent groundwork for a grouping of Southeast and Northeast Asian countries, the later proposal for a regularised ASEAN+1 Summit may not have been transformed into the first ASEAN+3 Summit. Those that were involved in the establishment of ASEM, including former Singaporean Prime Minister Goh Chok Tong, should also be recognised because it was only with the formation of ASEM that the grouping emerged as a reality. Former Japanese Prime Minister Hashimoto may also be regarded as one of the founding fathers, both because his initiative of having a regularised ASEAN+1 paved the way for the first ASEAN+3 Meeting, albeit unintentionally, and because of the way he changed Japan's reluctance to join the grouping that Mahathir had proposed.

Second, the Asian financial crisis was critical in institutionalising ASEAN+3. Although the first meeting of ASEAN+3 was planned before the Asian financial crisis, the institutionalisation of ASEAN+3 seems impossible without the crisis. Vietnam's decision to invite three Northeast Asian countries and the decisions of all the three countries to accept Vietnam's invitation were all coloured by the crisis in 1998.

Third, US behaviour was quite important in the formation of ASEAN+3. The major reason that EAEC was derailed was because of strong US opposition, which made Japan most reluctant to accept Mahathir's idea. Japan's changing attitude towards the East Asian grouping can partly be explained by a more relaxed attitude of the Clinton administration.[73] On the other hand, American behaviour may have indirectly strengthened the solidarity of ASEAN+3. Strong opposition by the United States to the AMF in 1997 may have given some impetus for the region's leaders to use the ASEAN+3 mechanism to strengthen financial cooperation – a move which subsequently led to the Chiang Mai Initiative. The clash between Japan and the United States over the EVSL in 1998 might have made both countries reduce their interest in APEC; the United States shifted its attention to the WTO and China's accession, while Japan shifted its focus to ASEAN+3. In many ways, ASEAN+3 institutionalised itself only while the United States did not pay particular attention to it.

Fourth, political leadership has been important to substantiate the ASEAN+3 framework. However, political leadership did not always exist. Despite the strong views of Dr Mahathir, ASEAN was not able to formulate consensus on various proposals to strengthen ASEAN+3. Overall, however, in the process of substantiating ASEAN+3 cooperation, it has been shown how it was leadership from the Northeast Asian countries that provided the necessary impetus to the grouping. In addition, competition between China and Japan regarding an FTA with ASEAN, though rather childish, contributed to promoting free trade within the region.

Finally, ASEAN+3 does not seem to have proven its continued viability as a substantive international institution playing the role more of a 'talk shop'. This is not to say that there is not evidence of regional programmes delivering concrete results, nor is it to imply that there is not a demonstrated commitment on the part of East Asian states to continue and deepen their various modes of engagement, but rather that the ratio of concrete outcomes that have a direct, positive impact on the states, markets, and societies in East Asia to policy pronouncements remains small. Whether ASEAN+3 crosses the bridge that divides substantive institutions from talk shops depends on the willingness of the ASEAN+3 members seriously to implement the EAVG's major proposals as opposed to the EASG's immediate measures. Political leadership seems critical whether ASEAN+3 can cross this bridge. While it is not yet clear if East Asia will follow the European model and have one or two leader states, or if it will develop its own path (based on its unique cultural and historical circumstances), what is still needed is for all states to commit firmly to advancing East Asian regionalism. It is only with such a commitment – one that can imagine the future and resolve the past – that future generations will look back on the events described in this chapter and elsewhere in this volume as the genesis of the East Asian Community.

Notes

1 For a vivid, journalistic account of the formation and development of APEC, see Yoichi Funabashi, *Asia Pacific Fusion: Japan's Role in APEC*, Washington, DC: Institute for International Economics, 1995.

2 For more on the development of APEC, see John Ravenhill, *APEC and the Construction of Pacific Rim Regionalism*, Cambridge: Cambridge University Press, 2001; Piamsak Milintachinda, Mario Artaza, and David Parsons, *APEC 2003 Outcomes and Outlook for 2004: What it Means for the Region*, Singapore: Institute of Southeast Asian Studies, 2004.

3 The most detailed chronicle on the formation of the ARF is Michael Leifer, The ASEAN Regional Forum, *Adelphi Paper No. 302*, Oxford: Oxford University Press, 1996. See Susumu Yamakage, *ASEAN pawa: Ajia Taiheiyo no chukaku he* (ASEAN Power: Toward the core of Asia Pacific), Tokyo: University of Tokyo Press, 1997, Ch. 9, too.

4 For further discussion on this Australia idea, see Grant Evans and Bruce Grant, *Australia's Foreign Relations in the World of the 1990s*, Melbourne: Melbourne University Press, 1991, pp. 111–13.

5 For a concise analysis of the genesis and development of the EAEC idea, see Koichi Sato, *ASEAN Rejime: ASEAN niokeru kaigi gaiko no hatten to kadai* (ASEAN Regime: Development of and challenges for conference diplomacy of ASEAN), Tokyo: Keiso shobo, 2003, pp. 84–103.

6 'Malaysia to initiate East Asian trade bloc', *Japan Economic Newswire*, 10 December 1990.

7 'Li Peng is supportive of East Asia market idea', *Japan Economic Newswire*, 13 December 1990.

8 'East Asia market proposal to be talked at ASEAN Summit', *Japan Economic Newswire*, 24 January 1991.

9 'Economic bloc', *Nihon Keizai Shimbun*, 22 June 1991.

10 B. McGowan, 'Trade bloc not endorsed', *The Courier Mail*, 18 March 1991.

11 Masanori Kikuta, 'US opposed plan to form new Asian economic group', *Japan Economic Newswire*, 5 March 1991.

12 See, for example, Noordin Sopiee, 'East Asian dream and what it means', *New Strait Times*, 19 January 1991.

13 Source: *The Twenty-third ASEAN Economic Ministers Meeting*, Malaysia, 7–8 October 1991. Online. Available http://www.aseansec.org/6126.htm.

14 Ibid.

15 Secretary Baker sent a letter to Japan's MOFA insisting Japan oppose the EAEC. In his memoir, Baker wrote: 'Mahathir was not seen as particularly pro-American and was considered likely to cause mischief if crossed, so I took a moderate line on his idea in public. In private, I did my best to kill it. Some East Asian APEC members were inclined to go along with it merely to placate the insistent Mahathir. At the APEC meeting in Seoul, Korean Foreign Minister Lee Sang Ok suggested his country might support Mahathir's proposal out of Asian solidarity. I reminded Lee that it was Americans, not Malaysians, who had shed their blood for Korea forty years before. My message was simple: All countries are not equal. The South Koreans got it, and did not press for an EAEG.', James Baker, *The Politics of Diplomacy: Revolution, War & Peace, 1989–1992*, New York: G.P. Putnam's Sons, 1995, pp. 610–11.

16 Online. http://www.aseansec.org/1163.htm.

17 See *Joint Communique Twenty-fifth ASEAN Ministerial Meeting*, Manila, 21–22 July 1992. Online. Available: http://www.aseansec.org/1167.htm.

18 See *The Twenty-fifth ASEAN Economic Ministers Meeting*, Singapore, 7–8 October 1993. Online. Available: http://www.aseansec.org/6128.htm.

19 Online. Available: http://www.aseansec.org/2081.htm.

20 Bertha Henson, 'PM: Time to forge Europe-E.Asia link', *The Straits Times*, 20 October 1994.

21 Goh told reporters that this idea was partly inspired by the view of other Europeans such as Klaus Schwab, Chairman of the World Economic Forum, who also felt the need to forge 'the missing link'. Source: Cherian George, 'Call for regions to hold top-level forum', *The Straits Times*, 15 October 1994.

22 Nirmal Ghosh, 'Manila supports PM Goh's Europe-Asia Summit idea', *The Straits Times*, 17 February 1995.

23 Lee Siew Hua, 'Thailand agrees to hold first Europe-Asia Summit', *The Straits Times*, 10 March 1995.

24 'Hashimoto gives up EAEC Meeting: Official', *Jiji Press Ticker Service*, 6 April 1995; 'Japan to skip proto-EAEC Meet, inviting SE Asia anger', *Japan Economic Newswire*, 10 April 1995.

25 'ASEAN drops bid to invite China, Japan, Korea to Phuket', *Japan Economic Newswire*, 10 April 1995.

26 Irene Ngoo, 'Many keen on Asia-Europe summit', *The Straits Times*, 3 May 1995.

27 Ibid.

28 Irene Ngoo and Tan Kin Song, 'Japan wants NZ, Aussies in Asia-EU Summit', *The Straits Times*, 25 July 1995.

29 Zulkifli Othman, 'Australia, NZ fail to get meet invitation', *Business Times*, 1 August 1995.

30 Koichi Sato, *ASEAN Rejime: ASEAN niokeru kaigi gaiko no hatten to kadai*, p. 90.

31 Asia–Europe Vision Group, created in 1998 at the initiative of South Korean President Kim Young Sum, as one of its 31 recommendations, 'encourages the Asian members of ASEM to increase dialogue among themselves'. *For a Better Tomorrow: Asia-Europe Partnership in the Twenty-first Century*, Asia–Europe Vision Group Report 1999, p. 39.

32 For details of Goh Chok Tong's and the Malaysian ideas, see Takashi Terada, 'Constructing an "East Asian" Concept and Growing Regional Identity: From EAEC to ASEAN+3', *The Pacific Review*, 2003, vol. 16, no. 2, pp. 262–4.

33 Hashimoto visited Brunei on 7–8 January, Malaysia on 8–9 January, Indonesia on 9–11 January, Vietnam on 11–12 January, and Singapore on 12–14 January.

34 Online.Available:http://www.mofa.go.jp/region/asia-paci/asean/pmv9701/policy.html.

35 Japan and ASEAN had two previous summits: Prime Minister Takeo Fukuda met with ASEAN leaders in Kuala Lumpur in 1977 and Prime Minister Noboru Takeshita in Manila in 1987. In other words, a 1997 summit between Japan and

ASEAN would not be so unnatural given the previous 10-year interval, but Hashimoto's intention was to have much more frequent meetings.

36 Teo Poh Keng, '"Hashimoto Doctrine" takes Japan step closer to ASEAN', *The Nikkei Weekly*, 20 January 1997.

37 Yang Razali Kassim, 'ASEAN and the Hashimoto doctrine', *Business Times*, 15 January 1997.

38 Felix Soh, Susan Sim, and Ho Wah Foon, 'Hashimoto Doctrine seen as move to engage ASEAN as equal partner', *The Straits Times*, 22 January 1997.

39 'Summit between ASEAN, Japan, China, S. Korea proposed', *Japan Economic Newswire*, 20 February 1997, and 'Mahathir hints at Japan-ASEAN summit before G-7 talks', *Japan Economic Newswire*, 27 March 1997.

40 For more information on the meeting in New Delhi see: 'ASEAN to make final decision on new membership May 31', *Japan Economic Newswire*, 7 April 1997.

41 Sato Koichi, 'EAEC koso to ASEAN+3 hikoshiki shunokaigi' (EAEC idea and ASEAN+3 informal leaders meeting), *Toa No. 404*, February 2001, p. 64.

42 Eisuke Sakakibara, *Nihon to sekai ga furueta hi* (The Days Japan and the World were Shaken), Tokyo: Chuokoronshinsha, 2000, p. 165.

43 'Hard day for Thailand's foreign exchange, stock markets', *Xinhua*, 15 May 1997.

44 Eisuke Sakakibara, *Nihon to sekai ga furueta hi*.

45 The Thai government initially requested assistance from Japan but the Japanese government was reluctant to make a bilateral scheme as the information about the Thai financial situations was not sufficiently transparent. The Japanese wanted 'the IMF to act as a tough guy' and suggested the Thai government go to the IMF. Disappointed, the Thai government officially asked the IMF, on 29 July, to take an initiative to make a rescue package. Eisuke Sakakibara, *Nihon to sekai ga furueta hi*, p. 177.

46 For more on the AMF refer to Chapters 6 and 7.

47 Eisuke Sakakibara, *Nihon to sekai ga furueta hi*, pp. 182–90.

48 Online. Available: http://www.mofa.go.jp/mofaj/kaidan/kiroku/s_hashi/arc_97/asean97/kaigi.html.

49 On the latter point, see Saiful Azhar Abdullah, 'New sense of confidence to meet economic problems in the region', *New Straits Times*, 18 December 1997.

50 'Vietnam invites 3 state leaders to ASEAN Hanoi summit', *Japan Economic Newswire*, 3 August 1998.

51 Ralph Cossa, 'A Chance to Patch Up the US–Japan Alliance', *International Herald Tribune*, 22 September 1998.

52 Kwan Weng Kin, 'From "Japan passing" to "Japan bashing"?', *The Straits Times*, 19 November 1998.

53 Siti Rahil Dollah, 'China calls for E. Asian-ASEAN finance dialogue', *Japan Economic Newswire*, 16 December 1998.

54 East Asian Vision Group Report, *Towards an East Asian Community: Region of Peace, Prosperity and Progress*, 31 October 2001, p. 44.

55 'The Meeting between the ASEAN Heads of State/Government and the Leaders of the People's Republic of China, Japan and the Republic of Korea', *Press Release*, Hanoi, 16 December 1998.

56 Ibid.

57 Source: *Chairman's Press Statement on ASEAN Third Informal Summit*, Manila, 28 November 1999.

58 'East Asian nations to scrutinize short-term capital flows', *Jiji Press Ticker Service*, 18 March 1999.

59 Justin Marozzi, 'ASEAN Single Currency Mooted', *Financial Times*, 25 July 1998.

60 Maria Teresa, 'E. Asian Economic and Security Forum pushed', *Japan Economic Newswire*, 8 October 1999.

61 Luz Baguioro, 'Manila pushes for an Asian currency', *The Straits Times*, 8 January 1999.

62 Online. Available: http://www.aseansec.org/691.htm.
63 *Final Report of the East Asia Study Group*, ASEAN+3 Summit, Phnom Penh, 4 November 2002, p. 64.
64 *Towards an East Asian Community: Region of Peace, Prosperity and Progress*, p. 6.
65 Ibid., p. 16.
66 *Final Report of the East Asia Study Group*, p. 13.
67 Ibid., pp. 3–6.
68 Based on this decision, an ASEAN–China Expert Group on Economic Cooperation was created; its report was submitted to the ASEAN+China summit in 2001. Online. Available: http://www.aseansec.org/newdata/asean_chi.pdf.
69 Online. Available: http://www.aseansec.org/13196.htm.
70 Source: *ASEAN-People's Republic of China*. Online. Available: http://www.aseansec.org/4979.htm.
71 Online. Available: http://www.mofa.go.jp/region/asia-paci/pmv0201/speech.html.
72 See, for example, Sun Yuting, 'China opposes Japanese leaders' visits to Yasukuni Shrine', *Zhongguo Xinwen She News Agency*, 29 September 2005; or 'China says its ocean gas project not issue for talks with Japan', *Japan Economic Newswire*, 29 September 2005.
73 For a more thorough discussion of this topic, please refer to the chapter by Evelyn Goh and Amitav Acharya in this volume.

4 Building a Northeast Asian community

A multilateral security approach

Shin-wha Lee and Hyun Myoung Jae

Introduction

Multilateral security cooperation efforts in East Asia have started to develop since the early 1990s, though the level of cooperation in the region (especially in Northeast Asia) still remains primitive when compared to the level of cooperation efforts in Europe or North America, which have their beginnings in the late 1950s and early 1960s.

The creation of the Association of Southeast Asian Nations (ASEAN) in 1967 could be seen as the first institutionalised effort to promote cooperation in Southeast Asia. However, ASEAN was unable to play any significant role in promoting regional cooperation during the first decade of its existence, as member states were often more preoccupied with addressing domestic issues. Nevertheless, ASEAN became the focus of international attention in 1976 and 1977, when ASEAN member states reaffirmed their commitment to promoting peace, freedom and political independence in the Southeast Asian region during their annual summit meeting. Though cooperation efforts since then have mostly been focused on addressing economic issues, there have been recent efforts to increase security cooperation within the frameworks of ASEAN and the ASEAN Regional Forum (ARF). These efforts, however, have mostly remained at the level of exchanging information or ideas on issues of common concern, and have been insufficient in institutionalising any specific regulations and enforcement authority aimed at promoting regional security.

The level of security cooperation in Northeast Asia lags further behind that found in Southeast Asia. The region lacks not only an institutional mechanism for intergovernmental multilateral cooperation, but also a regional power with the legitimacy to assume a leading and responsible role in regional collaboration. In addition, the greatest obstacle to establishing a multilateral cooperation regime in the region is the historical legacy of mutual distrust and confrontation that was left by the vestiges of colonial domination and war.

Even in the era following the Cold War, many traditional and military issues remain as existing and potential threats to regional security. There has been little progress on political or security regionalism,[1] while economic regionalism has developed to some extent in Northeast Asia since the Cold War. Moreover, there is little public awareness or political will for cooperation on regional security issues since traditional military issues are still regarded by the general public and academics, as well as by many policy-makers, as matters of diplomatic and polit-ical competition, rather than that of cooperation.

Despite these barriers to cooperation, it is encouraging to note that discus-sions on various issues concerning regional cooperation, including security cooperation, have been pursued at both the Track I (intergovernmental) and Track II (non-governmental) levels in recent years. One distinct example is the six-party talks process (a special multilateral arrangement between the two Koreas, the United States, Japan, China and Russia which was initiated in August 2003 with the aim of peacefully resolving the North Korean nuclear issue), which has triggered hopeful prospects of a new framework for security cooperation in Northeast Asia. Of course, this also depends on whether the talks are successful in bringing about a multilateral solution to the North Korean nuclear issue.

Moreover, countries in the region are seeking to formulate a broader concept of security, which would deal not only with traditional (military and political) issues, but also non-traditional (economic, environmental, human rights, labour and transnational crime issues) security issues. In the process, the governments and peoples of Northeast Asia have become increasingly aware of the need for greater discussion and cooperation in addressing such issues. However, as any discussion or proposals on the institutionalisation of regional multilateral cooper-ation efforts would first require a concrete examination of how to coordinate respective national interests and different policy directions, the task of constructing a regional security cooperation regime that would satisfy all the countries involved will not be an easy feat.

With these considerations in mind, this chapter aims at further increasing awareness of the need for intergovernmental cooperation strategies so as to effec-tively prevent and respond to any crisis situations that might occur in the region. The chapter thus intends to analyse existing forms of multilateral security coop-eration in East Asia (especially in Northeast Asia), and will proceed to examine the possibility of constructing a security cooperation regime in the region as part of an important step towards building a Northeast Asian community.

The chapter will first examine the definition and logic of multilateral security cooperation by looking at the expanding concept of security within the context of the changing international security environment, especially after the events of September 11, together with the notions of multilateralism and cooperative secu-rity. Second, the development of multilateral security cooperation efforts in the Asia–Pacific, East Asia and Northeast Asia and its significance in establishing a security regime in the region will be reviewed. Third, the positions of the main state actors in the Northeast Asian region with regards to regional multilateral security cooperation and the prospects for further cooperation will be evaluated. The countries chosen here include the United States, Japan, China, Russia and South Korea. Fourth, the challenges and opportunities security cooperation will pose for the region, with particular focus on why multilateral cooperation in

Northeast Asia remains difficult despite various intergovernmental and non-governmental efforts in recent years, will be explored. This section also discusses the 'complementary' aspects of comprehensive security and the role that non-traditional issues could play in consolidating ongoing confidence-building efforts. The concluding section highlights the need for multilateral security cooperation, as well as presenting possible action plans for cooperation in this area.

Theoretical approaches to multilateral security cooperation

A broader concept of security

The traditional concept of security was developed with the aim of promoting national security and thus countering the threat of war or other external threats to security. This traditional concept of security forms a major part of the realist security paradigm by providing an 'absolute' concept of security that aims to promote national security through relative power. Accordingly, most of the security study and policy literature during the Cold War focused on analysing and enhancing a state's defence and military capabilities. Nevertheless, there was also increasing criticism of the limited scope of issues and actors that could be addressed using the traditional concept of security. In particular, the oil shocks of the 1970s and the consequent rises in the prices of oil and raw materials increased international awareness of energy security. Likewise, the international trade disputes of the 1980s increased international awareness of the importance of economic security, while increased knowledge of the negative political and social consequences of environmental degradation increased demands to place environmental issues on the regional and global security agenda.

In 1983, Barry Buzan proceeded to maintain the need to expand the concept of security so that it would include various economic, environmental, social and political elements within the international context, and would thus overcome the limits of a state-centred concept of security that had mainly focused on promoting military security.[2] Richard Ullman also maintained that a broader concept of security would help expand the legitimate scope of policy-making.[3] Since the end of the Cold War, an increasing number of scholars and policy-makers have endorsed this position as non-traditional security or 'low-politics' issues like disease, famine, environmental degradation and transnational crime have emerged as real threats to national security along with traditional security issues. Accordingly, the concept of 'comprehensive security' has become an essential part of security thinking since the Cold War.[4]

'Cooperative security' has also emerged as an important concept in security thinking as interstate cooperation is increasingly necessary in addressing transnational and non-military security issues like human rights violations, refugee crisis situations, global warming, natural disasters and international financial crisis situations. Accordingly, economic, environmental and human security issues have become an integrative part of the security agenda. As the urgency and significance of these newly emerging security issues have increased, it has thus become imperative to seek a new approach in not only redefining and carrying out research on security, but also developing policies in response to such threats.

If traditional and military security issues have been addressed using a state-centred approach, comprehensive security issues are addressed using a multilateral approach, which would include the participation of intergovern-mental and non-governmental organisations, as well as state actors. This is because of the far-reaching and transnational impact that these issues could bring to the region as a whole. For instance, the Indian Ocean tsunami of December 2004 brought extensive, long-term environmental and economic damage to the region, forcing the international community to utilise a multilat-eral approach in enhancing environmental security and national safety through research, prediction and disaster preparation programmes, as well as in providing coordinated humanitarian aid to victims of disaster areas. Such a multilateral approach, which transcends national interests, contributes to facilitating the insti-tutional process of multilateral cooperation, and in turn serves as a useful mechanism in coordinating and resolving various transnational issues at the international or regional levels, as is discussed by Schreurs in Chapter 10.

Concepts and significance of multilateral security cooperation and regional multilateral security

Multilateral security cooperation is an institutional process that is established among a group of countries with the aim of undermining the potential effects of political, military, economic, environmental, social and cultural factors that would incite conflict; thereby promoting international/regional peace and secu-rity. This concept of multilateral security cooperation refers to the logic of 'cooperative security', which aims to undermine or remove military and non-military threats to security through dialogue, confidence-building and preventive diplomacy measures. Multilateral security cooperation also seeks to address secu-rity issues without designating a particular enemy. In this regard, it can be distinguished from the concept of 'collective defence', or a coalition of nations that is established with the aim of protecting the group from a designated enemy and preventing an outside attack through a military alliance like the North Atlantic Treaty Organisation (NATO).[5]

Multilateral security cooperation could also be distinguished from 'collective security', a type of coalition-building arrangement, under which a group of states agree on non-aggression and consider an aggressor against any one member state as an aggressor against all other member states. Thus, this provides the grounds for states within the arrangement to take collective action towards an invading state. The UN system is a distinct example of collective security.[6]

Meanwhile, the concept of 'common security', which aspires to preserve the state of mutual existence through interstate dialogue and compromise, is similar to the concepts of cooperative security and multilateral security cooperation.[7] This also applies to the concept of 'comprehensive security', which transcends the traditional concept of military security and aims to promote regional peace and security by responding to both traditional and non-traditional threats to security through interstate cooperation.[8]

The ultimate objective of multilateral security cooperation is to construct a security cooperation regime, which enhances the equal rights and duties of states participating in the regime, and allows them to exchange their views and coordinate their differences on common security issues. This, in turn, helps increase mutual assurance and allows states to peacefully manage existing, as well as preventing potential, conflicts by systematising and institutionalising a forum for dialogue.

There are three types of multilateral security cooperation: (1) the application of confidence- and security-building measures; (2) special cooperative measures in resolving particular regional conflicts; and (3) the establishment of a 'regional multilateral cooperation regime', which aims to increase dialogue, as well as cooperation, on regional political and security issues among states in the region. Among these, the first two types of multilateral security cooperation have the objective of resolving conflicts in the region through the implementation of various technical measures or agreements. The third type endeavours to create a 'process', which would contribute to building peace and stability in the region. Moreover, the third type of multilateral security cooperation does not undermine the role of existing security cooperation regimes. Instead, it can be seen as a framework, which complements the role of existing defence regimes or international/regional organisations.[9]

Indeed, while states during the Cold War had tried to resolve their security issues by siding with either the United States or the Soviet Union, the structural change in the international order after the Cold War, which could be represented by the coexistence of a US hegemony and the multi-polar leadership of the EU, Japan and China, has increased the need for a new approach to security. This new approach is represented by the ongoing debate and effort to establish a multilateral security cooperation regime in the East Asian region. In particular, there has been a growing consensus that confidence-building and cooperative security efforts, based on multilateral dialogue, are necessary in preventing regional conflicts and for constructing a peace regime in the region. In light of the non-traditional, as well as the traditional, threats to security and recent emphasis on the concept of comprehensive security, a more wide-ranging security strategy would be necessary in effectively responding to these various security threats.

In this context, the concept of a 'multilateral security cooperation regime' could be defined as a mutual cooperation regime in which three or more states that have a common interest in international/regional security issues get together to discuss and come up with a solution to comprehensive security issues, with the aim of promoting their common security. Considering that the concept of regional multilateral security cooperation first emerged as an idealist attempt to resolve the intense confrontation and conflict between the countries of Western and Eastern Europe during the Cold War, regional multilateral security cooperation aims to promote reconciliation and cooperation among states in a region by addressing regional security issues through dialogue and the non-use of force. Accordingly, this would help bring about the peaceful resolution of ongoing conflicts, as well as prevent future conflicts through crisis management.[10]

As the concept of security since the Cold War has expanded to include the non-traditional aspects of security through the concept of comprehensive security, the debate on regional multilateral security cooperation has increased within Asia and Europe. In the case of East Asia, there was much debate on the issue of institutionalising ongoing regional multilateral security cooperation efforts. This debate included not only a discussion of the scope of subregional countries that would be included in the cooperation framework, but also the approach that would be used in promoting cooperation efforts. That is, this refers to the question of whether the scope of multilateral cooperation would include the entire Asia–Pacific region or be limited only to the Northeast Asian region, and the question of whether efforts to promote multilateral security cooperation would be focused exclusively at the Track I level or also include the Track II level.

Northeast Asian multilateral security cooperation

Development of a multilateral security cooperation regime in East Asia and Northeast Asia

Since the mid-1980s, various ideas have been proposed with regard to promoting multilateral security cooperation in East Asia, in general, and Northeast Asia, in particular. Interest in early proposals has abated, though some have continually received the attention of states and are currently being pursued at the governmental level. On the other hand, new proposals and ideas on regional security cooperation have emerged in recent years and are attracting the attention of policy-makers and academics in the region.

The proposal to construct a security cooperation regime that would be applicable to the entire Asia–Pacific region could be represented by the scheme presented in 1985 by Soviet General Secretary Mikhail Gorbachev to establish an 'All-Asian Security Forum'. As an extension to his first proposal, Gorbachev made a second proposal calling on the need to establish a security forum in Asia that would be modelled after the Conference on Security and Cooperation in Europe (CSCE).[11] Furthermore, in September 1988, Gorbachev proposed to create a negotiating body that would examine and materialise his earlier proposals. However, efforts to implement Gorbachev's proposals were eventually aborted because of the negative attitudes of states in the region like China, not to mention the fact that the Cold War provided an unfavourable global, as well as regional, environment for cooperation. Former Australian Foreign Minister Gareth Evans also suggested a similar model for security cooperation during the ASEAN Post-Ministerial Conference (PMC) in July 1990. Applying the CSCE framework to the Asian region, Evans proposed to establish a Conference on Security and Cooperation in Asia (CSCA), which would address regional security issues like the Korean question. This met with the same fate as Gorbachev's proposals.

At the same time, there was some progress with regard to Canada's 1991 proposal to construct a North Pacific Cooperative Security Dialogue (NPCSD). At the time, Canada took the initiative to create a non-governmental forum for multilateral security dialogue, which would include the participation of scholars and officials from the two Koreas, the United States, Japan, China, the USSR and Canada. Its main objective was to create an environment for cooperation in the North Pacific region.

The results of these various efforts manifested in the establishment of the ARF in 1994. The ARF is the first and only intergovernmental forum for multilateral security dialogue in the Asia–Pacific region and was established under the initiative of ASEAN. As of 2005, 25 countries in the Asia–Pacific region, including North Korea, as well as the EU presidency, are participants in this high-level consultative forum, which aims to promote constructive dialogue and cooperation on various political and security issues in the region. Upon its inauguration, the ARF declared that it would gradually institutionalise its measures and procedures for resolving regional issues. This institutionalisation process would be carried out in the following three stages: (1) promotion of confidence-building measures (CBMs); (2) development of a preventive diplomacy mechanism; and (3) elaboration of approaches to conflict. However, despite these aspirations, the forum still lacks a specific plan, not to mention the compulsory measures that would help implement this process.[12]

The Shanghai Cooperation Organisation (SCO), which is based in Beijing, was founded in January 2004 following a summit decision in June 2002. It includes the participation of China, Russia, Uzbekistan, Kazakhstan, Tajikistan and the Kyrgyz Republic. In addition, there have been several proposals on the various forms of multilateral security cooperation efforts that could be pursued within the region, which have been made by the governments of Mongolia, South Korea and Malaysia since the mid-1980s. These proposals, however, have failed to materialise in any concrete form of cooperation in the region.

There have also been several proposals to promote multilateral security cooperation in the Northeast Asian region. The Korean proposal for a Northeast Asia Security Dialogue (NEASED) during the ASEAN Regional Forum Senior Officials Meeting (ARF SOM), held in Bangkok in 1994, is one such example. The main purpose of the NEASED would be to promote confidence building in the Northeast Asian region through interstate dialogue on issues of direct interest to the countries in the region (the two Koreas, the United States, Japan, China and Russia). Dialogue would be carried out based on the principles of state and territorial sovereignty, non-intervention, the peaceful resolution of conflicts, peaceful coexistence and democracy. South Korea has made continuous efforts to realise the NEASED because it would be able to contribute to promoting peace and stability in the Northeast Asian region, and could also serve as a framework for managing tensions on the Korean peninsula and contribute to the process of peaceful Korean reunification. However, little progress has been made in implementing this proposal due to the negative and passive attitudes of North Korea and China repectively.

Meanwhile, the Council for Security Cooperation in the Asia–Pacific (CSCAP), a non-governmental forum that was established in June 1993 through the collaboration of government-affiliated think tanks, has been successful in promoting multilateral security dialogue at the Track II level. Through the Council's strategic partnership with the ARF, it has been able to contribute to the forum by drawing upon new solutions to sensitive issues, which were introduced during its informal dialogue process.[13] Of course, there have also been some differences among CSCAP members on a common agenda due to regional differences and conflicting views over certain issues.

In addition, the Northeast Asia Cooperation Dialogue (NEACD), which was established in May 1993 by the Institute on Global Conflict and Cooperation (IGCC) with the support of the US State Department, has played a positive role in facilitating non-governmental multilateral security dialogue in the Northeast Asian region. The NEACD aims to build trust and promote cooperation in the region through informal dialogue between foreign and defence ministry officials, as well as academics from the two Koreas, the United States, Japan, China and Russia. This forum has been useful in exchanging views on the security situation in Northeast Asia. For example, a North Korean representative participated in a recent NEACD meeting and expressed the position of the North Korean government on the nuclear issue. The NEACD not only discusses traditional security issues, but also facilitates dialogue on non-traditional issues that are related to promoting cooperation in trade, investment and technology, as well as issues related to environmental protection and cooperation in combating terrorism, drug trafficking, organised crime and illegal migration. There have even been suggestions of raising the level of dialogue to the intergovernmental level because of the active dialogue that is carried out on various security issues within the forum.[14]

In summary, countries in the Northeast Asian region have attempted to increase regional confidence-building and cooperation efforts within various frameworks in the East Asian or Asia–Pacific regions, parallel to the growing trend of regional cooperation in other regions. This results in the point made by Breslin in Chapter 2 that there is a disjunctive between security regions and other regional forms in East Asia. At the same time, the increase in regional cooperation efforts is also related to the fact that the issue of political and security cooperation or regionalism among Northeast Asian countries has emerged as an important issue in the policy debates of Northeast Asian countries.

Since the establishment of the ARF was the result of an ASEAN initiative, ASEAN member states want to maintain their leadership in managing the ARF. Accordingly, security issues in the Northeast Asian region, such as the Korean question, will not be the primary security concerns of the ARF as initial concerns would mainly evolve around the South China Sea issue and other security issues in the Southeast Asian region (though it had been emphasised during the 2003 ARF meeting that peace and stability on the Korean peninsula would be vital to promoting security and economic growth in the wider Asia–Pacific region). Accordingly, there are increasing claims within the Northeast Asian region to develop an independent cooperation forum or a separate framework for dialogue within the ARF process that would address security issues unique to that region.[15]

Significance of multilateral security cooperation efforts in Northeast Asia

The institutionalisation of regional multilateral security cooperation efforts could contribute to promoting peace and security in the Northeast Asian region in many ways. First, the construction of a regional multilateral security cooperation regime could regularise dialogue among states in the region and, in turn, provide the opportunity for increased mutual understanding and cooperation on major security issues.

Second, because a multilateral security cooperation regime aims to enhance mutual interest and confidence-building by conveying state intentions and increasing the transparency of state activities, developing and implementing various mutual reassurance measures (MRMs) and CBMs are important in promoting multilateral security cooperation in Northeast Asia. This is because this process can contribute to accelerating arms reduction efforts and thereby help to resolve regional, as well as international, security threats.[16]

Third, the institutionalisation of regional security cooperation could help in guaranteeing a trade-friendly and economically sound region. Indeed, there is a high possibility that the economy-first policies of states in the region could contribute to increased regional security cooperation. For instance, China has continually made an effort to consolidate its cooperation efforts within the international community, as well as within the region, so as to maintain its high level of economic development. Moreover, there are prospects that China will actively make an effort to increase multilateral security cooperation in the region in order to consolidate its position as a regional power, and thus undermine the regional influence of the United States and Japan.

Fourth, a multilateral security cooperation regime could contribute to promoting regional peace and stability by providing fundamental principles and codes of conduct for interstate relations in the region. As confidence-building in Europe first started with the adoption of fundamental principles, a stable regional order could be constructed in Northeast Asia by establishing a code of conduct in carrying out regional multilateral security dialogue and cooperation efforts. Provisions that could be applied in regulating state relations in the Northeast Asian region would include those that relate to guaranteeing state and territorial sovereignty, the non-use of force, non-intervention in internal affairs, as well as specific provisions that relate to promoting economic cooperation, environmental protection and cooperation in combating terrorism, drug trafficking, organised crime and illegal migration.[17] Thus, the institutionalisation of multilateral security cooperation efforts is viewed as a step towards strengthening preventive diplomacy, as such efforts could decrease or remove altogether the possibility of conflict.

Country positions on multilateral security cooperation

Northeast Asia is not easy to define because it is more than a geographical entity. As a region, China, South Korea, North Korea and Japan are at its core, while the Russian Far East and Eastern Siberia, as well as Mongolia and Taiwan, are also among the countries included in its domain. The region also involves the United States, which is a significantly engaged power, though it does not necessarily fit into the region in geographical terms.[18] Nevertheless, the significance of Northeast Asia in the context of global politics seems more prominent than its geographical grouping. In terms of military capabilities, the United States, Russia and China are the three largest nuclear states in the world; North Korea is alleged as becoming one; and Japan, South Korea and Taiwan all have the potential of becoming one. Over the past 12 years, these countries have increased their arms build-ups through missile proliferation, thus increasing the possibility of a regional arms race.[19] Economically, the United States and Japan remain indisputable superpowers, while China is the third largest Asia–Pacific economy after the United States and Japan. These three countries are also among the world's largest trading countries.[20]

Although the six-party talks process among these countries has provided an opportunity for Northeast Asia to build a new regional framework for cooperation, the geopolitical and diplomatic calculations of the six countries remain ambiguous and contradictory, thus making predictions of the future course of regional community building unclear.[21] These countries have also displayed different positions on multilateral security cooperation, which would in turn act as an important variable in institutionalising such cooperation efforts in the region. In fact, Northeast Asian countries have long preferred bilateral security cooperation based on traditional alliances, and most of them have considered multilateral security cooperation as something for the future. This half-hearted attitude towards multilateral cooperation also originates from the geopolitical and historical legacy of distrust in the region. In particular, the Cold War security order in the region and its ideology still remain the source of conflict and have made it difficult for states to coordinate their differences in the name of universal values.

Accordingly, cooperation efforts have been pursued in a bilateral and rather hierarchical manner, providing little room for progress with regard to multilateralism after the end of the Cold War. For instance, trilateral relations among the United States, South Korea and Japan were merely seen as a linkage of South Korea's and Japan's bilateral relations with the United States, rather than the manifestation of a trilateral agreement among the three countries.[22] Nevertheless, as countries began to recognise the national, as well as regional, benefits of multilateral cooperation, government positions on multilateral cooperation underwent a gradual change. The following is a brief summary of each country's positions on multilateral cooperation.

United States

In the case of the United States, the main direction of US policy towards East Asia is focused on maintaining and consolidating US bilateral alliances in the region, so as to deter the rise of any potential powers there. These bilateral security arrangements were concluded during the Cold War era in line with the US containment policy towards the Soviet Union and China. With the end of the Cold War, the United States has pursued a more comprehensive security policy, which includes various efforts to promote multilateral security cooperation so as to respond effectively to the political, military and economic changes that have been taking place in the region.[23] American preferences towards multilateral cooperation in Northeast Asia were first expressed by former Secretary of State James Baker at the 1991 APEC Summit.[24] However, because diplomatic priorities were based on its bilateral alliances in the region, the United States continually emphasised the importance of its alliance with South Korea and Japan, as stipulated in the East Asian Strategic Initiative (EASI), which was part of the US Department of Defense's *East Asian Strategy Report* for 1991.[25]

This 'dual attitude' or conflicting attitude towards multilateral security cooperation was the result of the first Bush administration's need to reduce its security responsibilities in the region after the end of the Cold War. It could thus be assumed that the United States had concluded that the establishment of a multilateral security cooperation regime in the region would partially reduce its security responsibilities there. At the same time, there was also anxiety that discussions on multilateral security would weaken existing bilateral security arrangements and thus undermine US influence in the region.

In contrast, the Clinton administration recognised the limits of existing US bilateral security arrangements in the region in maintaining US security interests, and began to shift its policy on multilateral cooperation in East Asia. Following the first North Korean nuclear crisis in 1993, the United States began to recognise the importance of multilateral cooperation in addressing security issues on the Korean peninsula and proposed to initiate a four-party talks process that would include the participation of the two Koreas, the United States and China. Thus, US support for multilateralism in the East Asian region was the result of US attempts to use multilateral security cooperation as a complementary plan in pursuing existing US security policies that were based on its bilateral security arrangements within the region.[26] With the economic recession in the United States and increased uncertainty in the Northeast Asian region after the Cold War, this could also be seen as an attempt to share the costs of maintaining security in the region through a multilateral security framework. In addition, by accommodating the positions of South Korea, Japan and Russia, which had already actively expressed the need to construct a multilateral security dialogue regime in the region, this could also be seen as an attempt to maintain and expand US influence in the region.

However, after the second Bush administration came into office in 2001, and especially after the events of September 11, the United States has regressed to its original emphasis on bilateral alliance relationships in the region. As the 'war on terrorism' became one of the most important policies of the United States, the US–Japan alliance was perceived as the cornerstone of East Asian security, while US bilateral relations with China also became an important part of maintaining security in the region. Despite the launch of the six-party talks process, it would therefore be difficult to see this as an expression of US support for multilateral security cooperation in the region.

China

Like the United States, China had also placed more priority on its bilateral relations in the region. This was the combined result of deeply rooted diplomatic attitudes, past failed attempts at multilateralism, and possible limitations on China's newly acquired power in the region.[27] In particular, China was against any kind of multilateral cooperation in the region during the Cold War era because it perceived such efforts as part of US attempts to realign its relations with countries in the region and assume a more advantageous position. However, China's views on multilateral cooperation changed following the Cold War era as economic cooperation and interdependence continued to increase in the region. This was also the result of domestic economic reforms, which increased political/economic security and prosperity in the country, and expanded China's influence in the region. Moreover, China became increasingly aware of the need for a multilateral security cooperation regime in the region so as to mitigate anxiety about the country's military build-up efforts, and at the same time, to check Japanese efforts to remilitarise.[28] Accordingly, China has adopted a more flexible approach to resolving relevant security issues in the region through multilateral dialogue and negotiation, and has actively participated in various multilateral security cooperation fora like the ARF.

China thus recognises the need for multilateral security cooperation in the Northeast Asian region in order to maintain its high level of economic growth. Moreover, China's interests will not be limited by issues like that of the South China Sea. Although China is ready to play a constructive role in the establishment of a multilateral security cooperation regime in the region, it still prefers to participate in larger regional fora like the ARF or carry out a security dialogue at the non-governmental level. In short, although China still has anxieties about the limits that a multilateral security framework could place on its power, it is also examining the possibilities of actively participating in various ongoing multilateral cooperation efforts.

Japan

Japan, on the other hand, had not placed much importance on multilateral cooperation because there was no need to replace Japan's strong bilateral security relationship with the United States, which was sufficient in maintaining Japan's national security. This was also due to the lack of common security issues that could be dealt at the regional level. Though there were pending territorial issues with other countries in the region, Japan also preferred to resolve these issues bilaterally with the respective countries.

However, as the danger posed by traditional security threats sharply decreased and various factors of potential conflict emerged after the Cold War, Japan was faced with the inevitable choice of re-examining its security strategy. This was also due to the change in US strategy towards the region, as mentioned earlier in this chapter. In addition, the Gulf War of the early 1990s played a decisive role in altering Japan's diplomatic and security strategy. At the time, Japan was criticised for its 'checkbook diplomacy', though it had contributed approximately US$13 billion to the war effort. Japan thus realised the limited role it could play as a 'half state', or a country with only economic power in the international community, and sought to increase its political and diplomatic role in the international community. This explains Japan's recent efforts to become a 'normal state' and its active participation in the international effort to promote non-traditional security (for example, in the areas of environmental and human security). Japan was also faced with the need to pacify the anxieties of its neighbours with regard to an increased Japanese role in the region that would be the result of its dynamic foreign policy in the Post-Cold War era.

Accordingly, Japan started to work towards increasing multilateral cooperation in the region. In line with these efforts, former Foreign Minister Nakayama proposed to make the ASEAN PMC 'a political framework for promoting security in the region'[29] at the ASEAN PMC held in July 1991. This was later developed into the Miyazawa Doctrine, which called upon the need to increase security dialogue among states in the Asia–Pacific region, and was proposed by Prime Minister Miyazawa during his tour of Southeast Asia in 1993. Japan's interest in promoting a multilateral security dialogue during the ASEAN PMC is also seen to be the result of its judgement that security cooperation efforts within the framework of ASEAN would eventually help promote its role in the region, as well as in the international community. For this same reason, Japan played an essential role in establishing the ARF process.[30]

Since the mid-1990s, Japan has actively pursued its multilateral security policy in the region and has emphasised the need to hold trilateral summit and defence minister meetings with the United States and China that would discuss the issue of constructing a security regime in the region, and would mainly address security issues like the Korean question. The institutionalisation of such cooperation efforts to resolve North Korea's nuclear programme or missile issues would include substantial efforts to institute confidence-building measures. Japan's pursuit of substantive cooperation can therefore be interpreted as an attempt to buffer the effects of being a potential target for North Korea.[31] Nevertheless, such enthusiasm towards multilateral security cooperation does not necessarily mean that Japan's security alliance with the United States has weakened. On the contrary, Japan still regards this alliance as one of the most important factors in maintaining its national security, as well as the basis of its 'sound multilateral efforts' in the region.[32] This is confirmed by the increased military role of Japan after the September 11 terrorist attacks, and the important role that the US–Japan alliance has in carrying out US security strategy in the Asia–Pacific region.

Russia

Russia has continually made an active effort to promote multilateral security cooperation in Northeast Asia. Emphasis on the need for a security cooperation framework first started in 1969, when Brezhnev proposed to create an 'Asia Collective Security'. Since 1985, the Soviet Union has continually called on the need for multilateral cooperation, as part of Gorbachev's policies of perestroika and glasnost. Accordingly, the 1986 proposal for an 'Asian Helsinki Conference' resulted in the 1988 proposal to create a cooperation regime that would help relieve military tensions in the Asia–Pacific region, as well as expand economic cooperation. Such Russian efforts, however, were aborted due to US impediments.

The country's strategy on multilateral cooperation has also been in transition since the collapse of the Soviet Union in the early 1990s, which was soon replaced by the Russian Federation. The greatest change was that Russia was left with little power, compared to its Cold War predecessor. As a result, Russia's policy on multilateral cooperation and regional integration was reduced to promoting its interests in the Northeast Asian region compared to past Soviet policies, which focused on promoting Russian interests at the global level. In light of this, the proposal made by former President Boris Yeltsin in 1992 at the Korean National Assembly to set up 'a multilateral security cooperation regime that would address security issues in the Asia–Pacific region' is different from past proposals. With its economic recessions and social instability, Russia is no longer able to address its security issues via a military approach, and is now working towards addressing such threats through a more comprehensive and multilateral approach. However, Russia has been unable to sufficiently carry out its efforts due to its weak economy. This explains why it has been unable to make an active contribution to the Tumen River Area Development Programme (TRADP), the Gore–Chernomyrdin Committee, the Hashimoto–Yeltsin Plan, or the SCO, though they all demonstrate Russia's changed attitude towards multilateral cooperation.[33]

After the September 11 attacks, US–Russian relations have grown closer because of Russia's increasing cooperation and coordination with the United States on the 'war on terrorism'. This presents another aspect of Russia's economic development strategy and its role in the Northeast Asian region. Increased US–Russian cooperation will thus become another important variable in promoting security cooperation in the region.

South Korea

Being surrounded by regional powers, South Korea has been highly dependent on its security alliance with the United States in deterring the North Korean threat and thereby maintaining national security. In short, peace and stability on the Korean peninsula has been maintained through South Korea's and Japan's security alliances with the United States, and this has played a balancing role with regard to the DPRK–PRC–Russia coalition. At the same time, the development of inter-Korean relations has contributed to the process of building a peace regime on the Korean peninsula.[34] In light of this, South Korea's approach to multilateral cooperation had been based on promoting trilateral security cooperation with the United States and Japan.

Nevertheless, South Korea has played a more proactive role since the late 1980s in promoting multilateral cooperation in the region by examining ways and means in which South Korea could play an initiating role in promoting cooperation.[35] In particular, South Korea has annually emphasised the need to create a multilateral cooperative forum for security dialogue since its 1994 proposal to establish the NEASED. In short, as part of its comprehensive diplomatic policy, the Korean government has played an active role in promoting multilateral cooperation in the region that would not only address the North Korean issue, but also discuss the issue of building a Northeast Asian community.

One distinct example of South Korea's efforts was the establishment of the East Asian Vision Group (EAVG) and the East Asian Study Group (EASG) in 1999 and 2000, respectively. The EAVG was established at the Track II level as the result of a proposal made by former President Kim Dae-Jung at the ASEAN+3 Summit held in Hanoi in 1998. The EAVG was made up of eminent persons from the region and was given the task of presenting a long-term vision for East Asian cooperation in the twenty-first century. In 2001, the EAVG submitted its final report entitled 'Towards an East Asian Community: Region of Peace, Prosperity and Progress', which included recommendations on promoting economic, financial, political/security, environmental, social/cultural, educational and institutional cooperation in the region, including propositions on developing the annual summit meetings of ASEAN+3 into the 'East Asian Summit'.[36] In late 2004, the 10 ASEAN countries, together with China, South Korea and Japan, decided to hold the first East Asian Summit in 2005 in Kuala Lumpur, Malaysia, which was a major step towards the creation of an East Asian Community.

The EASG was also established through a proposal made by former President Kim Dae-Jung at the ASEAN+3 Summit in 2000. It was organised at the Track I level, and had a secretariat which was officially launched in 2001. The EASG submitted its final report at the ASEAN+3 Summit held in Cambodia in 2002. The report included the group's assessment of EAVG recommendations and its implications for the East Asian Summit. These two reports suggest that economic cooperation will be the cornerstone in building an East Asian community, though they do not underestimate the important role of political and security issues in promoting cooperation in the region.

In summary, the security environment in the Northeast Asian region is undergoing change in the midst of competition among the United States, Japan, China and Russia for regional power. That is, the security situation in the region is undergoing rapid change in the midst of various conflict situations brought about by US plans to construct a missile defence system, Chinese and Japanese competition for regional hegemony, territorial issues, the Taiwan question, the US 'war on terrorism' and the remilitarisation of Japan, among others. At the same time, it has become more important for countries in the region to adopt a collective and multilateral approach in addressing regional security issues, and discuss ways to relieve military tensions and build trust through a multilateral security cooperation regime that would parallel efforts to maintain existing bilateral security frameworks in the region. That is, Northeast Asian countries have more or less arrived at a consensus on the need to build a *bi-multilateral cooperation framework* that would help promote peace and security in the region.

Challenges and opportunities for multilateral security cooperation in Northeast Asia

Despite the growing awareness of the need for a regional cooperative framework that would deal with new security challenges and opportunities in the region, scepticism still remains strong in the region due to the pre-existing belief that it has a poor history of institutional frameworks (formal or informal) that could address relevant issues at the regional level. Such scepticism is due to a combination of the following complex issues.

First, the greatest barrier to the establishment of a recognised framework for cooperation in Northeast Asia is the historical legacy of conflict and distrust that remains among countries in the region as a result of colonisation and war (World War II, the Korean War and the Cold War). Even after the Cold War, various traditional and military security threats still remain in areas of potential conflict. The possibility of war recurring between the two Koreas, the North Korean nuclear issue, the Taiwan Strait conflict, anxiety over Japanese remilitarisation, and the competition between China and Japan for regional hegemony can be seen as examples. In particular, Japan's reluctance to provide reparations for its militarist acts during World War II remains an important barrier to regional reconciliation. Moreover, the level of public awareness and political will about regional security cooperation issues still remains low in the region.

Second, because relations between countries in the Northeast Asian region since the Cold War era have developed based on their respective bilateral alliance relations with the United States, a 'change in thinking' is needed to construct a multilateral security cooperation regime in the region that would complement existing bilateral security arrangements.

Third, it is highly likely that states will act contrary to agreed measures if their duties within the regime undermine their national interests. In particular, the sense of common security in Northeast Asia is relatively weak as the region has not experienced a large-scale war over the last 50 years. In addition, economic and cultural disparities among states in the region remain as barriers to substantiating security cooperation.

Fourth, because the region lacks a legitimate power that could neutrally and actively take the initiative in promoting multilateral cooperation in the region, multilateral security cooperation remains at the level of exchanging information and views on common issues, and has not resulted in the establishment of any concrete standards or measures for cooperation. In addition, none of the countries in the region are likely to take the initiative in adopting sanctions towards a state that has violated an agreement, and are unwilling to accept the risks of deteriorating interstate relations. Moreover, it is difficult to institute regulations and norms that would have the capability to employ coercive measures towards a state that has violated agreed measures.

Fifth, the unnecessary duplication of efforts, and competition between intergovernmental or non-governmental regional security cooperation regimes, could also serve to undermine their synergising effect. These problems have been the result of diplomatic competition among the participating countries. In fact, though the management of cooperative security would be a response to the urgent need to maintain peace and security in the region, there is also anxiety that China and Japan will exert their respective efforts to assume an initiating role in promoting regional multilateral security cooperation efforts so as to increase their influence in the region. South Korea also has ambitions to play a visible role in constructing a regional cooperation regime so as to stabilise and increase its influence in the region. Furthermore, as briefly mentioned earlier, there is increasing anxiety that the weapons build-up policies of countries could lead to an arms race in the region.[37] In fact, countries are continuing to competitively pursue their respective military build-up policies despite the emphasis on the importance of denuclearisation and counter-terrorism.

In summary, the following four conditions should be satisfied in order to develop a stable and effective regional security cooperation regime: (1) a shared value of mutual security and cooperation; (2) preference among the regional powers for a regime; (3) disbelief in the idea of promoting security through expansion; and (4) an awareness of the high costs of war and the high costs of the individualistic pursuit of (military) security.[38] Unfortunately, in light of the challenges mentioned above, the current security situation in the Northeast Asian region does not sufficiently meet these four conditions for institutionalising a security cooperation regime in the region.

Nevertheless, examples of existing multilateral security cooperation regimes like the OSCE and the ARF are suggestive of the factors that could play a catalytic role in developing multilateral security cooperation efforts in Northeast Asia. As Northeast Asian countries value economic growth as one of the most important objectives in their national policies (for example, China's economic reforms and opening up policies), regional peace and security will be an indispensable condition for continued trade and economic growth. Accordingly, countries will need to work towards promoting multilateral security cooperation in the region in order to develop their national economies. Furthermore, countries that were hostile towards each other during the Cold War period have worked towards normalising their diplomatic relations and are currently seeking to promote military cooperation and exchanges. As one example, China has been working towards promoting its bilateral military cooperation efforts with the United States, Japan and South Korea. Japan and South Korea have also expressed their interest in the construction of a multilateral security cooperation regime so as to complement their respective bilateral security alliances with the United States.

Although it is true that countries in the Northeast Asian region are competitively working towards expanding their military capabilities, this competitive relationship could also provide the opportunity for states to increase their awareness of the need for multilateral security cooperation in the region. Against this backdrop, various strategies have been proposed in order to promote such efforts, namely military dialogue at the working and leadership levels, humanitarian aid and joint rescue training projects. Moreover, it would also be important to provide a concrete strategy to systematise and regularise multilateral security cooperation efforts based on ongoing bilateral cooperation efforts. Plans to promote confidence-building would therefore be a prerequisite to security cooperation. Currently, there are debates on holding regular seminars on security cooperation, constructing hotlines, exchanging liaison officials, carrying out training observation programmes, sharing information, and so on. A concrete and feasible plan to implement these efforts should also be examined.

These efforts to promote multilateral security cooperation in the region would be more effective if simultaneously pursued with comprehensive security cooperation efforts, which would also include non-traditional security issues. Though confidence-building or traditional security issues such as arms control are vital to promoting multilateral security cooperation, an increasing number of experts have called for the need to pursue these efforts within the framework of comprehensive security, which would include non-traditional concerns such as economic, environmental, health and human security.

The need to address non-traditional issues including human security issues in the Northeast Asian region has grown proportionally with the increase in poverty and illegal migration after the financial crisis of 1997. The SARS (Severe Acute Respiratory Syndrome) epidemic of 2003, the 'yellow dust' phenomenon and air/marine pollution have emerged as health and environmental security issues. Moreover, the debate on the North Korean issue, which has mostly focused on its traditional security aspects over the last decade, now includes debate on the famine situation and economic difficulties in the country, as well as the issue of North Korean defectors.

Scholars and policy-makers engaged in this debate view non-traditional security as an independent variable in achieving sustainable regionalism. They regard non-traditional security cooperation among countries in the region as a potential stepping stone towards developing regional cooperation efforts on traditional security issues. For instance, regional approaches towards transnational issues such as environmental degradation cannot only help resolve this issue, but also set the stage for exchanging and coordinating views on more sensitive issues and thereby serve as a catalyst in building mutual trust in the region.

Thus it can be said that the process of building an effective regional security regime in Northeast Asia would be a long and tedious task. During this process, non-traditional security issues like environmental degradation, human rights violations and transnational crime will not receive the same amount of attention as traditional security issues. Nevertheless, the process itself will be able to promote dialogue and the exchange of views, and be significant in that it will ultimately contribute to set the stage for political dialogue, promoting regional security and peace. Once a cooperative regional regime is established, the regime will have the authority to promote interstate cooperation effort regardless of whether or not it succeeds in addressing and resolving particular non-traditional security issues.

Conclusion

It is argued that the increase in instability factors since the end of the Cold War has escalated conflict in the region, which could possibly lead to a military showdown.[39] Therefore, in order to remove the factors of conflict and instability, and construct a new international order, multilateral mechanisms (such as the OSCE), which would complement the 'prudence of realist power politics', should also be instituted in the Northeast Asian region. The possibility of unnecessary competition and distrust, misunderstanding and conflict can be minimised only when there is a multilateral cooperation regime in Northeast Asia that could serve as a regional 'safety valve'.[40]

Currently, the ARF provides the only formal multilateral institutional framework for security cooperation in the Northeast Asian region. However, the ARF remains insufficient in dealing effectively with sensitive issues that are limited to the Northeast Asian region, and still remains a loose forum for dialogue, not to mention the fact that it is an institution established under the initiative of ASEAN. Therefore, in order to address various security issues in the region, including the Korean question, it would be worth considering the possibility of establishing a 'Northeast Asian Security Cooperation Regime' that is either independent of, or within the framework of, the ARF. For example, in addressing the issue of the Korean peninsula, such a regime would not replace existing security frameworks in the region like the ROK–US and US–Japan security alliances or the Trilateral Coordination and Oversight Group (TCOG) established in 1999. Rather, it would complement and reinforce these security arrangements.

Though the current six-party talks process is a multilateral mechanism that was established among the two Koreas, the United States, Japan, China and Russia with the aim of peacefully resolving the North Korean nuclear issue, the six parties should examine the possibility of addressing other security issues in the region. During a trip to China in July 2004, Condoleezza Rice, former National Security Advisor and current US Secretary of State, proposed that the six-party talks process should be expanded into a regular forum for security dialogue in the Northeast Asian region after it achieves its initial aim of resolving the North Korean nuclear issue.[41] This regular forum could address conventional weapons and missile issues in the region, but also discuss issues related to bringing about a peace agreement on the Korean peninsula. However, experts have pointed out that it would be inappropriate to expand this multilateral framework into a high-level regional military regime like the OSCE or NATO,[42] since the six-party talks process was first initiated with the aim of addressing the specific issue of resolving the North Korean nuclear issue. Moreover, the present situation in Northeast Asia is not one in which either China or Japan, which both seek regional hegemony in constructing a multilateral security cooperation regime in the region, could take the initiative in establishing such a regime. Nor is it one in which South Korea could secure a balancing role considering its geopolitical position between China and Japan.

In conclusion, it appears that efforts to construct a framework for security cooperation in the Northeast Asian region will continue because of the number of security issues that must be commonly addressed, regardless of what the future will bring for the region. That is, it is likely that these efforts will develop into a *bi-multilateral cooperative mechanism*, which will complement ongoing efforts to realign existing bilateral relations. Therefore, in order to get the most out of the synergy effects of this mechanism, governments in the region need to make a concerted effort to devise a systematic security policy that would include increasing public awareness of ongoing international and regional trends, while at the same time accommodating various views on security issues. On the other hand, scholars and experts should present concrete measures on how to address and solve ongoing transnational security issues, and thus provide 'pressure and support' to various multilateral fora, as well as promote efforts to construct an intergovernmental cooperation regime.

Notes

1 Samuel Kim, 'Northeast Asia in the Local-Regional-Global Nexus: Multiple Challenges and Contending Explanations', in Samuel Kim (ed.) *The International Relations of Northeast Asia*, Lanham, MD: Rowman & Littlefield, 2004, pp. 3–65.
2 Barry Buzan, *People, State and Fear*, London: Harvester, 1983.
3 Richard Ullman, 'Redefining Security', *International Security*, 1983, vol. 8, no. 1, pp. 129–53.
4 David Capie and Paul Evans (eds), *The Asia-Pacific Security Lexicon*, Singapore: Institute of South East Asian Studies, 2002.
5 Conflict Research Consortium, University of Colorado, 'Collective Security', International Online Training Program on Intractable Conflict. Online. Available: http://www.colorado.edu/conflict/peace/treatment/collsec.htm.
6 Mark Lagon, 'Collective Security and the United Nations: A Definition of the UN Security System', *The National Interest*, 1995; Conflict Research Consortium, 'Collective Security'.
7 Capie and Evans, *The Asia-Pacific Security Lexicon*.
8 'The Concepts of Comprehensive Security and Cooperative Security', *CSCAP Memorandum No. 3*. Online. Available: http://www.cscap.org/publications.htm. Also, Mohamed Hassan and Thangam Ramnath (eds), *Conceptualising Asia-Pacific Security*, Kuala Lumpur, ISIS Malaysia, 1996; Korean Ministry of National Defense,

International Cooperation Division, 'The Concept of Regional Multilateral Security Cooperation'. Online. Available: http://www.mnd.go.kr/cms.jsp?p_id = 0050503000 0000.

9 Korean Ministry of National Defense, 'The Concept of Regional Multilateral Security Cooperation'.

10 Ibid.

11 The CSCE was created in 1975 as a multilateral forum for dialogue and negotiation between the East and West during the Cold War and was renamed the Organisation for Security and Cooperation in Europe (OSCE) in 1994. The OSCE is the largest regional security organisation in the world with 55 participating states from Europe, Central Asia and North America. It addresses a wide range of security issues so as to promote early warning, conflict prevention, crisis management and post-conflict rehabilitation mechanisms in the region. For details, see http://www.osce.org/general/.

12 'The ASEAN Regional Forum: A Concept Paper', Unpublished paper prepared by the ASEAN Senior Officials and presented to the ARF in August 1995.

13 Peter Katzenstein and Nobuo Okawara, 'Japan, Asia-Pacific Security, and the Case for Analytical Eclecticism', International Security, 2001/02, vol. 26, no. 3, pp. 153–85.

14 Institute on Global Conflict and Cooperation, 'The Northeast Asia Cooperation Dialogue'. Online. Available: http://www-igcc.ucsd.edu/regions/northeast_asia/ neacd/neacddefault.php. Also, Institute on Global Conflict and Cooperation, 'Track Two Diplomacy in Northeast Asia: Debrief from the Recent Meetings of the NEACD and US-DPRK Dialogue', IGCC Policy Seminar, 27 April 2004, UC Washington Center. Online. Available: http://www-igcc.ucsd.edu/NEACD policy-seminar.php.

15 Patrick Cronin and Emily Metzgar, 'ASEAN and Regional Security', 1996, No. 85. Online. Available: http://www. ndu.edu/inss/strforum/SF_85/forum85.html.

16 Gerald Segal, 'North-East Asia: Common Security or à la carte?', International Affairs, 1991, vol. 67, no. 4, pp. 755–67.

17 Dennis Blair and John Hanley, 'From Wheels to Webs: Reconstructing Asia-Pacific Security Arrangements', *The Washington Quarterly*, 2001, vol. 21, no. 1, pp. 7–17.

18 Gilbert Rozman, *Northeast Asia's Stunted Regionalism: Bilateral Distrust in the Shadow of Globalization*, New York: Cambridge University Press, 2004, pp. 3–4; Samuel Kim, 'Northeast Asia in a Local Regional-Global Nexus', p. 5.

19 Thomas Christensen, 'China, the US-Japan Alliance, and the Security Dilemma in East Asia', *International Security*, 1999, vol. 23, no. 4, p. 65; Ashley Tellis and Michael Wills, 'Strategic Asia by the Numbers', in *Strategic Asia 2004–05: Confronting Terrorism in the Pursuit of Power*, Washington, DC: The National Bureau of Asian Research, 2004, p. 500.

20 Tellis and Wills, 'Strategic Asia by the Numbers', p. 496.

21 Foreign Press Center, Japan, 'Prospects for an East Asian Summit are Both Optimistic and Cautious', 3 December 2004. Online. Available:http://www.fpcj/e/shiryo/jb/ 0455.htm.

22 Victor Cha, *Alignment Despite Antagonism: The US-Korea-Japan Security Triangle*, Stanford, CA: Stanford University Press, 1999.

23 US Department of Defense, *The United States Security Strategy for the East Asia-Pacific Region*, 1998.

24 James Baker, III, 'America in Asia: Emerging Architecture for a Pacific Community', *Foreign Affairs*, 1991/92, vol. 70, no. 5, pp. 1–18.

25 US Department of State Dispatch, 'The Evolving Security Environment in the Asia-Pacific Region', 4 November 1991, vol. 2, no. 44. Online. Available: http://usembassy.org.nz/about/what/nz_usrelations/evolve.pdf#search= 'Department%20of%20Defense,%20East%20Asia%20Strategic%20Initiative%20 (EASI).

26 Michael Yahuda, *The International Politics of the Asia-Pacific, 1945–1995*, London: Routledge, 1996, p. 144.

27 Paul Evans, *Asia's New Regionalism: Implications for Canada*, Asia Pacific Foundation of Canada, 2003.

28 Alastair Johnston, 'Is China a Status Quo Power?', International Security, 2003, vol. 27, no. 4, pp. 5–56.

29 *Far Eastern Economic Review*, 1 August 1991, p. 11.

30 Ralph Cossa, 'Asian Multilateralism: Dialogue on Track II', *JFQ Forum*, 1995. Online. Available: http://www.dtic.mil/doctrine/jel/jfq_pubs/jfq1007.pdf.

31 Paul Midford, 'Japan's Leadership Role in East Asian Security Multilateralism: The Nakayama Proposal and the Logic of Reassurance', The Pacific Review, September 2000, vol. 13, no. 3, pp. 367–97.

32 Masashi Nishihara, 'The Role of the Japan-US Alliance for Northeast Asian Security', *Japan Close-up*, September 1996, p. 7.

33 Gilbert Rozman, 'Russian Foreign Policy in Northeast Asia', in Samuel Kim (ed.) *The International Relations of Northeast Asia*, pp. 218–19.

34 Shin-wha Lee, 'South Korea's Strategy for Inter-Korean Relations and Regional Security Cooperation', in See Sang Tan and Amitav Acharya (eds) *Asia-Pacific Security Cooperation: National Interests and Regional Order*, New York and London: M.E. Sharpe, 2004, pp. 106–26.

35 For instance, the Korean Ministry of National Defense is examining ways in which South Korea could play a leading role with regard to cooperation efforts on counter-terrorism and piracy.

36 East Asia Vision Group Report, *Towards an East Asian Community: Region of Peace, Prosperity and Progress*, 31 October 2001.

37 Thomas Christensen, 'China, the US-Japan Alliance, and the Security Dilemma in East Asia'.

38 Robert Jervis, 'Security Regimes', *International Organization*, 1982, vol. 36, no. 2, 357–78.

39 Recited in Peter Katzenstein, Robert Keohane and Stephen Krasner, 'International Organization and the Study of World Politics', International Organization, 1998, vol. 52, no. 4, pp. 645–85.

40 Y. Yoon, 'Multilateral Cooperation in Northeast Asia and Inter-Korean Relations', 2001. This paper was presented at the Trilateral International Seminar on 'Peace and Cooperation in Northeast Asia' on 13 April 2001, which was held in commemoration of the 81st anniversary of the foundation of *Dong-A Ilbo*.

41 'Six-Party Talks Process: Now and Beyond', *Yonhap News*, 24 November 2004.

42 This was stated by a high-level US official, on condition of anonymity, at a conference in Europe on the security situation in Northeast Asia in which the first writer had participated in October 2004.

5 The ASEAN Regional Forum and security regionalism

Comparing Chinese and American positions

Evelyn Goh and Amitav Acharya

Introduction

The emergence of a multilateral approach to security was a distinctive feature of the security environment of the Asia–Pacific region in the 1990s. This was most obviously manifested in the formation of the ASEAN Regional Forum (ARF) in 1994, as the region's first security-oriented dialogue forum. After almost a decade since the establishment of the ARF, though, security regionalism still faces a number of important challenges.

The ARF is ostensibly geared to the idea of 'cooperative security' whose key features include inclusiveness (both likeminded and non-likeminded states) and reassurance as opposed to deterrence. As such, the ARF's security agenda includes confidence-building measures, preventive diplomacy and what has been called in the ARF vocabulary the 'elaboration of approaches to conflicts'. At the time of its formation, the ARF sparked some hope that it would generate a gradual shift in the security architecture of the Asia–Pacific region towards multi-lateral regionalism, reducing the dependence of states on balance of power approaches centred on bilateral security alliances and arrangements. For all practical purposes, however, the ARF has remained a 'consultative' forum, as opposed to being a 'problem-solving' organisation. It has adopted the non-legalistic, consensus-based approach of ASEAN, with minimal institutionalisation. While it has a moderating impact on regional geopolitics, it has not, as yet, ostensibly reduced the dependence of regional countries on bilateral security arrangements. Reasons for this, particularly in the Northeast Asian context, were elaborated upon in the previous chapter.

Hence, while the ARF remains the key regional forum for security issues, critics find the ARF to be weak and ineffective, a 'talk shop' with little to show in terms of concrete measures of confidence-building and preventive diplomacy. One of the major reasons behind this pessimism is the attitude of the United States and China, the two major powers of the Asia–Pacific. Their mutual engagement was a key rationale of the ARF. Both China and the United States initially opposed the idea of a regional multilateral security forum, but subsequently changed their minds and participated in the ARF. Yet, to a considerable extent, both powers have been reluctant players in the multilateral game, albeit for different reasons. The reasons behind this reluctance, and the prospects of their future involvement, are some of the most crucial factors that will determine the ultimate success or failure of the ARF, and provide useful insights into the prospects for East Asian regionalism in the medium term.

This chapter examines the perspectives and positions of the United States and China towards the ARF.[1] It identifies the similarities and differences in their respective position on the ARF's purpose, agenda and approach to regional security cooperation. It addresses two main questions: what explains the variation in great power behaviour towards multilateral institutions; and second, under what conditions, if at all, can the ARF engender a more positive engagement of the two powers? Finally, despite the limitations of multilateralism in the region, in the concluding section the chapter outlines a number of factors which suggest that East Asia's future security order need not necessarily rely primarily on balancing mechanisms.

Great powers and multilateral institutions

International relations theory offers several insights into the engagement of great powers in multilateral security cooperation. The most well known, and controversial, of them, hegemonic stability theory, posits that a hegemonic power may create multilateral institutions in order to legitimise its primacy by offering a collective good; for example, free trade or security to followers. Hegemonic stability theory has been the dominant explanation for the American sponsorship of global economic institutions (the Bretton Woods institutions), and, to a lesser extent, regional security groups after World War II, for example the North Atlantic Treaty Organisation (NATO).[2]

While hegemonic stability theory's power-centric perspective on why a hegemon may create multilateral institutions has been popular with neoliberal scholars, structural realists have focused on why great powers may oppose multilateralism out of distinctive interest and utility calculations. According to Steve Weber, great powers shun multilateralism for fear of being constrained by weaker states. This response is especially likely when power asymmetries between the great powers and the weaker members of the multilateral group are high; as in this situation, the potential benefits of the former's participation will be limited (since weak powers would have little to offer to the stronger powers) compared to the costs measured in terms of the hegemon's loss of autonomy.[3]

A recent variation of hegemonic stability theory, developed by John Ikenberry, has addressed this question by arguing that a hegemonic power may still seek multilateral cooperation despite uncertain returns and loss of autonomy. The key reason is legitimacy. From this perspective, material dominance alone is unlikely to last in the absence of a social framework that legitimises the power and leadership of the hegemon. Multilateral institutions provide a potent avenue for such legitimacy. Through them, hegemonic powers consent to 'bind' themselves to specified restraints in dealing with their weaker partners, in return for the latter's acceptance of their primacy. International orders that ensure such 'institutional binding' last longer and are generally more stable than those which are simply based on unilateral or bilateral relationships between the hegemon and the weaker states.[4]

In this chapter we explore the extent to which the attitudes of the United States and China are conditioned by considerations of power, interest and legitimation. We also suggest the need to pay attention to ideational transitions and identity formation in explaining the redefinitions of interests, which drove their evolving approaches to the ARF. We first examine their respective positions towards the ARF, and identify conditions which may engender a deeper engagement by both powers in the regional grouping.

China's approach to the ARF

China's position on the relevance and role of the ARF has evolved somewhat. Initially, China saw multilateralism as a threat to its sovereignty and security since it would give lesser regional actors an opportunity to 'gang up' against Chinese territorial interests and security objectives in the region. It was also suspicious that the ARF may develop into a tool in the hands of the Western powers for interfering in the domestic affairs of the Asian member states. Prior to the inaugural ARF meeting in Bangkok in 1994, China strongly opposed any discussion of the South China Sea dispute at the ministerial session, although it did not succeed in this objective.

This initial position changed in the mid-1990s, following the second meeting of the ARF in Brunei in 1995. At this meeting, China accepted the idea of multilateral discussion with ASEAN on the South China Sea issue. The shift was due to three perceived benefits of the ARF.

First, Beijing had begun to see the ARF as an important vehicle for airing its own security perceptions and advancing its security interests. Multilateral dialogues are a good way of reining in its neighbours' suspicions regarding its 'hegemonic' ambitions, and dampening the talk about a China 'threat'. Some analysts believe that through the ARF, China can project itself as a responsible regional actor interested in regional peace and stability and promoting the 'economic security' of the region.

Second, as Thomas Christensen has argued, the revitalisation of the US–Japan alliance might have led China to 'consider more positively the benefits of multilateral forums that might reduce mutual mistrust in the region'.[5] In other words, just as China's partners in multilateralism continued to see the ARF as a way of constraining China, China was beginning to recognise the value of the ARF as a useful means of influencing their thinking about its position and role in the regional security architecture.

Third, after the first few meetings of the ARF, China was reassured that the ARF would not develop into an anti-China bandwagon, nor would the United States be able to influence its course so decisively as to undermine Chinese strategic interests in the region.

This apparent shift in China's position on the ARF in some ways complements ASEAN's position. The ASEAN states, despite their persisting fears of China, have refused to join a US-led containment strategy.[6] ASEAN's desire to contain China with US support is tempered by a number of factors. The first is its own lack of military self-reliance. China's power well exceeds that of the combined strength of Southeast Asian states. For the ASEAN states, a containment posture towards China therefore implies increased dependence on the United States. Such dependence, in turn, runs counter to their domestic political concerns and regional norms, both of which explain Malaysia's official view that there is no need for a US military presence in Asia because there is no China threat.[7] Added to this is the concern that full-scale participation in US containment strategy towards China may be dangerously provocative to Beijing. For example, Lee Kuan Yew, the most enthusiastic proponent of the balance of power concept in Southeast Asia, sees an adversarial Sino-US relationship as a threat to regional stability. In his view, balancing Chinese power may stroke nationalist and hardline sentiments in China, with the consequence that 'the medium and small countries of the region have to live with the results of an aroused and xenophobic China'.[8]

Moreover, there exists within ASEAN a growing feeling that China will, over the next 20 years or so, seriously challenge, if not supplant, the US military dominance in the Asia–Pacific. As this happens, at least some ASEAN states could move towards a more conciliatory attitude, if not an outright bandwagoning posture.[9] Even if this may seem far fetched now, this scenario should not be ruled out. Differences have already emerged among the ASEAN countries in dealing with China over the Spratlys conflict, which has a potential to divide ASEAN into 'moderate' (Singapore, Thailand) and 'hardline' (Philippines and Malaysia) positions vis-à-vis China. For these reasons, US balancing strategies vis-à-vis China will not receive ASEAN's full backing unless they are accompanied by a multilateral process aimed at creating a general regional climate of restraint and moderation.

The 1997 Asian crisis also made it more difficult for the United States to make any efforts to revive ideas about containing China. China's political gain from the crisis, owing to its pledge not to devalue its currency, may not have altered the strategic balance in Asia, but it provided Beijing with an opportunity to present itself as a force for regional stability and secure recognition from other Asian countries as a 'responsible' regional power. This, as noted, enables Beijing to dampen talk about the 'China threat', thereby raising the political costs of an outright containment strategy.[10]

During interviews with Chinese officials in Beijing over the last few years, the authors were able to get the following sense of why China has come to place a great value on multilateralism than before.

The ARF helps China's security interests in four ways:

1   To 'learn directly from others what are the key problems in the region, not only between China and its neighbours, but also generally'. This is 'better than China's inward-looking view of the region as before'.

2   Through participation in the ARF process, China could 'learn about international arrangements, including the experience of other international organisations, in Europe'. Multilateralism is thus 'helping to internationalise Chinese diplomacy'.

3   'Through the ARF process, China, despite facing pressure on certain issues, such as the Spratlys, could also gain a broad sense of regional security, thereby helping it to broaden its views on security.'

4   Finally, the ARF has 'opened a new window' for Chinese Foreign Ministry officials. 'It has told leaders in Beijing how the outside world looks at China.' And 'when you know how the outside world thinks of China', it helps China to develop more sensitive policies.

Despite a noticeable positive turn in Beijing's attitude towards the ARF, available evidence suggests that too much optimism is unwarranted. While China's declaratory position on multilateralism is not too far from that of the other actors, including the United States, and given that the 1997 Asian crisis has dampened the momentum for multilateral approaches in general (with the exception of ASEAN+3, which was partly a regional response to the crisis), China's cautious approach to the ARF is indicated in the following positions:

•   China supports ASEAN's leadership in ARF. Without ASEAN's sponsorship, it is extremely unlikely that China would have joined any multilateral security forum in the Asia–Pacific, especially if the impetus for such a forum was seen to come from the United States. Furthermore, without Chinese involvement in the ARF, fears of a 'China threat' would have been far more pronounced, creating much greater uncertainty and predictability in the regional security environment.

•   China remains unwilling to take a more activist role in the ARF. China does not have a roadmap for the ARF, and has shown no initiative in moving the ARF's security agenda. It has been primarily in a reactive, rather than proactive, mode.

•   China wants to keep the ARF as a forum for confidence building, rather than conflict resolution. The ARF should be a consultative process, rather than a problem-solving mechanism. Its opposition led the ARF to change the third stage of its security agenda from 'conflict resolution' to 'elaboration of approaches to conflicts'.

•   China supports a preventive diplomacy role for the ARF, but limited only to interstate conflicts. Its chief worry is that including intrastate conflicts in the ARF's preventive diplomacy agenda will lead outsiders to 'interfere' in Taiwan's affairs, which for Beijing is strictly an internal issue.

An assessment of China in the ARF

It may still be too early to make a definitive assessment of China's posture towards the ARF. What is quite clear, however, is that China has increasingly used multilateral fora to project a new image as a 'responsible' and 'constructive' regional player and reassure its neighbours that it does not pose a threat to regional security and stability. Since the ASEAN Summit meeting in Bali on 7–8 October and the Bangkok Summit of the Asia–Pacific Economic Cooperation (APEC) on 20–21 October 2003, a perception has emerged in the region and in the West that China has hijacked the agenda of regional multilateralism and is using it to further its own strategic objectives which might culminate in a Chinese 'Monroe Doctrine' in Asia.

Such assessments are misleading. China's increasing diplomatic standing in the region is due to a number of developments since 1997, including its pledge not to devalue the renminbi during the Asian economic crisis, its offer of a free trade agreement to ASEAN, the signing of a Declaration on a Code of Conduct in the South China Sea between China and ASEAN in 2003, meaningful coop-eration with ASEAN to combat the SARS outbreak in early to mid-2003 (and ASEAN refraining from criticising China over Beijing's initial secrecy over the SARS outbreak), and its decision to accede to ASEAN's Treaty of Amity and Cooperation in Southeast Asia.

China's recent 'gains' are, however, not necessarily at the expense of the United States. ASEAN countries such as the Philippines, Singapore and Thailand have considerably enhanced their security cooperation with the United States. Further progress in China's relations with Southeast Asia and its security role in the region are subject to several factors. These include Sino-ASEAN economic tensions arising from the competitive nature of their respective economies, the as yet uncertain gains of a free trade agreement between China and ASEAN, and the continuing misgivings in Southeast Asia about China's military build-up. More importantly, the increasing acceptance of China's diplo-matic role in the region has much to do with Beijing's decision to work within ASEAN-led dialogues and processes. The mechanisms and processes that have contributed to improved Sino-ASEAN relations are mainly ASEAN-based. China, which at one point was deeply suspicious of ASEAN-led multilateralism, is now taking a cue from the 'ASEAN Way'. Any further progress in China's rela-tions with ASEAN will remain contingent on this approach. An assertive and unilateral Chinese stance in reordering Asia and its regional institutions could undermine its recent diplomatic gains. If China continues to work within the evolving multilateral framework in East Asia, however, it will make a significant contribution to the prospects for stability in Asia.

The US approach to the ARF

The ARF provides three potential sets of goods for Washington. First, it is a site of international society at the regional level. In spite of its inclusion of the EU countries, the ARF is centred upon the 'Asia–Pacific', drawing together East

Asia, Australia and New Zealand, and the Americas. It reinforces the identity of the Asia–Pacific as a region, and allows the United States and China to interact and engage with each other within the context of a shared neighbourhood and its concerns.

Second, growing this 'Asia–Pacific' notion also affirms the US identity as an integral regional player with legitimate interests in East Asia. This helps to justify US forward deployments and security postures in the region. This is a concern shared by certain East Asian states, which see significant interests in maintaining US commitments to the region. For instance, former Singapore Prime Minister Goh Chok Tong observed in 2001 that through the ARF, ASEAN had 'changed the political context of US engagement in Southeast Asia' because Southeast Asian countries had 'exercised their sovereign prerogative to invite the United States to join them in discussing the affairs of Southeast Asia'.[11] As a result, 'no one can argue that the US presence in Southeast Asia is illegitimate or an intrusion into the region'.[12]

Third, the ARF provides an additional testing ground for theories and expectations of socialisation regarding the engagement of China. In particular, as the only regional level forum for security issues, it is a proving ground for Chinese sociability in the security realm.

Initially, the Bush (Senior) administration was cold to suggestions by the Australians, Canadians and Japanese for a regional dialogue on security issues in Asia in 1990 and 1991.[13] This reluctant and suspicious attitude towards a multilateral security forum was derived from the Bush administration's struggle to understand and shape the security structure in the Asia–Pacific after the Cold War.

By late 1991, though, the Bush administration had moderated its attitude towards a regional multilateral security forum.[14] This change in attitude appears to have come about as a result of gathering regional doubts about the continued commitment of the United States to East Asia in the wake of the Cold War. The Bush administration began to appreciate the utility of a regional multilateral security dialogue in helping to reassure friends and allies in the region about its commitment in light of the budget cuts following the Cold War, planned troop reductions and the US withdrawal from the Subic Naval Base and Clark Airfield in the Philippines.

The momentum for the ARF gathered from 1992 onwards, and by the time the first ARF meeting was held in Bangkok in July 1994, Washington had declared its full backing for the forum.[15] This change of heart became much more pronounced from 1993 onwards with the new Clinton administration, which manifested a marked inclination towards values-driven strategy, liberal institutionalism and multilateralism.

Washington's support for the ARF might be construed as a low-cost, low-stakes policy during a time of transition. As some Bush administration officials have argued, by 1992 even the Republicans saw that given the change of opinion within the region, there was 'no reason to lie down across the railroad tracks and say do or die, we will oppose this'.[16] American acquiescence to the ARF was reactive – there was no benefit in opposing, and little cost and some gain in supporting the initiative. The costs would be low because only the secretary of state would be involved, and not the defence secretary or intelligence chiefs; there would be no treaties to be ratified by a sceptical Senate; and no dues to be paid to a secretariat. At the same time, Washington wanted to strengthen ties with ASEAN, which was becoming more important economically. Finally, it would also put to the test the issue of whether there was a 'China threat' to the region because ARF participants could have the opportunity to observe 'up close' whether China would 'play by the rules' in a multilateral security forum dealing with sensitive security issues.[17]

From ASEAN's viewpoint, by 1993, assurances about continued US interest in the region had become less important than the need to engage China in considerations about the ARF.[18] The key tenet of engagement was the assumption that by persuading the Chinese to participate in various international fora, it would be possible to condition and socialise Beijing into accepting international norms of acceptable behaviour.[19] The ARF had significant potential as an important element of an engagement strategy. It could help to address the difficult issue of how to engage China politically and on security issues, as opposed to the main focus of the engagement lobby which at the time was on economic issues.

In the context of a heated domestic debate about China policy centred on most favoured nation status, China's human rights record, and China's actions during the 1996 Taiwan Straits crisis, the ARF proved to be useful to the Clinton administration in 'selling' its engagement strategy towards China. Thus, Assistant Secretary of State Stanley Roth declared that 'facilitating the integration of the People's Republic of China into regional institutions like the ARF and APEC . . . can only encourage moderation in Chinese behaviour', helping to bring about 'a China that plays by the rules, rather than a China that seeks to make and enforce the rules'.[20] Even the Commander-in-Chief of the US Pacific Command acknowledged the importance of 'regional dialogues where we engage China, together with others, to fathom their intentions and to ease our misperception'.[21]

On balance, however, even though there is evidence aplenty of a remarkably sympathetic approach to multilateralism by the Clinton administration, in terms of rhetorical support and participation, the Clinton administration failed to specify how bilateralism and multilateralism related to each other, and left unexplained 'how a preference for maintaining power-balancing alliances could be reconciled with an inclination to seek instruments for threat reduction and region-wide security collaboration'.[22] Furthermore, there were significant limits to the discourse on the norms of 'cooperative security' and 'security pluralism': there was not a wide following for the more liberal notion of security pluralism within the administration, and the Clinton administration did also strengthen its alliances with Japan, South Korea and Australia.[23]

Fundamentally, Washington's East Asia policy under Clinton did not evolve very far away from its basis of containing potential threats to regional stability and US hegemony by maintaining a ring of alliances and a posture of forward deployment in the region.[24] Within the framework of the broader US policy towards East Asia, the evidence so far shows that bilateral alliances are its mainstay, supporting a strategy of containment and deterrence in order to retain the US preponderance of power in the region. Secondary to this basic element, engagement with China consists of an important complement, but this is largely conceived of, and carried out within, a bilateral context in the form of summits, official and military exchanges, trade and other Sino-American contacts.[25] On the multilateral front, Washington places most emphasis on economic fora like the WTO and APEC. Other multilateral 'shaping' strategies vis-à-vis China are supplementary, in spite of Washington labelling the ARF 'complementary'. As Secretary of State Warren Christopher told the ARF in 1995, Washington was working with the region to build a regional cooperation architecture in order 'to reinforce our treaty alliances and our policy of engagement'.[26]

Judging from the first term, it would seem that the George W. Bush administration has reinforced the emphasis on containment and military alliances, while reducing the Clintonian focus on multilateralism. Washington now takes a more sceptical view of China and has labelled it a 'strategic competitor'. Furthermore, the Bush administration's 2001 Quadrennial Defence Review (QDR) adopted an explicit agenda of promoting US primacy in the Asia–Pacific region.[27] It identifies a subregion, 'East Asia Littoral', spanning the south of Japan through to the Bay of Bengal, within which US forward-deployed forces would be more widely dispersed to cope with contingencies. This implicitly divides the region into littoral and continental sections, the latter of which is dominated by China, indirectly identified in the QDR as 'a possible competitor with a major resource base'.[28]

Furthermore, the events of 9/11 and the ensuing war against terrorism have exacerbated certain trends. First, some bilateral US alliances, such as those with Japan and the Philippines, have been strengthened. At the same time, however, the Bush administration's inclination towards unilateralism has also been deepened in the war against terror and the campaign in Iraq.[29] Its ambivalence towards multilateralism notwithstanding, the Bush administration has brought its intense focus on counter-terrorism to multilateral institutions such as the ARF and APEC, which have post-9/11 adopted anti-terrorism as their main focus.[30] Such an overarching emphasis on terrorism at the expense of other regional security issues and the deep-seated institutional problems within the ARF may work to the detriment of the forum as an effective security institution.

An assessment of the United States in the ARF

Yet, even if Washington views the ARF as a supplementary tool in its China and East Asia policies, the United States has supported and participated in the regional security forum. In terms of concrete issues, the United States tends to utilise the ARF as a supporting forum for declaratory statements and garnering support for the perpetration of international norms deemed important by the United States, rather than as a potential regional norms generator. In particular, the United States has consistently pushed its international non-proliferation and arms control agenda in the ARF, exhorting others to ratify, observe and support the entry into force of international conventions like the Nuclear Non-proliferation Treaty, the Comprehensive Test Ban Treaty, the Missile Technology Control Regime and the Chemical Weapons Convention (1997).

This tendency has also been manifested in the two other key issues: human rights and anti-terrorism. Madeleine Albright, in particular, used the ARF to state strongly the reservations and disagreements of the United States with ASEAN about policy towards Myanmar's military regime, and to express the US government's concerns about its human rights record.[31] In the wake of the terrorist attacks on 11 September 2001, Secretary of State Colin Powell read the campaign against terrorism as the prime issue of common interest for states in the ARF, which 'has perhaps given a focus to the ASEAN meetings and ARF that might not have existed before'.[32]

A major problem is that in spite of the plethora of increasingly 'non-traditional', and 'new' security issues discussed at the Forum, the ARF has little real contribution to make in regional security issues that are critical from the American point of view. The Taiwan issue, peaceful reunification of the two Koreas, and the India–Pakistan nuclear contest rank top on US priorities, and a regional institution that cannot help to address these issues represents low stakes for the superpower. Thus, when multilateralism is mentioned in conjunction with the Asia–Pacific in official US documents or speeches, it is APEC, with its economic liberalisation focus and summit-level meetings, and not the ARF, which is highlighted.[33]

Some observers have painted a two-way split within the ARF in recent years, between ASEAN and China, which prefer to concentrate on general dialogue to avoid disagreements; and the United States, Australia, Canada and Japan, who seek to move on to develop the ARF's potential in preventive diplomacy and conflict resolution.[34] Washington has indeed been urging since 1998 that '[w]hile the confidence building foundations must be solid, the ARF must move forward if it is to remain vital and relevant' because the 'traditional security challenges the ARF was created to address must still be met'.[35] At the same time, at the Track II level, the US Council for Security Cooperation in the Asia–Pacific (CSCAP) has played a leading role in developing the concept and principles of preventive diplomacy.[36] In 2000, Washington also suggested the need for greater institutionalisation of the ARF.[37] For example, the US Assistant Secretary of State for East Asian and Pacific Affairs, James Kelly, called ARF a 'limited forum', and pointed out that 'progress in both deepening the debate on security issues and in sharpening its focus has been slow'.[38]

On the positive side, from the American point of view, the ARF has contributed to regional security in two ways. First, and probably most important, the ARF has, since 2000, provided opportunities for official US–North Korea contact. Albright's meeting with North Korean Foreign Minister Paek Nam Sun at the ARF Meeting in Bangkok in 2000 led to the visit of a North Korean envoy to the United States, and Albright's trip to North Korea in October that year. The

2002 ARF Meeting in Brunei also provided an occasion for Paek to meet with the new US Secretary of State, Colin Powell.[39] Note, however, that on this issue, the ARF is not useful in and of itself, but rather as a facilitating meeting place.

Second, ARF meetings have provided a useful forum at which the United States could reassure the region during periods of tension or crisis, such as during the Korean peninsular nuclear crisis in 1993/4; Washington's reassurance after the revision of the US–Japan treaty guidelines in 1999 that it was not directed at any particular country; in the aftermath of the bombing of the Chinese Embassy in Belgrade in 1999; and after the EP3 incident in 2001. ARF meetings have also been used by other participants to clarify or criticise US security policies: for instance, China and North Korea expressed their concerns and suspicions about Washington's Missile Defence plans at the 2001 ARF Meeting.[40] At the 2001 ARF Meeting in Hanoi, ASEAN also formally requested that China and the United States ease bilateral tensions, while the main mediation efforts of Japan, South Korea and ASEAN over the EP3 incident were conducted outside of the Forum.[41] This set of limited benefits derived from the ARF supports the case of those who argue that it is fundamentally a 'talk shop', which serves an important, but essentially low-profile, function.

The quality of US participation derives from the fact that it is a global superpower taking a back seat in a regional security enterprise in its relatively dangerous backyard. This disjuncture breeds ambivalence, both within Washington and amongst its dialogue partners. The United States has so far chosen to accord the ARF a subsidiary role in its East Asian strategy because of its limited efficacy, and because the constraints on US influence through this channel render it low stakes. On the other hand, there are those who insist that ASEAN must eventually make way for the United States and other great powers in the driver's seat if ARF is to count.[42]

Comparative analysis

A comparison between the US and Chinese approaches to the ARF reveals a similar pattern. First, both professed deep scepticism of a multilateral approach to security in the immediate period following the Cold War. Second, this attitude softened somewhat in the mid-1990s. In both cases, this shift occurred because the initial misgivings about the negative impact of multilateralism on their respective security interests and postures were assuaged by other ARF members, including the ASEAN states. Nevertheless, neither has taken a proactive role in developing the ARF.

Despite these apparent similarities, there are major differences in what shapes the respective motivation and attitude of the two countries towards multilateralism. The Chinese approach to the ARF has been more reactive and cautious than that of the United States. While the United States feared the impact of multilateralism in undermining the rationale for its bilateral alliances, China feared the potential of multilateralism to develop into an anti-China bandwagon that would compromise its security interests and territorial claims in the region.

This indicates that concern for sovereignty was a more powerful factor in shaping Chinese attitudes towards the ARF than that of the United States. Interestingly, both powers have been especially wary of confidence-building measures: the United States is particularly concerned that they would constrain its naval deployments and supremacy in regional waters, while China has been wary of defence transparency as a threat to national sovereignty and security (and partly because it might reveal weaknesses in China's defence capabilities).

The fact that sovereignty plays a more important factor in China's position on the ARF is further indicated by its stubborn resistance to a full-fledged role for the regional group in preventive diplomacy, and its determination to limit any such role to interstate conflicts only.

Unlike the United States, China had little previous experience in security multilateralism at the regional level right up to the 1990s. Thus, its initial misgivings about multilateralism might have been partly due to unfamiliarity and inexperience. This was clearly not the case with the United States, which has been involved in regional defence cooperation within the NATO and Organisation of American States (OAS) frameworks. Thus, the US resistance to the ARF might be explained as stemming from utility calculations (the fear that the costs of multilateralism would outweigh its benefits for the US strategic posture).

In this sense, Washington's reservations about multilateral security institutions in the Asia–Pacific stem also from its habit and identity. Washington has become used to its position and status as the paramount power in the region. This relates especially to its being the strategic 'hub' from which regional bilateral alliance 'spokes' emanate. Multilateralism ARF style involves ceding this primacy in manner, if not in substance. The modality of interaction is different, and it runs counter to habit for the United States. Thus there is a tension between Washington refraining from hegemonic domination of a small/middle-power-led institution, and a reactive, 'back-seat' posture which in fact contributes to the lack of progress.[43]

Washington's relative ambivalence towards the ARF may also be explained by incomplete strategic ideational transformation after the Cold War. During times of conceptual uncertainty, there is a tendency to rely on 'the devil we know', even more so if the devil in this case is a tried, tested and triumphant one. Thus, Washington clings to the validity of its Cold War grand strategy and the bilateral alliances which formed the core of its East Asia policy. At the same time, the various administrations since the Cold War have recognised the need or exigency to try to think outside of the Cold War box. Therefore we see the coexistence of bilateral security arrangements with Clinton's push for multilateral security dialogue, and, more recently, George W. Bush's penchant for more unilateralist security policies. Multilateral approaches have consistently ranked lower than bilateralism.

Parallel to this is Washington's strategic indecision regarding China. The uncertainty about how to approach China is a prominent element of the strategic ideational transition in Washington following the Cold War. The debate about the China 'threat' is a manifestation of a plethora of interrelated issues, including trade, human rights, nuclear proliferation and strategic competition. Sino-American relations have been characterised by summitry and personal diplomacy, as well as a series of bilateral crises throughout the 1990s, trends which have not helped to clarify China policy. Although there is recognition in the 'engagement' camp that Chinese attitudes to the world must change, this tends to be presented as vague hopes that Chinese perceptions and priorities will be altered by development and liberalisation. The idea of 'socialisation' through multilateral fora is under-conceptualised, and so the *de facto* official approach is a minimalist one of 'join us, and we will sit back and wait for you to show us that you are not disruptive', rather than a proactive one that seeks out ways to draw out Beijing and Washington.

In responding to calls for multilateralism in Asia–Pacific security, both the United States and China have shown a preferences for bilateralism. For the United States, this has meant a continuing emphasis on its bilateral alliances. For Beijing, which does not maintain the kind of conventional treaty-based military alliances in the region, bilateralism is the preferred mode of conflict management, in addressing its disputes with neighbouring states.

Ways forward for Asian regionalism?

Given the differences, what sort of changes in the domestic and international environment might induce greater involvement of the two powers in the ARF? What impact might this have on the prospects for East Asian regionalism in general? The first is a prior improvement in their bilateral relations, which is governed by considerations that are to some extent quite distinct from the forces driving multilateralism. Domestic politics, bureaucratic alignments and economic imperative are important factors in shaping the US policy towards China. For China, nationalism and sovereignty, both largely domestic variables, are critical in shaping its policy towards the United States. The interaction between these factors will be key to the health of Sino-American relations, which in turn will shape their attitude towards regional multilateral security institutions.

To be sure, closer ties between Beijing and Washington may develop along a 'Concert' model (a great power condominium which excludes lesser states from decision making).[44] This could bring more harm than benefit to the ARF. However political and economic considerations make it unlikely that Sino-American relations would develop to the exclusion of other powers in the region. Overall, improved bilateral ties between China and the United States are likely to augur well for the ARF.

Second, domestic politics will play a role in shaping the US attitude towards the ARF. Changes of administrations in Washington have, in the past, produced important shifts in the overall US policy towards multilateralism. Witness, for instance, the first Clinton administration's turn to greater multilat-eralism at the regional level (although at the global level, the Bush Senior administration was equally multilateral, suggesting thereby that a more pro-multilateral approach at the global level does not necessarily translate into increased support for multilateralism at the regional level). The current US disdain for multilateralism under the George W. Bush administration again shows the importance of domestic factors in shaping the US policy towards both regional and global multilateralism.

China's domestic political structures make it less likely that major shifts in attitude towards multilateralism would respond to leadership transitions. Yet, this cannot be entirely ruled out. Leadership changes in China, even within the framework of its communist power structure, may produce shifts in the use of nationalism as an instrument of foreign policy. A long-term dark horse is democratisation, which may make a major difference to the way China views multilateral cooperation. Some relatively sudden democratic transitions without a prior development of institutions of power sharing can produce a narrow nationalism, at least in the short term. On the other hand, democratic states, including newly democratic states, are known to acquire a less rigid view of sovereignty (Thailand under Chuan Leekpai), which may be conducive towards multilateralism. Shifts in China's attitude towards multilateralism will depend in part on the manner in which its democratisation takes place, if and when it does occur.

Third, another important factor which will shape the attitude of the United States and China towards the ARF concerns the fate of US bilateral alliances in the region. While appearing to be stable for the present, many US alliances in the region have underlying problems that cloud their long-term viability. These factors include: domestic public opinion in Japan against US bases, peace and reunification in the Korean peninsula, and renewed nationalism in the Philippines against US–Philippine defence cooperation. Any undermining of the alliances due to the above factors might make the United States turn more unilateral. This, in turn, however, could increase the level of support for multilateralism in the rest of the region, which can no longer count on the US security umbrella as a collective good. In this situation, Beijing might turn more multilateral to demonstrate greater unity with the region and isolate the United States. This outcome would not enhance the prospects for the ARF.

Fourth, the ongoing war on terror might engender a positive shift on the part of the United States and China towards regional multilateralism. The United States has already shown a willingness to turn to APEC and ARF in developing and strengthening anti-terror measures. China has gone along with this move. The fallout of 9/11 has allowed China to seek some measure of US understanding, if not support, of its own challenges of domestic terrorism. So far, the United States has resisted this move, but faced with an escalation of the global anti-terror campaign, the United States may offer the kind of understanding of the Chinese predicament as it has to Russia.

An initial reason for China's misgivings about the ARF was its lack of any significant previous experience in regional multilateral security cooperation. Since then, however, Beijing has been actively engaged in developing the Shanghai Cooperation Organisation (established in June 2001), from the original

Shanghai Five grouping of Russia, China, Kazakhstan, Kyrgyzstan and Tajikistan established in 1996, through which China now addresses security issues related to terrorism, separatism and extremism.[45] This indicates that the real choice for China is not multilateralism versus bilateralism, but which kind of multilateralism. A compact grouping with a focused security agenda geared to what Beijing sees as genuine transnational challenges is more preferable to Beijing than the kind of overarching and broad-brush approach that the ARF represents. Thus, an important challenge for the ARF will be to develop synergies with subregional security approaches which could make Beijing view security multilateralism in a more favourable light.

The factors mentioned above may not lead to similar or parallel shifts in the attitudes of the United States and China towards the ARF. Greater American enthusiasm for the ARF may produce suspicions on the part of China and vice versa. However, as China's regional power rises and the United States maintains its global hegemony, multilateralism could become, for both players, an important tool for reassuring the region. A future US administration stepping back from the extreme unilateralism of the current incumbent could find engagement within the ARF useful in signalling this shift and legitimising US leadership in the region. Chinese leaders are also increasingly aware that the rise of Chinese power needs to be backed by efforts at reassurance of its nervous neighbours. A powerful China cannot pursue its interests effectively in the absence of a regional perspective that views it as a constructive and legitimate leader. Both the United States and China have an interest in seeking greater legitimacy from their neighbours, and multilateralism offers both an important avenue for seeking such legitimation.

Implications for future East Asian security architecture

A cursory look at East Asia's security architecture would seem to suggest that US post-war bilateral defence arrangements have done a better job in adapting to the post-Cold-War and post-9/11 challenges than the region's multilateral security institutions.[46] The US–Japan alliance has been revitalised against the rise of China and then readjusted to meet the requirements of the war on terror. This and the US–Australia alliance have been used to support US interventions in Afghanistan and Iraq. The United States has enhanced its bilateral security cooperation with Singapore, securing greater access to military facilities there. Thailand and the Philippines have been accorded major non-NATO ally status by the Bush administration.

In contrast, East Asia's multilateral security institutions appear to be struggling. In the early 1990s, the emergence of a variety of multilateral security dialogues and institutions offered the promise to dilute, if not altogether supplant, the centrality of US bilateral security arrangements. However, the Asian economic crisis that occurred in mid-1997 put paid to that expectation. ASEAN, the anchor for Asia–Pacific cooperative security arrangements, was especially hard hit. While it could not be blamed for failing to prevent the economic crisis, its inability to arrest the strategic and political fallout from the crisis, including renewed bilateral tensions among its members, was damaging to its credibility as a regional security community.

The ARF, the only multilateral security organisation in the Asia–Pacific, has been slow to move from confidence building to preventive diplomacy. It has had little role in managing the crisis in the Korean peninsula, even though North Korea is a member. Potential alternatives to the ARF, such as the Shangri-la Dialogue organised by the International Institute for Strategic Studies, have emerged, partly by exploiting the ARF's limitations.

APEC, severely weakened by the 1997 crisis, has seen its trade liberalisation agenda overshadowed by the proliferation of bilateral trade deals. APEC has sensibly turned its attention to promoting a human security agenda and fighting terrorism on the economic front. APEC is the only Asia–Pacific organisation to provide for a heads of government summit. Over the past years, this has proven to be a timely and important venue for consultations to address urgent regional security issues, such as East Timor (in 1999) and terrorism (in 2001 and 2003). The future of APEC may well be decided by its increasing turn towards security issues.

Conclusion

Despite the limitations of multilateralism, however, a security order relying primarily on balancing mechanisms need not be East Asia's destiny. First, the long-term outlook for US bilateral alliances remains uncertain. There are serious uncertainties over the future of the US–South Korean alliance, much of it due to growing domestic opposition in South Korea to Washington's hardline stance towards North Korea. Similarly, the revival of the US–Philippines defence relationship is a move that may not necessarily survive the current preoccupation of both governments with terrorism in the south. Domestic opinion in the Philippines remains predisposed against too close a security nexus between Washington and Philippine security agencies. The US–Australia alliance remains robust, but Australian Prime Minister Howard's desired role as something of a local American 'deputy sheriff' has not endeared him to the region and has alienated large segments of domestic Australian public opinion.

Second, US bilateral alliances have thrived by being adaptive. One aspect of this adaptation is their willingness to become more inclusive, and thereby narrow the political gap between bilateralism and multilateralism. For example, bilateral exercises involving the United States and formal treaty allies such as Thailand (Cobra Gold) now routinely include third-country participation and observation. Bilateral structures operating under multilateral norms of transparency and inclusiveness may be one of the more important developments in the emerging Asian security order.

Third, new forms of regional security cooperation in East Asia are emerging. These include ad hoc and informal multilateral approaches, a prime example being the six-party talks over the Korean peninsula. Another new development, straddling both economic and security arenas, is the ASEAN+3 (APT) framework. The APT challenges the neoliberal and largely utilitarian view of regionalism represented by APEC. As an East Asian framework, it is more attuned to its members' sense of regional identity than either APEC or the ARF. A key factor affecting the APT's prospects will be the role of China in East Asian regionalism. Through the APT, China has an unprecedented opportunity to shape the agenda of East Asian security cooperation, perhaps supplanting a weakened ASEAN that is at the same time increasingly dependent on China's markets.[47]

China's growing involvement in multilateralism is a welcome development, and vindicates the strategy of China's neighbours and policy advocates who saw engaging China through multilateral institutions as a superior approach to regional order than containing China. China has been able to use multilateralism as a means to dampen the talk about a 'China threat' and discredit containment. In return, ASEAN has gained the Chinese pledge not to use force in the Spratlys and its accession to the Treaty of Amity and Cooperation. Nevertheless worries remain as to whether China will turn its engagement in regional institutions into a lever for regional dominance. While Chinese officials increasingly appear to be putting more emphasis on APT, and while the Bush administration has used other fora such as APEC to address security issues, successful East Asian regionalism would have to include the central participation of the United States since it remains the key security player in the region. Whether the ARF is necessarily the only option to make this come true is more debatable, but in the absence of other alternative institutions that encompass both these major powers, it seems reasonable to put regional efforts into developing security regionalism within this one.

Notes

1   The section on the United States is somewhat longer than that on China because the existing literature on the United States in the ARF is more limited.
2   See Robert Keohane, *After Hegemony: Cooperation and Discord in the World Political Economy*, Princeton, NJ: Princeton University Press, 1984; Robert Gilpin, *The Political Economy of International Relations*, Princeton, NJ: Princeton University Press, 1987; Andrew Walter, *World Power and World Money: The Role of Hegemony and International Monetary Order*, New York: Harvester Wheatsheaf, 1993.
3   Steve Weber, 'Shaping the Postwar Balance of Power: Multilateralism in NATO', in John Gerald Ruggie (ed.) *Multilateralism Matters: The Theory and Praxis of an Institutional Form*, New York: Columbia University Press, 1993, pp. 236–8.
4   John Ikenberry, *After Victory: Institutions, Strategic Restraint, and the Rebuilding of Order after Major Wars*, Princeton, NJ: Princeton University Press, 2001.
5   Thomas J. Christensen, 'China, the US-Japan Alliance, and the Security Dilemma in East Asia', *International Security*, Spring 1999, vol. 23, no. 4, pp. 49–80.
6   Amitav Acharya, 'ASEAN and Conditional Engagement', in James Shinn (ed.) *Weaving the Net: Conditional Engagement with China*, New York: Council on Foreign Relations, 1996, pp. 220–48.
7   Amitav Acharya, 'Containment, Engagement, or Counter-Dominance: Malaysia's Response to the Rise of Chinese Power', in Alastair Iain Johnston and Robert Ross

(eds) *Engaging China: The Management of an Emerging Power*, London: Routledge, 1999, pp. 129–51.

8   'S.M. Lee, Kissinger Rap US Policy Towards China', *The Straits Times Weekly Edition*, Singapore, 20 November 1993, p. 5.

9   On balancing and bandwagoning, see Stephen M. Walt, 'Alliance Formation and the Balance of World Power', *International Security*, Spring 1985, vol. 9, no. 4, pp. 7–8.

10 The ASEAN countries have acknowledged China's positive role in the economic crisis; as the Malaysian Foreign Minister put it, 'Asean is grateful to China for all its assurance not to devalue the renminbi despite pressures upon it to do so'. 'Abdullah: China Can Help ASEAN to Rally', *New Straits Times*, Kuala Lumpur, 29 July 1998. Online. Available: http://ftdasia.ft.com/info-api/sh.

11 Goh Chok Tong, keynote address to US–ASEAN Business Council annual dinner, Washington, DC, reprinted in *The Straits Times*, Singapore, 15 June 2001.

12 Ibid.

13 Gareth Evans, 'What Asia Needs is a Europe-Style CSCA', *International Herald Tribune*, 27 July 1990; Joe Clark, Canadian Secretary of State for External Affairs, remarks before Foreign Correspondents Club of Japan, Tokyo, 24 July 1990; Statement by Japanese Foreign Minister Nakayama at ASEAN Post-Ministerial Conference, Kuala Lumpur, 22 July 1991.

14 James Baker, 'America in Asia: Emerging Architecture for a Pacific Community', *Foreign Affairs*, Winter 1991/2, vol. 70, no. 5, pp. 5–6.

15 Winston Lord (A/S EAP) pointed out the critical preventive diplomacy and trust-building role of the ARF, declaring that the United States wanted to discuss the Cambodian situation, the Spratlys dispute and the Korean problem at the Forum, as well as develop greater transparency in regional defence establishments. 'US to Boost Asia Ties Through APEC, Regional Forum', *The Straits Times*, 21 July 1994.

16 Richard Solomon in David Capie, 'Power, Threats and Identity: Rethinking Institutional Dynamics in the Pacific, 1945–2000', Ph.D. Thesis, York University, Toronto, 2001.

17 Michael Pillsbury, 'The Future of the ARF: An American Perspective', in Khoo How San (ed.) *The Future of the ARF*, Singapore: Institute of Defence and Strategic Studies, 1999, p. 139.

18 Ralf Emmers, 'The Influence of the Balance of Power Factor within the ASEAN Regional Forum', *Contemporary Southeast Asia*, August 2001, vol. 23, no. 2, pp. 281–2.

19 See Shinn, *Weaving the Net*.

20 Stanley O. Roth, Remarks at Closing Plenary Session of the World Economic Forum, Hong Kong, 15 October 1997.

21 Statement of Admiral Richard Macke, USN, Commander-in-Chief, Pacific Command, to the Hearing of the House Committee on International Relations, Asia and Pacific Subcommittee on 'US Security Interests in Asia', 27 June 1995.

22 William T. Tow, *Asia-Pacific Strategic Relations: Seeking Convergent Security*, Cambridge: Cambridge University Press, 2001, p. 189. See pp. 186–90 for the full critique.

23 Capie, 'Power, Threats and Identity', chapters 5 and 6.

24 See Tow, *Asia-Pacific Strategic Relations*, p. 193, footnote 94.

25 On the general preference in Washington for bilateralism over multilateralism, see Ralph Cossa, 'Bilateralism, Multilateralism, and the Search for Security in East Asia', Paper presented at Conference on 'Multilateralism, Bilateralism and the Search for Asian Security', St Antony's College, Oxford, May 2000.

26 Opening Intervention by US Secretary of State Warren Christopher, ARF Ministerial, Bandar Seri Begawan, Brunei, 1 August 1995.

27 This has been reinforced at the global level by the National Security Strategy, which states the aim to keep forces 'strong enough to dissuade potential adversaries from pursuing a military build-up in hopes of surpassing, or equalling, the power of the

United States'. White House, National Security Strategy of the United States of America, September 2002. Online. Available: http://www.whitehouse.gov/nsc/print/nssall.html on pp. 21–2.

28 The QDR is online. Available: http://www.defenselink.mil/pubs/qdr2001.pdf. A more hopeful analysis based on a similar division of East Asia into a US-dominated maritime region as opposed to a China-dominated continental region was presented in Robert Ross, 'The Geography of the Peace: East Asia in the Twenty-first Century', *International Security*, Spring 1999, vol. 23, no. 4, pp. 81–118.

29 See Kumar Ramakrishna, '9/11, American Praetorian Unilateralism, and the Impact on State-Society Relations in Southeast Asia', June 2002, Working Paper No. 26, Institute of Defence and Strategic Studies, Singapore; Evelyn Goh, 'Hegemonic Constraints: The Implications of September 11 for American Power', *Australian Journal of International Affairs*, 2003, vol. 57, no. 1, pp. 77–97.

30 A/P EAP James Kelly, 'US-East Asia-Pacific Relations', Statement before the Subcommittee on East Asia and the Pacific, House International Relations Committee, 14 February 2002.

31 Albright, Statement to the ARF, 27 July 1997; Secretary of State Madeleine K. Albright, Intervention at the ARF Plenary, Manila, Philippines, 27 July 1998.

32 Secretary Colin Powell, Roundtable with ASEAN Journalists, Washington, DC, 25 July 2002. Online. Available: http://www.state.gov/secretary/rm/2002/12207.html. The United States also chose the ARF meeting as the venue at which to sign an anti-terrorism agreement with ASEAN, which is viewed with some anxiety by Beijing. See 'China Wary of US-ASEAN Anti-Terrorism Pact', Agence France Presse, 30 July 2002.

33 A notable recent example is the Bush administration's new *National Security Strategy*, September 2002. Online. Available: http://www.whitehouse.gov/nsc/print/nssall. html on p. 19. But this US focus on APEC is interesting given the recent East Asian turn to more regional trade liberalisation foci such as ASEAN+3, the China–ASEAN FTA and other bilateral FTAs, and given Washington's own focus on security issues at APEC.

34 Sheldon Simon, 'The ASEAN Regional Forum Views the Councils for Security Cooperation in the Asia Pacific: How Track II Assists Track I', *NBR Analysis*, July 2002, vol. 13, no. 4, pp. 10–11.

35 Albright, Intervention at the ARF Plenary, 27 July 1998.

36 Simon, 'The ASEAN Regional Forum Views the Councils for Security Cooperation in the Asia Pacific', p. 15; Preventive Diplomacy: Charting A Course for the ASEAN Regional Forum, CSCAP CSBM International Working Group Report, Pacific Forum CSIS, July 2002. Online. Available: http://www.csis.org/pacfor/issues/3–02.htm.

37 Deputy Secretary of State Strobe Talbot, Intervention at the ARF, Bangkok, Thailand, 27 July 2000.

38 A/P EAP James Kelly, 'US Policy in East Asia and the Pacific: Challenges and Priorities', Testimony before the Subcommittee on East Asia and the Pacific, House Committee on International Relations, 12 June 2001.

39 'ASEAN Regional Forum: Powell, North Korea's Peak Hold Brief Talks', *The Nation*, Bangkok, 2 August 2002.

40 'N. Korea and US Spar at ASEAN Forum', *Financial Times*, London, 26 July 2001.

41 Gaye Christoffersen, 'The Role of East Asia in Sino-American Relations', *Asian Survey*, May/June 2002, vol. 42, no. 3, pp. 394–5.

42 For example, see Ron Huisken, 'Civilizing the Anarchical Society: Multilateral Security Processes in the Asia-Pacific', *Contemporary Southeast Asia*, August 2002, vol. 24, no. 2, pp. 198–200.

43 This parallels what Paul Dibb has observed to be a larger problem in US East Asian policy. In order to gain the willing participation of other states in its concept of inter-national order, the United States has to conduct 'strategic restraint' to convey its

willingness to limit its use of military power and to stay within international norms. As a result, it has to 'walk a tightrope between too little and too much use of force and between too much and too little involvement with its allies'. Paul Dibb, 'Will America's Alliances in the Asia-Pacific Region Endure?', *Working Paper No. 345*, Canberra Strategic and Defence Studies Centre, May 2000, p. 15.

44 See Amitav Acharya, 'A Concert of Asia?', *Survival*, Autumn 1999, vol. 41, no. 3, pp. 84–101.

45 Uzbekistan joined the Shanghai Cooperation Organisation in June 2001 when it made the transition to the SCO from the Shanghai Five.

46 These arguments can be found in Amitav Acharya, 'Seeking Security: The East Asian Way', *The Straits Times*, 30 December 2004.

47 For further discussion of China and Japan's potential role in the APT process, see Chapter 3 by Tanaka in this volume.

6 Financial cooperation and domestic political economy in East Asia

Natasha Hamilton-Hart

Introduction

Regional cooperation on financial issues has begun to take shape in East Asia. The series of financial crises that hit East Asian and other emerging markets in 1997–8 made it clear that Asia lacked effective mechanisms for crisis prevention and management. Many policy-makers and commentators argued that there was a need for more effective regional mechanisms as a complement to global institutions such as the IMF. Several initiatives for cooperation on financial issues have since been made. These include the creation of modest liquidity support facilities to be drawn on in the event of future currency crises, technical assistance for monitoring financial flows and markets, and diplomatic coordination. Whether these initiatives are precursors to more ambitious forms of cooperation remains subject to contestation. Some analyses see them as the foundation of much more ambitious regional cooperation schemes, possibly even leading to a common East Asian currency, while sceptics see regional cooperation as very much a side-issue for most countries and therefore unlikely to go much beyond rhetorical statements of intent. Aspects of this debate are presented in the next chapter by Thomas in his discussion of financial as well as economic aspects of regional cooperation to date.

Much of the debate over the likelihood of further financial cooperation has centred on the issue of whether countries in the region stand to gain from financial cooperation on a regional basis. As reviewed below, there are fairly strong indicators that many, though perhaps not all, countries in East Asia would make overall gains from certain types of financial cooperation, despite the costs involved. However, national policies regarding currency cooperation are frequently not determined by estimates of aggregate gains. Overall gains can coexist with losses for some actors, who may be in a position to influence policy. Hence the structure of domestic interests, institutions and political coalitions in particular countries can affect the likelihood of cooperation. After reviewing initiatives for regional cooperation, this chapter presents a preliminary map of the interests and institutions that will shape national polices on financial cooperation.

Initiatives for financial cooperation in East Asia

This section summarises the main ideas and initiatives for regional cooperation in the area of finance. Its starts with an overview of the broader cooperative context in which these initiatives have been made, briefly reviewing initiatives for economic integration and cooperation. It then describes initiatives for crisis prevention and crisis management, and some tentative proposals for currency cooperation that have been associated with officially sponsored studies.

Context: initiatives for economic integration and cooperation

Specific proposals for cooperation on financial issues have been put forward not only in the context of the financial crises of 1997–8 but also in the context of broader schemes for regional economic integration and cooperation. After 1998 the two primary regional arenas for economic cooperation then extant, the Association of Southeast Asian Nations (ASEAN) and the Pacific-wide Asia–Pacific Economic Cooperation (APEC) group, were both subject to relative de-emphasis.[1] ASEAN underwent a period of reduced confidence in its relevance and capacity, as it was unable to respond to the financial crisis, and its members' commitment to ongoing trade liberalisation also came under question.[2] The momentum for Asian–Pacific regional trade liberalisation under the auspices of APEC stalled in the aftermath of the crisis, amidst increasingly divergent priorities among its members. Conversely, East Asia (Southeast Asia and Northeast Asia) emerged as a relatively new arena for regional cooperation, under the banner of ASEAN+3 (APT) meetings which brought together the members of ASEAN with China, Japan and South Korea.[3] Bilateralism also emerged as a major post-crisis trend in the region, as many countries shed their previous reliance on multilateral trade negotiations in favour of bilateral trade and economic agreements.[4]

By 2004, some of the momentum behind APT initiatives had slowed in the area of finance, as discussed below, whereas the trend towards bilateralism in trade and economic cooperation continued unabated. APEC remained sidelined as a forum for significant economic cooperation but ASEAN, in contrast, regained at least some of its profile as a vehicle for more ambitious initiatives. After initial post-crisis concerns that members of ASEAN would retreat from trade liberalisation commitments made under the ASEAN Free Trade Area agreement signed in 1992, which envisaged tariff reductions to levels of 0 to 5 per cent, members actually recommitted themselves to an accelerated liberalisation timetable in most product areas.[5] Further underlining efforts by ASEAN members to ensure its continued relevance as an organisation, the idea that its members would establish an 'ASEAN Community', comprising three pillars of security, economic and socio-cultural cooperation, was formally adopted at the summit level in October 2003.[6]

The economic cooperation component of the ASEAN Community is proceeding under the heading of creating an 'ASEAN Economic Community'

(AEC), with the goal of economic integration involving the 'free flow of goods, services, investment and a freer flow of capital'.[7] While it is ostensibly an ASEAN-specific scheme, it is predicated on the idea of promoting integration among a much more extensive set of countries than the members of ASEAN alone. As in the case of the earlier AFTA and ASEAN Investment Area initiatives, the idea is to reduce internal barriers among ASEAN members specifically in order to promote the competitiveness and attractiveness of member countries as sites for investment and trade partnerships with non-ASEAN economies. The major speeches and studies informing the AEC proposal underline this outward-looking agenda.[8] Bilateral pacts and other trade cooperation initiatives, such as the proposed China–ASEAN free trade agreement, further reinforce ASEAN's long-term economic ties to both the broader East Asian region and the global economy.

Under the stewardship of the ASEAN Economic Ministers, supported by regular Senior Officials Meetings, the AEC has taken on some specific proposals for enhancing integration and cooperation. In principle, members have accepted the goal of strengthening extant ASEAN liberalisation and facilitation measures regarding trade in goods and services as well as investment, and have identified 11 priority economic sectors for integration: electronics, automotives, wood-based products, rubber products, textiles and clothing, agricultural products, fisheries, information technology, healthcare, air travel and tourism.[9]

Implementing the roadmaps for accelerated liberalisation in these priority sectors remains in its early stages, and resistance to implementation can be expected from the less competitive domestic interests involved in several of the sectors (for example, automotives and textiles) in some ASEAN countries. Nonetheless, to the extent that the AEC promotes domestic economic restructuring, the changes that it will reflect are likely to be significant for other regional cooperation agendas. As discussed in a later section, as economies become less oriented to serving the preferences of inward-looking or protected sectors, the configuration of each country's domestic political economy is likely to become more supportive of at least certain types of financial cooperation.

Regional organisations for financial cooperation

Some organisational infrastructure relating to financial cooperation in East Asia predates the financial crisis of 1997–8.[10] ASEAN had no regular meeting of finance ministers until 1997 but most ASEAN countries were members of SEANZA (Southeast Asia, New Zealand and Australia), a central bank group established in 1957 which also included Japan and South Korea since the 1960s. Another central bank group, SEACEN (Southeast Asian Central Banks), was established in 1966. Both groups organised training of central bank officials and meetings of central bank governors and officials. The first ASEAN initiative in the financial area was the establishment in 1972 of the Central Banks and Monetary Authorities Committee. Later, the Committee on Banking and

Finance held its first meeting in 1977. Financial cooperation remained, in practice, at a low level until the 1990s. In 1991, the Executives' Meeting of East Asia–Pacific central banks (EMEAP) was set up as a result of a Japanese proposal for a new central bank forum. It has held biannual meetings at the senior official level since then, and the first meeting of EMEAP central bank governors was held in July 1996.[11]

Since 1997, the most significant regional financial cooperation initiatives have mainly taken place under the auspices of the ASEAN+3 group. The first APT informal summit was held in 1997, regular meetings of APT finance and central bank deputies have taken place since 1999 and APT finance ministers began to meet officially in 2000.[12] Regular Asia–Europe meetings (ASEM) have also been a forum for regional dialogue on financial cooperation.[13] In association with the APT and some non-Asian donors (notably Australia), the Asian Development Bank (ADB), headquartered in Manila, is hosting nascent efforts at regional surveillance and financial monitoring. ASEAN and the Manila Framework Group (associated with APEC) have also been involved in some initiatives for exchanging financial information and dialogue on financial cooperation but in practice have been relatively inactive on these issues.[14]

Crisis prevention and management

The depth and largely unexpected nature of the currency and financial crises of 1997–8 provided an obvious impetus for developing regional crisis prevention and management capacities. However, even before the crisis, Japanese officials had been considering the merits of some kind of regional crisis management facility.[15] In the early stages of the crisis they raised the idea of an 'Asian Monetary Fund' (AMF) privately with Asian governments. Strong opposition from the United States and a lack of Chinese support, however, meant that the proposal was shelved.[16] In the absence of a viable alternative, the crisis economies were forced to comply with much criticised IMF rescue schemes. Regional countries did make commitments to provide 'second line of defence' funding as part of IMF bailout packages, but by far the most significant amount of non-IMF financing that was actually disbursed came from Japan, under its New Miyazawa Initiative for Asian recovery.[17]

While the AMF was not revived, a set of bilateral currency swap agreements was created, which provides for some financial support during future crises. In some analyses, they are potentially the starting point for more ambitious forms of cooperative crisis prevention and management, such as regional–multilateral financial support facilities similar to the AMF idea, reserve pooling or even monetary cooperation.[18] The plan to establish these bilateral swap facilities, known as the Chiang Mai Initiative, was announced by the APT finance ministers in May 2000.[19] The intra-ASEAN swap facility was also increased to US$1 billion in November 2000. A series of bilateral swap arrangements were negotiated under the CMI over the next three years. As shown in Table 6.1, while the early pacts were all anchored by Japan, later swaps included a broader range of countries as both swap providers and recipients. By the end of 2003, 16 bilateral swaps had been concluded, potentially mobilising US$36.5 billion in financing. In addition to the swaps negotiated under the CMI, Japan has committed US$5 billion to Korea and US$2.5 billion to Malaysia under the New Miyazawa Initiative.

In 2004, momentum towards the further development of the CMI appeared to slow. No new bilateral swaps were signed in the first half of the year and no moves were made to take up proposals to develop the CMI further. A major officially sponsored study, published in 2004 and presented to APT officials in March, recommended options such as multilateralising the swaps, earmarking a portion of each country's foreign reserves for use under the CMI, a comprehensive regional surveillance system and centralised reserve pooling.[20] However, in May 2005, APT finance ministers moved to strengthen the CMI, signalling moves to integrate economic surveillance capabilities, adopting a collective decision-making process, increasing the size of the bilateral swaps and improving the drawdown mechanism.[21] The results of this began to be seen in the second half of 2005, when South Korea and the Philippines increased the size of their swap to $1.5 billion, the Japan–Indonesia swap grew to $6 billion and the PRC–Indonesia swap expanded to $2 billion.[22]

Swaps and financial support during a crisis fall mostly in the category of crisis management, although they have limited potential to deter crises, particularly if associated surveillance mechanisms actually act to prevent significant imbalances and vulnerabilities from developing. Crisis prevention efforts made loosely under APT auspices include cooperation on financial monitoring, regulatory capacity and standard setting. China has arranged training courses on economic reforms and development, South Korea has hosted a working visit by senior officials and organised a training programme on financial restructuring, and Japan has offered funds and technical assistance for monitoring capital flows.[23] In addition, new initiatives for information gathering and analysis have been located within the ADB, which has developed a prototype for a regional early warning system, which may be the beginning of some regional surveillance capacity. The idea of developing a regional surveillance capacity, widely considered necessary if regional crisis management facilities are to function properly, remains contested: while it is on the APT agenda, it remains still underdeveloped in policy terms.[24]

Other moves that could provide regional countries some protection from the vulnerabilities associated with capital mobility – and hence form part of regional crisis-prevention efforts – include cooperation in capital account monitoring and technical assistance with financial regulation.[25] Another crisis-prevention initiative aims to improve the region's self-sufficiency in long-term finance and reduce its reliance on bank financing, thereby reducing its vulnerability to currency destabilisation and speculative pressures. Towards this end, in 2001 the APT, in association with the ADB, took up an initiative to develop regional bond markets and close the gap between ratings on Asian bonds and the needs of local institutional investors.[26] This developed into the Asian Bond Markets Initiative, under which a multilateral Asian Bond Fund to guarantee bond issues was launched. A series of working groups were also formed to continue the process of conducting studies on credit guarantee mechanisms, regional clearing and settlement and impediments to cross-border bond investments. The outputs from these groups will be fed into a roadmap for information sharing and bond market development, which is – as of late 2005 – still being discussed by the ASEAN+3 Finance Ministers.[27] Also under the Asian Bond Markets Initiative, technical assistance for capacity building to support regional bond markets has been provided by Japan, with offers of support also made by South Korea and Malaysia.[28]

Monetary cooperation

Monetary cooperation was not even considered seriously in the region until the 1990s.[29] Japan gave more attention to the idea of increasing the use of the yen as an international currency from late 1980s and, in 1994 and 1995, the Japanese Ministry of Finance, MITI and the Economic Planning Agency all released reports mentioning the desirability of greater international and regional use of the yen.[30] In the mid-1990s, one of the main intellectual proponents of some kind of a yen bloc, C. H. Kwan, argued that the idea was 'no longer ahead of its time'.[31]

The academic and ideational groundwork for monetary cooperation in the region began to build after 1997. In early 1999, Miyazawa Kiichi, then Japanese Finance Minister, suggested that Asia adopt a currency basket based on the yen, the dollar and the euro,[32] an idea that Japanese Ministry of Finance officials have since promoted in public speeches on regional cooperation in Asia. Building on ideas among many Japanese (and other) policy-makers that over-reliance on the US dollar had been a factor behind the crisis, calls to increase the use of the yen as an international currency have gained at least verbal support.

A number of ongoing research projects investigating the viability of monetary cooperation in the region have also received official support and funding. One of these, the Kobe Research Project, was endorsed by the ASEM Finance Ministers Meeting held in January 2001 and which presented its reports in July the following year. Led by Japanese academics working in cooperation with officials and academics from Europe and Asia, the project's reports contain several technical studies pointing to the benefits of greater monetary cooperation, as well as discussions of preconditions and modalities.[33] The Japanese Ministry of Finance has also co-sponsored a three-year research project on future financial arrangements in East Asia, which includes studies of cooperative currency arrangements in the region.[34]

Overall, while the idea that Asia might benefit from various forms of currency cooperation has been raised by policy-makers and commentators in several East Asian countries, there is no serious political support for concrete moves towards currency cooperation in the near term.[35] Much of the intellectual groundwork towards legitimating the idea of currency cooperation has been officially sponsored (most of it, directly or indirectly, by Japan) but the idea remains largely in the realm of academic study and technical, quasi-official discussion. Nonetheless, efforts to develop regional capacity for cooperation in this area moved forward in February 2005, when representatives from regional central banks met in Bangkok for an informal meeting. It is planned that this new effort, known as the 'Asian Bellagio Group', will 'help coordinate policies and ideas among central banks, finance ministries and academics', although its efficacy is still to be proven.[36]

Table 6.1 Bilateral swaps under the Chiang Mai Initiative

Parties	Currencies	Date agreed	Size ($bn)
Japan–Korea	$/won	4 July 2001	2
Japan–Thailand	$/baht	30 July 2001	3
Japan–Philippines	$/peso	27 August 2001	3
Japan–Malaysia	$/ringgit	5 October 2001	1
PRC–Thailand	$/baht	6 December 2001	2
Japan–PRC	yen/renminbi	28 March 2002	3
PRC–Korea	renminbi/won	24 June 2002	2
Korea–Thailand	$–won/baht	25 June 2002	1
Korea–Malaysia	$–won/ringgit	26 July 2002	1
Korea–Philippines	$/peso	9 August 2002	1
PRC–Malaysia	$/ringgit	9 October 2002	1.5
Japan–Indonesia	$/rupiah	17 February 2003	3
PRC–Philippines	renminbi/peso	31 August 2003	1
Japan–Singapore	$/S$	10 November 2003	1
Korea–Indonesia	$/rupiah	24 December 2003	1
PRC–Indonesia	$/rupiah	30 December 2003	1

Source: ADB, 'Chiang Mai Initiative (CMI): Current Status and Future Directions', Public statement, 12 May 2004.

Note: Although funds potentially available under the bilateral swaps are said to amount to US$36.5 billion, the amounts shown here do not sum to US$36.5 billion because some of these agreements are two-way arrangements and hence are counted twice.

Aggregate costs and benefits from financial cooperation

The likelihood of these initiatives and ideas regarding financial cooperation developing further depends in part on whether they offer gains for participating countries. That is, whether the costs of cooperation are outweighed by the aggregate benefits it may bring. Even if, as discussed in the following section, the distribution of costs and benefits at the domestic level also counts, the issue of overall costs and benefits may have some impact on decisions taken for or against cooperation. This section discusses the potential advantages of specifically regional cooperation on money and finance, as complements to cooperation at the global level.[37] Current research suggests that enhanced regional crisis prevention and management mechanisms offer scope for overall gains if properly designed. There is also increasing acceptance of the idea that regional monetary cooperation, initially in the form of a common currency basket, would offer net benefits to several East Asian countries.

Crisis prevention and management

Regional mechanisms for crisis prevention and management incur two main types of cost. The first relates to the commitment and use of funds to be disbursed during a future crisis. Differences among likely fund-providing countries and likely users hampered negotiations on the swap facilities established as part of the Chiang Mai Initiative. Providers wish to minimise the risk of losses and thus attempt to ensure that emergency liquidity support funds are not disbursed without conditions. Further, the distribution of foreign lending to the region adds to the potential costs of a regional support facility. European banks are collectively by far the largest foreign bank lenders to East Asian countries and American banks are increasing their share of foreign loans to Asia.[38] A regional facility could therefore see fund-providing countries in the region carry a disproportionate share of future bailout costs. The second cost relates to the development of adequate regional surveillance systems: the data gathering and analysis associated with genuine surveillance efforts is intrusive, time consuming and may duplicate efforts spent meeting IMF surveillance requirements.[39]

Despite these costs, it is likely that there are overall gains to be realised from greater cooperation at the regional level, if regional initiatives are appropriately designed. The diversified sources of international investment flowing to East Asia point to the necessity to engage non-regional players in future crisis management efforts but regional cooperation does not exclude efforts in wider arenas. One incentive that has been frequently raised by policy-makers in Asia since 1997 is in fact a desire to improve the functioning of global institutions for financial crisis prevention and management by presenting the region's interests more forcefully at the global level. Coordination could secure a greater say in global negotiations and organisations such as the IMF, where Asia still lacks influence proportionate to its economic weight.[40]

The development of some type of crisis management capacity at the regional level holds out the possibility for embedding local preferences regarding financial and economic policy into regional standards and rescue packages. There is some doubt over whether the Chiang Mai Initiative swaps, which might be the first step towards creating a regional liquidity fund, will provide for this. In the first phase China and Japan succeeded in linking all but 10 per cent of these facilities to IMF conditionality, a stipulation which Malaysia in particular had opposed.[41] Even though this was increased to 20 per cent in the second phase, as Dieter and Higgott have noted, this undermines the potential for greater regional autonomy that would be one of the benefits of a regional facility.[42] However, the fig leaf of IMF conditionality is useful to donor countries as a way of deflecting criticism of bailout exercises that are likely to involve unpopular or intrusive measures. Once a regional facility is established, it would be politically difficult for the IMF to block disbursements that donor countries wish to make. As Narine noted, financial independence means that remaining an adjunct to the IMF would be unlikely.[43]

Even if there are no distinctive shared preferences on financial management in Asia, and even if regional countries are very dissimilar in terms of economic structure, there are nonetheless advantages to regional crisis management and prevention. Proximity on its own can create shared risks from contagion and, in the case of East Asia, substantial interdependence reinforces this incentive to respond to crises in neighbouring countries.[44] While there are also significant economic links with the United States, the asymmetry in these ties and US global, political and economic engagement dilutes its interest in Southeast Asia. Regional actors are also less likely to be distracted by experiences and activities elsewhere than the IMF, which has a global mandate. In addition, local actors may be better informed and thus better able to devise appropriate crisis management and prevention schemes. Overall, therefore, regional interdependence through real and perceived linkages can fuel the contagion of crises among countries in a region, creating strong incentives to act collectively to prevent and manage them.

Monetary cooperation

There is debate among economists over whether economic preconditions for a common currency basket peg or a shared regional currency exist in East Asia. Even if some flexibility is built into the arrangement, to the extent that currency values are fixed, individual countries lose monetary policy autonomy. Is this loss of autonomy likely to be worth it? One indicator that several countries are prepared to sacrifice some autonomy in favour of stability is that most of the region appears to be extremely reluctant to follow a free floating exchange rate regime.[45] Hence, in addition to Malaysia's introduction of a formal peg to the US dollar, China and Hong Kong have maintained their *de facto* pegs and several other countries appear to have reverted to pre-crisis exchange rate regimes which accorded the US dollar predominant rate in revealed currency baskets.[46]

Reducing the overwhelming reliance on the US dollar in currency baskets, international transactions and reserve holdings could yield benefits given the distribution of regional trade. Regional exports to the United States dropped from a peak of 29 per cent of total regional exports in 1986 to average less than 20 per cent of total regional exports in the years immediately preceding the financial crisis.[47] Currency regimes which give overwhelming predominance to the US dollar thus expose countries to fluctuations in exchange rates vis-à-vis markets which are collectively more significant. While the level of intra-regional trade remains lower than it is in Europe, it is now significant at 51 per cent of total trade in 2000, compared to 42 per cent in 1980.[48]

Reduced reliance on the US dollar could also serve as a way of reducing the potential for the United States to abuse its position as the issuer of the world's most widely used currency.[49] Such a shift appears more feasible if private decisions regarding which currency to use in international transactions are seen as being significantly influenced by government choices regarding exchange rate baskets, official reserves and intervention currencies.[50]

The more economies are similar in terms of trade structure, sensitivity to external shocks and inflation rates, the fewer trade-offs they face in adopting similar monetary policies. In this regard, Japan, Taiwan, Singapore, Korea and Hong Kong are better candidates for monetary cooperation than the whole of East Asia, which is much more diverse.[51] The gains from a common currency basket might not be evenly distributed among different countries,[52] but even an otherwise negative assessment of the prospects for currency cooperation concludes that, 'On standard optimum currency area grounds, then, the economies of East Asia would seem to be more or less as plausible candidates for internationally harmonised monetary policies as the members of the European Union.'[53] Further, studies of monetary cooperation which take into account the dynamic effects of such cooperation suggest that many of the preconditions for monetary cooperation as set out in Optimum Currency Area theory are in fact endogenous.[54] Another significant benefit from monetary cooperation would be the gains from reducing the region's extremely high foreign reserve holdings.

Given the potential gains from monetary cooperation and the apparent sub-optimality of the weight given to the US dollar in exchange rate regimes, the question arises as to why much of the region has returned to US-dollar-oriented regimes, rather than seeking out alternative arrangements. The general explanation often advanced is a lack of political will, compounded by international collective action problems. Since international political obstacles that might account for coordination failure among a group of countries are only relevant if there is domestic demand for cooperation, the next section attempts to specify the domestic factors that might explain the existence or otherwise of political will regarding regional financial cooperation.

Domestic interests and institutions in East Asian countries

The interests and political power of particular subnational economic actors in East Asia are likely to influence national policies regarding regional cooperation. As yet, the structure of domestic interests regarding financial cooperation has received very little attention in the case of East Asia, even though the European case suggests that it is likely to be among the determinants of cooperation.[55] The reason for examining the interests and influence of subnational sectors lies in common problems of institutional design and collective action which can produce perverse policy outcomes. What promises gains for the country as a whole is not necessarily in the interests of particular economic groups, which may well enjoy political influence that is disproportionate to their economic significance. The influence of Japan's agricultural sector in preventing substantial agricultural trade liberalisation is a widely cited example of how even relatively small subnational groups may, if the political system empowers them sufficiently, steer national policy in a direction that benefits the group but inflicts overall losses on the country as a whole.

This example points to the importance of subnational distributional issues in explaining cooperation outcomes. Different groups at the domestic level form preferences regarding cooperation on the basis of the perceived distribution of its costs and benefits. Their preferences, as aggregated through formal and informal political institutions, frequently have a significant effect on cooperation outcomes.[56] National policies regarding cooperation are likely to be somewhat affected by the relative economic importance of particular domestic groups. Their political weight, however, will often be a function of domestic institutions that privilege or exclude certain actors. Work on regional cooperation that has taken national-level interests and political coalitions seriously in the Southeast Asian context has so far concentrated on trade.[57] We know very little about the domestic political economy of cooperation on money and finance in the region.

Distributional issues and preference aggregation

Before turning to East Asian cases, some discussion of the distributional issues that arise in connection with financial cooperation is necessary. In the case of cooperative crisis management and prevention, there are of course major international distributional issues that need to be resolved if free riding is to be avoided. However, there are also domestic distributional issues which may be relevant. First, there is some scope for divergent preferences on crisis management at the domestic level in countries that are likely to be providers of emergency financing facilities. This cleavage will form between domestically oriented economic actors and international investors and traders, who have a direct interest in the financial stability of foreign countries with which they have trade and investment links. The internationally oriented actors can be expected to favour their country's contribution to crisis management facilities that provide funds to countries in which they have significant economic interests. Second, while it is in some cases reasonable to assume that, given the economy-wide costs of a serious financial crisis, most domestic players have a long-term interest in effective management and prevention systems aimed at protecting their own currencies and financial systems, this assumption may not always hold true. If politically privileged economic actors can use their influence to secure bailout packages from their own government they may be able to deflect the costs of the crisis to the public and emerge relatively unscathed. The ongoing contention over the extent to which Indonesia's bank owners and major debtors were ever made to pay for emergency central bank support during the crisis in 1997–8, for example, suggests that if some groups believe they can insulate themselves from the effects of a crisis they have little incentive to support crisis prevention and management efforts.

With regard to monetary cooperation, models of domestic preferences hold that the distributional consequences of monetary cooperation are likely to lead to a basic division of interests on two critical issues.[58] First, as regards the trade-off between monetary policy independence and exchange rate stability, producers of traded goods and cross-border investors and traders will favour exchange rate stability over monetary independence, because they are relatively sensitive to exchange rate fluctuations and risks.[59] They are thus likely supporters of monetary cooperation that will stabilise exchange rates. Conversely, producers in the non-tradables sector (and those producers of traded goods who are relatively insensitive to international prices) depend more on domestic economic conditions and are thus likely to prioritise monetary independence over exchange rate stability.

The second issue relating to monetary cooperation on which domestic preferences are likely to diverge is macroeconomic policy, since monetary cooperation requires countries to adopt coordinated macroeconomic policies. While in theory this requirement is neutral as to actual macroeconomic policy settings, in the European case the convergence criteria for cooperation dictated prioritising low inflation and fiscal restraint.[60] In the foreseeable future, monetary cooperation in Asia would also be likely to include commitments to moderately low levels of inflation. The distributional consequences of low inflation favour business actors and investors in particular, who tend to favour conservative monetary and fiscal policies.[61] These groups are thus more likely to support monetary cooperation that entrenches a commitment to low inflation than mass-based political parties with left or labour constituents, who tend to favour more expansionary macroeconomic policies.

How the preferences of different economic groups get translated into national policy depends on institutional context as well as the economic weight of particular actors. First, the extent to which domestic interest groups influence policy at all varies with the degree of insulation of government policy-makers. This insulation does not simply correspond with variations in levels of democracy. Regardless of the level of democracy, the influence of sectional interests can vary according to nature of the domestic support base of a government and according to the design of political institutions. Institutions which centralise political decision making, for example, offer fewer points of entry for sectional interests to block policy.[62] Further, political systems vary with regard to the particular groups that they empower or exclude from influence, whether this is through electoral system design (for example, the over-representation of rural electors in Japan) or other mechanisms which privilege or disempower groups such as the financial industry, labour or big business.

Domestic preferences in East Asia

Applying this kind of analysis to East Asia means identifying the potential domestic winners and losers from regional cooperation and assessing their influence in national policy-making. One source of national policy preferences on financial cooperation can be fairly safely discounted at the outset: mass public opinion regarding financial cooperation, particularly that which falls short of adopting a common currency, is unlikely to be important in most East Asian countries. Electoral constraints on economic policy do exist but the details of foreign economic policy are generally insulated from mass politics, leaving interest groups as the most plausible category of political actor influencing government policies on financial cooperation. A preliminary outline of the structure of domestic interests in regional countries suggests that there should be domestic support for financial cooperation in many East Asian countries, and that this is likely to increase if countries continue to restructure their economies in favour of internationally oriented and competitive sectors, although the situation varies from case to case.

For both crisis management and monetary cooperation, the degree of engagement with the international economy is an important factor affecting whether domestic groups will favour cooperation. Regional interdependence creates further grounds for favouring crisis management at the regional level and regional monetary cooperation. Trade and cross-border investment levels in the region suggest that groups with an interest in exchange rate stability are significant in almost all East Asian economies except the new members of ASEAN (Burma, Cambodia, Vietnam and Laos) and North Korea, which are not considered here.[63] If the distribution of exports is taken as a measure of regional interdependence, most East Asian countries have a significant stake in the economic welfare of their neighbours: exports to East Asia in 2000 ranged from 38 per cent in the case of Japan to 64 per cent in the case of Hong Kong.[64] However, the economic weight of the export sector varies a lot among different countries in the region. While in world terms all countries in the region except Japan have relatively high trade levels, with the ratio of exports to GDP above 30 per cent for all countries except Indonesia, China and Japan, the difference between Japan, where the ratio of exports to GDP is less than 15 per cent of GDP, and Malaysia, where exports amount to more than 100 per cent of GDP, is striking.

The importance of exports to East Asia varies from country to country. As shown in Table 6.2, exports to the region are moderately significant when expressed as a percentage of GDP for Korea, China, Thailand and Indonesia, but much more important for Malaysia (a function of Malaysia's much higher level of overall trade dependence). The significant outlier in the region is clearly Japan, for which exports to the region are only 3.9 per cent of GDP, which suggests that the economic interest groups with a strong stake in regional markets remain comparatively small and therefore political incentives to respond to their preferences may be correspondingly weak. Given Japan's overwhelming economic size compared to the rest of the region, its active participation is critical for the development of regional cooperation schemes. However, these aggregate figures on the size of the trade sector underplay its economic significance as a source of growth, in contrast to the more stagnant domestically oriented sectors of the Japanese economy. Potentially, therefore, Japanese policy-makers may look to the internationally oriented sectors as the most promising sources of future economic growth.

Cross-border investment, another indicator of whether domestic groups are sensitive to exchange rate movements, is comparatively high for most countries if one uses a broad measure of cross-border capital exposure (assets and liabilities, bank loans as well as direct investment). Again, however, the situation varies across the region in terms of the composition of cross-border investments and liabilities. With the exception of Japan, investment outflows are concentrated in the East Asian region but liabilities are more widely disbursed.[65]

The political influence of particular domestic economic actors does not necessarily coincide with their economic importance. An assessment of how political institutions in East Asian countries are likely to filter support or opposition for policies regarding financial cooperation is not possible in this chapter. However, some general observations can be made. As regards macroeconomic policy preferences which affect a country's ability to commit to monetary cooperation targets, left–right political balances in most of the region tend to favour business and investor interests and hence a preference for relatively low inflation. More populist politics in the Philippines and post-1998 Indonesia are exceptions. If actual inflation levels are taken as a proxy for the preferences of dominant domestic actors, average inflation rates in 1982–9 show that Indonesia, the Philippines, China and Hong Kong had averages above 6 per cent per year; Korea, Thailand, Malaysia, Taiwan, Singapore and Japan had average inflation rates of below 6 per cent.[66]

It is not clear how political systems in the region are likely to affect the aggregation of domestic preferences regarding the trade-off between monetary independence and exchange rate stability. According to several analyses, political institutions under-privilege trading interests in much of Southeast Asia and Japan. If true, this might explain national policies that do not support financial cooperation even if it would yield overall benefits for an economy. In the case of Southeast Asia, a high proportion of trade is accounted for by foreign-owned companies, a legacy of a development model in which export-led growth has been dependent on FDI. Further, politically influential local business actors are frequently concentrated in the non-tradables sector, such as property development, generally considered to have more to gain from monetary independence than exchange rate stability. This combination of a politically marginalised trade sector and a privileged non-tradables sector was widely blamed for perverse macroeconomic policy choices in Indonesia, Malaysia and Thailand before the 1997–8 crisis.[67] In the case of Japan, the electoral system has until recently privileged the voices of domestically oriented economic actors, which are not expected to support financial cooperation.

Before concluding that this type of domestic political economy will always tend to prioritise monetary independence over exchange rate stability, however, the assumed preferences of groups in the non-tradables sector need further attention. Part of the non-tradables sector, financial services providers, are conventional supporters of domestic price stability and fiscal restraint, and hence constitute a potential constituency for monetary cooperation that might entrench these macroeconomic policy goals. Financial sector actors in East Asian contexts also often have significant international operations or exposure, making them sensitive to exchange rate fluctuations, making it necessary to revisit the conventional political economy assumption that the non-tradables sector is domestically oriented. Hong Kong, for example, illustrates the way a domestic political economy dominated by finance and property sector interests will in fact tolerate a high level of domestic price and output adjustment in order to maintain exchange rate stability.[68]

The preceding summary suggests that the domestic political economy of financial cooperation in the region varies from country to country. Japan, the Philippines and Indonesia have political economies that may limit their support for cooperation in practice. In general, the smaller, more open economies have more to gain from financial cooperation but, in parts of Southeast Asia, the interests that might gain most from cooperation may not be influential politically because a significant part of the trade sector is foreign owned. However, more study of the preferences of politically influential actors in the non-tradables sector is required before firm conclusions can be drawn. Further, the independent preferences of policy-makers have not been covered here. Such independent preferences are likely to be important in countries like Singapore, with relatively insulated policy-makers.

Prospects for further financial cooperation

Given that some forms of regional financial cooperation do appear to offer gains, the modest progress made so far in terms of tangible regional schemes is often thought to represent some form of coordination failure at the international level. International coordination failure is a possibility as collective action among a group of formally sovereign states is subject to several difficulties. In the absence of an undisputed regional hegemon to monitor the costs of compliance, do countries in the East Asia have enough confidence in each other to allow them to overcome the collective action problems inherent in some forms of cooperation? Asia is sometimes portrayed as a region in which interstate political rivalries and mistrust make cooperation all but impossible, but this picture is rather misleading because it ignores the many ways in which regional countries have engaged each other in dialogues and ventures to increase levels of interdependence.[69] A more detailed summation of this perceived dichotomy is elaborated upon by Baviera in the concluding chapter. Political suspicion and resentments do intrude into some relationships, particularly between Japan and China, but all major countries in the region have already accepted some significant limits on their autonomy in order to reap the benefits of economic integration.

A related obstacle sometimes cited in the case of Asia is a purported absence, in comparison with Europe, of an intellectual tradition of regional thinking.[70] Work by serious historians of Asia, however, strongly refutes this assertion and the impact of Europe's (very uneven) intellectual history of support for the idea of regionalism is open debate.[71] While political relationships and ideational worldviews affect cooperative behaviour, there is also a domestic political economy component to the kind of international trust necessary for cooperation. Cooperation requires that governments be in a position to make credible commitments to cooperation targets. In the case of financial cooperation, the credibility of commitments to particular macroeconomic settings or financial policies will be affected by the structure of domestic political coalitions and institutions, as well as the economy-wide effects of such policies.

Table 6.2 International trade and investment profiles

	Trade (% GDP, 1995)	Investment (% GNP, 1995)	Regional exports (% GDP, 1995)
China	40	7.9	12.6
Hong Kong	297	n.a.	15.6
Indonesia	53	6.8	14.0
Japan	17	n.a.	3.9
Korea	67	n.a.	12.5
Malaysia	194	14.7	47.6
Philippines	80	5.2	9.9
Thailand	90	6.1	17.7

Sources: World Bank, *World Development Report*, Oxford: Oxford University Press, various years; Randolph Henning, 'The Complex Political Economy of Cooperation and Integration', p. 87.

The review of the costs and benefits of financial cooperation in East Asia given here suggests that in addition to looking at the international politics of the region, more attention should be directed to dynamics at the domestic level. The domestic political economy of East Asia is mixed with regard to cooperation. While most economies, with the exception of Japan, are quite strongly internationally oriented and thus have economic profiles that suggest strong constituencies for cooperation, in political terms some of the actors with most to gain may be relatively weak. There are also some significant differences among countries in East Asia in terms of how supportive their domestic political economy is to further cooperation on finance. With an economy that is still much more domestically oriented than that of its neighbours, Japan has limited incentives to invest in regional cooperation. This means that official Japanese cooperation initiatives, which have been led by relatively insulated policy-makers and academics, do not at present have the support of a strong domestic constituency. On the other hand, a broad convergence across much of East Asia in the priority given to domestic price stability defuses some of the domestic political obstacles to monetary cooperation that were important in the European case. For crisis management and prevention initiatives, potential gains and losses at the domestic level are more evenly distributed than on trade, which means that cooperation on finance is likely to be subject to weaker sectoral and political pressures either for or against cooperation. This allows policy-makers some leeway in pushing ahead with regional initiatives but also reduces the political urgency of the regional cooperation agenda.

Notes

1 See, for example, Webber's analysis contained in: Douglas Webber, 'Two Funerals and a Wedding? The Ups and Downs of Regionalism in East Asia and Asia-Pacific after the Asian Crisis', *The Pacific Review*, 2001, vol. 14, no. 3, pp. 339–72.

2 For further discussion of this point see: Simon Tay, Jesus Estanislao and Hadi Soesastro (eds), *Reinventing ASEAN*, Singapore: Institute of Southeast Asian Studies, 2001.

3 For more on this see: Richard Stubbs, 'ASEAN Plus Three: emerging East Asian regionalism?', *Asian Survey*, 2002, vol. 42, no. 3, pp. 440–55.

4 See, for example, John Ravenhill, 'The New Bilateralism in the Asia Pacific', *Third World Quarterly*, 2003, vol. 24, no. 2, pp. 299–317.

5 Mohamed Ariff, 'Trade, Investment and Interdependence', in Simon Tay, Jesus Estanislao and Hadi Soesastro (eds) *Reinventing ASEAN*, Singapore: Institute of Southeast Asian Studies, 2001, pp. 45–66.

6 Source: ASEAN, 'Declaration of ASEAN Concord II (Bali Concord II)', 7 October 2003. Online. Available: http://www.aseansec.org/15160.htm.

7 Ibid.

8 See: George Yeo, 'Building an ASEAN Economic Community', Speech at the AFTA Seminar, Jakarta, 31 January 2002. Online. Available: http://www.aseansec.org/13080.htm. Also, 'Recommendations of the High-Level Task Force on ASEAN Economic Integration', 7 October 2003. Online. Available: http://www.aseansec.org/hltf.htm and Denis Hew and Hadi Soesastro, 'Realizing the ASEAN Economic Community by 2020: ISEAS and ASEAN-ISIS Approaches', *ASEAN Economic Bulletin*, 2003, vol. 20, no. 3, pp. 292–6.

9 Source: 'Recommendations of the High-Level Task Force on ASEAN Economic Integration', 7 October 2003.

10 The source for this paragraph is Natasha Hamilton-Hart, 'Co-operation on Money and Finance: How Important? How Likely?', *Third World Quarterly*, 2003, vol. 24, no. 2, pp. 293–7.

11 The group comprises Singapore, Malaysia, Indonesia, Thailand, the Philippines, China, Hong Kong, South Korea, Japan, Australia and New Zealand.

12 Nick Thomas, 'Building an East Asian Community: Origins, Structure, and Limits', *Asian Perspective*, 2002, vol. 26, no. 4, pp. 83–112.

13 See, for example, speeches at the 2001 Finance Ministers Meeting. Online. Available: http://www.mof.go.jp/english/asem.

14 For more on this see: Ramkishen Rajan, 'Financial and macroeconomic co-operation in ASEAN: issues and policy initiatives', in Mya Than (ed.) *ASEAN Beyond the Crisis: Challenges and Initiatives*, Singapore: Institute of Southeast Asian Studies, 2001, pp. 126–47; Haruhiko Kuroda and Masahiro Kawai, 'Strengthening Regional Financial Cooperation in East Asia', in Gordon de Brouwer and Wang Yunjong (eds) *Financial Governance in East Asia: Policy Dialogue, Surveillance and Cooperation*, London: RoutledgeCurzon, 2004, pp. 136–66.

15 Bilateral repurchase agreements (most of which involved Japan) were made among regional countries in the 1990s and a (never utilised) ASEAN Swap Arrangement had existed since 1977. See Natasha Hamilton-Hart, 'Co-operation on Money and Finance: How Important? How Likely?'.

16 Despite Chinese opposition at this time, the head of Hong Kong's Monetary Authority, the territory's *de facto* central bank, made a strong, but not unqualified, argument in favour of regional cooperation (see: Joseph Yam, 'Asian Monetary Cooperation', *Per Jacobsson Lecture*, Hong Kong, 21 September 1997. Online. Available:http://www.info.gov.hk/hkma/eng/speeches/speechs/joseph/speech_210997b.htm). Taiwan also offered to anchor an Asia-only fund of US$50 billion but this idea too was vetoed by the United States and China (for more information on this see: 'Thanks, but No Thanks for Taipei's APEC Plan', *The China Post*, 28 November 1997).

17 As discussed by Seiichi Masuyama, 'The Role of Japan's Direct Investment in Restoring East Asia's Dynamism: Focus on ASEAN', in Seiichi Masuyama, Donna Vandenbrink and Chia Siow Yue (eds) *Restoring East Asia's Dynamism*, Singapore: ISEAS, 2000, pp. 213–58; Christopher Hughes, 'Japanese Policy and the East Asian Currency Crisis: Abject Defeat or Quiet Victory?', *Review of International Political Economy*, 2000, vol. 7, no. 2, pp. 219–53.

18 Examples of such analysis can be seen in: Heribert Dieter and Richard Higgott, 'Exploring Alternative Theories of Economic Regionalism: From Trade to Finance in Asian Co-operation?', *Review of International Political Economy*, 2003, vol. 10, no. 3, pp. 430–54; Fred Bergsten and Yung Chul Park, 'Toward Creating a Regional Monetary Arrangement in East Asia', *ADB Institute Research Paper Series No. 50*, December 2002; ADB, 'Chiang Mai Initiative (CMI): Current Status and Future Directions', *Public statement*, 12 May 2004. Online. Available: http://aric.adb.org.

19 As discussed by Jennifer Amyx, 'Japan and the Evolution of Regional Financial Arrangements in East Asia', in Ellis Krause and T. J. Pempel (eds) *Beyond Bilateralism: US-Japan Relations in the New Asia-Pacific*, Stanford, CA: Stanford University Press, 2004, pp. 198–218.

20 Source: ADB, 'Chiang Mai Initiative (CMI): Current Status and Future Directions'.

21 Source: *The Joint Ministerial Statement of the Eighth ASEAN+3 Finance Ministers Meeting*, Istanbul, Turkey, 4 May 2005.

22 'Philippine, S. Korean Central Banks Ink bilateral Swap Deal', *Asia Pulse*, 18 October 2005; 'Indon-Japan Currency Swap Deal Doubles to US$6b', *Business Times Singapore*,

1 September 2005; 'China, Indonesia Sign Swap Pact Up To 2bn dollars', *BBC Worldwide Monitoring*, 17 October 2005.

23 For more information see: Nick, Thomas. 'Building an East Asian Community: Origins, Structure, and Limits', *Asian Perspective*, 2002, vol. 26, no. 4, p. 97.

24 As discussed by Fred Bergsten and Yung Chul Park, 'Toward Creating a Regional Monetary Arrangement in East Asia', *ADB Institute Research Paper Series No. 50*, December 2002.

25 Ramkishen Rajan, 'Financial and macroeconomic co-operation in ASEAN: issues and policy initiatives', in Mya Than (ed.) *ASEAN Beyond the Crisis: Challenges and Initiatives*, Singapore: Institute of Southeast Asian Studies, 2001, pp. 126–47.

26 This is reviewed in: Norman Chan, 'Governor's Statement', *Address to the Thirty-fourth Asian Development Bank Annual Meeting*, Honolulu, 9–11 May 2001. Online. Available: http://www.info.gov.hk/hkma/speeches/speechs/norman/20010510e.htm.

27 Source: *The Joint Ministerial Statement of the Eighth ASEAN+3 Finance Ministers Meeting*, Istanbul, Turkey, 4 May 2005.

28 Source: *The Joint Ministerial Statement of the ASEAN+3 Finance Ministers Meeting*, 15 May 2004. Online. Available: http://www.aseansec.org.

29 One case of bilateral cooperation has endured: Brunei and Singapore, which inherited a shared currency as a result of colonial arrangements, continue to have their currencies exchangeable at par value.

30 C. H. Kwan, 'A yen bloc in Asia', *Journal of the Asia Pacific Economy*, 1996, vol. 1, no. 1, p. 3.

31 Ibid., p. 15.

32 See: James Areddy, 'Miyazawa Suggests Asia Adopt Tricurrency Link', *The Asian Wall Street Journal*, 18 January 1999, p. 3.

33 The Reports of the Kobe Research Project are online. Available: http://www.mof.go.jp/jouhou/kokkin/tyousa/kobe_e.htm and have also been published as an ADB study.

34 The project is located at the Australia–Japan Research Centre of the Australian National University.

35 More analysis on this point is contained in: Hamilton-Hart, 'Co-operation on Money and Finance: How Important? How Likely?'.

36 Grace Ng, 'Asian central banks to work together on monetary policy', *The Straits Times*, 26 February 2005.

37 An overview of the rationales for different types of regional financial and monetary cooperation after the crisis is provided by Yunjong Wang, 'Instruments and Techniques for Financial Cooperation', in Gordon de Brouwer and Yunjong Wang (eds) *Financial Governance in East Asia: Policy Dialogue, Surveillance and Cooperation*, London: RoutledgeCurzon, 2004, pp. 189–215.

38 This point is noted by Natasha Hamilton-Hart, 'Capital Flows and Financial Markets in Asia: National, Regional, or Global?', in Ellis Krause and T. J. Pempel (eds) *Beyond Bilateralism: US-Japan Relations in the New Asia-Pacific*, Stanford, CA: Stanford University Press, 2004, pp. 133–53.

39 As discussed by Jennifer Amyx, 'Japan and the Evolution of Regional Financial Arrangements in East Asia'.

40 This point is made in: Randolph Henning, *East Asian Financial Cooperation*, Washington, DC: Institute for International Economics, 2002.

41 See: Jennifer Amyx, 'Japan and the Evolution of Regional Financial Arrangements in East Asia'.

42 See: Heribert Dieter and Richard Higgott, 'Exploring Alternative Theories of Economic Regionalism: From Trade to Finance in Asian Co-operation?'.

43 Shaun Narine, 'ASEAN and the Idea of an "Asian Monetary Fund": Institutional Uncertainty in the Asia Pacific', in Andrew Tan and Kenneth Boutin (eds) *Non-*

Traditional Security Issues in Southeast Asia, Singapore: Institute of Defence and Strategic Studies, 2001, p. 240.

44 For more on this point see: Ramkishen Rajan, 'Examining the case for an Asian Monetary Fund', *Visiting Researcher Series No. 3*, Singapore: Institute of Southeast Asian Studies, February 2000; Fred Bergsten and Yung Chul Park, 'Toward Creating a Regional Monetary Arrangement in East Asia'.

45 In this respect East Asia is not exceptional. See: Guillermo Calvo and Carmen Reinhart, 'Fear of Floating', *Quarterly Journal of Economics*, 2002, vol. 117, no. 2, pp. 379–408.

46 The finding is common to several studies of post-crisis exchange rate policies in the region. See, for example, the report of the study group on Exchange Rate Regimes for Asia, Kobe Research Project. Online. Available: http://www.mof.go.jp/jouhou/kokkin/tyousa/kobe_e.htm.

47 Source: Randolph, Henning. 'The Complex Political Economy of Cooperation and Integration', p. 85.

48 Source: Kwanho Shin and Yunjong Wang, 'Monetary Integration Ahead of Trade Integration in East Asia', Paper prepared for Linkages in East Asia: Implications for Currency Regimes and Policy Dialogue Conference, Seoul, 23–24 September 2002, p. 26.

49 See: C. H. Kwan, *Yen Bloc: Toward Economic Integration in Asia*, Washington, DC: Brookings Institution Press, 2001.

50 See: ibid., pp. 146–7, and Ronald McKinnon, 'Euroland and East Asia in a Dollar-Based International Monetary System: Mundell Revisited', in Guillermo Calvo, Rudi Dornbusch and Maurice Obstfeld (eds) *Money, Capital Mobility and Trade: Essays in Honor of Robert A. Mundell*, Cambridge, MA: MIT Press, 2001, pp. 413–29, for contrasting views on this point.

51 Ibid., pp. 162–9.

52 See: Gordon de Brouwer, 'Does a Formal Common-Basket Peg in East Asia Make Economic Sense?', in Gordon de Brouwer (ed.) *Financial Markets and Policies in East Asia*, London: Routledge, 2002, pp. 286–314.

53 Barry Eichengreen and Tamim Bayoumi, 'Is Asia an Optimum Currency Area? Can it Become One? Regional, Global and Historical Perspectives on Asian Monetary Relations', in Stefan Collignon, Jean Pisani-Ferry and Yung Chul Park (eds) *Exchange Rate Policies in Emerging Asian Countries*, London: Routledge, 1999, p. 360. Increasingly, recent economic studies have estimated that there are potential gains from currency cooperation in the region. See, for example, John Williamson, 'The case for a common basket peg for East Asian currencies', in Collignon *et al.*, *Exchange Rate Policies in Emerging Asian Countries*, pp. 327–43; Ramkishen Rajan, 'Examining the case for currency basket regimes for Southeast Asia', *Visiting Researcher Series No. 1*, Singapore: Institute of Southeast Asian Studies, January 2000; Takatoshi Ito, 'A Case for a Coordinated Basket for Asian Countries', Paper prepared for the report of the study group on Exchange Rate Regimes for Asia, Kobe Research Project, 2002. Online. Available: http://www.mof.go.jp/jouhou/kokkin/tyousa/kobe_e.htm and Gordon de Brouwer, 'Does a Formal Common-Basket Peg in East Asia Make Economic Sense?'.

54 This conclusion is supported by a review of recent theoretical and empirical studies contained in Kwanho Shin and Yunjong Wang, 'Monetary Integration Ahead of Trade Integration in East Asia'.

55 This conclusion is made by Randolph Henning, 'The Complex Political Economy of Cooperation and Integration', in Gordon de Brouwer and Yunjong Wang (eds) *Financial Governance in East Asia: Policy Dialogue, Surveillance and Cooperation*, London: RoutledgeCurzon, 2004, pp. 83–100.

56 This is noted in: Peter Alexis Gourevitch, 'Squaring the Circle: The Domestic Sources of International Cooperation', *International Organization*, 1996, vol. 50, no. 2, pp. 349–73;

Andrew Moravcsik, *The Choice for Europe: Social Purpose and State Power from Messina to Maastricht*, Ithaca, NY: Cornell University Press, 1998.

57 As seen, for example, in: Etel Solingen, 'ASEAN, *Quo Vadis?* Domestic coalitions and regional cooperation', *Contemporary Southeast Asia*, 1999, vol. 21, no. 1, pp. 30–54.

58 See, for instance, Jeffry Frieden, 'Invested Interests: The Politics of National Economic Policies in a World of Global Finance', *International Organization*, 1991, vol. 45, no. 4, pp. 425–51; Matthew Gabel, 'Divided Opinion, Common Currency: The Political Economy of Public Support for EMU', in Barry Eichengreen and Jeffry Frieden (eds) *The Political Economy of European Monetary Unification*, Boulder, CO: Westview, 2001, pp. 49–76.

59 The level at which the exchange rate is set introduces distinctions between importers and exporters (and between import-competing producers of traded goods). This issue is ignored in the following discussion on the basis that gains from currency over- or undervaluation are short run and are therefore less likely to affect decisions regarding long-term institutionalised exchange rate arrangements.

60 This point is made in: Kathleen MacNamara, *The Currency of Ideas: Monetary Politics in the European Union*, Ithaca, NY: Cornell University Press, 1998.

61 Source: Jonathan Kirshner, 'Disinflation, Structural Change, and Distribution', *Review of Radical Political Economics*, 1998, vol. 30, no. 1, pp. 53–89.

62 For an application that develops this idea in the case of Southeast Asia, see Andrew MacIntyre, *The Power of Institutions: Political Architecture and Governance*, Ithaca, NY: Cornell University Press, 2003.

63 Comparing countries only in terms of trade and cross-border investment levels may underestimate sensitivity to exchange rate fluctuations.

64 Source: Kwanho Shin and Yunjong Wang, 'Monetary Integration Ahead of Trade Integration in East Asia', p. 26.

65 Source: Natasha Hamilton-Hart, 'Capital Flows and Financial Markets in Asia: National, Regional, or Global?'.

66 Source: C. H. Kwan, *Yen Bloc: Toward Economic Integration in Asia*, p. 169.

67 See, for example, K. S. Jomo (ed.), *Southeast Asian Paper Tigers? From Miracle to Debacle and Beyond*, New York: Routledge, 2003.

68 Source: Linda Y. C. Lim, 'Free Market Fancies: Hong Kong, Singapore, and the Asian Financial Crisis', in T. J. Pempel (ed.) *The Politics of the Asian Economic Crisis*, Ithaca, NY: Cornell University Press, 1999, pp. 101–15.

69 This conclusion is reached in Takashi Terada, 'Directional leadership in institution-building: Japan's approaches to ASEAN in the establishment of PECC and APEC', *The Pacific Review*, 2001, vol. 14, no. 2, pp. 195–220.

70 This obstacle is discussed further by Barry Eichengreen and Tamim Bayoumi, 'Is Asia an Optimum Currency Area? Can it Become One? Regional, Global and Historical Perspectives on Asian Monetary Relations'.

71 See, for instance, Anthony Milner and Deborah Johnson, 'The Idea of Asia', in Jogn Ingleson (ed.) *Regionalism, Subregionalism and APEC*, Melbourne: Monash Asia Institute, 1997, pp. 1–19; Sun Ge, 'How Does Asia Mean? (Part 1)', *Inter-Asia Cultural Studies*, 2000, vol. 1, no. 1, pp. 13–47.

7 Developing a regional economic community in East Asia[1]

Nicholas Thomas

Introduction

In pre-modern times membership of a state was limited, allowing states to meet their obligations with relative ease. In the post-Westphalian system, where all those born into a state or being considered permanent residents of a state can claim membership of the polity, the demands placed on a state have grown exponentially. As globalisation has advanced not only have these demands grown but also they have become increasingly complex. The contemporary state can no longer address all the needs of all its peoples and societies through unilateral actions and programmes. It has little choice but to interact with other states, to help secure the necessary advantages and thus assure its legitimacy..

The inherent weakness of global processes is that they are simply too broad to offer a coherent, timely response to particular issues. There are too many actors, with differing agendas and capacities, for any one process either to proceed smoothly or to be concluded quickly. This can be most clearly seen in the Uruguay Round of the GATT as well as in the failure of the WTO Cancun Meeting. States are therefore faced with a stark choice – to commit to a global process of indeterminate time and uncertain outcome or to address their needs via smaller scale-processes.

Regions have emerged as a midway stage between the unilateral state and the global community. Väyrynen posits that the definition of what a region is can differ between physical (geographical and strategic) or functional (economic, environmental, and cultural) regions as well as the level of analysis employed (national, regional or global).[2] This implies a fluidity in the boundaries of a region, depending on the issue. While this fluidity can be seen in the fact that no state currently within a regional association interacts exclusively with its regional partners, the distinction between physical and functional criteria is becoming-blurred, a point which Breslin addressed in terms of the new regionalism literature in Chapter 2. As regions develop they take on a wide variety of aspects, so as to address the needs of their constituent members. Hence, just as nations can form states, so states can form regions, with each successively higher level of administration needing to be responsive to a wider community of interests and increasing diversity.

In the immediate aftermath of the 1997 Asian crisis, ASEAN and APEC were both subjected to severe criticism for their lax responses in addressing the needs of their constituent states, economies, and peoples. Nearly a decade on and the regional economic and financial landscape has changed significantly. Integration in the ASEAN and ASEAN+3 zones has accelerated, aided by member states' unwillingness to again suffer the economic and social impositions of a regional crisis. At the same time APEC is suffering from an identity dilemma, seemingly unable to decide if it should be an economic or security body, but with little to show in the way of concrete developments in either area.

This chapter explores the development of economic and financial regionalism in East Asia since 1997, within the ASEAN+3 zone. In the first part of the chapter particular attention is paid to the creation of regional economic trade and invest-ment zones, such as the ASEAN Free Trade Area and the ASEAN Investment Area. It is shown how a web of independent but mutually reinforcing agreements has emerged with ASEAN at the centre. This chapter then moves on to review other economic initiatives undertaken at the subregional and bilateral levels. In the second part of the chapter, efforts to financially integrate the region are reviewed. In this section the operationalisation of the Chiang Mai and Asian Bond Fund Initiatives as well as the proposed development of a regional stock exchange are examined to ascertain their impact on the regional economic architecture. Finally, the role played by the emerging regional policy communities in creating an Asian Economic Community is analysed. In concluding, the future potential of this accelerated economic regionalism to create an Asian Economic Community is considered.

Economic and financial regionalism

It is widely recognised that the catalyst for the current wave of enhanced region-alisation was the 1997 Asian crisis. In the aftermath of the crisis, regional states acted to ensure that they would be protected against such a serious degradation in their capacities and resources. What has developed since is a web of economic and financial regimes, whose cumulative purpose is to safeguard the region's economic welfare, at both the state and regional levels.

This web has several key strands. Economically, the region has seen the promotion of regional, subregional, and bilateral agreements for freer trade in goods and services. Financially, a network of currency swap arrangements, known as the Chiang Mai Initiative, has supported these economic activities. Other proposals, such as a regional currency union, an Asian Monetary Bond Fund, and an Asian Monetary Fund, are also being discussed as future financial activities. The third strand is a growing array of policy dialogues. These dialogues include the ASEAN+3 Economic Ministers' Meetings, the ASEAN+3 Finance Ministers' Meeting, meetings of central bank officials, as well as a number of combined meetings such as the Manila Framework Group and those between ASEAN+3 Finance and Central Bank Deputies. Combined, these strands have the potential to accelerate regional economic integration, leading to the eventual realisation of an ASEAN Economic Community (as announced at the 2003 Bali Summit) and an East Asia Free Trade Area (as proposed by both the East Asian Vision Group and East Asian Study Group). To understand how the region has addressed the issues linked to the resolution of the Asian crisis, it is necessary to examine the three strands in the web of economic and financial integration separately, before their combined effect on the region can be evaluated.

Economic regionalism

At the conclusion of the 2003 Bali Summit, the leaders announced their intent to create an ASEAN community. One of the three pillars supporting this community is to be an ASEAN Economic Community (AEC). As the ASEAN Concord II (released at the 2003 summit) stated:

> The ASEAN Economic Community is the realisation of the end-goal of economic integration as outlined in the ASEAN Vision 2020, to create a stable, prosperous and highly competitive ASEAN economic region in which there is a free flow of goods, services, investment and a freer flow of capital, equitable economic development and reduced poverty and socio-economic disparities in year 2020.[3]

In essence, the AEC is a combination of the ASEAN Free Trade Area (AFTA), the ASEAN Investment Area (AIA), and the ASEAN Framework Agreement on Services (AFAS), when they are all fully operational. Although the goal is a logical result of regional economic plans currently being implemented, these plans have a less than optimal history of delivering results on time or as envisaged. Despite this, there is a clear momentum towards the economic integration of the region, particularly in the area of free trade agreements, unified investment regimes, harmonisation of product lines and standards, as well as in the development of common financial and monetary policies.

AFTA is currently the only 'regional' free trade agreement in East Asia, although it focuses on the ASEAN group rather than on the broader ASEAN+3. AFTA was created in 1992 to promote intra-ASEAN trade. Indeed it was only following the establishment of AFTA that there was an ASEAN policy of promoting the free movement of capital for enhancing economic cooperation.[4] Prior to this, ASEAN members made their own intra-regional agreements for capital flows.[5] Following the crisis, AFTA was used to develop mechanisms to help restore stability by encouraging the use of ASEAN currencies for payment of traded goods and services.[6] This enhanced interdependence on regional currencies was designed to boost the currencies' demand, thereby reducing the impact of negative speculation. When examining the trade patterns of AFTA members it can be seen that intra-ASEAN trade has steadily increased since

AFTA's inception. In part that can be attributed to improved economic performance in the member countries, coupled with readily accessible markets in close geographic proximity, most notably China. Moreover, the regulatory aspects of AFTA provide an overarching framework that encourages trade with other Southeast Asian states.[7]

This is not to say that AFTA is not without its problems. Adherence to ASEAN's principles of consensus and non-interference has meant that some countries have been able to retain preferential positions for selected domestic markets. However, as Southeast Asian countries fully accede to the World Trading Organisation (WTO) these trade barriers will be gradually removed.[8] Indeed global efforts towards trade liberalisation offer an alternative option between balancing domestic imperatives and regional realities. Where regional and domestic concerns exist regarding market penetration by external actors, global frameworks for liberalisation offer a way to overcome these concerns without triggering national sensitivities.

Although AFTA came into force in January 2003 – later than planned – it remains hampered by imperfect implementation coupled with enforcement problems. The former problem is especially visible in the elimination of unnecessary and unjustifiable non-tariff measures (NTMs).[9] The latter problem can be seen when disputes arise where the issue of compensation arises. One example of this was seen in the petrochemical dispute between Singapore and the Philippines, where the Philippines resisted paying compensation claimed by Singapore due to their ongoing protection of the local petrochemical industry. It was only after Singapore threatened to withdraw tariff concessions granted to the Philippines that the Philippines relented.[10] This type of behaviour reinforces the perception that, at this stage, regionalism in East Asia is still fragile and more concerned with maximising national interests rather than achieving common regional goals.

Nonetheless, there are also indications that this national-oriented mindset is gradually changing. Among the recent recommendations handed down by the High Level Task Force (HLTF) on ASEAN Economic Integration was a set of recommendations for the creation of a dispute settlement mechanism (DSM) relating to all economic agreements. The mechanism will include: (1) a legal unit with the ASEAN Secretariat to provide legal advice on trade disputes; (2) an ASEAN Consultation to Solve Trade and Investment Issues (ACT), to 'provide quick resolution to operational problems'; (3) the establishment of an ASEAN Compliance Body – 'modelled after the WTO Textile Monitoring Body and [sic] make use of peer pressure'; and (4) an enhanced ASEAN DSM 'to ensure expeditious and legally binding decisions in resolving trade disputes'.[11] If effectively implemented, this new DSM architecture could provide a much needed boost to the development of the AFTA. More importantly, it will represent a significant step forward in formalising regional economic integration, as states will have to abide by the decision of a supranational institution. To do so will require a partial abdication of state sovereignty in order to gain greater economic benefits.

While internal problems need to be resolved before AFTA can consider further evolution as a regional trade association, ASEAN is also helping promote this process by establishing free-trade-type agreements with Northeast Asian countries.[12] The most developed of these is the Framework Agreement on the China–ASEAN Closer Economic Cooperation Agreement (CECA). For some ASEAN countries, this has already led to economic benefits as tariffs on goods are reduced immediately under an Early Harvest Programme (EHP). The benefits from this EHP are uneven, being more directed towards the four less developed ASEAN states – Cambodia, Laos, Myanmar, and Vietnam (CLMV). While negotiations have advanced between China and ASEAN, they have highlighted the difficulties ASEAN faces in coordinating the needs and agendas of all 10 member states. Partly reflecting that difficulty, Singapore announced in May 2004 that it would seek a bilateral agreement with China, which would be informed by the aims of the larger China–ASEAN CECA.[13] However, despite these difficulties in coordinating the talks, China and ASEAN announced that they had agreed to remove completely all tariffs on merchandised goods by 2010, with the implementation of the cut to be phased in from 1 July 2005.[14] At this point, the first group of products under the EHP had their associated tariffs reduced to between 5 and 0 per cent.[15]

At the 2003 Bali Summit, Japan and ASEAN agreed to establish a Closer Economic Partnership to strengthen economic integration.[16] This agreement was realised in early 2004 when Japan launched parallel bilateral trade talks with the Philippines, Malaysia, and Thailand. These talks are a reflection of Japan's regional FTA strategy with ASEAN, which it sees as being built upon a series of bilateral agreements with Southeast Asian states, rather than the top-down approach of the Chinese government. As Tanaka noted in Chapter 3, Japanese motives for moving forward with FTA agreements with Southeast Asia must also be seen in the context of China–Japan rivalry for regional economic leadership. That said, each of the three bilateral talks holds its own challenges. The Philippines is most interested in the liberalisation of labour flows so that Japan will accept nurses and other care workers as immigrant labourers.[17] Malaysia is less keen on a full FTA with Japan, and is more focused on improving sectoral economic cooperation. Malaysian negotiators instead handed their Japanese counterparts a list of over 200 areas for closer economic cooperation. For their part, Japan is keen that Malaysia lower or eliminate tariffs on automobiles and farm produce, which Japan sees as being more realisable with an FTA package.[18] Meanwhile, Thailand has indicated a more flexible approach to the negotiations; in particular, expressing a willingness to leave contentious sectors – such as agriculture – off the table until later in return for an opportunity to fully liberalise other sectors, such as telecommunications.[19]

On an individual scale, these different issues and negotiating approaches presage the difficulties the two sides will face in developing a bilateral Japan–ASEAN Free Trade Agreement. Nonetheless, in April 2005, Japanese and ASEAN negotiators commenced regional discussions. While the pattern of these initial discussions reflected Japan's earlier bilateral trade preferences (in so far as on the first day Japan held FTA negotiations with those ASEAN countries with which it had not yet opened talks), the aim was to use these talks as a basis to create a truly subregional free trade area. According to official Japanese estimates, such a trading group would be worth in excess of US$18.5 billion and generate an additional 260,000 jobs.[20]

South Korea has also expressed a commitment to a bilateral agreement with ASEAN. To this end, in March 2004, South Korea and ASEAN launched a joint study on a free trade agreement. During 2004 five rounds of the joint study group were held, with ASEAN positive regarding the outcome but South Korea being more cautious; possibly as a result of the domestic unease that stemmed from the earlier South Korea–Chile agreement. The two sides originally planned to decide on whether to open formal FTA talks after reviewing the results at a bilateral Economic Ministers' Meeting held in September 2004, but this was deferred until the bilateral summit in November 2004 in Laos. It was not surprising therefore that during the ASEAN+1 (South Korea) Summit a decision was taken to commence negotiations, with the aim of eliminating tariffs on 80 per cent of traded goods.[21]

Over the first six months of 2005 a further three rounds of negotiations were held between the two sides, with a view to implementing the agreement in 2007 or 2008. At the conclusion of the second round of negotiations in April 2005 a draft FTA was announced, allowing a formal agreement to be signed during the bilateral summit in Malaysia. In addition, South Korean officials declared their intent to develop and sign supplemental agreements with ASEAN covering investment and the services sector in 2006.[22] Not only were these agreements seen as a logical evolution in South Korea's relationship with ASEAN, but South Korean officials were also concerned with the impact China–ASEAN and Japan–ASEAN FTAs would have on South Korea's regional trading relationships.[23] In terms of regional integration, the Korea–ASEAN FTA (and the related Korea–Singapore FTA) was an important agreement as it extended the FTA provisions to encompass the Kaesong Industrial Complex in North Korea, thereby creating a mechanism for the inclusion of the DPRK in regional trade arrangements.[24]

Beyond the ASEAN+1 FTA negotiations, preliminary discussions have also been held to create a +3 FTA. In other words, a trilateral FTA involving China, Japan, and South Korea. As a start to these discussions an investment treaty involving all three states is currently underway, with the Business Forum[25] also undertaking joint projects on intellectual property protection.[26] These efforts are also supported by interlocking studies between the three states on a bilateral basis. For example, China and Japan are studying the potential impact of a China–Japan FTA;[27] while South Korea and Japan have held four rounds towards concluding an FTA.[28]

However, the disparities between the three economies will lead to win–loss calculations by the three governments; calculations that will likely require other benefits to be introduced to ensure all three states reach agreement (such as additional services agreements or the resolution of competing territorial claims). For instance, it is estimated that the positive change in GDP as a result of a trilateral agreement would be very mixed: 1.74 per cent for South Korea, compared with

5.91 per cent for China, and 0.61 per cent for Japan.[29] Such an agreement would also force structural change to the domestic economies. For some sectors likely to be most affected – such as South Korea's agricultural sector – this is a domestic political challenge likely to become part of the electoral landscape.[30]

That such agreements can bring tangible benefits to the signatory countries, and also spur the development of a regional economic bloc, is not disputed. However, problems are very likely to emerge during discussions relating to capacities of countries to negotiate these agreements – particularly the CLMV group – as well as the ability of individual countries to overcome powerful domestic lobby groups, such as farmers, whose interests may be negatively affected.[31] The latter issue nearly derailed South Korea's first FTA with Chile, and has been raised as a likely obstacle in South Korea's FTA talks with Japan.[32]

More broadly ASEAN and its member states are looking for ways to even out the results of economic integration, particularly in light of the challenges to Southeast Asian economies that are presented by China's high rate of growth. Southeast Asian economic ministers and officials are increasingly discussing the need to 'balance' the China–ASEAN economic relationship with other alternatives, so that the impact of China's rising dominance on the regional economy can be mitigated. Indeed, this need is in part behind the move to develop closer ties with Japan and South Korea. It is also spurring the expansion of the ASEAN+ model to include India and, most recently, Australia and New Zealand.

In contemporary times India has been trying to develop closer ties with ASEAN since September 1994, when Indian Prime Minister Rao signalled a new 'Look East' policy. In the two years prior to this policy India and ASEAN had been developing linkages in trade, investment, and tourism. Following this announcement, cooperation gradually expanded to encompass a wide range of other sectors, such as science and technology. In 2002 the two sides held their first Leaders' Summit in Phnom Penh.[33] This was followed in 2003 by India's accession to the Treaty of Amity and Cooperation and the adoption of a *Framework Agreement on Comprehensive Economic Cooperation*, the purpose of which is to develop an ASEAN–India Regional Trade and Investment Area (RTIA).[34] As with the China–ASEAN FTA, the RTIA contains an early harvest programme that began operations in November 2004. The RTIA was expected to commence on 1 January 2006, with a phased implementation to take approximately 10 years. In practical terms this means that even as the China–ASEAN FTA is being implemented, its uniqueness will be balanced by the opening of the Indian (and possibly Japanese) markets for ASEAN goods and services.[35] However, the start date for the RTIA has been delayed until 2007, following an impasse on the rules of origin.[36]

Australia and New Zealand have also been attempting to develop a regional economic association with ASEAN, both singularly and within the context of an ASEAN–CER arrangement.[37] As the 1997 Australian foreign policy White Paper noted, '[t]he Government will give priority to developing links between ASEAN and CER, as well as working closely with individual ASEAN countries, both as an ASEAN dialogue partner, and within the broader regional forums such as APEC and the ARF'.[38] In April 2004, the ASEAN economic ministers offered the suggestion that their respective leaders seek to negotiate an FTA arrangement with the CER countries. While there is a valid perception that the retirement of Malaysian Prime Minister Dr Mahathir Mohamad created an opening for this offer to be made, it is also true that an ASEAN–CER FTA provides a further balancing point against the rise of China, and to a lesser extent India, while providing an additional impetus for deeper ASEAN integration. Following an invitation of both countries to the 2004 Vientiane Summit, ASEAN–CER negotiations commenced in February 2005 and are expected to be completed within two years.[39]

These ASEAN-level agreements are supplemented by a number of signed and planned bilateral agreements between individual ASEAN+3 states. Singapore is the most advanced of the ASEAN states in this respect. In January 2002, Singapore and Japan signed the Japan–Singapore Economic Agreement for a New Age Partnership (JSEPA). Two years later this was followed up in November 2004 when the Korea–Singapore FTA was signed after two years of discussions.[40] Thailand has also been very active in signing bilateral FTA agreements with other regional states. As is also the case with Singapore, Thailand has chosen to partner with states from outside the region that can act as gateways to other economic areas (such as the Middle East, South America, or Europe). However, unlike Singapore, most of the agreements are yet to be fully implemented.

The combination of AFTA and ASEAN FTAs with China, Japan, and South Korea, supplemented by individual agreements between regional states in Southeast and Northeast Asia, could provide the necessary building blocks for the creation of an East Asian FTA. However, using the current state of negotiations between China and ASEAN as a template, such a pan-Asian FTA is unlikely to be achieved in the medium term. That said, the collapse of the WTO talks at Cancun and the problems in the Hong Kong round of talks should provide an additional impetus to all regional free trade talks, in so far as the inability of all states to progress global talks spurs regional and bilateral negotiations.[41] However, what the Cancun collapse also demonstrated is that the region is still far from acting as a bloc, with some regional countries in support of the 'Singapore proposals' and others firmly against them. Ultimately what will be required is a mindset and a mechanism similar to that encapsulated in the recommendations put forward by the HLTF on ASEAN Economic Integration. Through the implementation of such an approach, the region will be able to develop transparent and accountable processes, so that states which 'opt in' do so in acceptance of the binding conditions. However, as the EU has shown – in the recent cases of state breaches of mandated deficit levels – the real challenge is not in getting states to accept the binding conditionalities, but to accept the power of regional organisations to levy penalties against members. In this area, the region still has a long way to go.

Complementing ASEAN's trade liberalisation scheme is the ASEAN Investment Area (AIA). The AIA, an outcome of the 1998 Hanoi Summit, is designed to 'attract greater and sustainable levels of foreign direct investment (FDI) into the region and to realise substantially increasing flows of FDI from both ASEAN and non-ASEAN sources'.[42] As Lawan suggested:

> the AIA thus indicates a new direction for ASEAN to balance deeper regional integration and 'Open Regionalism'. While it enhances intra-ASEAN economic integration, it also opens the door to non-ASEAN investors. Moreover, individual ASEAN countries have also unilaterally liberalised their trade and investment regime, by keeping their margin of preference as low as they can so that market access is more available for non-ASEAN enterprises.[43]

The objectives of AFTA are also supported by the operations of the Asia–Pacific Economic Cooperation (APEC) group. As Soesastro noted, the umbrella nature of APEC provides a sense of cohesiveness between the different subregional trade and investment initiatives.[44] This helps prevent divisive problems arising, such as new forms of trade discrimination or the development of new sets of interests resistant to broader regional trade and investment liberalisation efforts.[45] However, there are limits to this claim. For APEC to function as a supranational 'glue' for subregional initiatives, it needs to maintain a primary relevance for East Asia trading regimes. Although APEC remains a highly relevant institution it is focused on sustaining unilateral trade liberalisation rather than institutionalising region-wide FTAs.[46] For those East Asian states for whom APEC does not produce substantive institutional cohesion, other regimes, such as political or security coalitions, may provide the additional impetus to generate a regional identity able to prevent these divisive problems from arising.[47] The AFTA/APEC relationship is another example of deeper regional ties being balanced with membership in larger, extra-regional organisations.

Other subregional initiatives

The 1990s also witnessed the growth of other subregional initiatives, such as the Greater Mekong Subregion (GMS) development project, as well as the creation of 'growth triangles'. Growth triangles are an attempt to create capital for three countries either by tapping into an existing resource and infrastructure base whose benefits can be spread across a transborder region or by identifying areas of potential resource development.[48] These triangles are important for wider regionalisation efforts as they not only have a direct impact on their operating zones but also stimulate positive flow-on effects for neighbouring areas. As Chavez notes in the next chapter, the GMS and other such subregional initiatives bind provinces in contiguous areas together, but, in terms of supporting wider regionalism, need to adopt wider social and development goals if they are to contribute positively to region-building projects.

The GMS project involves a deeper commitment from members than is the case with growth triangles.[49] The potential in the GMS has long been recognised but it has only been in the last decade that socio-political conditions enabled the integrative process to proceed.[50] Working with the Asian Development Bank (ADB) and the United Nations Development Programme (UNDP), the countries in the project identify areas of cooperation across seven areas – transport, energy, telecommunications, environmental, human resource development, trade and investment, and tourism.[51] Although there is no formal GMS Secretariat, the number of ministerial summits, Senior Officials Meetings and related fora encourages a high degree of policy cooperation between participating states. Hence, the integration between the GMS members represents a compressed form of what is occurring in the wider ASEAN+ area.

Subregional cooperative efforts such as the GMS form strong bases for wider regional integration, as they encourage small-scale transnational development to take place that would not otherwise occur.[52] In many respects the challenges faced by these projects mirror broader regional issues. First, given wide social, economic, and political disparities the benefits may be unequally distributed between participating countries. Second, states have to provide long-term commitment to the project's objectives.[53] This means that participating states have willingly to accept constraints on their ability to allocate resources unilaterally – a key aspect of state sovereignty. In addition both the growth triangles and the GMS are heavily dependent on private sector investment. This raises issues of government transparency and accountability in providing accurate information to investors. In some cases regional governments are not accustomed to providing timely economic and financial data, and may even regard such information as secret. Although this change can be seen as an encroachment on state sovereignty, the added value of the subregional initiatives encourages governments to change management practices and adopt new governance policies, for example in the harmonisation and standardisation of customs procedures to facilitate subregional trade and investment.[54]

Hence it can be said that there are concrete expressions of commitment to economic integration within the ASEAN+3, ASEAN and different subregional groupings. Taken together, these initiatives hold the potential to form an East Asian Economic Community. However, a key stumbling block in the creation of such a community is that while the ASEAN and subregional endeavours are – to a certain extent – being coordinated (in so far as they involve the same actors), the ASEAN+1 and +3 efforts are proceeding in a more chaotic manner; with regional rivalries based on economic balance of power equations and regional fears playing as much a role in their development as the presumption of deliverable economic benefits. It is suggested that those ASEAN+ agreements need to be better coordinated with clearer economic and policy end-point objectives if the ideal of an AEC is to be realised. However, beyond economic integration, truly to realise the creation of an AEC will also require deeper regionalisation of the financial sector. This is the topic of the next section.

Financial regionalism

The rehabilitation and deeper integration of the region's financial activities was considered a key step towards recovery after the 1997 Asian crisis. While issues such as currency regulation mechanisms, banking reform, corporate governance, and reforms of state–market relationships were left to individual countries to address – either by themselves or in conjunction with international organisations or donor groups – other ideas, such as regional currency swaps, an Asian Monetary Fund, or the launching of an Asian Bond Fund to bolster East Asian financial regionalism, have gained varying degrees of acceptance in markets and policy fora.

The most significant swap arrangement to date is the Chiang Mai Initiative (CMI). Launched in May 2000, the CMI envisaged a 'network of bilateral swap and currency repurchase agreement facilities among ASEAN countries, China, Japan, and the Republic of Korea'.[55] In this respect the CMI built on the ASEAN Swap Arrangement developed in March 1997 and the currency swaps that Japan had already undertaken in 1999 as part of the New Miyazawa Initiative.[56] By mid-2002, most of the bilateral swap arrangements (BSAs) either had been concluded or were under negotiation between the +3 countries and the core five ASEAN economies (Thailand, Malaysia, the Philippines, Indonesia, and Singapore).[57] To date, US$36.5 billion has been pledged in BSAs.[58] The importance of the CMI, especially in terms of a confidence-building measure for other regional initiatives, should not be underestimated. As Hiwatari observed, '[m]ost notably, the initiative was the only proposed post-crisis regional financial arrangement actually realised'.[59]

Originally, the CMI was seen as the basis for creating an ASEAN Monetary Fund (AMF) and a common regional currency. Although the latter idea has been shelved for the future, the concept of an AMF keeps reappearing on policy agendas. Initially proposed by Japan in the aftermath of the crisis as a more regionally responsive alternative to the IMF, the concept was dropped in the face of severe US pressure as well as Japan's unwillingness to take on the estimated US$100 billion funding commitment.[60]

Moving away from the notion that an AMF would act as a lender of last resort, as is the case with the IMF, contemporary reconceptualisations of the AMF see it as focusing on regional financial crisis management and prevention.[61] While the CMI is the only post-crisis arrangement realised:

> [t]he prospects that an AMF, or some kind of regionally based financial institution, will take form are quite good. How effective an AMF would be, however, is a different matter. Its chances of becoming a meaningful regional institution hinge on how Asia-Pacific states see the future.[62]

In April 2004, ASEAN finance ministers began considering plans to create a more meaningful form of the CMI, which brings the currency swap arrangement even closer to the concept of an AMF. Under this proposed arrangement regional states would create a common fund of US$100 billion that could be drawn upon by any state in the event of a liquidity crisis. In terms of burden sharing, Japan (which proposed this new arrangement) would contribute 40 per cent, with the remainder shared between South Korea, China, Thailand, Malaysia, the Philippines, Indonesia, and Singapore. As an initial proposal, this concept represents a midway point between the CMI and the AMF, one that is more acceptable to regional countries as well as the United States. At a meeting of the ASEAN's finance ministers in May 2005, an agreement was reached to double to size of the current funding available under the CMI and to enlarge the amounts that could be drawn upon without IMF support.[63]

While this new proposal would appear to deepen further the region's financial architecture, a great deal still rests on how preoccupied regional states are with how 'sovereignty, state building, and security' will affect the AMF's (or related institutions') ability to act to prevent future financial shocks.[64] As with economic matters, the more regional states are able to transcend their present condition of 'together yet separate', the more robust and viable the region will be as an organisational entity.

The CMI can also be seen as the first step in the eventual creation of an Asian currency. The opening move in developing this single Asian currency was put forward in October 1998 by then Japanese Minister of Finance, Miyazawa Kiichi, who called for Asian currencies to be pegged to a basket of the yen, dollar, and euro. Although there was only a lukewarm response to that aspect of the Miyazawa Initiative, an alternative option – the rapid internationalisation of the yen – had a better reception within Southeast Asia.[65]

The implementation of such a plan remains technically difficult. Undoubtedly, the greater internationalisation of the yen would improve the economic outlook of all East Asian economies. As the 1999 World Bank Annual Report noted, 'A Japanese recovery is crucial to the stabilisation and prosperity of Asian economies.'[66] However, despite any improvement in Japan's economic situation, the US economy is likely to remain vibrant enough for its dollar to be attractive to regional and international markets.[67] Until this situation changes any attempt to 'force' the development of a yen bloc would cause macroeconomic stresses in all regional economies.

That said, given a trend towards deepening regional integration across a multiplicity of sectors, some form of currency union appears inevitable. First, it is more likely that East Asian states would prefer adopting a currency union rather than moving towards a yen bloc. The former option would give all member states an (in principle) equal say in monetary affairs, whereas the adoption of the yen would take a large part of monetary policy (and with it the Keynesian control of their national economies) away from subscribing states and place it in the hands of the Japanese government. As has already been noted, this would be a highly difficult position for many regional states to accept. Second, in an area of deepening ties, a currency union would result in substantial savings when undertaken in tandem with FTAs, harmonisation of educational and legal standards, and liberalised labour and migration laws.[68] However, the wide economic disparities between the ASEAN+ members, coupled with their differences towards economic sovereignty and openness, mean that the adoption of any such measure is likely to be in the longer term.

One initiative to develop further the web of regional financial ties is the Asian Bond Fund (ABF). Announced in June 2003, the ABF supports 'the development of a regional market in government and semi-government bonds' through the issuance of US$1 billion of foreign currency reserves from participating countries to invest in dollar-denominated bonds'.[69] In May 2005, funding for the second round of the ABF (ABF 2) was realised. This new round added a further US$2 billion to the regional bond market. Unlike the first round, the ABF 2 was issued in local currency bonds.[70]

The creation of the ABF and the ABF 2 meets several pressing needs of regional markets. First, they offer an additional mechanism by which governments can protect themselves against another crisis. As Lejot *et al.* concluded, '[g]overnments maybe become better able to fund themselves securely, with fewer risks of flight capital leading to contagion and chronic illiquidity'.[71] Second, they help integrate underdeveloped or isolated markets with their more mature regional counterparts. This improves the operations of these markets as it requires them to adjust their practices to higher regional and global finance market standards. This is a critical step, both in avoiding future crises as well as in creating a regional market based on shared norms and regulatory understandings. Third, they address ongoing concern related to the CMI, namely that the pool of available funds was insufficient to protect a market under speculative attack. Taken together, it is intended that the two rounds of the bond funds and the CMI will provide an enhanced regional shield against such problems.

Policy dialogues

Regional cooperation in both economic and financial areas has spawned integrated policy communities at the ASEAN and ASEAN+3 levels. This is primarily due to these issues being of immediate concern to the region's leaders in the wake of the 1997 Asian crisis. Over the last six years, these communities have gone further than their political, social, environmental, or strategic counterparts in fostering an interdependent regional community. It is pertinent, therefore, to review their recent operations so as to evaluate this sector's ability to promote an economically integrated East Asia.

Public policy dialogues

The first ASEAN+3 Economic Ministers' Meeting (AEM+3) in May 2000 had a brief to foster economic growth and industrial development across the region. The AEM+3 is supported by the Senior Economic Officials from the ASEAN+3 countries (SEOM+3). At their second meeting (October 2000) the ministers began delineating what issues and programmes fell under their jurisdiction, deciding that any particular project would have to be regional in nature and outcomes, and involve a minimum of two ASEAN and two Northeast Asian countries. This is a useful benchmark in evaluating other ASEAN+3 schemes to see if they should be categorised as regional, ASEAN, or subregional.

In 2001, the ministers began using this benchmark to promote a series of projects – ranging from ICT development, to increasing regional SME competitiveness, to environmental and e-learning training initiatives. Throughout 2002, the AEM+3 and SEOM+3 meetings focused on the implications of developing economic links with external partners, and how ASEAN should be advancing the development of AFTA, as well as where it could go after AFTA was fully operationalised.

In September 2003, the ministers 'agreed to sign the Protocol to amend the ASEAN Framework Agreement on Services that would enable the application of the ASEAN Minus X formula in the implementation of member countries' services commitments'.[72] The concept, that some states can run faster in pursuing a more integrated region, can be seen in the recent Protocol to amend the ASEAN–China CECA as well as in the initial decision by the Philippines not to participate in the Early Harvest Programme.[73]

Another scheme that seeks to achieve a similar result is the '2+X' option, where two or more ASEAN states undertake the liberalisation of a specific sector, which other member states can then choose whether or not to join in. Singapore, Thailand, and Brunei, for example, have signed an aviation agreement that liberalises all air-cargo services between the three countries. This agreement, which was originally only between Singapore and Thailand, may expand to include other member states as well.[74] In a similar move, Singapore and Indonesia have signed an agreement on the mutual recognition of telecommunications equipment, which allows 'phone equipment made in either country [to] be used without additional testing'.[75] As Singaporean Prime Minister Goh noted, 'It takes two to tango', but if other countries want to join in, the option is available. In this way, sectoral agreements and their accompanying policy relationships within a subregional (bilateral+) relationship could become the nexus for faster regional liberalisation within AFTA, or with other economies in Northeast or South Asia. What both the 'ASEAN-X' and '2+X' also indicate is that ASEAN is prepared to leave behind its rigid adherence to consensus decision making in functional areas in order to secure economic benefits.

Complementing the work of the AEM+3, and also beginning operations in 2000, is the ASEAN+3 Finance Ministers' Meeting (AFM+3). It is the AFM+3 which reviews policies relating to 'regional financial cooperation initiatives, including, the Chiang Mai Initiative (CMI), Monitoring of Capital Flows, the Early Warning System (EWS) and the Asian Bond Market Initiative (ABMI)'.[76] Arising out of this policy dialogue, an ASEAN+3 Study Group comprising senior finance and central bank officials was formed in May 2001 to review economic programmes and suggest reforms. As a spin-off from this meeting, an informal process involving finance and central bank deputies started in April 2002, to discuss economic and policy issues.[77] At each stage, a new avenue for coordinating regional financial policy is created, which over time supports the development of a regional financial community.

Unlike the AEM+3 and the AFM+3, the Executives' Meeting of East Asia–Pacific central banks (EMEAP) is the only region-wide economic policy forum that operated before the 1997 Asian crisis, although, as Hamilton-Hart noted in the previous chapter, there were other groupings revolving around Southeast Asian or Southeast Asian/Australasian central banks even before EMEAP.[78] Prior to the crisis EMEAP was concerned with information exchanges and networking between the deputy governors. In 1996, the first Governors' Meeting was held, and working groups to examine ways to 'enhance financial stability and market developments in the region' were formed.[79] Since then, the networks between central bank officials have increased allowing for more comprehensive regional policy formulation. It was as a result of these networks and working groups that EMEAP was able to push successfully for the development of the aforementioned ABF. It is also reviewing ways to decrease the level of home currency exchanges in offshore markets, to 'restrain exchange rate volatility and restore latitude to monetary policy'.[80] Thus, what began as a space for information exchange has developed into a forum for policy creation, where new regional mechanisms better placed to protect the regions' economies are considered.

The need to coordinate more closely the recovery efforts led to the creation of the Manila Framework Group (MFG) in 1997. The MFG draws together central banks as well as finance ministers from nine East Asian countries, in addition to Australia, New Zealand, Canada, and the United States.[81] Its purpose is to provide a forum to discuss issues affecting regional financial stability.

Both EMEAP and the MFG include East Asian as well as Western members. However, with the development of ASEAN+3, there has been a marked strengthening of ties between the East Asian members of these organisations. In 1999, Vietnam hosted the first of what has become an annual series of meetings of (what might be termed) the ASEAN+3 MFG; in other words, the MFG members plus the missing East Asian members minus the Western participants.[82] Regardless of the merits of such a group, its creation under ASEAN+3 auspices was indicative of a trend towards economic and financial regionalism under an established pan-Asian political structure. This ties the East Asian region into a distinct political–economic bloc, but allows for the maintenance of extra-regional ties.

Private sector and Track II dialogues

Supporting the operations of governments and central banks in regional financial arrangements is the private sector. Although most regional governments have already developed abiding ties with their local private sectors, little has been done to translate that experience and knowledge into a regional setting. Given the key role of local and multinational companies in advancing the overall trend towards greater intra-regional trade, this is a necessary move if intra-regional development is to be taken further.

To address this gap in regional policy fora, the private sector East Asian Business Council (EABC) was launched. The EABC was initially mooted in 1999 during the Manila Summit, when all 13 heads of states were present for the first time. The EABC held its first meeting in April 2004 to discuss possible areas for industrial collaboration between ASEAN corporations and their +3 counterparts, with the aim of deepening economic collaboration and investment. Unlike its national equivalents, the structure of the EABC ties it explicitly into regional policy processes by requiring it to present its recommendations directly to the ASEAN Economic Ministers' and Senior Officials' Meetings.

One of the most interesting policy dialogues to emerge in recent times is the Asian Bellagio Group. This group is a working committee of ASEAN+3 central bank officials, finance ministry representatives, and academics formed 'to discuss ways to stabilize Asia's volatile currency markets and deal with the global economic imbalances caused by the massive twin US deficits'.[83] Although it is currently only a committee with no ability to enforce joint monetary action, its creation as well as the name of the committee are seen as a broad indication of closer policy coordination on regional monetary issues.[84]

Between them, these public and private sector dialogues have the capacity to promote deeper regional integration in the economic and financial sectors. However, as indicated from the activities and outputs shown in the first two sections of this chapter, there is a pressing need to unify better the objectives of the policy communities within the overarching goal of the ASEAN Economic Community. As Breslin and Hamilton-Hart highlighted in previous chapters, this will require coordination horizontally across the regional policy-makers but also vertically: down into domestic constituencies and up into the global arena.

Conclusion

This chapter began from the position that regional economic and financial integration was expanding and deepening in East Asia but it was not yet clear as to where it would lead. It is possible that, at a particular stage in a region's development, the benefits of a state entering into a competing extra-regional arrangement might be overshadowed by the costs to the other regional endeavours that the state is involved in. Hence, a 'tipping point' can be envisaged where states will begin to choose further regional developments over new extra-regional agreements. It could be further suggested that such a point would likely arise in sectors where cooperation was most advanced, whose accumulated influence on state policy-making would then allow for the coalescence of a region around these two key sectors.

It is in the economic and financial sectors that the most mature example of East Asian regionalisation can be identified. This is not surprising as these were the sectors most affected by the 1997 Asian crisis, and thus were the two most needing to be enhanced if a repeat crisis was to be avoided. As Breslin noted in Chapter 2, these have also been two sectors most affected by globalisation and have, hence, needed to be the most responsive to change and development. While regional cooperation in these sectors has advanced since the crisis, the outcomes from the 2003 Bali Summit could indicate a tipping point being reached in this area. In particular, the decision to create an ASEAN Economic Community, supported by a new dispute resolution mechanism, might presage the emergence of an AEC, where member states surrender part of their sovereignty for greater benefits at the regional level.

It can be concluded that, if economic and financial forms of regionalism are not yet at a tipping point, they are getting closer. It is clear that there is a vision of the region, an AEC, which places a high value on deeper economic and financial integration as the engine of future regionalisation. Indeed, across all policy dialogues is the clear recognition that economic and financial integration is the keystone for any future region-building efforts. What is needed now is the domestic and regional capacity and political will to see this vision joined with reality.

Efforts to join the two can especially be seen in the last two years, where regional economic and finance ministers have actively sought to address shortfalls in their respective areas by adopting new mechanisms to overcome existing problems, and in doing so create new processes to strengthen the region further. What is notable about the policy dialogues in this area is that ministers and their senior officials are meeting twice yearly, with a similarly busy schedule for regional central bank governors and deputy governors. New policy initiatives are also being developed to allow the region to respond better to Asian and international challenges. This hectic (and expanding) pace of meetings reflects the importance placed on these two areas in terms of their ability to protect the region against another crisis, and is vital if a regional community is to be created. However, while these efforts appear to be well placed, to tip this sector over into a deeper form of regional integration, much depends on the timely and comprehensive implementation of the proposed initiatives.

Notes

1 Certain aspects of this chapter have been previously published in *Asian Perspectives* and the *Journal of International and Area Studies*.
2 Raimo Väyrynen, 'Regionalism: Old and New', *International Studies Review*, 2003, vol. 5, no. 1, pp. 26–7.
3 *Declaration of ASEAN Concord II*, paragraph B1, 7 October 2003.
4 Lawan Thanadsillapakul, *Open Regionalism and Deeper Integration: The Implementation of ASEAN Investment Area (AIA) and ASEAN Free Trade Area (AFTA)*, Thailand: Institute of International Business and Economic Law Studies, 2000, pp. 9–10.
5 Lawan, *Open Regionalism and Deeper Integration*.
6 As *The Hanoi Declaration* in part stated, 'We encourage wider use of ASEAN currencies in intra-ASEAN trade settlements.' See Paragraph 13 of *The Hanoi Declaration*, Sixth ASEAN Summit, Hanoi, Vietnam, 16 December 1998.
7 This is not to say that intra-ASEAN trade is dominant. Extra-AFTA trade (particularly with Europe and North America) far outweighs regional trading patterns. However, intra-regional trade is increasing. As one report noted, 'Between 1993 and 2000, intra-ASEAN exports grew to 87.7 billion US dollars from 43.26 billion dollars, while the bloc's total exports to all markets increased to 696 billion dollars from 374

billion dollars.' Source: 'Tariff Among ASEAN Countries Reduced Sharply', *Xinhua*, July 2001, p. 27.

8 The APEC Bogor Declaration on free trade is an additional pressure on Southeast Asian economies to remove protective trade barriers.

9 See: 'ASEAN Free Trade Area Council Meeting Ends in Phnom Penh', *BBC Monitoring*, 22 September 2003.

10 See: 'Philippines, Singapore settle petrochem tariff dispute', *AFX News Limited*, 9 September 2003.

11 These quotes are drawn from the Recommendations of the High-Level Task Force on ASEAN Economic Integration. Submitted to the ASEAN Economic Ministers Meeting, September 2003.

12 It should also be noted that ASEAN is planning a bilateral FTA with India, and has signed a Closer Economic Partnership with Australia and New Zealand. Though these extra-regional agreements may generate closer ties between ASEAN and these countries over the longer term, the core economic relationship is likely to be focused on East Asia.

13 The Singapore–China FTA negotiations were officially launched in November 2004. Source: 'Singapore, China to Launch FTA Talks in November', *Japan Economic Newswire*, 14 May 2004.

14 'China, ASEAN agree to end tariffs', *The China Daily*, 26 October 2004.

15 'ASEAN-China to Implement First Phase of FTA on 1 July', Malaysian National News Agency, 7 June 2005.

16 See: *Framework for Comprehensive Economic Partnership Between the Association of Southeast Asian Nations and Japan*, 8 October 2003.

17 'Japan to propose letting qualified Filipino nurses work indefinitely', *Japan Economic Newswire*, 25 October 2004.

18 'Japan Pushing for FTAs to shore up presence in Asia', *Japan Economic Newswire*, 17 September 2004; 'Japan calls for Malaysia to scrap tariff on farm exports', *Japan Economic Newswire*, 21 July 2004.

19 Junichi Fukazawa. 'First round of FTA talks with ASEAN reveals snags', *Yomiuri Shimbun*, 17 February 2004.

20 'Japan, ASEAN kick off first round of formal FTA negotiations', *Japan Economic Newswire*, 12 April 2005.

21 'S. Korea, ASEAN Start FTA Study Talks', *Asia Pulse*, 8 March 2004; 'ASEAN Seeks Completion of FTA Talks with S. Korea by 2007', *Asia Pulse*, 6 September 2004.

22 'South Korea, ASEAN reach draft framework free trade agreement', *BBC Monitoring Asia Pacific – Political*, 21 April 2005. The third round of negotiations in early June 2005 began to flesh out the details in specific non-agricultural sectors. Source: 'S. Korea, ASEAN to Discuss Trade Framework Agreement this WK', *Asia Pulse*, 7 June 2005.

23 'S. Korea, ASEAN Hold First Meeting to Discuss Free Trade Pact', *Asia Pulse*, 21 February 2005.

24 'South Korea Hopes to Sign FTA with ASEAN Late 2005', *Global News Wire – Asia Africa Intelligence Wire*, 10 June 2005.

25 The Business Forum groups key private sector and labour organisations from the three states. Its creation, in 2002, was designed as a preliminary step in developing closer economic and trade relations in Northeast Asia.

26 'Trilateral Cooperation on FTA, Energy Urged', *The Korea Times*, 23 October 2004.

27 'Joint Japan-China study to examine FTA impact', *The Daily Yomiuri*, 19 October 2004.

28 In terms of regional economic importance, it is worth noting that if the Japan–Korea FTA was successfully concluded it would create a market worth US$5 trillion or approximately 75 per cent of the East Asian economy. Source: Tim Shorrock, 'Asia Shifting Towards Economic Regionalism', *Inter-Press Service*, 28 June 2004.

29 'Scholars question benefits of FTA between S. Korea, China, Japan', *Asia Pulse*, 13 September 2004.

30 Ibid.

31 CLMV = Cambodia, Laos, Myanmar, and Vietnam.

32 'Japan may halt FTA talks with S. Korea for ones with other nations', *Asia Pulse*, 25 February 2004.

33 See: *Joint Statement of the First ASEAN-India Summit*, 5 November 2002, Phnom Penh, Cambodia.

34 See: *Framework Agreement on Comprehensive Economic Cooperation Between The Association of Southeast Asian Nations and the Republic of India*, signed 8 October 2003, Bali, Indonesia.

35 It is worth noting that this seems to be an explicit goal of the Indian negotiators. An Indian official was reported to remark that 'India was ready to do everything that China had done to open its market'. Source: Hatakeyama Noboru, 'FTA Movements in the Asia Pacific Region', *Journal of Japanese Trade & Industry*, 1 May 2004.

36 'ASEAN, India delay FTA target until January 2007', *Japan Economic Newswire*, 26 September 2005.

37 The CER (Closer Economic Relationship) is the FTA between Australia and New Zealand.

38 Department of Foreign Affairs and Trade, *In The National Interest*, Canberra, 1997, p. 66.

39 'ASEAN, Australia, New Zealand to further cooperation projects, FTA negotiations', *Xinhua*, 26 September 2005.

40 'S. Korea, Singapore conclude FTA', *Xinhua*, 29 November 2004.

41 See analysis in: Amy Kazmin, 'Singapore and Thailand seek bilateral deals', *Financial Times*, 8 October 2003.

42 Joint Press Release, *Inaugural Meeting of the ASEAN Investment Area Council*, Manila, Philippines, October 1998.

43 Lawan Thanadsillapakul, *Open Regionalism and Deeper Integration*.

44 Hadi Soesastro, 'East Asia Economic Cooperation: In search of an Institutional Identity', Paper presented at the Fourteenth Asia-Pacific Roundtable, Kuala Lumpur, June 2000.

45 See: Asia–Pacific Economic Cooperation (APEC), August 1994, *Achieving the APEC Vision*, Second Report of the Eminent Persons Group, Singapore: APEC Secretariat.

46 Soesastro, 'East Asia Economic Cooperation', p. 5.

47 For an analysis of APEC's utility to East Asian countries see: 'APEC Ministers to focus on stability and reputation', Agence France Press, 2000, 6 September 2000.

48 Examples of growth triangles include – the Greater Southern China Economic Zone (PRC, Hong Kong, and Taiwan), the Singapore–Johore–Riau (SIJORI) triangle, the Indonesia–Malaysia–Thailand (IMT) triangle, and the Tumen River triangle (Siberia province, Russia, the DPRK, and Jilin province, PRC). Derived from Ricardo Tan, Filologo Pante, and George Abonyi, 'Economic Cooperation in the Greater Mekong Subregion', in Kiichiro Fukasaku (ed.) *Regional Co-operation and Integration in Asia*, Paris: OECD, 1995.

49 The six members of the GMS are: Vietnam, Cambodia, Laos, Thailand, Myanmar, and Yunnan province, PRC.

50 As early as 1957 a report was issued by the Committee for the Coordination of Investigations of the Lower Mekong Basin. This report focused on the economic complementarity between Cambodia, Laos, Thailand, and Vietnam.

51 For a detailed overview on the GMS see: http://www.adb.org/gms.

52 Abdul Karim Haryati, 'BIMP-EAGA still vital for Sabah's domestic mart', *Malaysia Economic News*, 20 June 2001.

53 Tan *et al.*, 'Economic Cooperation in the Greater Mekong Subregion', p. 238.

54 On this point, with reference to the GMS, see the Proceedings of Ministerial, Forums and Working Groups Meetings. Online. Available: http://www.adb.org/GMS/gmsproc.asp.
55 See: the Joint Ministerial Statement of the ASEAN+3 Finance Ministers Meeting, 2000.
56 For more information see: Ngiam Kee Jin, 'The Future of Financial Cooperation in East Asia', *The Journal of East Asian Affairs*, Spring/Summer 2003, vol. XVII, no. 1, pp. 121–47.
57 Ibid., p. 127.
58 It should be noted that a number of the BSAs (such as the Japan–China BSA) allow each party to request the other to provide support up to the total amount. Thus, while the face value of all regional CMI BSAs to date is US$26.5 billion, their worth is actually US$36.5 billion.
59 Nobuhiro Hiwatari, 'Embedded policy preferences and the formation of international arrangements after the Asian financial crisis', *The Pacific Review*, 2003, vol. 16, no. 3, pp.331–59.
60 Hiwatari, 'Embedded Policy Preferences', p. 345.
61 See comments by: Ramkisken Rajan. *Examining the Case for an Asian Monetary Fund*, ISEAS Working Paper No. 3, Singapore: ISEAS, 2000; and the analysis contained in: Natasha Hamilton-Hart, 'Co-operation on Money and Finance: How Important? How Likely?', *Third World Quarterly*, 2003, vol. 24, no. 2, pp. 283–97.
62 Shaun Narine, *Explaining ASEAN: Regionalism in Southeast Asia*, Boulder, CO: Lynne Rienner, 2002, p. 187.
63 Anthony Rowley, 'Moves to Bolster Regional Currency Swap Arrangement', *Business Times Singapore*, 5 May 2005.
64 Narine, *Explaining ASEAN: Regionalism in Southeast Asia*, p. 187.
65 Ramangkura Virabongsa, 'Japan must introduce an Asian Currency', *Japan Echo*, 26 June 1999.
66 World Bank, 'East Asia and Pacific', *The World Bank Annual Report 1999*, New York: Oxford University Press.
67 Moreover, there remain substantial questions as to the qualitative gains for such a regional basket (offset against the political and administrative costs of such a decision), whether or not advantages would be enjoyed by all member economies and what would be the inflationary effect of such a basket. See, for example, Kenichi Ohno, 'Exchange Rate Management in Developing Asia: Reassessment of the Pre-crisis Soft Dollar Zone', *Asian Development Bank Institute Paper*, Japan: Tokyo, 1999.
68 This point is made in Donald Brash's speech: 'The Pros and Cons of a Currency Union – A Reserve Bank Perspective', 22 May 2000.
69 Anthony Rawley, 'Asian Bond Fund set for launch', *The Business Times Singapore*, 2 June 2003.
70 'Asian Central Banks Unveil Details of Second Asian Bond Fund', *Channel News Asia*, 12 May 2005.
71 Paul Lejot, Douglas Arner, Liu Qiao, Mylene Chan and Marshall Mays, *Asia's Debt Capital Markets Appraisal and Agenda for Policy Reform*, HKIEBS Working Paper No. 1072, Hong Kong, September 2003, p. 29.
72 'AEM approves recommendations of HLTF to formalise AEC', *Financial Times Information*, 2 September 2003.
73 In April 2004, the Philippines announced it would be seeking to reopen EHP discussions with China. See: Christine A. Gaylican, 'RP to revive Early Harvest Program talks with China', *Philippine Daily Inquirer*, 19 April 2004.
74 Karamit Kaur, '3-nation open skies agreement on cargo', *The Straits Times*, 26 February 2004.
75 Raju Chellam, 'Singapore, Indonesia sign accord on phone testing', *The Business Times*, 22 April 2004.

76 The Joint Ministerial Statement of the ASEAN+3 Finance Ministers Meeting, 7 August 2003, Makati, The Philippines.

77 The Joint Ministerial Statement of the ASEAN+3 Finance Ministers Meeting, 10 May 2002, Shanghai, People's Republic of China.

78 At this point it should be noted that EMEAP does include Northeast and Southeast Asian members, it does not include representatives of the CLMV central banks, but it does include the Australian and New Zealand central banks. So while it is a regional institution, in this context it is more appropriate to define it as an open regional institution.

79 EMEAP Press Release, July 1996.

80 Kenichiro Watanabe, Hiroshi Akama, and Jun Mifune, 'The Effectiveness of Capital Controls and Monitoring: The Case for the Non-Internationalization of Emerging Market Economies', *EMEAP Discussion Paper*, January 2002, p. 1.

81 Myanmar, Laos, Cambodia, Malaysia, and Vietnam are not represented in the Group. In addition Hong Kong is also a member – separate from China.

82 Chairman's Statement, *First ASEAN + China, Japan, Korea (ASEAN+3) Deputy Finance Ministers and Deputy General Bank Governors Meeting*, 18 March 1999. Cambodia was not yet a full member of ASEAN so there was no Cambodian representative at the Hanoi meeting.

83 'Asian Officials Agree to Forex Stability Panel', *Global News Wire – Asia Africa Intelligence Wire*, 8 March 2005.

84 'Asian central banks to work together on monetary policy', *The Straits Times*, 26 February 2005.

8 Regionalism beyond an elite project

The challenge of building responsive subregional economic communities

Jenina Joy Chavez

Introduction

During its first summit, the Association of Southeast Asian Nations (ASEAN) declared, among other things, its intention to pursue 'cooperative action in their national and regional development programmes' and to 'develop awareness of regional identity and exert all efforts to create a strong ASEAN community'.[1] The ASEAN Concord, signed in Bali, Indonesia, in February 1976, which became the basis of future agreements of the organisation, was updated in October 2003 when ASEAN came back to Bali for its Ninth Summit. After more than 25 years, and with the addition of four new members, perspectives are mixed as to how far the organisation has progressed in terms of developing a community.

The ASEAN Concord II stated '(t)he framework to achieve a dynamic, cohesive, resilient and integrated ASEAN Community'[2] by establishing an ASEAN Security Community (ASC), an ASEAN Economic Community (AEC) and an ASEAN Socio-Cultural Community (ASCC). It was in Kuala Lumpur during the Second Informal Summit in December 1997 that the idea of an ASEAN Economic Region and the vision of 'an ASEAN community conscious of its ties of history, aware of its cultural heritage and bound by a common regional identity' were born.[3] ASEAN Vision 2020 became a mainstay in ASEAN-speak but it would take five more years, at the Eighth ASEAN Summit in November 2002 in Phnom Penh, before the concept of an ASEAN Economic Community would emerge.

The time lapse, and the slow pace by which economic initiatives were implemented in the organisation, is indicative of the difficulty of adjusting economic policies within the ASEAN region and underscores the lack of cohesion among members. This is, in part, due to the structure of domestic interests, institutions and outlook in various ASEAN countries as discussed by Hamilton-Hart in Chapter 6. Initiatives in security moved relatively faster, reinforcing the high political motivation that first brought the members together, although largely aided by the exigencies of external factors and the involvement of actors from outside the region. When the ASEAN Economic Community came into being, it was overshadowed by ASEAN's declaration at the very same summit to advance

East Asian cooperation and deepen ASEAN–China cooperation. This raises the question of whether economic integration in the region is feasible without external stimuli and, if so, whether it is relevant to speak of an ASEAN community at all.

Will the three interrelated communities – the ASC, the AEC and the ASCC – bring about the dynamism, cohesion, resilience and integration that have so far evaded ASEAN? This is a major challenge that confronts the organisation. ASEAN, being the oldest and the broadest integration initiative in the Asian region, is also an important indicator of the acceptability and viability of a wider East Asian community, or even a pan-Asian community. On the other hand, ASEAN's success can be measured by, and indeed depends on, how much resonance it has with the populations of ASEAN countries – that is, how popular or how relevant ASEAN is to them.

The inadequacy of the growth model that guided ASEAN, the apparent China threat, the differential level of development by new ASEAN members, and various developments external to Asia and globally – increasing regionalism in North America and Western Europe, the march of globalised trading regimes, and so on – all provided the momentum for ASEAN to move more swiftly towards economic integration in the early 1990s. ASEAN has also encouraged various forms of regionalism and subregionalism to address diverse needs, to respond to different actors and to service a range of political exigencies. These new forms are both formal and informal and have varied records of success and failure.

This chapter gives a critical assessment of ASEAN's attempt at integration, specifically economic integration. It looks at the different modes of regional cooperation practised in ASEAN and examines their contribution to the development of an ASEAN identity. It argues that ASEAN's preoccupation with trade and investment liberalisation limits the scope and possibility for deeper economic cooperation in the subregion. The expansion of ASEAN initiatives to include the bigger economies in East Asia provides an added impetus towards integration, but belies the lack of a more coherent vision of a community within ASEAN itself. The case of the Brunei–Indonesia–Malaysia–Philippines East Asian Growth Area (BIMP–EAGA) highlights how a narrow focus on economic concerns constrains community building even among areas that supposedly have deeper shared cultural and historical roots, are at a more even stage of development and are more physically proximate to each other. Finally, the chapter proposes that meaningful regional integration necessarily looks beyond the mere opening up of markets and tackles fundamental economic, political and social cooperation. In the case of ASEAN, this means fostering greater links in agriculture, confronting common social and environmental issues, and democratising the vision of a community to make ASEAN an everyday reality to ordinary citizens. All this is crucial to maximise ASEAN's gains from and contributions to initiatives that advance Asian regionalism.

Asian economic regionalism in perspective

Regionalism in East Asia has grabbed attention, not so much by way of how it manifested politically, but by how growth was aided by sustained flows from the economically stronger to the economically weaker countries in the region. In the 1980s, while far from the integration already taking place in Europe, the economic interaction in the region was so dynamic that it gave birth to the phenomena that would be termed the 'Asian Miracle'.

East Asia's development has been described as following the flying geese model, which entails the relocation of production from a lead economy in search of lower costs to follower economies that will take up the lower value chain of the production process.[4] In this model much of the output is exported back to the lead economy, while the followers gain industrial and economic strength that eventually elevates them to the status of secondary geese. This relationship is maintained by the export-oriented investment flows from the leading or secondary geese to the followers, which are used to develop the next generation of productive capacity.[5]

This path highlights the primary role of strong linkages between trade and foreign direct investment (FDI) in driving regional integration. Japan was the primary goose that helped boost the productive and investing capacities of the secondary geese, Asia's newly industrialised economies (NIEs) of South Korea, Taiwan, Singapore and Hong Kong. Japan and the NIEs then replicated the process by extending it to the ASEAN-four (Malaysia, Thailand, Indonesia and the Philippines), although with less impressive results than in the case of Japan and the NIEs themselves.

The impact of the flying geese phenomenon on regional integration, particularly trade–investment integration, is significant. In many instances utilised to 'jump trade barriers and to take advantage of host-country Generalised System of Preferences (GSP) privileges and underused Multifibre Arrangement (MFA) textile quotas', investments from the bigger Asian economies to the smaller ones were also undertaken as a result of their own restructuring (stemming from industrial upgrading and innovations) and to take advantage of the market opportunities inside the region. The host economies, in turn, benefited from the access to the investing countries' savings and technology, and access to their markets.[6]

This pattern of trade–investment flows also explains the high degree of vertical specialisation in the region, or the 'slicing up of the production process into distinct steps, allowing specialisation across locations (locational decentralisation) and firms (outsourcing)'.[7] This is partly reflected in the growing levels of intra-industry trade and underlies East Asia's focus on labour-intensive manufacturing industries.[8] From the mid-1980s, intra-industry trade growth registered increasing contributions to total trade growth. From less than 50 per cent between 1986 and 1995, intra-industry trade growth accounted for three-quarters of the total trade growth in East Asia in the latter half of the 1990s (see Table 8.1).

The 'flying geese' model has had its time. It is no longer a sufficient model on which to base expansion and sustained economic growth in the region.[9] Predicated on the drive to conquer markets outside of East Asia, and with much of the intra-regional exports being further processed for exports destined for North America and Europe, the model has resulted in the emergence of almost uniform exports from countries in the region, especially in Southeast Asia, making them compete for the same markets.

The patterns of the past resulted in an increased 'homogeneity of the region's manufacturing industrial structure', and with primary markets outside the region, 'the negative implication is that host economies become more vulnerable to fluctuations in the world economy'.[10] The global economic downturn in 1995–6 caused drastic declines in the demand for the region's products, 'with a cascading effect through the region's production networks'.[11] The same effect occurred in 2001 when a decline in the demand for information technology (IT) products saw a fall in the export volumes of countries such as Malaysia, Thailand and the Philippines.[12]

This suggests that ASEAN now requires a different vehicle to support integration, and that will correct the limitations and negative impacts of the flying geese. While the entry of Cambodia, Myanmar, Laos and Vietnam to ASEAN created opportunities for older member states to unload the lower value-added production sectors, the pace of progress attained in expanding higher value-added manufacturing in ASEAN has slowed down in recent years. The 1997 Asian crisis dealt a heavy blow to Southeast Asia's manufacturing and industrial capacity. This was exacerbated by the downturn in the United States, which has traditionally been the major market for Southeast Asia's high-end exports.

The economic crisis negatively affected the inflow of investments to Asia. When it recovered, it was mainly due to mergers and acquisitions, and it has been the bigger economies of East Asia that have captured most of the inflows, while Southeast Asia lost its relative attraction. Malaysia, Singapore and Thailand lost some of the attraction they had in the early 1990s towards the end of the 1990s. Indonesia fell from grace as a favourite FDI destination, although Vietnam has emerged as a potential new one. Table 8.1 indicates that early into the new millennium, FDI flows to Asia have become highly concentrated. The top three destinations – China, Hong Kong and Singapore – account for 81 per cent of FDI flows, with China alone eating up almost 58 per cent.

Since 1990 China has been importing more from Southeast Asia than it has been exporting to it. Table 8.2 shows that in 2002–3, the growth of Southeast Asia's exports to China (59 per cent) outstripped the growth of China's exports to Southeast Asia (40 per cent). Growth in China, therefore, created opportunity for Southeast Asia by offering a large domestic market that can absorb high levels of imports, and by the Chinese themselves becoming investors in Southeast Asia, in the process creating greater opportunities for economic integration.

For Southeast Asia, China is a competitor to its labour-intensive manufacturing industries. China has taken great strides in technology absorption and improvements in industrial capacity, and has been moving not only into production areas ASEAN has left behind, but also into newer areas ASEAN markets only recently entered. The biggest 'threat' from China is its advance into production areas where ASEAN still has significant interests, before ASEAN producers can shift into higher value-added production. The so-called 'China threat' and more recently the 'China opportunity', therefore, are urgent ones for ASEAN to address, to maximise the opportunities it provides for ASEAN's own growth.

ASEAN attempts at economic integration

A string of failed economic cooperation initiatives makes it difficult for ASEAN to address current economic integration issues. The ASEAN Industrial Project (AIP, 1976), the ASEAN Industrial Complementation scheme (AIC, 1981), the ASEAN Industrial Joint Venture (AIJV, 1983), the Brand-to-Brand Complementation scheme (BBC, 1988) and the ASEAN Industrial Cooperation scheme (AICO, 1997) were all failed attempts to enable ASEAN firms to pool resources and share in production to enhance and upgrade their industrial capacity and benefit from shared markets. Members were so unconvinced of these initiatives that they undertook their own national projects that directly competed with the regional ones. For instance, Malaysia's decision to start its own automobile industry sidetracked the ASEAN car that was hoped to be produced from the initiatives in the 1980s. AICO, on the other hand, happened too slow and too late to be substantially helpful. It was initiated at a time when Southeast Asia had already undergone economic liberalisation programmes so that the preferential margins from AICO were small.[13]

As with its formation, ASEAN needed an external push to take the issue of integration seriously. It was not until the aggressive moves towards regionalism in the North (the formation of the European Union, consolidation of the North American Free Trade Agreement), and their inroads to the region via APEC (Asia–Pacific Economic Cooperation) did ASEAN leaders see the need for a more economically integrated ASEAN.

In 1992, the Fourth ASEAN Summit in Singapore agreed to establish the ASEAN Free Trade Area (AFTA), although it would take a full year before the Comprehensive Effective Preferential Tariff (CEPT) scheme would be in place. The original target was for AFTA to be realised in 15 years or by 2008. This was accelerated in 1998 during the Sixth ASEAN Summit in Hanoi to 10 years or 2003. The ultimate goal of AFTA is the complete abolition of tariffs for the ASEAN-six by 2010, and 2015 for the newer members, with flexibility on some sensitive products until 2018. By the beginning of 2003, 99.55 per cent of tariff lines in the inclusion list of ASEAN-six had been reduced to the 0–5 per cent range; more than 60 per cent of these tariff lines had been further brought down to 0 per cent by end 2003. The major development in 2004 was Malaysia's inclusion of automobile parts into the CEPT scheme, one year ahead of the original committed date (2005). Only products transferred from the general exception and highly sensitive lists maintain tariffs above 5 per cent.[14]

This acceleration notwithstanding, AFTA has failed substantially to rally intra-ASEAN trade. It prompted a marginal increase in intra-ASEAN trade in

Table 8.1   Vertical specialisation in and FDI flows to East Asia

	Share of total trade growth due to intra-industry trade growth		
	1986–90	*1991–5*	*1996–2000*
East Asia	42.5	46.9	75.0
	Ratio of merchandise trade to merchandise value added		
	1980	*1990*	*2000*
Asia	93.8	115.6	168.5
China	12.1	23.7	32.9
NIEs[a]	216.5	259.3	365.5
Others[b]	39.4	52.4	84.3
	FDIs		
	% of total FDI (2002)	**Ratio to GDP** *1980*	*2003*
China	57.7	0.5	35.6
Hong Kong SAR	15.0	623.8	236.5
Taiwan	1.6	5.8	11.9
Singapore	8.4	52.9	161.3
Korea	2.2	2.1	7.8
Indonesia	–	13.2	27.5
Malaysia	3.5	20.7	57.2
Philippines	1.2	3.9	14.5
Thailand	–	3.0	25.8
Vietnam	1.3	0.2	50.6

a Includes Hong Kong SAR, Korea, Singapore and Taiwan Province of China.

b Includes Bangladesh, Pakistan and the ASEAN-four (Indonesia, Malaysia, the Philippines and Thailand).

Sources: International Monetary Fund, *World Economic Outlook*, Washington, DC: IMF, September 2002; UNCTAD, as cited in Asian Development Bank, *Asian Development Outlook*, 2004; UNCTAD, *World Investment Report 2004: The Shift Towards Services*, New York: The United Nations, 2004.

the 1990s, but the percentage remains at less than a quarter of the total ASEAN trade. Growth in intra-ASEAN exports pales in comparison with ASEAN exports to East Asia and China (see Table 8.2).

It has long been claimed that increasing intra-regional trade was never AFTA's objective in the first place. Rather, AFTA is seen to be a platform for the region's competitiveness and outward orientation. This partly explains why the preferential nature of the CEPT is eroded by some members' unilateral moves to realign CEPT rates with their commitments to the World Trade Organisation (that is, many CEPT rates become the Most Favoured Nation rates, as was the case with the Philippines). It cannot be discounted, however, that the lack of complementarity among the ASEAN nations makes them such fierce competitors that preferential treatment of each other becomes a less attractive option than enticing new foreign investments into the region. Further, rather than look hard at the issue and resolve the dilemma, ASEAN chooses instead to introduce new initiatives, with the same motivation of providing such platforms to external investors, in the hope that the new areas will marginally increase economic interaction within ASEAN.

During the Fifth Summit in Bangkok in December 1997, the Framework Agreement on Services (AFAS), which seeks the free flow of services in the region by 2020, was established. The initial package of commitments came into force in March 1998, and the Sixth Summit in Hanoi in December 1998 mandated the start of the second round of negotiations from 1999 to 2001. The third round of negotiations started in 2002 and concluded at the end of 2004. AFAS now covers 11 priority integration sectors including, among others, air transport, finance, telecommunication, tourism and healthcare services. New initiatives in services and investments give rise to increased movements of professionals and skilled persons, and to address this, ASEAN started taking small steps towards establishing Mutual Recognition Arrangements (MRAs) with the creation of an Ad-Hoc Expert Group for this purpose.[15] Another bold attempt is the establishment of an ASEAN Investment Area (AIA), which seeks national treatment of ASEAN investors by 2010. By 2003, seven members – Brunei, Indonesia, Myanmar, Philippines, Thailand, Singapore and Malaysia – had opened all sectors for inclusion in the AIA, with the initial exclusions already phased out.

Services and investments are very suitable areas for cooperation in ASEAN because, unlike in goods (both agriculture and manufactures), ASEAN countries exhibit more diversity in these areas. Nevertheless, it remains a challenge for ASEAN to realise the vision of integrated service and investment areas without unnecessarily causing a diminution in the productive sectors of weaker members, or the crowding out of smaller domestic investments. The outcome and impact of these newer initiatives will determine how broad ASEAN's idea of integration is.

More significantly, the move towards new areas of economic cooperation is being overtaken by ASEAN's expansion to include bigger East Asian economies, particularly China. On the one hand, this is precisely a response to the China

Table 8.2   Direction of intra- and inter-subregional trade, and total exports growth rate (%), September 2002–September 2003

Exports from/to	East Asia	China	Southeast Asia	South Asia	Total exports
East Asia	29.8	28.3	22.2	0.6	18.5
China	35.5	–	39.6	10.2	40.5
Southeast Asia	27.6	59.0	20.1	-20.3	16.2
South Asia	23.8	41.5	15.5	28.7	14.9

Source: International Monetary Fund, *Direction of Trade Statistics*, 2003, as cited in Asian Development Bank, *Asian Development Outlook 2004*, Manila: ADB, 2004.

'threat' or 'opportunity', and is in recognition of the existing trade and economic dynamics between ASEAN and these countries (that is, there is more robust economic interaction between ASEAN and the rest of East Asia than there is within ASEAN itself). On the other hand, as will be discussed in the next sections, it is the issue of weak economic cohesion within the ASEAN itself that puts the heaviest obstacle to realising a genuine ASEAN community.

Subregionalism, ASEAN-X, ASEAN+X: solution or dilution?

Over the years, the ASEAN decision-making process has come to be known as the 'ASEAN Way', for the manner in which the organisation dances around sticky political issues, preserves consensus and protects individual member country's sovereignty within the organisation. Many observers attribute the ASEAN Way to much of the slowness, and failure, of ASEAN efforts at integration. According to Narine, 'ASEAN is dedicated to protecting and enhancing the sovereignty of its member states . . . because most of its member states are – or perceive themselves to be – institutionally weak'.[16] Added to this, ASEAN members lack common economic and political interests, accounting for the group's weakness and emphasising the fact that greater international cooperation should be motivated by domestic factors if ASEAN is to remain relevant.[17]

An extension of the ASEAN Way, or in some instances perhaps a defence against it, are the different modes of cooperation practised in ASEAN. Apart from ASEAN itself as a grouping, there are three general forms of regionalism ASEAN has embarked on since the 1990s. These are ASEAN-X, the 'cog and wheel' model of subregionalism and the 'hub and spoke' model of expansion. These three modes are supposed to cover multiple levels of needs. Yet, as the phrase states, the proof of the pudding is in the eating. The successful development of these three modes along these lines is best gauged against whether or not they actually deepen Southeast and East Asian integration.

ASEAN recognises and appreciates the readiness of some of its members to move more readily than others into cooperative schemes. This is particularly true of trade and economic liberalisation. The cooperation mode popularly known as 'ASEAN-X' is a way around the sticky consensus process in the group. This means that members are free to decide how fast and how far they want to go into the cooperative scheme at a given time. Only those countries signing specific arrangements will be bound by, and therefore benefit from, such arrangements. An individual country member will only enjoy the same benefits that it is willing to give to other members. Notwithstanding such flexibility, the regional grouping agrees to adopt common milestones or dates or deadlines where commitments are supposed to be harmonised within a range (for example, 0–5 per cent tariff by 1 January 2003).

ASEAN-X is the mode of regionalism practised in the various industrial complementation schemes (AIP, AIJV, BBC, AIC and AICO). Countries (or firms from member countries) cooperate with other countries that have similar interests in the same projects. The AICO, for instance, requires only that a minimum of two companies in two different ASEAN countries form an AICO Arrangement to qualify for the scheme. The AICO Arrangement need not be a legal entity but an 'umbrella association' to enable the participating companies to enjoy the privileges offered by the programme (a maximum tariff preference of 0–5 per cent upon approval of project).[18] The biggest draw to the AICO is the tariff privilege for companies participating in the programme, which was set at 0 per cent for Brunei, Cambodia, Indonesia, Lao PDR, Malaysia and Singapore starting in 2003.[19]

ASEAN-X has thus far been unable to significantly promote cooperative ventures in ASEAN industries. To date, there is yet to be a recognisable ASEAN brand or assembly that can be said to have resulted from the AICO. After seven years of AICO's implementation, only 118 project applications have been approved (as of 20 January 2004), with only one project involving a relatively big group of four countries cooperating.[20] The small number of projects that applied for AICO accreditation does not match the long-winded negotiation process that yielded the AICO agreement. Waivers of national equity requirements (the last one ended in 2004) also controvert aims for resource pooling and production sharing among ASEAN firms, and instead cause AICO to be exploited primarily by regionally based transnational corporations.

AFAS is also adopting the ASEAN-X approach. While it is still too early to pass any judgement on the efficacy of the approach, the move again underlines the fact that despite many past and new initiatives, ASEAN is still not ready to tackle AFAS as a potential mechanism to develop a truly regional service industry.

Another mode of cooperation is a unique Asian invention called growth polygons. Growth polygons group provinces or states from different countries (or in the case of the Greater Mekong Subregion, smaller and/or newer members with provinces in more advanced countries). They are designed to be a subregional answer to the declining competitiveness of areas or countries that face rising price factors, particularly land and labour costs. The polygons are supposed to serve as the new centres of development from the different member countries, hence the 'cog and wheel' metaphor. The more popular growth polygons are BIMP–EAGA, the Singapore–Johor–Riau growth triangle (SIJORI), and the Greater Mekong Subregion (GMS), which groups Cambodia, Laos, Vietnam, Myanmar, Thailand and the Chinese province of Yunnan.[21]

Subregional arrangements were acknowledged by the Fourth ASEAN Summit in Singapore in January 1992. It recognised the arrangements of ASEAN members among themselves, or between ASEAN member states and non-ASEAN states. The grouping together of regions/countries/provinces in search of factors (land and labour) already deemed too expensive on the home front, and those that are abundant in these factors, has been the original tack and remains one of the more important aspects of the growth polygon concept. In ASEAN, the sensitivity of having to change national laws in order to cooperate with a neighbour is avoided by making the growth polygon arrangement between provinces and/or states, and not necessarily between countries. Cooperative ventures, therefore, need not imply national legislation, which has always been a difficult process in ASEAN countries.[22] We return to the issue of growth polygons in the next section on the BIMP–EAGA.

The third mode is very similar to the second, except that instead of focusing inwards it focuses outwards – hence the 'hub and spoke' model. ASEAN is the hub that extends its reach towards other partners, with ASEAN+3 (a forum with Japan, China and South Korea) as the most popular articulation these days. The ASEAN Plus X concept supposedly answers the need for ASEAN to forge stronger links with its traditional 'sponsors' and the bigger markets in the region. In this manner, part of the extreme competitiveness between and among ASEAN members can be tempered.

ASEAN has been developing framework agreements with the ASEAN+3 countries individually and collectively. Japan is central to the ASEAN Vision 2020, and South Korea is in the East Asian Vision Group. ASEAN as a group is also negotiating a free trade agreement with China, the outline accord of which was approved in December 2002. The Framework Agreement foresees the full implementation of the China–ASEAN Free Trade Agreement (CAFTA) by 2010 for ASEAN-six, and 2015 for the newer ASEAN countries of Cambodia, Lao PDR, Myanmar and Vietnam. Prompted by short-term interests in the Chinese agricultural markets, an Early Harvest Programme Acceleration Agreement for the CAFTA took effect in January 2004, where China, Singapore and Thailand agreed to eliminate tariffs on all fruits and vegetables ahead of CAFTA's full implementation. Negotiations for the CAFTA were particularly fast paced with the FTA being launched on 1 July 2005, taking less than three years to complete.

Will the combined strength of the three East Asian economies and the fastest growing economies in Southeast Asia provide a counterbalance to the economic dominance of North America and Western Europe in the region? For ASEAN, a more relevant question is whether expansion to include the bigger East Asian economies dilutes the already weak basis for economic integration in the ASEAN region.

ASEAN analysts do not necessarily think that the outward expansion of ASEAN is a dilution of its own integration, provided that it can become the core of ASEAN+3. The success of these initiatives also depends on the 'political will to deepen co-operation' which 'implies a willingness to surrender some national sovereignty in promoting regional interest'.[23] There are troubling signs, however, highlighted by the CAFTA negotiations that bring to question how centrally ASEAN can steer the ASEAN+X initiatives. The CAFTA process is more akin to a network of 10 bilateral negotiations with China, and barely capitalises on ASEAN's regional strength. The lack of a mechanism to manage a consensus that can be brought to China for negotiation as a bloc is a big setback for ASEAN. China, in effect, got 10 new deals, while ASEAN members only made one each. The CAFTA process may have answered the short-term needs of members, but the issue of a regional agenda becomes even more urgent as ASEAN goes further down the expansion route. Unless ASEAN is able to articulate a truly regional interest and agenda in the bigger groupings, then belonging to the organisation will bring few benefits to its members.

Subregional groupings for subregional communities: the case of BIMP–EAGA[24]

Of the three modes of regionalism practised by ASEAN, the growth polygon concept holds the most potential for community building in that it builds on existing linkages and/or proximity. It is also by far the most aggressive, at least theoretically, in terms of matching needs and resources, and is based on concrete activities and projects that can be implemented on the ground. The challenge is in enhancing the community-building aspect of the model, away from the idea of growth polygons as little more than special economic zones.

Although in itself a promising experiment, the subregional grouping/growth polygon concept has not taken off beyond the economic imperative. The concept suffers from a number of concerns that have yet to be adequately addressed. Growth polygons are built around observable comparative advantage between points of the polygon. A hub or a key economy around which much of the prospects and initiatives for the polygon revolve is crucial. The hub's relationship with the other points is usually based on the need for a single resource, for example land and water resources. Because of this, the vulnerability of the hub is passed on to the other members of the polygon, and distributional conflicts within the subregional groupings become critical. Finally, projects conceptualised for growth polygons tend to be large-scale ones that require huge investments.

This is due in part to the heavy involvement of multilateral institutions like the Asian Development Bank. The result: ambitious initiatives that are bigger and more expensive than might be needed in the subregions.

The failure of subregionalism to embrace broader cooperation highlights the limitation of economic growth as an objective. The failure to bring in other stakeholders to the process jeopardises the success of cooperation, especially during times of economic slowdown. The case of the Brunei–Indonesia–Malaysia–Philippines East Asian Growth Area (BIMP–EAGA) is a case in point.

BIMP–EAGA is composed of contiguous geographical areas, with Brunei Darussalam as the only complete country member. The other member territories are the Indonesian provinces of West, Central, South and East Kalimantan, Central, North, South and Southeast Sulawesi, Maluku and Irian Jaya provinces; the Malaysian states of Sabah and Sarawak and the federal territory of Labuan; and the Philippines' Mindanao (Regions 9–12 and the Autonomous Region of Muslim Mindanao) and Palawan. BIMP–EAGA has a population base of 50 million and a total land area of 1.56 million square kilometres.

Including the vast bodies of water at its centre, BIMP–EAGA is the biggest subregional grouping. The EAGA subregions are linked by a long history of trading activities between their many points. To this day, barter trade is still widely practised, especially between the Labuan, Mindanao, Sabah and East and West Kalimantan areas. Local currencies are even accepted and local languages spoken in reciprocal fashion. To this extent the subgrouping is already a de facto community.

Another unique feature is that this is a grouping of the lesser economically developed areas of Indonesia, Malaysia and the Philippines, with the exception of Brunei. With few exceptions, the three subregions also register per capita incomes lower than the respective national averages (see Table 8.3). Together with Brunei, the area's production is largely natural resource based. Of the four partners, only Philippines–EAGA (P-EAGA) exports agricultural products, with the three other subregions specialising in non-edible primary products such as oil, gas, timber and petrochemicals.

The establishment of BIMP-EAGA has formalised and strengthened nascent economic linkages inside the subgrouping. It has also attracted national focus on the erstwhile neglected regions. Various transborder agreements – on travel and trade routes, travel tax exemptions, port tariffs, customs, immigration and quarantine – were clinched at the initial stages of the BIMP-EAGA. The growth area facilitated economic interaction never before seen in the subregion. Between 1994 and 1995 there were 253 trade missions from BIMP-EAGA to Mindanao alone.[25] The 1997 Asian crisis and the ensuing global economic downturn, however, stalled many BIMP-EAGA initiatives.

In 2001, moves towards reviving BIMP–EAGA started. The Asian Development Bank, which bankrolled the formation of the subgrouping, took a renewed interest. Business opportunities were underscored, particularly the establishment of new air and sea links for moving people and cargo within the

EAGA via the Davao–Manado (Sulawesi) and Zamboanga–Bongao (Tawi-tawi) –Sandakan routes. The objective is to make the transport of exports cheaper by going through the back door (for example, Sulawesi to the United States via General Santos, Mindanao to Singapore via Bitung), rather than via the ports in the capitals.[26] Another new policy focus post-crisis has been SME development, which has attempted to broaden the positive impact of the subgrouping.

Although the post-crisis recovery was slow for Southeast Asia, some EAGA partners were relatively insulated. This was attributed to the predominantly resource-based production in those areas that were less dependent on high-value-added exports, which contracted significantly during the crisis.[27] At least for the P-EAGA, this also highlights the importance of agriculture.

Table 8.3   Basic economic indicators for BIMP–EAGA (latest comparable data)

	Population Total (million)	Growth rate (%)	Incidence of poverty (1999)	GDP (1999) Per capita $ (nominal)	Growth rate (%)	Unemployment (%)
Total BIMP–EAGA	50.2	–	–	–	–	–
Brunei	0.4 (2002)	–	–	–	–	–
Indonesia	231.2 (2002)	1.5	20.43	810 (2003)	5.1 (2004)	9.6 (2004)
Kalimantan	11.6	2.0	19.5	1,059	3.1	–
Sulawesi	15.0	1.7	20.8	422	3.4	
Malaysia	22.7 (2002)	2.6	8.1	3,780 (2003)	7.1 (2004)	3.5 (2004)
Sabah	2.6	4.0	25.0			
Sarawak	2.1	2.1	6.6	–	–	–
Philippines	80 (2003)	2.4	34.2	1,080 (2003)	6.1 (2004)	11.8 (2004)
Mindanao	18.1	2.4	47.8	698.4	5.0	7.6
Palawan	0.8	3.6	69.3	417.1	5.0	19.6

* All figures are for 2000, unless otherwise indicated.

Sources: Asian Development Bank, *Sub-regional Cooperation Strategy and Programme Status Report 2002*, Manila: ADB, 2002; Asian Development Bank, *Asian Development Outlook 2004*, Manila: ADB, 2004; Mindanao Economic Development Council, *BIMP-EAGA Member Countries*. Online. Available: http://www.medco.gov.ph/medcoweb/bimpcountryprof.asp.

The vast agricultural area in the BIMP–EAGA places it an auspicious position for cooperation in agriculture. Unlike the broader ASEAN, BIMP–EAGA has developed for implementation potential on-the-ground projects in fisheries and agriculture. Such projects include research, information exchange and actual joint ventures, for instance in seaweed production, processing and export, and roasted edible coconut. Containing a majority Muslim population, BIMP–EAGA has a flagship project on halal food (similar to the ASEAN Accreditation Scheme for the Halal Food Establishment).[28]

Another insight is the limitation of anchoring cooperation to the expectation of growth. This constraint is caused by the almost exclusive focus on big business activities, and big private sector actors in the subregion. As a result, the crisis crippled what could have been a more dynamic community. It also highlighted the lack of a broader base for the subregional initiative. Unfortunately, even BIMP–EAGA initiatives in agriculture and fisheries remain at the level of enterprise and do not, as yet, deal directly with producers (farmers and fishers). In September 2003, the Eighth BIMP–EAGA Ministerial Meeting provided new impetus to the BIMP–EAGA. The lists of projects and initiatives for the revitalised BIMP–EAGA are long and detailed, but again focused almost exclusively on the economic initiatives. In 2004, the focus broadened to include tourism and natural resource development, enhancing air and sea linkages, and tapping the China market.[29] With the exception of the revival of the BIMP–EAGA Friendship Games,[30] no initiative was pursued to popularise BIMP–EAGA to the peoples of the growth polygon.

The level of BIMP–EAGA's *de facto* community may be shallow, mostly at the level of clans and families, but the areas share many socio-cultural experiences beyond just economic backwardness. Transmigration, terrorism, refugees and refugee repatriation are experiences with which all EAGA populations have an affinity. In cases like this, solidarity advocates stress that regional and subregional cooperation will have more potential if it is not just state led or if it is a multi-actor-led process. Real communities need to build people-to-people relations and work together in acknowledging a solidarity on the issues that most affect them.[31] The importance of this point is returned to in the conclusion.

The challenge of deepening integration

Integration is almost always defined as an economic process. Integration is considered 'shallow' if it relies solely on trade liberalisation agreements between members; and becomes 'deep' when domestic policies are harmonised and the economic performance of members converges.[32] By this definition alone, ASEAN integration should be deemed shallow or only in the process of developing, if the new initiatives towards an economic community are included. On the other hand, it can be said that ASEAN's own organisational integration has not been allocated that much importance economically, something which becomes glaringly obvious during periods of economic downturn.

Between 1984 and 1993, the newly industrialised Asian economies, and all of the ASEAN-4 except the Philippines, grew at an average rate of at least 6.5 per cent, with Thailand posting the highest real GDP growth for the period at 8.7 per cent. From 1994 to 1999, all these countries experienced drastically lower average growths, with Thailand plummeting the most to only 2.8 per cent real growth. The only exception was again the Philippines, which experienced a higher average at 3.6 per cent versus the 1984–93 average real growth of only 1 per cent. Note that the years from 1994 to 1996 were still relatively high-growth years for these countries. It was only between 1997 and 1999 that GDP growth really nose-dived (see Table 8.4).

Recovery was apparent in 2000, but this was cut short by the downturn in the United States and the rest of the developed world. As a result, Singapore and Taiwan experienced economic contraction for the first time in three decades. In the ASEAN-4, the highest growths were achieved by Indonesia and the Philippines, traditionally the slowest growing countries in this group. The contraction was largely brought about by sluggish exports as the more developed markets scaled back orders. The stronger showing of Indonesia and the Philippines, on the other hand, was supported by better than expected agricultural growth.

The economic slump once again brought agriculture to the forefront. Yet, the preoccupation of regional initiatives in Southeast and East Asia has had very little to do with agriculture. The absence of a more proactive treatment of agriculture by ASEAN, the various subregional and bigger East Asian regional initiatives has limited to a great extent their potential to achieve deeper regional integration. With the exception of Malaysia and Singapore, agriculture accounts for around 40 per cent of total employment in Southeast Asia, with the percentages being significantly higher for the newer members (Cambodia and Laos). Agriculture, therefore, becomes an important arena of cooperation for a range of interests. First, the industrial sector's demand for labour has slowed down significantly, and for some countries this has been the case for quite some time now. Second, there is great space for the development of economic (backward and forward) linkages in agriculture. How ASEAN deals with agriculture (especially in times of crisis) will determine whether or not ASEAN can develop a broader base for itself.

Since its inception, ASEAN has recognised the need to cooperate in food production and supply. The First ASEAN Summit made mention of the need to develop cooperation in agriculture, at first quite narrowly defined as cooperation in the production of basic commodities in the individual member states. This widened in the Second Summit when the cooperation was extended to give 'priority of supply and purchase in critical circumstances based on the principle of first refusal'.[33] The Ministerial Understanding on ASEAN Cooperation in Food, Agriculture and Forestry, passed in October 1993 in Brunei, provided the framework for cooperation based on the concept of Joint Promotion of ASEAN Agricultural Products. The agreement is broad, covering the areas of joint promotion in intra- and extra-ASEAN trade, harmonisation of quality standards, trade and investment promotion, technology and human resources development, complementarity of ASEAN products and private sector participation.[34] Still, the realised initiatives in agriculture have been lacklustre considering the many possibilities for the sector. Cooperation in agriculture is strongest in the areas of research and training, and somewhat less advanced in the promotion of access to extra-ASEAN markets.

Even the innovative ASEAN Food Security Reserve (AFSR), an emergency rice reserve arrangement, is now being promoted as a way of boosting intra-ASEAN trade, eclipsing the original intent of mutual assistance in times of need. The AFSR Agreement entered into force on 24 July 1980. It is unclear how the AFSR remains relevant in the face of liberalisation in the rice sector and ASEAN members' other trade commitments outside of AFTA.

ASEAN has not been able to forge stronger linkages in the region's agricultural sector. Owing to the highly politicised character of the agricultural

Table 8.4 Real GDP growth in East Asia: 1984–93, 1994–9, 2000–4 and 2005–7 (forecast)

	1984–93 average	1994–9 average	2000–4 average	Forecast 2005	2006	2007
Newly industrialised Asian economies						
Hong Kong SAR	6.5	2.8	4.8	5.7	4.1	4.6
Korea	8.2	5.5	5.4	4.1	5.1	4.9
Singapore	7.5	7.1	4.2	4.1	4.5	4.4
Taiwan province of China	8.3	6.1	3.3	4.2	4.5	4.6
ASEAN-four						
Indonesia	6.7	2.7	4.6[a]	5.5	6.0	6.5
Malaysia	6.9	5.8	5.1	5.7	5.3	5.8
Philippines	1.0	3.6	4.3	5.0	5.0	5.0
Thailand	8.7	2.8	5.1	5.6	5.8	6.0
Brunei Darussalam	–	2.3	–	–	–	–
Cambodia	–	5.1	5.9	2.3	4.1	4.7
Lao PDR	5.0	6.3	6.0	7.0	6.5	5.8
Myanmar	1.1	7.1	12.7	–	–	–
Vietnam	6.0	7.3	6.6	7.6	7.6	7.5
China	10.5	9.4	8.5	8.5	8.7	8.9
Japan	3.7	1.3	1.3	0.8	1.9	–

a The 2001–4 average.

Sources: International Monetary Fund, *World Economic Outlook, September 2002 and April 2004*, Washington, DC: IMF, 2002 and 2004; Asian Development Bank, *Asian Development Outlook 2005*, Manila: ADB, 2005.

sector, it has been an area subject to most sensitivity and protection from ASEAN's economic initiatives. This is because the focus tends to fall on just how fast ASEAN can liberalise the sector. In fact, agriculture was considered AFTA's litmus test when it was first established. Very little has been discussed in terms of addressing the repercussions of liberalisation to member countries' agriculture. CAFTA is another reason why ASEAN needs to focus more seriously on agriculture, because competition in the sector is expected to be more intense.

Fisheries are another area where ASEAN should develop regional mechanisms. The Philippines signed its first bilateral agreement on fisheries with Indonesia in early 2002. Although not a BIMP–EAGA initiative, the agreement was prompted by strong advocacy from the tuna industry (both canners and fishers) for the establishment of joint management of tuna fisheries in the Celebes and Sulawesi Seas and the definition of allowable catch in the Indonesian exclusive economic zone (EEZ). Fisheries constitute a common property resource pool for the BIMP–EAGA, and it is in such areas that regional and subregional groupings should be extremely sensitive.

Beyond big investments and export production, regionalism should play a role in protecting common property resources and community rights, and in finding ways of addressing difficult social and political issues. The issue of small producers, especially small farmers and artisan fishers, is particularly critical as they tend to be excluded from the more formal regional fora, yet they are the first to be marginalised in the event of policy restructuring and adjustment.

In August 2002, thousands of Filipino and Indonesian migrants from various EAGA points were expelled from Sabah (another EAGA point) and other areas in Malaysia. While some left voluntarily, the issue was particularly sensitive as a sizeable number of migrants have been settling in and around Sabah for decades, some dating as far back as the World War II period. Malaysia temporarily halted deportations in September 2002, and has implemented occasional amnesty periods since then, but the crackdown on migrants still continues. The issue of refugee repatriation is not being discussed, much less resolved, either at the EAGA or the ASEAN level. The most that governments are willing to do, particularly Indonesia and the Philippines where most of the migrants come from, is to monitor the repatriations closely. More broadly, ASEAN members became even less willing to discuss the sensitive issue of labour movement multilaterally after September 11.[35]

Economic integration results in labour movements, and while unauthorised labour movement is not encouraged, it is a reality that ASEAN countries are facing. In ASEAN, Thailand and Malaysia receive the greatest numbers of migrant labour, mostly from Indonesia and the Philippines. A deeper integration will necessitate individual ASEAN countries yielding part of their sovereignty in the interest of fostering greater understanding within the organisation and within the region. The process will not be easy, but it is a requisite step towards more meaningful regionalism. By developing commonly agreed standards, ASEAN will not only make regulation of labour issues more transparent, but also build the confidence of regional workers in the organisation that just might start the process of socialisation of the idea of a regional community.

The issue of labour movement is made more urgent by ASEAN's expanding ties with bigger East Asian countries. However, instead of emphasising the imperative to discuss labour movement issues within the region, the expansion seems to have given added incentive to evade it instead. During the Eighteenth ASEAN Labor Ministers Meeting in May 2004, China emphasised differences in Asian and Northern countries' conception of labour rights and discipline.[36] By framing the issue by way of the 'Asian values' argument, ASEAN effectively skirts an ultra-sensitive issue. Even as 'Asian values' are exhorted, there is nothing 'Asian', that is nothing regional, in the ensuing response. Each country conveniently retreats to its national laws.

Alternative regionalism

Cooperation should stress bridging the gap between prosperous and less prosperous areas in the region. Regionalism and subregionalism should be a source of development inspiration that will support a truly Asian articulation of development – versus the more restrictive options of only opening trade and investment opportunities. This will help strengthen the 'internal cohesion' of ASEAN and help bring the newer members up to a more comparable development level with the rest of the organisation. In doing this, ASEAN can learn from the European Union, which employed a 'regional policy that mobilised large resource transfers to the poorer member-economies'.[37] Unfortunately, the first bold attempt of East Asian economies to arrive at some financial mechanism, the Asian Monetary Fund, was effectively thwarted by strong pressure from the United States and the IMF, and the open non-support of China.[38] This has dimmed the prospects of developing financial mechanisms that go beyond balance of payments assistance, and that will straddle alternative approaches to development finance.

A more integrated Southeast and East Asia will necessarily steer the focus away from just the economic elements, and give attention to the social and political aspects (beyond the security dimension) of cooperation. Only with a deeper integration will the issue of an ASEAN identity become relevant. It remains to be seen whether the citizens of ASEAN countries can identify themselves with 'ASEAN'. The most that people recognise would be the high-profile ASEAN Summit, and the popular ASEAN Games, and for travellers, visa-free entry to ASEAN countries. There is little knowledge, much less a connection with any, of the other initiatives of the organisation. This is because ASEAN has been 'socialised' among the 'foreign policy elites within the foreign affairs ministries and academic institutions of the ASEAN countries' and 'between leaders of the ASEAN states'.[39] It is 'an elite-driven institution' that does not resonate with the public consciousness within the ASEAN states, resulting in a shallow ASEAN identity.[40]

Acharya argues that it is time to broaden policy making in Asian states.[41] Track II dialogues, or those that involve academics and non-governmental actors, have proved useful in opening up the discussion of sensitive security issues and generating transparency, and argue for the inclusion of the NGO community (Track III) in the process. Acharya believes that civil society has certain strengths in dealing with transnational issues such as human rights, refugees and the environment,[42] which are issues that Curley and Schreurs address in the next two chapters. Beyond the formal dialogues, however, regional and subregional organisations should be in touch with communities on the ground, and tackle the issues that directly affect them, to give them an opportunity to take ownership of the regional/subregional initiatives. Indeed, in nearly 40 years of ASEAN's existence, the development of such inclusive regional institutions have not been seriously contemplated. It is high time they were given attention.

Notes

1 ASEAN Leaders, *Declaration of ASEAN Concord*, Singapore: ASEAN Secretariat, 1976.
2 ASEAN Leaders, *Declaration of ASEAN Concord* II (Bali Concord II), Jakarta: ASEAN Secretariat, 2003.
3 ASEAN Leaders, ASEAN Vision 2020, Jakarta: ASEAN Secretariat, 1997.
4 The phrase 'flying geese' was originally used by Kaname Akamatsu in his writings in Japanese in the 1930s. In 1962, his work 'A Historical Pattern of Economic Growth in Developing Countries' was published in *The Developing Economies*, Preliminary Issue No. 1, pp. 3–25. Comprehensive discussions of the model can be found in Pekka Korhonen, 'The theory of the flying geese pattern of development and its interpretations', *Journal of Peace Research*, 1994, vol. 31, no. 1, pp. 93–108, and Kiyoshi Kojima, 'The "flying geese" model of Asian economic development: origin, theoretical extensions and regional policy implications', *Journal of Asian Economics*, 2000, vol. 11, no. 4, pp. 375–401.
5 Jenina Joy Chavez, 'From Flying Geese to Cog and Wheel: Some Issues on Subregional Economic Zones', *Asian Exchange*, 1998, vol. 14, no. 1, pp. 9–32.
6 Chia Siow Yue and W. Dobson, 'Harnessing Diversity', in W. Dobson and Chia Siow Yue (eds) *Multinationals and East Asian Integration*, Ottawa: IDRC/ISEAS, 1997. Online. Available: http://www.web.cdri.ca/es/ev-68168-201-1-D0_TOPIC.html.
7 International Monetary Fund, *World Economic Outlook*, September 2002, pp. 128–9.
8 Ibid.
9 Two interesting critiques of the 'flying geese' model can be found in Martin Landsberg and Paul Burkett, 'Contradictions of capitalist industrialization in East Asia: a critique of "flying geese" theories of development', *Economic Geography*, 1998, vol. 74, no. 2, 87–110, and Shigehisa Kasahara, 'The flying geese paradigm: a critical study of its applications to East Asian regional development', *UNCTAD Discussion Papers*, April 2004, No. 169.
10 Chia Siow Yue and W. Dobson, 'Harnessing Diversity'.
11 Ibid.
12 United Nations Conference on Trade and Development, Trade and Development Report, Geneva: UNCTAD, 2003. Online. Available: http://www.unctad.org/en/docs/TDR2003ch1_en.pdf.

13 Ibid.; also see Hadi Soesastro, 'ASEAN in 2030: The Long View', in Simon S. C. Tay, Jesus P. Estanislao and Hadi Soesastro (eds) *Reinventing ASEAN*, Singapore: Institute of Southeast Asian Studies, 2003, pp. 273–310.

14 ASEAN Secretariat, *ASEAN Annual Report 2003–2004*, Jakarta: ASEAN Secretariat, 2004, p. 17.

15 Ibid., p. 19.

16 Shaun Narine, *Explaining ASEAN: Regionalism in Southeast Asia*, Boulder, CO: Lynne Rienner, 1999, pp. 193–209.

17 Ibid.

18 Since AFTA is supposed to have realised a CEPT rate of 0–5 per cent for most of its products, the AICO is said to have come too late in the game to afford substantial benefits for the region's industries.

19 ASEAN Secretariat, *ASEAN Annual Report 2003–2004*, Jakarta: ASEAN Secretariat, 2004, p. 21.

20 Ibid.

21 J. J. Chavez, 'From Flying Geese to Cog and Wheel', pp. 9–10.

22 Ibid.

23 Hadi Soesastro, 'ASEAN in 2030', pp. 273–310.

24 This section takes from J. J. Chavez, 'From Flying Geese to Cog and Wheel', pp. 9–32, and 'Co-opting Cooperation: The Asian Development Bank and Sub-regional Economic Zones', in *Creating Poverty: The ADB in Asia*, Bangkok: Focus on the Global South, 2002, pp. 23–9.

25 Joji Ilagan-Bian, 'Crisscrossing Mindanao', *Philippine Daily Inquirer*, 1 July 2002.

26 Ibid.

27 Asian Development Bank, *Sub-regional Cooperation Strategy and Programme Status Report: Southeast Asia*, 2002. Online. Available: http://www.adb.org/Documents/CSPs/SERD/reg_in225_02.pdf.

28 *Information on the BIMP-EAGA*. Online. Available: http://www.medco.gov.ph/medcoweb/bimpeaga.asp.

29 A China mission to BIMP–EAGA was organised in April 2004 in Davao City and Puerto Princesa City in the Philippines, and a China–ASEAN Expo in Guangxi, China in November 2004. Information from Mindanao Economic Development Council, 'New Strategies and Directions for the Resurgence of the BIMP-EAGA Initiative', November 2004 (unpublished presentation materials).

30 International Games Archives, 'BIMP–EAGA Games'. Online. Available: http://www. internationalgames.net/bimpeage.htm.

31 Interview with Gus Miclat, Executive Director, Initiative for International Dialogue, Davao City, Philippines, 18 November 2004.

32 W. Dobson, 'East Asian Integration: Synergies Between Firm Strategies and Government Policies', in W. Dobson and Chia Siow Yue (eds) *Multinationals and East Asian Integration*, Ottawa: IDRC/ISEAS, 1997. Online. Available: http://www.web.idrc.ca/es/ev-68133-201-1-DO_TOPIC.html.

33 ASEAN Secretariat, *Joint Communiqué*, The Second ASEAN Heads of Government Meeting, Jakarta: ASEAN Secretariat, 1977.

34 Ministerial Understanding on ASEAN Cooperation in Food, Agriculture and Forestry, Bandar Seri Begawan, Brunei Darussalam, 28–30 October 1993. Online. Available: http://www.aseansec. org/6181.htm.

35 Graziano Battistella, 'Unauthorized Migrants as global workers in ASEAN', Paper presented at the IUSSP Regional Population Conference on Southeast Asia's Population in a Changing Asian Context, Chulalongkorn University, Thailand, 10–12 June 2002.

36 Ronald Montaperto, 'Smoothing the Wrinkles', in *Comparative Connections (An E-Journal on East Asian Bilateral Relations)*, Second Quarter 2004. Online. Available: http://www.csis.org/pacfor/cc/0402Qchina_asean.html.

37 Gwendolyn Tecson, 'Confronting Regionalism in Asia: A View from the Philippines', in Ryokichi Hirono (ed.) *Regional Co-operation in Asia*, ASEAN Development Experience, Singapore: ISEAS, 2003, Vol. 3, pp. 73–91.

38 For further discussion on this topic, see Chapter 3 by Akihiko Tanaka in this volume.

39 Narine, *Explaining ASEAN*, pp. 193–209.

40 Ibid.

41 Amitav Acharya, *Regionalism and Multilateralism*, pp. 276–86.

42 Ibid.

9 The role of civil society in East Asian region building

Melissa G. Curley

Introduction

How is a discussion of civil society relevant to the debate about processes of regionalism and relationalisation in Asia? With its Western intellectual heritage, is the concept of civil society present and comparable across East Asian states?[1] Countries in East Asia are united by what Alagappa describes as 'the distributional consequences arising from the embrace of capitalism and economic reform, along with the integration of national economies in the global capitalist economy'.[2] Although civil society manifests itself in different ways in East Asian states, it is clear that the non-state sphere has become an important factor for political elites to consider.

In the previous chapter and as discussed elsewhere in this volume, the numerous challenges facing East Asian elites and peoples in forging an East Asian regional identity and community were discussed. While the region remains dominated by traditional security challenges and the influence of the state, the growing array of civil society organisations (CSOs) in East Asia have an important role to play in the future development of policy-making at the domestic level and in regional identity and community building.

This chapter focuses on the role that civil society is playing in community and region building in East Asia. It addresses how civil society in individual regional states, as well as at the regional level – in the form of regional networks and transnational constituencies of ideas – is reacting to processes of regionalisation and globalisation. Regional civil society is not conceived of as a coherent movement but as an emergent and changing space where CSOs from countries in East Asia work at both the domestic and regional levels, collectively organising themselves across diverse issue areas.

This chapter utilises a sociological interpretation of civil society understood as

> an intermediate associational realm situated between the state on the one side and the major building blocks of society on the other (individuals, families and firms), inhabited by social organisations with some degree of autonomy and voluntary participation on the part of its members.[3]

Actors within civil society are taken to include a broad spectrum of organisations in the space between the market and the state including NGOs, international NGOs (INGOs), government-organised NGOs (GONGOs), family foundations, voluntary associations, youth groups, professional organisations, think tanks, community groups, user committees, and so on. As NGOs are often used as a shorthand for civil society, the distinction is made in the chapter between the term NGOs and CSOs, where NGOs are considered as part of the wider category of CSOs. As highlighted above, civil society comprises different types of groups and organisations whose mission and membership vary from country to country. While NGOs are a significant and often vocal representative voice of civil society in some East Asian societies, it is a mistake to take them as representative of civil society per se.

Rather than conceiving of regional civil society as a collection of regionally based CSOs, this chapter analyses the emergence of a 'regional space' in which CSOs are acting. The first section locates the civil society debate in East Asia by reviewing recent literature on civil society in particular countries, and at the regional level. A typology for understanding how different political and economic systems impact on the development of civil society is outlined, before being applied to the East Asian context. Civil society in East Asian countries is then outlined, before implications for the process of region building are considered. The role of civil society and CSOs in the development of an East Asian region is the focus of the second section. Examples of the activities undertaken by CSOs, the areas of alternative security, national identity and human rights, and the environment are explored in a bid to understand the sector's potential impact on regional processes. Regional CSOs' links with 'transnational civil society' and their need to secure sustainable funding sources is then considered, before some conclusions are offered.

Definitions and conceptual limitations

Civil society is not a unitary category and it is important to recognise that its application to East Asia has limitations. As Schak and Hudson note, the application of European idealisations of civil society to the Asian state is problematic.[4] Scholars of civil society in Asia deploy different notions of its composition and application such that 'there are major discrepancies between approaches that emphasise civil society as a space or level, whatever falls within in, and approaches that identify it with one or more western political projects'.[5] Some key assumptions of European civil society – such as the division between the private and public sphere, the role of the voluntary sector and the state, and a moral or normative function – do not apply uniformly to Europe or indeed to East Asian states. As Alagappa stated:

> Civil society in Asian countries, as elsewhere, is an arena of power, inequality, struggle, and cooperation that is populated by a wide array of

voluntary and nonvoluntary groups whose political orientations, interests, resources, capacities, and methods span a wide spectrum. These non-state groups, operating in urban and rural areas and at times in foreign countries, function independently or in small networks to advance specific causes and interest that may diverge and conflict with one another.[6]

It is also important to be aware of assumptions made about civil society and competing and contradictory expectations of its value in regional debate and dialogue. How is the concept of civil society operationalised in regional political practice and discourse? States and international organisations have interests in the actions of civil society. As detailed below, the state acts in different ways towards CSOs and their agendas, and in more authoritarian regimes attempts to co-opt and influence CSOs in line with its agenda. The state in many regional countries, however, has become increasingly aware of the value and use of civil society as a partner and implementer of domestic and regional policy objectives. Governments throughout the region acknowledge the limitations that the forces of globalisation and liberalisation place on policy-making and implementation. Some also recognise the role that CSOs can play in addressing complex socio-economic problems, such as the delivery of social welfare and provision of health services.

The point is that 'civil society' in East Asia is a space under contestation, where actors who form part of civil society must negotiate their own agenda alongside that of other major players with considerable power, such as domestic governments and international donors. Although of relevance, the question of whether these activities form part of a global or transnational civil society cannot be dealt with at length due to lack of space.

Locating the civil society debate in East Asia

Before considering to what extent civil society can be understood as a regional space of actors, it is useful to review civil society in the region via the lens of particular country contexts. First, domestic civil society is relevant for our discussion both as a reaction to, and result of, the forces of economic globalisation taking place in the region (a corollary example was seen in Chapter 6 where Hamilton-Hart discussed the links between domestic and regional financial sectors). Second, in reference to processes of regionalisation, the non-state public sphere is an actor in this process. In a region with multiple political systems and where regime legitimacy exists to varying degrees, nation building and changing state–society relations warrants ongoing scholarly attention. The non-state sphere, including civil society and the CSOs within it, form an important space to better understand how the processes of globalisation impact on individuals at the grassroots level, and how individuals and groups within states act to lobby domestic and international structures around those concerns.

There is a rich literature in international relations that theorises about change in international politics which recognises the significance of transnational actions.[7] This literature and debate centres on interactions between 'multiple channels of contact among societies, and the resultant blurring of domestic and international politics'.[8] The analytical value of studying these interactions depends on the focus of enquiry. For our purposes, does a vibrant civil society support the development and maintenance of democracy? Can civil society be nurtured from the 'outside' or must it emerge as an indigenous phenomenon?[9]

In terms of East Asian region building, there are a number of ways the category of 'civil society' may relate to processes of integration and cooperation. First, as an analytical concept, civil society can help build a more accurate picture of the diversity of civil society–government relations in the region as discussed below, and what these relations can tell us about the prospects for intraregional cooperation among CSOs. As noted by Baviera in the concluding chapter, there are countries in the region where civil society is virtually nonexistent. An understanding of the regulatory systems, capacities and focus of civil society in particular countries provides us with important indicators for cooperation. For example, the analysis of the NGO communities in various East Asian countries does suggest that NGOs in countries with less regulation and more flexibility to define their work programmes may be more likely to cooperate internationally together on certain topics (for example, human rights or democratisation), and be able to forge and maintain transnational alliance networks, than those NGO communities more closely associated with the state.

This is not to say that innovative spaces have not emerged in all regional countries for a range of NGO activities. At the regional level, the East Asian Vision Group (EAVG) and East Asian Study Group (EASG) have highlighted the potential for incorporating NGOs into the creation of more participatory and consultative regional policy-making approaches. Likewise, as the ASEAN+3 (APT) process expands, its vision of developing a 'community of caring societies' will engage and seek the partnership of CSOs. Indeed CSOs are already lobbying governments and regional fora, on specific interest areas. This is discussed in more detail below.

Civil society in East Asia: a review

Research in this area has engaged with how the notion of civil society could be applied and related to the development of East Asia, in terms of democratisation, identity, regional action and advocacy, and institutional architecture. A landmark attempt to explore how civil society and NGOs could contribute to the future of regionalism in East Asia was a project undertaken by the Japan Centre for International Exchange (JCIE) in the mid-1990s because of a perceived need

> to have a clearer picture of the present state of development of the 'demand side' of the nonprofit sector in Asia Pacific in order for the philanthropic

activities by the supply side of private foundations and corporations to be effective and relevant.[10]

That project documented the growing interest that already existed within CSOs in the region – in this instance philanthropic organisations, NGOs and research institutes – on the topic of civil society and the contribution it could make to an emerging regional community. The project demonstrated that government–NGO relationships were an important structural factor in the potential for cooperation in the region. It also identified that the emergence of intergovernmental regional organisations such as APEC gave rise to parallel dialogue and cooperation in both the private sector and civil society.

Yamamoto pointed to lack of resources (human resources and finances), language differences, and the degree to which a 'conducive environment' was available to CSOs as constraining factors. This continues to be the case a decade on. The project also recognised the state's limited ability to solve problems arising from globalisation and liberalisation, and that a widening of space for NGOs and CSOs had emerged in response to the expanding needs of citizens. Another important concern was how NGOs and CSOs could develop cooperative relations with their governments without compromising their social agendas, a challenge they continue to face.

More recent scholarship has focused on the development of civil society in a variety of ways: the role of NGOs in Asia, on the relationship between civil society, democratisation and political change, and the existence of an international or global civil society, in which East Asian CSOs are active.[11] This is reflective of increasing state, donor and scholarly interest in the linkages between civil society, democratisation and political change, and the non-profit sector's role in providing social safety mechanisms under conditions of globalisation and economic restructuring.

Comparative research on NGO–state relations in East Asia has usefully demonstrated that different political systems, government regulations and other 'determining factors' play a crucial role in how NGO activities impact and manifest themselves in different state contexts.[12] Shigetomi has argued that structural features of the state, NGOs' agendas and abilities to implement programmes, and other factors, such as available resources and levels of economic and material need within the country, determine why NGO–state relations differ in various countries.

Shigetomi pointed out that NGO activities directed towards regional conferences and agencies (such as APEC or ASEAN) attract relatively more attention in the literature than their in-country activities. Shigetomi acknowledged that NGOs' in-country work programmes are more likely to have an international dimension as the processes of globalisation and political and administrative relations between nations grow stronger, and domestic development concerns are more profoundly affected by international agreements and international consensus.[13] Nevertheless, it is important to note when discussing the existence of a 'regional civil society' to distinguish between the role NGOs play in domestic context and the role they play in transnational/regional issues.

In this respect, two points should be borne in mind. First, many NGOs and CSOs in East Asian countries are primarily focused on domestic issues. The 'regional level' – whether for dialogue or for networking – realistically makes up a limited amount of their operation in terms of time and resources, in accordance with their needs assessment. Second, when examining INGO cooperation on a regional level, it is important to consider it as part of a more complex regional whole, where political and economic development varies, such that considerable diversity exists when talking about domestic civil societies. Therefore, it is necessary to be cautious about what conclusions can be drawn from the evidence of regional NGO cooperation and networking as evidence of a 'region-wide' or otherwise coherent movement. It appears more accurate to point to constituencies of CSOs organising around particular issues, whose local, state and international links evolve over time. In this space of activity, models of engagement differ, from the confrontational and activist (such as the Pak Mun Dam alliance and its lobby on the Thai government), to close NGO/CSO–state partnerships with government agencies to implement development programmes (as seen with many Chinese NGOs).

The relationship between governments and civil society development

Recent cross-country comparative research on civil society suggests that governments do more to shape and affect the manifestation of civil society than the existing literature has implied.[14] Previous typologies commonly located governments along the spectrum from left to right, or alternatively placed them along a spectrum from autocracies to liberal democracies.[15] Manor proposes the most relevant typology to explain the development of civil society and classifies governments/states according to: (1) state capacity to perform key tasks; (2) the degree of state centralisation; and (3) the manner in which the state seeks to make its influence penetrate downwards into society.

As illustrated in Table 9.1, Manor's typology divides governments into (1) low-capacity and centralised systems; (2) medium- to high-capacity and accommodative systems; and (3) high-capacity and centralised systems. According to this typology, governments in category 1 have low or very low state capacity to perform key administrative tasks (for example, designing and implementing development policies), are highly centralised, and have difficulty influencing society in ways other than coercion. Governments in category 3 are similar to those in category 1, in that they are highly centralised, but differ in that they have high capacity to influence society through government structures. These states often seek to influence 'by pursuing control, cooption, rule by diktat and at times coercion'.[16]

In contrast, governments in category 2 have medium to high capacity to perform state functions, but tend to be more decentralised, and 'seek to make their influence penetrate downward by way of accommodation, by encouraging bottom-up processes and independent power centres and by sharing powers and resources with diverse interests within and . . . beyond government – that is within civil society'.[17] In summary, the typology suggests that governments in categories 1 and 3 foster a negative environment for civil society to develop, while those in category 2 seek to embrace and strengthen it, giving organisations more room to operate and act autonomously.

The application of this typology to East Asian political systems (see Table 9.2) provides insight into the future prospects for regional cooperation, as it illustrates broad but significant differences in the state of civil societies in the region. Applying this typology to East Asia, one can see that countries are distributed throughout the range.[18]

The typology raises a number of issues for regional CSOs. First, indigenous CSOs in East Asia emerge from countries with varying economic development levels, where political systems also vary. Hence, civil society in category 2 countries are generally free and more vibrant that those in either categories 1 and 3, although their interests may focus on different concerns generally reflecting higher levels of development (with the exception of the Philippines). Second, it suggests that CSOs from category 1 countries (that is, low government capacity, suspicious of civil society, large economic need: Laos, Cambodia) may be more reliant on international funding for their own operational needs and their capacity to network and set agendas regionally is constrained by their limited resources. This is not to suggest that similar degrees of development are necessary for cooperation to occur. Indeed there is ample evidence that very successful cooperation and exchange programmes have been occurring between countries in the region with divergent political systems (and approaches to civil society) for some time via people-to-people contacts, for example.[19] It does suggest, however, that transnational regional networks of CSOs in East Asia develop a division of labour among themselves, according to the interests and capacities of the various organisations.

Civil society in East Asian contexts

Scholarship on civil society in individual East Asian countries provides further insight into the nuances of civil society in these categories. Particularly useful is the literature on China and Vietnam which has focused on the emergence of civil society in market socialist economies under economic transition.

Scholars disagree on the relevance and utility of the civil society concept for Confucian and Islamic societies. Regarding China, one group of scholars argue that the Western-centric concept of civil society is not applicable to China and has little analytical value due to the long historical presence of benevolent rule by a dominating state, tradition, orthodoxy and a high degree of state penetration by the state.[20] In contrast, other China scholars have used the concept to explain political developments in contemporary China and the late Imperial and Republican eras, while some Western historians of China have deployed civil society to understand the growth and transformation of Chinese cities as they accelerated during the Republican era and their historical relevance for contemporary China.[21] Similar debates abound over the applicability of civil society to Islamic societies, and specifically their utility in countries such as Indonesia and Malaysia. Returning to a point made in the introduction, disagreement over the definition of civil society, and different interpretations of its applicability to East Asian societies, makes regional comparison challenging.

Such themes are also explored in Kerkvliet's volume on organisations, groups and associations in Vietnam, and what socio-economic changes over the last decade have meant for civil society in that country.[22] Meanwhile Heng has highlighted, in relation to the media in Vietnam, how the lack of a clear division between the media and the state can result in civil society activity, 'because of and not despite the interlocking nature of state and civil society'.[23] Relatively little scholarship has been written on civil society in Laos and Myanmar,[24] although documentation and project reports from donors, INGOs, and international organisations working in these countries have important insights. Both these governments fall into category 1 of Manor's typology with civil society virtually non-existent or nascent in development, and with considerable suspicion directed towards any alternative institutions/groups that are autonomous from the state apparatus. Having said that, development partnerships between INGOs and state partners (such as is required in Laos, Vietnam and China) may provide important opportunities for the state to experiment with more accommodative forms of regulating civil society behaviour.[25] Such partnerships are also a means to maintain control of funding allocation and implementation, which Zweig has discussed for example in relation to the Chinese aid model.[26] Further research is required into these partnerships and their implication for our understanding of civil society development in authoritarian systems.

As noted above, the democratisation process in South Korea, Taiwan, Thailand and Indonesia since the beginning of the 1980s has seen growth in the organisation of civil society activities in those countries.[27] It is sufficient to say that civil society, and the type and interests of CSOs in each polity, differs, depending on: structural factors, organisational capacities, levels of economic need in the community, and the interaction between these conditions and the state's agenda. The case of China, however, warrants further attention for its insight into how CSOs are able to pursue their agendas within and through considerable state control of their activities.

Civil society in China

The literature on emergent forms of civil society in China has emphasised the need to locate the concept within rapidly changing economic and social conditions. Howell and Pearce argue that as rigidly imposed state categories of class,

Table 9.1 Types of governments: capacities and postures

1 Low-capacity/centralised	2 Medium- to high-capacity/accommodative	3 High-capacity/centralised
Low or very low state capacity; inability to perform many key tasks, except the use of coercive power	Medium or high state capacity; some or much emphasis on downward accountability and responsiveness	High or very high state capacity, with strong top-down emphasis
Often a high degree of centralisation, but since little institution building has occurred, power tends to be personalised; little penetration of lower levels	Less centralisation; an awareness that decentralisation improves regime legitimacy and developmental outcomes; substantial building of institutions (some autonomous); medium to strong capacity to penetrate lower levels	High degree of centralisation, with substantial institution building; but institutions mainly geared to top-down control and penetration of all levels, including local; power sometimes personalised
Aspirations to control, but they are achieved only to a very limited extent	Aspirations to yield some control, in order to gain legitimacy and improve developmental outcomes; middling to high achievement	Aspiration to control all levels and power centres (except the private sector), and control is widely achieved
Few (or virtually no) roots in society due to state incapacity, serious organisational weakness of ruling party, and unwillingness to be responsive	Middling or deep penetration of society via sharing of powers and funds, and via responsiveness to social groups; party organisations moderate to strong	Deep downward penetration by government and strong party organisation give solid roots in society, but their purpose is to co opt and control

1 *Low-capacity/centralised*	2 *Medium- to high-capacity/accommodative*	3 *High-capacity/centralised*
Suspicion and hostility towards independent power centres within government – towards autonomous institutions	Some or much encouragement to independent power centres within government – autonomous institutions and elected lower level bodies	Suspicion and hostility towards independent power centres within government – towards autonomous institutions
Little clarity in definition and perception of development and poverty	Define development and poverty in broad terms including need for empowerment; seek to tackle all aspects of poverty	Define development and poverty – for the most part – economistically; stress economistic solutions
Little legitimacy in the eyes of the populace	Legitimacy based on openness and responsiveness, *plus* economic and developmental performance, including growth	Legitimacy based on economic and development performance – mostly economistically defined – with emphasis on growth

Source: James Manor, 'Civil Society under Different Types of Governments'.

Table 9.2 Countries' location in the typology

1 Low-capacity / centralised		2 Medium - to high-capacity / accommodative		3. High / very high-capacity / centralised	
Laos	Indonesia	Taiwan*	Japan*	Malaysia*	PRC
Cambodia*		Thailand*		Singapore*	Vietnam
Myanmar*		South Korea		Brunei*	

Source: James Manor, 'Civil Society under Different Types of Governments', with additional inser-tions (*) by the author.

residence and political status are eroded by increasing complexity in economic relations, the resultant social differentiation has seen the rise of new grievances, needs and losers within the system. This in turn created two key changes in the 'intermediary sphere' – 'namely, the reform of existing mass organisations and the emergence of new intermediary organisations'.[28] A number of scholars have reviewed and continue to monitor the growth of the non-profit or non-governmental sphere in China.[29] If a common theme can be drawn from these analyses, it is that the Chinese Communist Party recognises and is encouraging certain types of CSOs to expand and meet increasing social welfare and envi-ronmental needs in the community, through the provision of specific services to members.[30] Nevertheless it remains reluctant to accept organisations that are advocacy based, or that 'challenge the party's power or the process of economic reform'.[31]

There is an increasing interest amongst scholars and commentators alike on what effect the expansion of social organisations in China will have on opportu-nities for free association and an emergent civil society. Under political systems where the state still plays a major role and society is undergoing immense change, the boundaries between the state, market and aspects of civil society are not clear. In these situations, defining autonomous spheres is problematic. Howell and Pearce have argued that the case of China 'demonstrates the need to think in terms of multiple civil societies existing across time and space, with diverse purposes, varying degrees of autonomy, and different political implications'.[32] Meanwhile, Saich cautions that an exclusive focus on 'state-dominated' theories, 'society-informed' concepts of social corporatisation, or ideas of purely 'state-led' civil society runs the risk of obscuring the complex dynamics of change in China. Importantly, this includes the extent to which groups are considered 'co-opted' by the state, as well as how they have been able to negotiate space through various strategies both to influence the policy process and to advance the cause of their members or target groups.[33]

In relation to the non-profit sector, Saich argues that while the state does exert extensive formal control over social organisations and foundations, the approaches mentioned above fail to take account of three main factors. These are (1) the increasing difficulty for authorities to enforce regulations uniformly across China, in a system that itself is rife with contradictions; (2) the fact that so-called 'subordinate' or 'co-opted' organisations often benefit from their institutional arrangements with the state; and (3) that many social organisations have derived strategies to negotiate relationships with the state which maximise members'/target group interests' or have found ways to deflect or avoid state intervention.[34]

Considering the implications of the above for regional civil society is complex. Currently CSOs that are linked to the state (such as those seen in China and Vietnam) do not provide the types of alternative voices in regional fora that are heard from organisations from more liberal polities, such as the Philippines or Thailand. The expectation that civil society *should* provide such an alternative and critical voice is an example of the conflicting view of civil society's utility. One such example is in relation to perspectives on the role of civil society in development. An alternative view of civil society is found within some grassroots movements and 'change-oriented' organisations whose view articulates a critical approach to the global economy and which advocates struc-tural changes to readdress fundamental power inequalities that characterise many development partnerships.[35] This interpretation differs from the more mainstream view that problems of poverty and inequality can be solved by the 'right' set of economic policies that leads to a consensual approach to develop-ment among civil society, the market and the state. In this context, development 'partnerships' are viewed as important mechanisms through which this consensus can be operationalised.

Returning to the point that state-linked organisations are not likely to provide critical voices, this is not to say that government-organised NGOs' (GONGOs) contributions are not valid and important at the regional level, but that their autonomy is limited to various degrees. The point is more that regional dialogue for CSOs has much potential, but certain parameters still exist primarily for organisations where the state is centralised and authori-tarian, and where its approach to civil society is supportive for social welfare and poverty alleviation work, but not for lobbying and advocacy which can be perceived to challenge the legitimacy of the state, particularly with respect to issues of democratisation and human rights. That said, the potential exists for GONGOs and CSOs from more controlled regimes to have an expanded capacity within the regional space. Such interaction can provide channels of communication and potential policy ideas to be communicated back to state partners.

The role of civil societies in East Asian region building

As Baviera illustrates in the concluding chapter, the end of the Cold War ushered in new political realities in East Asia. The breakdown of ideological tensions and their divisive power in the region was greatly diminished. In the 1990s, the region witnessed the resolution of the conflict in Cambodia, an expansion and overall improvement in diplomatic relations between China and Southeast Asian states, the admission of Vietnam, Cambodia, Laos and Myanmar to ASEAN, and a general improvement of relations among countries, groups and peoples in the region. At the same time, the deepening of the democratisation process in Taiwan, South Korea, Thailand and Indonesia saw civil society activism grow. The rise of civil societies in East Asia needs to be especially seen in the context of the changing socio-political and economic changes that took place in this period. Governments also came to realise that their ability to solve problems arising from rapid economic growth and industrialisation was limited by the impact of globalisation, which also widened the space for NGOs and CSOs to address the emerging needs of their society.

It is widely accepted that the 1997 Asian crisis played an important role in the evolution of the idea of an East Asian Community. Although the idea had been mooted in the early 1990s in the form of the East Asian Economic Caucus (EAEC), the events and aftermath of the crisis helped identity formation in the region by cementing a sense of common goals and mutual interests. The crisis shaped the emergence of a regional awareness by highlighting the commonalities across Northeast and Southeast Asian states, while at the same time giving rise to the idea that it was a result of extra-regional forces rather than poor domestic governance structures.

The emergence of new economic and security institutions such as APEC, the ASEAN Regional Forum (ARF), ASEAN+3 and now the East Asia Summit (EAS) has provided a focus and meeting point for regional CSOs to gather in parallel sessions to express their views on areas of interest, if not directly to leaders, via the media. Institutionalisation in the region has had a concomitant impact on modes of regional CSOs, with a parallel circuit of civil society actors meeting alongside APEC and ASEAN+3 summits. Despite this, Alagappa cautions that 'the dramatic growth in the number of civil society organisations has not, however, been accompanied by institutionalization of the nonstate public sphere' where civil society in many Asian countries is 'viewed largely in instrumental terms, as bringing about or preventing political change in the state and its institutions'.[36]

The 1997 Asian crisis also shed light on the stark development gap existing among East Asian countries, and the impact of the crisis on the regions' poor. Regional attempts to involve civil society actors in addressing these gaps are reflected in the EAVG's recommendation to establish an East Asian Forum, consisting of government and non-governmental representatives from various sectors to 'serve as an institutional mechanism for broad-based social exchanges, and ultimately, regional cooperation'.[37] The EAVG called for greater cooperation between governments and NGOs in policy development to encourage civil participation and responsibility, and to promote the use of state–civil society partnerships in addressing social problems.[38] While many remain sceptical about their potential for meaningful long-term structural change, the potential for state–civil society partnerships to make a positive impact exists if adequate resources and political will are provided.

Although the institutionalisation of the non-state sphere may be lagging behind the growth of CSOs, such growth nonetheless bodes well for the development of a critical mass as networks of organisations with similar concerns. Networks are emerging to address issues at a regional scale, as regional institutions themselves broaden and deepen. The ASEAN People's Assembly and East-Asian-based environmental lobby networks are two such examples. However, many questions remain about the relationship between CSOs and regionalism in East Asia: What is the potential for greater regional cooperation and collaboration via NGO networks, policy and advocacy networks? What are the current obstacles facing such groups? How do existing structural constraints such as funding availability and sustainability, and human resource limitations, place limitations on the pace of such future regional networking activities? In terms of developing constituencies at the regional level, to what extent can we see a common agenda emerging amongst regional civil society groups? Around which types of issues are groups likely to mobilise? What types of fora will they have to air views and forge common agendas for future action?

Recent cross-country research that focuses on the link between civil society and democratic change has analysed 'the specific functions and consequences of CSOs in promoting or preventing political change in the direction of open, participatory, and accountable political systems'.[39] Alagappa's comparative project posits a number of propositions, three of which appear relevant to our discussion on the nature and development of regional civil society. These are: (1) the growth of CSOs in general; (2) the composition and dynamics of civil society have changed dramatically over time in several countries; and (3) that growth in numbers of CSOs has, however, not been accompanied by the institutionalisation of the non-state public sphere.

The focus of domestic civil societies in East Asian countries noted in the first section differs considerably, suggesting that CSOs will bring to the region experiences and alliances reflective of their country context. For example, in states with high legitimacy (Japan), CSOs emphasise reform, accountability and representation, while the focus in states with less legitimacy (for example, Cambodia) is on organising resistance, developing counter-narratives and alternative institutions, and fostering support from domestic and international allies.[40] Differences in nature and form of CSOs can thus be said to revolve around the following variables: (1) support and resources from political societies within countries; (2) response from the state (i.e. support, cooption and/or suppression); and (3) types of international support. The assertion that growth in CSOs in general in the region has not been accompanied by institutionalisation of civil society within states suggests that CSOs remain vulnerable to resource shortages and are still subject to the political agenda of governments.

It is more accurate to think of the emergent cooperation by CSOs in the region as being multiple, existing across time and space, where purposes are diverse and groups have varying degrees of autonomy from the state, with different political implications depending on the context.[41] Rather than a unified regional movement, we can more easily identify likeminded groups coming together to form constituencies for action on certain areas of concern such as alternative security, the environment, and human rights and national identity.

Regional examples of mobilisation

Alternative and non-traditional security

Caballero-Anthony argues that CSOs in Southeast Asia have been contributing to an alternative discourse on security thinking within ASEAN states, one that reflects concerns of citizens in ASEAN countries such as food security, environmental degradation, depletion of fish stocks, and human rights.[42] CSOs are now actively involved in 'attempting to redefine concepts of security' by examining the recent emergence of fora such as the ASEAN People's Assembly (APA), established in 2000 by CSOs from the 10 ASEAN states. Caballero-Anthony's analysis traces the development of CSOs that have come together to push the state to consider alternative concepts of security and development. Building upon the momentum gained in earlier groups and fora such as Peace, Disarmament and Symbiosis in the Asia–Pacific (PDSAP) and regional NGO conferences on alternative security issues, she argues that the APA process is helping to build 'constituencies of peace' which intend not only to challenge the dominant discourse on security, but 'more importantly . . . to influence policies and programs that could engender "people-centred" security systems'.[43]

The APA provides insights in how CSOs in ASEAN countries are interacting with existing Track II networks (for example, CSCAP and ASEAN-ISIS)[44] in pushing their agendas of development and security with regional elites and policy-makers. Caballero-Anthony explores the APA advocacy on two fronts: developing a human rights scorecard, and producing a regional Human Development Report for Southeast Asia, emphasising that the APA's agendas 'have to be examined against the material environment that these actors work in'.[45] Referring to the Human Rights Scorecard, ongoing meetings of transnational NGO groups, members of the ASEAN-ISIS network and the Regional Working Group on Human Rights (RWGHR) with the APA, 'reflects an increasing constituency of human-rights advocates in the region – people and groups that are actively engaging officials at national and regional levels to push for the establishment of a regional human-rights mechanism'.[46]

Healthy scepticism exists regarding the utility of the APA in acting as a 'true' reflection of the 'grassroots' and some have criticised ASEAN for not paying enough attention to the APA's recommendations and its 'eagerness and vision'.[47] Caballero-Anthony rightly asserted, however, that common interest and avenues for CSOs have emerged despite the region's diversity discussed previously. It is often noted that NGOs in Vietnam, Laos and China are quasi-state institutions or GONGOs, whose operations, staff and agendas are closely aligned to that of the states. Counteracting such criticism, it is contended that common ground has been and is being found for regional cooperation. One such example of cooperation is between the Laos Women's Union, a mass organisation of the state, and *Gabriela*, an independent NGO in the Philippines, on incorporating gender mainstreaming in the set of indicators for the Southeast Asian HDR.[48]

This analysis suggests that civil society activism that challenges traditional notions of security is gaining momentum. Furthermore, it is representative of the evolution of a critical space in ASEAN in which different sectors of the ASEAN community can be involved in the process of redefining security.[49] If one accepts this argument, then NGO networking at regional conferences such as APEC and the upcoming EAS, and Track II dialogue between NGOs, research institutes and the state, represent avenues through which other potentially sensitive regional issues could be addressed.

The environment

Civil society cooperation on the environment is one area which has expanded rapidly in East Asia in the 1990s and 2000s. As noted by Schreurs in the following chapter, activism and cooperation has benefited from democratisation processes witnessed to varied degrees in South Korea, the Philippines, Indonesia, Thailand, Singapore and Malaysia over the last 15 years. While civil society is more limited in China, Vietnam and Laos, governments have recognised CSOs' utility in raising public awareness on environmental and conservation issues, and their efficiency in helping implement government and aid-partnered projects. As such, some environmental NGOs in China, for example, are not only tolerated, but encouraged, as they are perceived to be broadly supportive of the government's agenda, and indeed may provide public support for the goals and objectives of the state's environmental bureaucracy.[50] The expansion of CSOs and NGOs in the environmental area across East Asia, particularly their acceptance in highly centralised political systems, has meant that a critical mass of organisations has emerged.

Cooperation between environmental groups has taken the form of pooling domestic strength to speak with one voice to the government, and also forming alliances with likeminded international groups to lobby government(s) on particular issues. The Southeast Asia Rivers Network (SEARIN) and Rivers Watch East and Southeast (RWESA) are examples of regional environmental networks established around the environmental impact of damming the rivers, particularly the Mekong, and its potential impact on local people's livelihoods. SEARIN was established in 1999 by academics and NGO activists in Thailand who were campaigning on social and environmental issues within Thailand, particularly the impact of dams and government policies on resource management. Apart from campaign activities, the organisation supports grassroots-based research on river systems and livelihoods such as that conducted by villagers in Chiang Khong, in Chiang Mai province in Thailand, to document their local water ecosystems, to counteract the planned blasting of the Mekong in Chiang Khong's 10 km section of rapids, underwater rocks and sandbars which hinder commercial navigation, but which also serve as a spawning ground for fish. Their research aims to document fish stocks, species and vegetation in an attempt to lobby the Thai government against the blasting plan,[51] which is part of the wider plan to increase commercial navigation services from China to Vietnam via the Mekong. RWESA seeks to combine the knowledge, networks and resources of its 35 network partner organisations to campaign against 'destructive river development projects in East and Southeast Asia and to restore rivers to the communities who depend on them'.[52]

Apart from publishing research on the negative environmental and social impact of dams and river diversion projects, RWESA also lobbies regional organisations such as the Asian Development Bank and financial institutions such as the Japan Bank for International Cooperation (JBIC) against financing more dams and providing funding for previous environmental damage. INGOs such as Oxfam US are similarly taking a regional focus to their strategy on the Mekong via their Mekong River Basin Management Programme. One such activity of this programme in Cambodia has been to support fisherfolk living on the Tonle Sap Lake to document fish stocks in order to communicate their needs and concerns to the government, regarding the depletion of fish stocks and upstream water resource management.[53]

The benefits of seeking international alliances and support through collective numbers will enable environmental groups to speak more forcefully on a regional stage. And while the state remains undeniably in control of decisions at the heart of environmental issues, domestic and regional alliances look set to gain momentum in strength and power as the capacity and resources of such groups increase. The importance of support from INGOs, and sources of reliable and sustainable funding for domestic CSOs, is discussed further below.

The role of international support: INGOs and international aid donors

INGOs and international organisations (IOs), such as the World Bank and Asian Development Bank (ADB), and various bilateral donors, have a role to play in nurturing the future potential of regional civil society cooperation. Both the World Bank and the ADB have programmes in the East Asian region that fund and support, to varying degrees, domestic NGO programmes, regional exchange visits, networking opportunities among CSOs, and so forth. It is well documented that both institutions have taken engagement with civil society actors more seriously after sustained criticism in the 1980s and early 1990s that their programmes lacked the input and participation of key stakeholders in communities affected by large-scale infrastructure projects, and that funding should be more poverty focused. While mechanisms have been established to ensure project planning takes account of views of community stakeholders and relevant CSOs, the World Bank and the ADB remain the objects of much NGO criticism for their financing of projects such as hydroelectricity and population relocation. Nevertheless, greater transparency and the increased network and lobbying activities of region CSOs mean that dialogue between IOs and CSOs – both cooperative and conflictual – has likely improved CSOs' human resource capacity through a better working knowledge of IO bureaucracy, and how to lobby IOs and regional member governments more effectively to advance their interests.

INGOs provide support to domestic NGOs via funds and capacity building programmes, transferring knowledge about campaigning and lobbying, and so on. They are also able to assist domestic NGOs to overcome the constraints of civil society placed on them, particularly with sensitive issues such as national identity and independence. Baogang He, for example, argues that INGOs have been instrumental in providing support for NGOs involved in the East Timorese independence movement, including East Timor organisations in the overseas diaspora, INGOs (such as the Asia–Pacific Coalition of East Timor), and East-Timor-related NGOs in Australia.[54] He argues that INGOs supported the independence movement in different ways, including according legitimacy to secessionists by dealing directly with them, and placing pressure on Australian Prime Minister Howard, who wrote to then Indonesian President Habibie in December 1998 calling for free and fair elections.

Generally speaking, regional cooperation activities are lower in the priority of international donors whose aid allocations are structured largely according to country programme priorities. Such programmes centre on poverty reduction in sectors such as health, education and agriculture, and capacity/institution building as major funding priorities. While regional cooperation may take place via study trips and exchange visits to build local capacities, funding is smaller in scale compared with in-country priorities. While small-scale people-to-people exchanges provide invaluable insights for the participants, the potential for CSOs to participate and engage regionally with their counterparts is often beyond their funding and human resource capacity. For NGOs focusing on a specific sector or issue (such as health, landmines) the scope for meaningful regional exchange and dialogue may be limited, while strategic planning and day-to-day operational issues are the priority. In short, 'regional cooperation' may be a luxury for many smaller NGOs and CSOs that must prioritise their scarce resources.

The top-down agendas of donors which may build in regional cooperation activities into their funding schedule, without adequate consultation, can result in conferences and workshops organised around issues that are not crucial to all participants. In such cases, capacity and interest may be too different for much useful dialogue to take place. On the other hand, Keck and Sikkink observed that there is a downside to the intensive work of CSOs for their involvement in transnational advocacy networks. In relation to the global campaign for women's human rights, they note that many organisations were so focused on the intensive preparations for the Vienna and Beijing Conferences that they 'neglected their own communities'. While they argue that the conferences 'stimulated global awareness and networking . . . there was still a considerable distance between the new resolutions and changing actual practices'.[55]

Challenges and opportunities

This chapter began with the recognition that civil society in East Asia is not a unitary category and that attempts to impose a variety of idealised definitions and conceptions upon East Asian polities are fraught with conceptual and analytical confusions. Discussing 'regional' civil society in East Asia is difficult to sustain for a number of reasons. First, civil society, as it manifests itself in East Asian polities, is diverse. Recent literature has stressed institutional capacity and centralisation, rather than ideology or political systems (democratic, communist, authoritarian), to explain the degree to which Western expectations of civil society emerge. Despite this diversity, possibilities exist in more controlled environments for CSOs to act because of the difficulty of the state effectively to impose its regulatory control, and because individuals and groups appear able to utilise connections to the state and with the international arena for the benefit of their groups and organisations.

Cooperation at the regional level may gain momentum as groups form in tandem with increasing institutionalisation in East Asia. New institutions such as the EAS will provide CSOs with another region-wide forum to direct their advocacy and campaign activity; an opportunity via the media to increase awareness of their interests through visibility at the regional level; and will draw support from international partners such as INGOs and organisations for networking and campaign activities. CSOs from ASEAN will have the opportunity to meet with ASEAN leaders for the first time in a scheduled 15-minute meeting at the December EAS, a move which arguably reflects Malaysia's desire to make ASEAN less – or, at least, appear less – elitist.[56]

Growth in the civil society sector will also necessitate growth in sustainable forms of funding so that organisations can plan and increase their capacities and programme continuity. The development of philanthropy in the region will be crucial in the future as funding for non-profit organisations and charities is sought from within the region. East Asia is home to a cohort of very wealthy businesspeople and families, many of whom have already established family foundations. Further cooperation and networking among philanthropic institutions are needed to identify areas of need, in order to channel funds, and also to facilitate the evolution of family foundations into professional funding organisations with regularised systems of giving. One such current example is the

Conference of Asian Foundations and Organisations (CAFO) based in Manila, whose broad aim is to enhance transnational civil society and to expand opportunities for dialogue among different societal actors. In the recent past China has been reviewing its laws on fundraising and the role of foundations and how the institutionalisation of philanthropy may contribute to broader party policy on the role of CSOs in areas of social welfare and the environment. Growth in the quantity and quality of grant-making activity from regional foundations will undoubtedly contribute to multilateral CSO activity on regionalism issues.

Conclusion

Civil society activity across East Asia is diverse, ranging from very critical and activist organisations, such as those in the Philippines and Hong Kong, to GONGOs in countries like China and Vietnam, whose agenda is often closely aligned with that of the state. Advocacy and activities that criticise state and regional policies provide an important alternative voice for the marginalised, and contribute to the public debate about particular polities. At the same time, state–civil society partnerships can provide an important opportunity for state bureaucracies to develop and implement programmes more effectively and efficiently. A challenge for CSOs will then be how to develop more cooperative relations with governments without compromising social and political agendas. In countries where civil society is very nascent, such as Laos and Myanmar, this may be premature. However, the research on state–civil society relations in China and Vietnam, for example, indicates that an emerging space is available for CSOs to implement programmes relatively independently of the state in some cases, and that this can be achieved through and within existing political structures.

The diversity of political systems and various regulatory environments means, however, that regional cooperation among CSOs is more likely to emerge around issues where interests of the state, international organisations and CSOs converge, such as the environment, human trafficking, and so on. This is because many CSOs in the region remain under the influence of the state to varying degrees, which has implications for the types of internal political support, and international connections that may be tolerated. Nevertheless, national NGOs in East Asia have become more adept at developing links with INGOs to overcome the national limits of civil society. By creating links with grassroots organisations, mobilising people and organising collective action, international networks of INGOs and NGOs have made meaningful interventions in the international arena, challenging the state's dominance on issues of independence, succession and national identity in countries and territories such as East Timor and Tibet.[57]

East Asia remains a region dominated by traditional security issues, where the state remains the most important political unit, norms of sovereignty and territoriality are ever present, and where the capacity of non-state actors to influence policy making in general has been limited. Nevertheless, CSOs and NGOs with their ongoing connections to other transnational INGO networks will play an increasingly important role in the ongoing formation of an East Asian identity. Evidence suggests that CSOs are gaining capacity and momentum in terms of growth, international support and ability to pursue creative strategies to influence the state and further their particular mission or policy goals. While not yet mature, their future role in advancing East Asian regionalism cannot be ignored.

Notes

1 In this chapter East Asia refers to Northeast Asia, including Japan, China (Hong Kong Special Administrative Region (SAR) and Macau SAR, and Taiwan), South Korea and the Democratic Republic of Korea, and Southeast Asia, including Brunei, Cambodia, Indonesia, Laos, the Philippines, Malaysia, Myanmar, Singapore, Thailand and Vietnam. It excludes Australia, New Zealand and the South Pacific Islands.

2 Muthiah Alagappa, 'Introduction', in Muthiah Alagappa (ed.) *Civil Society and Political Change in Asia: Expanding and Contracting Democratic Space*, Stanford, CA: Stanford University Press, 2004, p. 7.

3 This definition is taken from the concept paper, 'Civil Society and Governance', from the Civil Society and Governance programme at the Institute of Development Studies in Sussex. Online. Available: http://www.ids.ac.uk/ids/civsoc/public.doc.

4 David C. Schak and Wayne Hudson, 'Civil Society in Asia', in Schak and Hudson, *Civil Society in Asia*, p. 2. See also Wayne Hudson, 'Problematizing European Theories of Civil Society', in David C. Schak and Wayne Hudson (eds) *Civil Society in Asia*, Aldershot: Ashgate, 2003, pp. 9–19.

5 David C. Schak and Wayne Hudson, 'Civil Society in Asia'.

6 Muthiah Alagappa, *Civil Society and Political Change in Asia*, p. 5.

7 See, for example, Robert O. Keohane and Joeseph Nye, *Power and Interdependence: World Politics in Transition*, Boston: Little, Brown, 1977; Robert Keohane, *International Institutions and State Power: Essays in International Relations Theory*, Boulder, CO: Westview, 1989.

8 Margaret E. Keck and Kathryn Sikkink, *Activists Beyond Borders – Advocacy Networks in International Politics*, Ithaca, NY: Cornell University Press, 1998, p. 29.

9 For a further discussion of this debate, see Jude Howell, 'Making Civil Society from the Outside – Challenges for Donors', *The European Journal of Development Research*, 2000, vol. 12, no. 1, pp. 3–22.

10 Tadashi Yamamoto, 'Summary Report on the Osaka Symposium on Philanthropic Development and Cooperation in Asia Pacific', in Tadashi Yamamoto (ed.) *Emerging Civil Society in the Asia Pacific Community*, Singapore/Tokyo: Institute of Southeast Asian Studies and Japan Centre for International Exchange, 1995, p. 42.

11 Recent works on these topics include: Lee Hock Guan (ed.), *Civil Society in Southeast Asia*, Copenhagen/Singapore: Nordic Institute of Asian Studies/Institute of Southeast Asian Studies, 2004; David C. Schak and Wayne Hudson (eds), *Civil Society in Asia*; Shinichi Shigetomi (ed.), *The State and NGOs – Perspectives from Asia*, Singapore: Institute of Southeast Asian Studies (ISEAS), 2002; Muthiah Alagappa, *Civil Society and Political Change in Asia*; Alejandro Colás, *International Civil Society*, Cambridge: Polity Press, 2002; Michael Edwards, *Future Positive – International Co-operation in the Twenty-First Century*, revised edn, London: Earthscan, 2004; Margaret E. Keck and Kathryn Sikkink, *Activists Beyond Borders*; Kendall Stiles (ed.), *Global Institutions and Local Empowerment – Competing Theoretical Perspectives*, Basingstoke: Macmillan, 2000; Marlies Glasius, David Lewis and Hakan Seckinelgin, *Exploring Civil Society – Political and Cultural Contexts*, London: Routledge, 2004, particularly the Introduction and Ch. 22.

12 Shinichi Shigetomi, *The State and NGOs*, pp. 4–5.

13 Ibid., p. 22.

14 Research conducted by the Civil Society and Governance Programme at the Institute of Development Studies, University of Sussex. Of the 22 country case studies, three are located in East Asia: China, the Philippines and Thailand. Online. Available: http://www.ids.ac.uk/ids/civsoc/.

15 Manor notes that two widely accepted typologies for understanding why civil society flourishes under some governments and not others are less helpful now than previously. Manor argues that the first is essentially redundant as there has been a move towards centrism, such that since the early 1990s many governments including those with leftist ideology (China, Vietnam) are in practice centrist. The second, while useful in political analysis, he suggests is not as useful in anticipating civil societies' prospects because some democracies operate in a highly centralised and top-down manner. James Manor, 'Civil Society under Different Types of Governments', Online paper, Civil Society and Governance Programme, Institute of Development Studies. Online. Available: http://www.ids.ac.uk/civsoc/PolicyBriefs/policy10.doc.

16 Ibid.

17 Ibid.

18 Manor has plotted China, the Philippines, Laos, Indonesia, South Korea and Vietnam, while the remaining countries are plotted by the author according to the characteristics outlined in Table 9.1.

19 See, for example, Melissa G. Curley, 'NGOs in China: The Role of International Organizations and South-South Cooperation', *Asian Perspective*, 2002, vol. 26, no. 4, pp. 187–90.

20 Alagappa, *Civil Society and Political Change*, p. 13.

21 Ibid.

22 Ben J. Tria Kerkvliet, Russell H. K. Heng and David W. H. Koh, *Getting Organized in Vietnam – Moving in and Around the Socialist State*, Singapore: Institute of Southeast Asian Studies (ISEAS), 2003.

23 Russell Hiang-Khng Heng, 'Civil Society Effectiveness and the Vietnamese State – Despite or Because of the Lack of Autonomy', in Lee Hock Guan (ed.) *Civil Society in Southeast Asia*, p. 159.

24 Exceptions include Kyaw Yin Hlaing, 'Burma: Civil Society Skirting Regime Rules', in Muthiah Alagappa, *Civil Society and Political Change in Asia*. Indeed Lee Hock Guan notes that his edited volume, *Civil Society in Southeast Asia*, lacked papers on Brunei, Cambodia, Laos and Myanmar 'because of lack of success in finding researchers in the region working on those countries'. Lee Hock Guan (ed.), *Civil Society in Southeast Asia*, p. vii.

25 For further discussion of this, see Melissa G. Curley, 'The Role of the Non-profit Sector in Transitional Asian Economies: The Case of Cambodia', Paper presented at the Fifteenth Biennial Conference of the Asian Studies Association of Australia (ASAA), Canberra, July. Online. Available: http://coombs.anu.edu.au/ASAA/conference/proceedings/Curley-M-ASAA2004.pdf.

26 David Zweig, *Internationalizing China: Domestic Interests, Global Linkages*, Ithaca, NY: Cornell University Press, 2002. See particularly Ch. 5.

27 Jie Chen, 'Burgeoning Transnationalism of Taiwan's Social Movement NGOs', *Journal of Contemporary China*, vol. 10, no. 29, pp. 613–44.

28 Jude Howell and Jenny Pearce, *Civil Society and Development – A Critical Exploration*, Boulder, CO: Lynne Rienner, 2002, p. 134.

29 Mary E. Gallagher, 'China: The Limits of Civil Society in a Late Leninist State', in Muthiah Alagappa (ed.) *Civil Society and Political Change in Asia: Expanding and Contracting Democratic Space*, Stanford, CA: Stanford University Press, 2004, pp. 419–54; Tony Saich, 'Negotiating the State: The Development of Social Organizations in China', *China Quarterly*, March 2000, no. 161, pp. 124–41; Nick Young, 'Searching for Civil Society', *250 Chinese NGOs: Civil Society in the Making*, Hong Kong: China Development Brief, 2001. See also their ongoing commentaries. Online. Available: http://www.chinadevel-

opmentbrief.com. Also, Sarah Cook, 'After the Iron Rice Bowl: Extending the Safety Net in China', *IDS Discussion Paper 377*, Sussex: Institute of Development Studies, 2000, p. 23; Baogang He, *The Democratic Implications of Civil Society in China*, London: Macmillan, 1997.

30 Cook notes that for the Chinese government, 'the main contribution of such organizations is their capacity to raise resources – for example through charitable activities, donations, and from the international development community – and to use these funds to provide services which complement or fill gaps in the formal system'. See Cook, 'After the Iron Rice Bowl', p. 23.

31 Howell and Pearce, *Civil Society and Development*, p. 135.

32 Ibid., p. 145.

33 Tony Saich, 'Negotiating the State: The Development of Social Organizations in China'.

34 Ibid., p. 125. This passage is based on a passage from Melissa G. Curley, 'NGOs in China', p. 177.

35 Howell and Pearce, *Civil Society and Development*.

36 Muthiah Alagappa, *Civil Society and Political Change*, p. 10. For figures on International NGOs in East Asia and their focus areas, see Baogang He, 'Transnational Civil Society and the National Identity Question in East Asia', *Global Governance*, 2004, vol. 10, no. 3, pp. 227–46. On the growth of CSOs in Southeast Asia in particular, see Mely Caballero-Anthony, 'Non-state Regional Governance Mechanism for Economic Security: The Case of the ASEAN People's Assembly', *The Pacific Review*, 2004, vol. 17, no. 4, pp. 567–85.

37 'Towards an East Asian Community: Region of Peace, Prosperity and Progress', *East Asian Vision Group Report, 2001*. Online. Available: http://www.mofa.go.jp/region/asia-paci/report2001.pdf.

38 Ibid., p. 24.

39 Alagappa, *Civil Society and Political Change*, p. 8.

40 Ibid., p. 50.

41 This description is based on that forwarded by Howell and Pearce in relation to China, see Howell and Pearce, *Civil Society and Development*, p. 145.

42 Mely Caballero-Anthony, 'Revising Human Security in Southeast Asia', *Asian Perspective*, 2004, vol. 28, no. 3, pp. 155–89.

43 Ibid., p. 167.

44 Council for Security Cooperation in the Asia–Pacific (CSCAP) and ASEAN–Institutes of Strategic and International Studies are both Track II (non-official) dialogue networks active in the discussion of both traditional and non-traditional security issues in the wider Asian region.

45 Mely Caballero-Anthony, 'Revising Human Security in Southeast Asia', p. 181.

46 Ibid., p. 183.

47 Kavi Chongkittavorn, 'Regional Perspective: An Effort to Connect Civil Society in Asia and Europe', *The Nation*, 21 June 2004.

48 Mely Caballero-Anthony, 'Revising Human Security in Southeast Asia', p. 185.

49 Ibid.

50 See Miranda Schreurs' chapter in this volume.

51 'Doing it for Themselves', *Bangkok Post*, 27 June 2005. See also SEARIN website at: http://www.searin.org/Th/Mekong/mek_research_a1_en.htm.

52 See RWESA's website at: http://www.rwesa.org/.

53 Interview with Oxfam US staff, May 2004, Phnom Penh.

54 Baogang He, 'Transnational Civil Society', p. 234.

55 Keck and Sikkink, *Activists beyond Borders*, p. 188.

56 Kavi Chongkittavorn, 'ASEAN gearing up for future challenges', *The Nation*, 9 September 2005.

57 Baogang He, 'Transnational Civil Society'.

10 Problems and prospects for regional environmental cooperation in East Asia

Miranda A. Schreurs

Introduction

In their eagerness to develop, states in East Asia (with the notable exceptions of Japan and Singapore) largely ignored the onset of environmental degradation, domestically as well as internationally. East Asia is a region where, because of widespread poverty, governments and societies have prioritised economic development over environmental protection. This could be expected when it is considered that East Asia was the poorest region in the world until the early 1980s. While there has been considerable wealth already for decades in some regions of East Asia, including in Japan, the Republic of Korea, Hong Kong, and Singapore, poverty was widespread throughout much of the region. From 1981 to 2001, however, more than 500 million people were pulled out of poverty, with progress being particularly extensive in China. During this period, those living in extreme poverty, at levels of US$1 or less per day, in East Asia fell from 58 to 16 per cent.[1]

The primary concern of governments in the developing states of the region has been to develop modern infrastructures and promote industry to bring employment opportunities to society. In this context, environmental protection has been viewed as a luxury that the region cannot afford. There are, however, many signs that these views, while still dominant, are being modified as the region experiences successful economic development. Governments, industry, and the public increasingly are becoming aware of the need to act to protect natural areas and to reduce pollution.[2] There is also a growing recognition that unless environmental protection measures are taken, pollution and resource depletion will create what a Chinese governmental official described as 'a bottleneck' that will hamper economic development.[3]

To the extent that environmental awareness is growing in the developing states of East Asia, it is still mostly in relation to local pollution and conservation issues. At the same time, however, there are signs of a growing concern with national, transboundary, and global environmental problems. The states of East Asia are being pushed by a variety of factors towards greater regional cooperation for environmental protection. These include the growing scale of environmental threats and the adverse impact they are having on the region's economy and quality of life; growing public concern with pollution and natural resource depletion; a greater political awareness that environmental degradation is a barrier to economic development; the influence of international norms and examples; the interventions of international and bilateral institutions and donors; and the efforts of non-governmental organisations (many of which are newly formed), academics, environmental institutions, and governmental bureaucrats to enhance the priority of environmental issues on domestic and regional political agendas.

Promoting regional environmental cooperation, however, is complicated by the many capacity shortfalls that plague the region. Despite the rapid economic development of the past two decades, environmental administrative capacity in much of the region remains weak. Environment ministries and agencies tend to be understaffed and underfunded. There is a lack of adequate environmental data. Monitoring of the environmental performance of firms and government agencies remains patchy. There are many environmental laws, often modelled on examples from more developed countries, but enforcement of these laws remains a challenge due to financial limitations at the local level, lack of data, and corruption, among other problems. Environmental groups are growing in number but remain small in scale and financially very weak. There are still few environmental engineers and conservation and pollution experts. Improving the potential for regional environmental cooperation in many cases means first addressing the multitude of capacity problems that exist at the local level.

There are also problems that stem from the unwillingness of many governments in the region to pool their sovereignty in regional environmental institutions in the way that has been done by the members of the European Union. As a result, despite greater regional awareness of the need for joint problem solving, there are still relatively few multilateral environmental agreements in East Asia.

This chapter examines several of the factors that are pressuring the states of East Asia to work together to address transboundary environmental problems. It considers the forms that environmental cooperation is taking and the efforts that are being made to address capacity problems. Environmental cooperation is examined as it is occurring among different groups and at different levels: within Southeast Asia, within Northeast Asia, across Northeast and Southeast Asia, and within the context of global environmental agreements. The chapter concludes by considering differences in the extent to which multilateral approaches are being embraced in Southeast and Northeast Asia and what the potential is for deeper environmental cooperation at the regional level in East Asia.

Environmental challenges in East Asia

East Asia is challenged by widespread pollution and environmental resource depletion problems. Here a very brief introduction to some of the environmental challenges affecting the region is provided. Population pressures in East Asia are enormous. China alone has a population of approximately 1.3 billion in 2005 (compared with about 540 million in 1949). Indonesia's population is over 213 million.[4] Large populations place great strain on natural resources. Economic growth rates in several states of the region, moreover, are among the highest in the world. With rapid economic growth, there are rising demands for energy, natural resources, and food. China, for example, is now the world's third largest market for automobiles.[5]

Rapid urbanisation, population growth, industrialisation, and growing consumption have combined to create truly serious pollution problems for the region. Few of East Asia's many large urban areas meet World Health Organisation (WHO) standards for air and water quality. China's State Environmental Protection Agency (SEPA), for instance, found that 63.5 per cent of 338 cities that it monitored for air quality suffered from medium to serious air pollution. The Chinese Institute of Environmental Science and researchers at Qinghua University have estimated that acid rain causes yearly losses in China estimated at 110 billion yuan (US$13.3 billion). Conservative estimates are that atmospheric pollution causes losses equivalent to 2 to 3 per cent of China's gross domestic product (GDP).[6] Similar problems plague other rapidly developing countries in Southeast Asia.

Pollution and excessive resource exploitation (in part a problem of large populations rather than of large per capita consumption) are taking a toll on East Asia's natural environment. Over-fishing and pollution have led to a loss of fish stocks in regional seas and have contributed to growing competition and, at times, conflict among regional fishing fleets.[7] Desertification is resulting in increasingly severe sand and dust storms in Northeast Asia causing problems not only for local communities, but more distant urban areas, including Beijing and Seoul.[8] Logging – both legal and illegal – has resulted in rapid depletion of the region's biologically rich tropical forests. Indonesia, which accounts for approximately one-tenth of the world's remaining tropical forests, was losing an estimated 1 per cent of its forests per year by the mid-1990s. While the country has put a little over one-fifth of its forests under protection, an estimated half of its remaining forests are considered to be under threat.[9] Conservation International's *Hotspots Revisited*, an updated analysis of the world's biologically rich hotspots (areas where biological diversity is among the highest in the world but loss of original habitat has already exceeded 70 per cent), includes many parts of Asia. The 2005 publication includes, as biological hotspots, the Philippine archipelago, the Japanese archipelago, Fiji, Polynesia and Micronesia, the East Melanesian Islands (Papua New Guinea, the Solomon Islands, Vanuatu), and the mountains of Southwest China.[10] Other areas throughout East Asia are at risk of being added to the list.

The Mekong River is one of the world's most sediment-rich and biodiverse river systems. This river system supports over 50 million people and stretches from Tibet, through China, along the Laotian, Myanmar, and Thai borders, through Cambodia, and into Vietnam. Yet, development of hydropower dams, diversion of water for irrigation purposes, salinisation, and pollution threaten the river's sensitive ecology. Trade in wildlife products, illegal poaching, logging, and human encroachment, moreover, threaten the region's many endangered species.[11] On a larger scale, the entire South China Seas region is threatened by pollution from land-based sources, oil spills, over-fishing, and extensive damage to mangroves and coral reefs, both of which are critical to maintaining healthy marine ecosystems.

While some of these problems are local or national in scale and impact, many of them are problems that have transnational characteristics. Trade in endangered species, for example, links importers with suppliers (including poachers). Demand in China for endangered species parts – for use in Chinese traditional medicines or as aphrodisiacs – is contributing to the poaching of tigers, rhinos, elephants, seals, bears, and other species not only in China but also in Vietnam, Laos, Cambodia, Thailand, Indonesia, and Myanmar.[12]

Slash and burn agricultural practices and the deliberate setting of fires to clear land for large plantation companies in Indonesia and other heavily forested areas has become a transnational issue because of the thick and dangerous haze caused by the burning. During dry spells, the fires have spread out of control and become so extensive that the smoke and soot produced travel for hundreds and even thousands of kilometres to neighbouring countries and regions. During the particularly serious forest fires in 1997 and 1998 over 6.5 million hectares were affected in Kalimantan (part of Borneo). These fires destroyed not only lowland forests, but also many animal species, including orang-utans. The fires also contributed to global carbon emissions and caused health problems for individuals as far away as Singapore and Malaysia.[13]

This is but a small sampling of the numerous environmental problems with transnational characteristics that are afflicting East Asia. Pollution and resource degradation are at or near crisis levels in many parts of both Northeast and Southeast Asia and, unless addressed, will have increasingly adverse impacts on human health, ecological systems, and economic activities.

Emerging environmental cooperation in East Asia

One of the more encouraging developments in East Asia in recent years has been the proliferation of cooperative efforts to address pollution, resource degradation, and health problems at the international/regional level. This is occurring at the bilateral and multilateral levels, and at the national and subnational levels, through international environmental agreements and through regional bodies – most notably the Association of Southeast Asian Nations (ASEAN). While some multilateral programmatic efforts already existed in Southeast Asia in the 1970s and the 1980s, their scale was limited. Since the early 1990s, however, governments in Southeast Asia have begun to pay more attention to environmental protection at both the national and international levels. There are also numerous indications that the governments in Northeast Asia are recognising the need to cooperate on environmental protection. In addition, region-wide initiatives for pollution control and conservation are becoming more common.

Bilateral environmental cooperation

There are a growing number of bilateral environmental cooperation agreements throughout East Asia. Most have been initiated by environment ministries that are either eager to share their own expertise with developing country counterparts or eager to create partnerships as a way of strengthening their own information base, to acquire information on best practices. Bilateral environmental cooperation can be a way to strengthen the momentum behind environmental policy change and to pressure governments to take action on specific policy matters. There are now dozens of bilateral cooperation agreements linking environment ministries throughout the region. For example, environment ministries launched the Indonesia–Singapore Environment Partnership in November 2002, with the idea of enhancing technical cooperation between the two nations. The partnership is supported by a Joint Working Group that has as its mandate developing joint programmes in such fields as air and water pollution, haze control, solid and hazardous waste management, and environmental education.[14] Similarly, in 2004 a Memorandum of Understanding on Environmental Cooperation was signed between China's SEPA and the Singapore Ministry of the Environment.[15] Bilateral cooperation agreements are now widespread between Northeast Asian countries as well.

Environmental cooperation through ASEAN

Importantly, cooperation is also moving beyond the bilateral to the multilateral level. Developments have been most pronounced in relation to ASEAN. ASEAN was established in 1967 on the model of the European Economic Community by five countries that had experienced years of conflict and tension among themselves: Thailand, Malaysia, Indonesia, the Philippines, and Singapore. Much as was the case with the European Economic Community, the initial goal of ASEAN was to promote peace and stability among historic rivals at a time when the Vietnam War was destabilising the region and there were fears that great power rivalries would spill over into other parts of Southeast Asia, as was already being witnessed in Laos and Cambodia. In many ways, given the historical situation, ASEAN's formation was a remarkable feat.

ASEAN expanded slowly in terms of both numbers of member states and policy reach. This was largely because of the unstable situation on the Indochina peninsula, the large shadow cast by China, and the lack of any strong champions of deeper integration for the region. The initial membership of five expanded to six when Brunei Darussalam joined in 1984. It was not until the latter half of the 1990s, however, that Vietnam (1995), Laos and Myanmar (1997), and Cambodia (1999) became members, bringing the membership of ASEAN to its current 10.

As was the case in Europe's early integration, ASEAN's initial focus was almost exclusively on economic cooperation and the eventual establishment of a common market. As economic cooperation deepened among ASEAN member states, slowly other social and environmental issues began to creep onto the agenda. The United Nations (UN) played an important stimulating role in this process. It was largely at the urging of the United Nations Environment Programme (UNEP) that ASEAN established a Sub-Regional Environmental Programme in 1977 and the following year introduced the first of what was to become a series of five-year environmental programmes that spell out broad environmental goals and philosophies.

In the 1980s ASEAN issued several environmental declarations, including the Manila Declaration on the ASEAN Environment (1981), which led to the establishment of a committee on the environment and called for cooperation on raising environmental awareness in the region;[16] the ASEAN Declaration on Heritage Parks and Reserves (1984) that created a list of sites in the region that would be recognised as special heritage parks and reserves;[17] and the Jakarta Resolution on Sustainable Development (1987) calling for regional cooperation in protection of the seas and tropical forests and addressing land-based pollution, air pollution, and urban pollution. Interestingly, this resolution also called for action and cooperation not only among member states, but also among governmental, business, professional, academic, and non-governmental organisation actors.[18] In addition, an Agreement on Conservation of Nature and Natural Resources (1985), which called on member states to develop national conservation strategies and plans for the protection of biological diversity and to introduce environmental impact assessments, was drawn up, but it has to date only received three ratifications and thus has not come into force.[19]

These declarations represented an important step forward in Southeast Asia's recognition of transnational and regional environmental matters and in the development of common goals and priorities for action. They have been limited in their effectiveness, however, as they tend to be simply goal statements that are difficult to enforce in the absence of a requirement that these goals be transposed into national regulations. There is, moreover, no means to ensure national compliance with the goals outlined in these agreements.

ASEAN's environmental activities picked up noticeably in response to the United Nations Conference on Environment and Development in 1992 and especially in response to the haze problems caused by wide-scale slash and burn agriculture in Indonesia, a problem that gained international attention in 1997 and 1998 when the fires burned out of control.

In 1994, ASEAN environment ministers concurred on the need to develop minimum standards for ambient air and river water quality and subsequently set up an Urban Air Pollution Monitoring and Control Programme. In 1995 a Cooperation Plan on Transboundary Pollution targeting atmospheric pollution, ship-borne pollution, and hazardous waste was formed. This was followed by the establishment of a Regional Haze Task Force, a Regional Haze Action Plan

(1997), and the ASEAN Agreement on Transboundary Haze Pollution (2002).[20] The last agreement entered into force in November 2003 after receiving the sixth instrument of ratification from the government of Thailand. The establishment of the Agreement on Transboundary Haze Pollution marks the first such agreement in the world and has led to the formation of regular Conferences of the Parties to the agreement and the formation of an ASEAN Coordination Centre for Transboundary Haze Pollution. The agreement could serve as a model for other transboundary environmental problems affecting the region.

There are clearly growing efforts within ASEAN to institutionalise regional environmental cooperation, enhance cooperative monitoring, and promote region-wide sustainable development. In 1997, ASEAN's first State of the Environment Report was introduced and in 1999 the ASEAN Regional Centre for Biodiversity Conservation was formed. ASEAN's Strategic Plan of Action for the Environment, 1998–2004, included several measures intended to promote cooperation related to monitoring, reporting, and controlling transboundary pollution related to forest fires; strengthening biodiversity conservation initiatives; and harmonising environmental databases. It also initiated a regional plan for marine environmental protection. Efforts to expand environmental awareness have been fostered through the 2000–2005 ASEAN Environmental Education Action Plan.

ASEAN also has formulated a draft Framework Agreement on Access to Genetic Resources (but has yet to reach agreement on a final document), revised its Declaration on Heritage Parks (that now extends to all 10 member countries), and adopted a framework for Environmentally Sustainable Cities and a Long-Term Action Plan for Water Resources Management. The ASEAN Environment Ministers 2003 Yangon Resolution on Sustainable Development specifically mentions the need to develop a plan of action 'to harmonise environmental policies, legislation, regulations, standards and databases' and consider the development of an ASEAN Environment Fund.[21]

ASEAN's environmental activities have attracted the attention of international organisations and bilateral donors. There are now efforts underway to enhance international environmental dialogues and develop cooperative projects among ASEAN member states in partnership with Australia, China, the European Union, Japan, South Korea, New Zealand, and the United States. One interesting example of this in the biodiversity area is the formation in 1999 of the Philippines-based ASEAN Regional Centre for Biodiversity Conservation (ARCBC), a regional network of national biodiversity institutions that with the support of the European Commission promotes information exchange, research, awareness raising, and human capacity development related to biodiversity in ASEAN member states.[22]

Environmental cooperation in ASEAN is still primarily intergovernmental. There are no bodies equivalent to the European Environment Agency, the European Parliament, the European Court of Justice, or the Directorate-General for the Environment within the European Commission, which have played crucial roles in environmental information dissemination, agenda setting, and enforcement within the European context.

In ASEAN's case, environmental cooperation remains a matter of negotiation and consensus building among member states. This is done largely through regular ASEAN Ministerial Meetings on the Environment, meetings of Senior Officials on the Environment, and working groups on specific issues: nature conservation and biodiversity, the coastal and marine environment, and multilateral environmental agreements. ASEAN Environment Ministers began meeting on a formal basis every three years beginning in 1981 and informally on an annual basis between these meetings beginning in 1994. The ninth informal meeting, held on 27 September 2005, saw the adoption of an ASEAN Strategic Plan on Water Resources and the issuance of a Joint Communiqué on Transboundary Haze Pollution.[23]

The first ASEAN+3 (Japan, China, and Korea) Environment Ministers Meeting was held in November 2002.[24] These meetings have been an opportunity for environment ministers, who are typically relatively weak within their own national systems, to build alliances with their counterparts in other countries, raise awareness of environmental matters, work together to promote common concerns, share knowledge about environmental best practices, and elevate environmental matters on national agendas. The addition of Japan, Korea, and China to these meetings is expected to lead to greater exchange of information and know-how related to environmental management. At the third meeting, in October 2004, the ASEAN Environment Ministers discussed implementation of the ASEAN Agreement on Transboundary Haze Pollution, the creation of the next medium-term environmental action plan for the region (the Vientiane Action Programme), and proposals to support environmentally sustainable cities within ASEAN.[25] The annual meeting of ASEAN Senior Officials on the Environment, who are responsible for working out concrete action plans, was expanded for the first time to be an ASEAN+3 meeting in 2004.

All of these developments suggest that multilateral environmental protection initiatives have taken a significant step forward as a result of ASEAN. Still, it is important to recognise that there remain many barriers to deeper cooperation, the most significant of which has been the lack of willingness of member states to pool their sovereignty in ASEAN institutions. The 'ASEAN Way' is premised on voluntary cooperation and informal procedures. This is in contrast with the European Union's establishment of agreements with the force of law and use of qualified majority voting, which can require member states to adopt environmental regulations that a weighted majority of states vote for. The 'ASEAN Way' has promoted consensus but also has limited the effectiveness of regional environmental protection efforts given that there is really no mechanism to enforce a change of behaviour on a state that does not itself choose to cooperate. A lack of enforcement agencies and tools restricts what ASEAN as a whole can really demand of its member states in terms of environmental change. Nevertheless, despite these still significant barriers to greater and deeper regional environmental integration, there are many indications that in the coming years ASEAN will adopt more international environmental agreements and work towards greater harmonisation of national environmental standards.

Movements towards greater regional cooperation in Northeast Asia

Northeast Asia has considerably less experience with regional humanitarian and environmental cooperation than Southeast Asia. This is largely a result of the region's long history of colonisation, warfare, and territorial disputes that has made the building of regional networks and programmes difficult.

In comparison with the politics of accommodation and cooperation that took root among Europe's largest economies – France, Germany, and Britain – in the decades following World War II, unresolved territorial questions and ideological differences left relations among Asia's largest economies cold and tense. Diplomatic relations were normalised between Japan and South Korea in 1965 and Japan and China in 1972, but between South Korea and Russia only in 1991 and between South Korea and China only in 1992. Amazingly, Japan and Russia have yet to sign a peace treaty formally ending World War II because of their dispute over the ownership of the four Northern Territory islands (Kurile Islands) seized by Russia in the closing days of the war. The Korean peninsula, moreover, remains one of the most heavily fortified in the world. In this context, it has been difficult to foster a sense of regionalism. Nevertheless, there have been encouraging developments to suggest that at least some degree of regional cooperation is not only possible, but inevitable.

Environmental cooperation in Northeast Asia is largely a product of the 1990s. The first official meeting of Senior Officials on the Environment in the Northeast Asian region was held in Seoul in 1993 following upon the 1992 United Nations Conference on Environment and Development. At this meeting, it was agreed that a Northeast Asian Subregional Programme on Environmental Cooperation (NEASPEC) should be established under the auspices of the United Nations Economic and Social Commission for Asia and the Pacific. Three areas of activity were initially agreed upon: energy and pollution control, managing deforestation and desertification, and capacity building. Since its formation, NEASPEC has broadened the range of activities it is involved in. It has established an environmental trust fund; engaged in numerous pollution reduction, nature conservation, and energy efficiency projects; and set up a Regional Training Centre for Reducing Pollution from Coal-Fired Power Plants, a Regional Network for Trans-boundary Environmental Monitoring, and a Northeast Asia Center for Environmental Data and Training.[26] The 10th meeting of senior officials on NEASPEC was held in Okinawa, Japan, in 2004.

In 1988, at Korea's suggestion, Japan and Korea began holding annual environmental symposia. With the cooperation of UNEP, in 1992 these meetings were reorganised as the Northeast Asian Conference on Environmental Cooperation (NEACEC). NEACEC brings together environmental officials, local government officials, environmental experts, and some non-governmental organisations from Korea, Japan, China, Mongolia, and Russia along with UNEP officials to meet and discuss regional environmental matters. These meetings serve largely as a forum for the exchange of information and ideas about regional and international environmental problems and policy solutions.

Following the example of ASEAN, annual Tripartite Environmental Ministers Meetings (TEMM) were initiated in January 1999 also at the urging of the government of Korea. TEMM brings together the environment ministers of China, Japan, and South Korea to encourage greater cooperation among them in sustainable development. TEMM held its sixth meeting in December 2004. At this meeting, the three ministers agreed to: promote the work of the Acid Deposition Monitoring Network in East Asia (EANET) and joint research on Long-range Trans-boundary Air Pollution (LTP); to expand habitat networks based on the Asia–Pacific Migratory Waterbird Conservation Strategy; to consider launching an expert network to consider technical issues related to dust and sandstorms (in collaboration with Mongolia); to consider the development of a joint environmental research institute among China, Korea, and Japan; and to promote the development of circular economies that are based on reduction, reuse, and recycling of materials.[27] TEMM has been important because it has forced environment ministers to consider regional environmental cooperation issues on an annual basis.

Most of the government-to-government meetings of environment ministers and senior environment officials in Northeast Asia have led to joint goal statements and/or the introduction of specific pollution-control programmes, nature conservation projects, capacity-building initiatives, or data-sharing agreements. There have been few formal international environmental agreements that have resulted from these gatherings. Nevertheless, that regional environmental issues are now considered important enough to justify annual environment ministerial conferences and more frequent meetings of senior environmental officials is a big step. Over time, the meetings appear to be producing more substantive results in the form of more significant projects and multilateral initiatives.

Broader East Asian environmental cooperation

There are now also broader regional environmental cooperation efforts, such as the Environmental Congress for Asia and the Pacific (ECOASIA), which brings together environmental officials and experts from 22 Asia–Pacific region countries to share information on environmental matters. ECOASIA members have jointly produced ECOASIA NET (Environmental Information Network for Asia and the Pacific), a database of environmental information for all member countries with the idea that making such information available online will promote sustainable development.[28] Another significant regional network that spans much of the region is the Acid Deposition Monitoring Network in East Asia (EANET). EANET has as its goals the modelling and monitoring of acid rainfall throughout

East Asia and working towards the reduction of sulphur dioxide emissions.[29] Perhaps most importantly, as briefly discussed above, through the ASEAN+3 process, environmental cooperation is beginning to take on a broader East Asian dimension as well.

Multilateral cooperation at the subnational level

Interestingly, bilateral and multilateral cooperation is not occurring simply at the national level. There are a growing number of cities and prefectures that are creating linkages with their counterparts in other Asian countries. For example, Kitakyushu, Japan, which had a notorious reputation as a highly polluted industrial area but now is known as a leader in industrial pollution control, has made the export of pollution control know-how to developing countries a major part of its revitalised image and has won international awards for its efforts. Kitakyushu's experiences with pollution control and movement towards a zero-emission society became the model for the United Nations Economic and Social Commission for Asia and the Pacific (UNESCAP)'s 'Kitakyushu Initiative for a Clean Environment', a project designed to promote regional cooperation among cities for environmental clean-up. Kitakyushu initiated two regional networks of urban communities, the Environmental Cooperation Network of Asian Cities, which involves seven cities from four Southeast Asian nations, and the 'East Asia (Pan-Yellow Sea) City Conference', involving 10 cities in East Asia to promote sustainable urban development.[30]

Recognising the potential that such exchanges hold for sharing pollution control and environmental protection knowledge among local officials, and even of creating a sense of competition among them, there are a growing number of international programmes fostering regional urban environmental cooperation. These include the WHO's Healthy Cities Programme, the United Nations Centre for Human Settlements, UNEP's Sustainable Cities Programme, and the United Nations Urban Management Programme, to name just a few.[31] In 2000 UNEP, the WHO, the Korea Environment Institute, and the Stockholm Environment Institute developed the Air Pollution in the Megacities of Asia Project. Noting that air pollution contributes to 20–30 per cent of all respiratory diseases, the project focuses on addressing urban air pollution in 22 Asian cities and is funded by the Korea Ministry of the Environment and the Swedish International Cooperation Agency. The project seeks to promote the collation of emissions data; a review of existing goals, policies, and strategies; development of best practices in urban air pollution management from selected European cities; development of recommendations for an urban area regional action plan; and promotion of regional cooperation in air pollution management.[32] Various bilateral programmes have been initiated as well. The Canadian International Development Agency and the Asian Institute of Technology, for instance, entered into a five-year agreement beginning in 2003 to improve urban environmental management policies and practices in the region through the Southeast

Asia Urban Environmental Management Applications (SEAUEMA) Project. The programme includes fellowships for graduate training in urban environmental management at the Asian Institute of Technology and funding for joint action research projects that address water and sanitation, solid waste, and air pollution.[33]

Given the impact that international transfer of best practices can have on improving environmental performance, cooperation at the urban level is important. Moreover, since already over half of the region's population lives in urban areas, the clean-up of urban environments should be a regional priority.

Capacity building for regional cooperation: the role of the UN

Without the key role played by the UN and its specific programmes, most importantly UNEP and the United Nations Development Programme (UNDP), it is doubtful that environmental cooperation would have progressed to the point where it is today in East Asia.[34] Using experiences it gained from developing cooperative environmental programmes and agreements in other parts of the world, the UN has helped launch numerous multilateral initiatives in East Asia. In the late 1970s, it was UNEP that persuaded ASEAN to develop an East Asian Seas Environment Action Plan, along the lines of UNEP's other Regional Seas Programmes. The plan was agreed upon in 1981 and a Coordinating Body on the Seas of East Asia (COBSEA) was set up as the decision-making body responsible for the implementation of the plan. COBSEA expanded beyond its original ASEAN membership of Indonesia, Malaysia, the Philippines, Thailand, and Singapore to include Cambodia, China, Australia, South Korea, and Vietnam in 1994. It now encompasses all the littoral states of the South China Seas. In 2002, UNEP and the Global Environment Facility (GEF) together launched a five-year multi-million-dollar initiative that includes over 400 institutions and 45 implementing agencies from the seven countries bordering the South China Sea and that has as its main goal fostering capacity building and collaborative environmental management in the South China Sea.[35]

Complementing these efforts, the UNDP together with the GEF and the International Maritime Organisation (IMO) initiated a five-year project, Partnerships in Environmental Management for the Seas of East Asia (PEMSEA), in 1999 after an earlier pilot project. The idea of the project is to demonstrate integrated approaches to coastal area management at sites in geographical areas in Brunei Darussalam, Cambodia, China, Indonesia, Malaysia, North Korea, the Philippines, Singapore, South Korea, Thailand, and Vietnam.

The UN also has worked to promote greater regional cooperation in Northeast Asia, although its efforts did not take root as quickly there due to geopolitical factors. In 1994, at the urging of UNEP's Regional Seas Programme, Japan, Russia, China, North Korea, and South Korea established the Northwest Pacific Action Plan (NOWPAP) for the Protection, Management and Development of the Marine and Coastal Environment of the Northwest Pacific Region. At the fourth NOWPAP Inter-governmental Meeting agreement was reached on the establishment of a Pollution Monitoring Regional Activity Centre, which is now located in the Pacific Geography Institute of the Far Eastern Branch of the Russian Academy of Sciences.[36]

Civil society initiatives

As also noted in the previous chapter, civil society is playing an increasingly important role in fostering regional cooperation as well. Critical to this process has been the 'political opening' of many countries in the region. South Korea, Russia, the Philippines, Indonesia, Thailand, Singapore, and Malaysia have all experienced some form of democratisation in the past 15 years, even if it is premature to suggest that there has been democratic consolidation in all of them. Others, such as China, Vietnam, Cambodia, and Laos, are permitting some international and local humanitarian aid and environmental group activities. Indeed, the 1990s and 2000s have seen something of an explosion in civil society activism in Northeast and Southeast Asia and this has contributed to environmental policy change domestically and efforts to promote regional cooperation regionally.[37]

In the more authoritarian states of the region there are still many restrictions on the permissible activities of environmental and humanitarian groups, where stepping over the line can mean having your office shut down or, worse, being sent to prison.[38] To the extent that environmental groups are perceived by the government as beneficial as a result of their efforts to raise environmental awareness in the public or implement projects that are in line with government goals, their activities tend to be tolerated and even encouraged.[39] Environment ministries are also increasingly recognising that environmental groups can be an important constituency for them as such groups can help provide public support behind goals that environment agencies/ministries themselves share.

Cooperation among local environmental groups

There are a growing number of cooperative initiatives among local environmental groups. In some cases, the efforts are among a group of domestic NGOs that have tried to strengthen their voice in domestic debates related to regional environmental matters by speaking in a single voice. An example of this was the effort made in 1995 by a group of 30 local environmental NGOs and institutes in Thailand to get the Thai government to reconsider its support of dam-building projects on the Mekong River Delta. These NGOs jointly presented a statement to their government that expressed their concern about the influence that dam-building interests were having in the development of the agreement for Cooperation on the Sustainable Development of the Mekong River Delta among the governments of Cambodia, Laos, Thailand, and Vietnam. They argued that the hydropower dams and water-diversion projects that were being supported by the Thai government would be ecologically destructive and would harm local communities.[40] Their efforts failed to prevent the Thai government's support of dam and water-diversion projects; nevertheless, their efforts have contributed to a growing awareness of the need to consider the ecological implications of development in the Mekong River Delta.

It is noteworthy that a similar, environmental NGO campaign that was extensively reported on by the media preceded (it is not possible to say definitively that it caused) Chinese Prime Minister Wen Jiabao's decision to suspend the building of a series of dams on the Nu River, including in the three parallel Rivers Area (a UNESCO World Heritage Site) pending further investigation. Environment activist, Yu Xiaogong, the founder and director of the Chinese NGO Green Watershed was awarded the Goldman Environment Prize for his efforts to protect the Nu River. International networks formed to protect the damming of the Nu River as well. The Southeast Asia Rivers Information Network publicly criticised the project and the Thai director of the Rivers Network submitted a protest letter that was endorsed by 82 environmental, community development, and human rights organisations in Thailand and Myanmar. Friends of Nature and Green Volunteers, both groups operating in Beijing, were then invited by their Thai counterparts to join the campaign. They won the support of some sympathetic journalists who found a way to release information about the dam project and its destructive potential through television and a website.[41]

In other cases, activists have established alliances with their counterparts in other countries, recognising that they may be able to have more impact on governments in this way than they can in pursuing their causes alone. A good example of this would be the June 2004 meeting of Buddhist nuns and monks from Cambodia, Laos, Thailand, and Myanmar who came together to share their experiences in promoting sustainable development and forestry protection in their own communities. This meeting, which was described as something that would have been 'unimaginable' five years earlier, led to a proposal to establish a Southeast Asian Monks' Federation for the Environment.[42]

Another example is the initiative by South Korean and Chinese environmental NGOs to establish new networks. In November 2000, Chinese environmental activists from Green Yanji, Greenpeace China, Green Plateau Institute, Siberia Tiger Forest Park, Dongbei University of Finance and Economics, and the Tibetan Antelope Conservation Project were invited to South Korea by Green Korea United to learn about how the environmental movement functions in South Korea. The groups adopted a joint agreement on mutual cooperation and participated together in the anti-SEMANGUM reclamation rally. Because of this meeting, individual groups agreed to establish some joint campaigns. Green Korea United and Green Yanji, for example, decided to work together on a campaign to protect the Tomen River and Mount Paekdu, which lie on the North Korean–Chinese border, from pollution.[43]

Meetings are happening on larger scales as well. Large numbers of advocates of animal welfare and conservation from around the Asian region met in Singapore in June 2004 for the biannual Asia for Animals Conference. At this conference issues ranging from zoo treatment of animals to animal welfare issues and trade in wildlife were discussed.[44] Another case of multilateral environmental NGO cooperation is represented by the First Asian Anti-Incineration Alliance Meeting (Founding Conference of Waste Not Asia), bringing together 36 environmentalists from China (Hong Kong), Japan, Korea, Malaysia, Thailand, Taiwan, the Philippines, India, Nepal, Pakistan, and Guam, held in Thailand in 2000. This newly founded international NGO grouping opposes waste incineration and instead supports waste reduction and material recycling.[45]

Linkages between international environmental NGOs and local environmental groups

Many of the groups operating in both Northeast and Southeast Asia are branches of international NGOs. These groups have come to play an indispensable role in environmental and health education, environmental awareness raising, environmental monitoring, and policy implementation. In Vietnam, for example, CARE International has received the Vietnamese government's agreement to promote health education related to HIV/AIDS and the spread of the avian influenza virus, and to engage in small economic development projects on improving sanitation and access to safe drinking water. The UNDP has established an office in Vietnam that includes among its goals the promotion of sustainable development and achieving the Millennium Development goals of reducing poverty and improving access to safe drinking water.[46] Both WWF and IUCN (The World Conservation Union) began work on capacity building and nature conservation in Vietnam in the mid-1980s and helped the country to produce its first National Conservation Strategy. The WWF helped the Vietnamese government to produce a biodiversity action plan in 1995. Operations were extended to Cambodia in 1993 and Laos in 1997 and an Indochina Ecoregion Programme was established in an effort to work both locally with villagers and nationally and transnationally with the governments of Vietnam, Cambodia, and Laos on conservation efforts in two of the richest ecosystems in the world: the Greater Annamites and the Central Indochina Dry Forests.[47]

International environmental NGOs and institutions have opened offices throughout East Asia. Their role has been critical in a number of respects. They bring expertise, financial backing, and a degree of international legitimacy to the environmental protection cause in a region that has until recently paid but scant attention to pollution problems. They have also helped to train local staff, foster international linkages, and provide funding for specific projects. The explosion of groups in the region has been quite astounding.

The IUCN now has country programmes in Bangladesh, Cambodia, China, Laos, Nepal, Pakistan, Sri Lanka, Thailand, and Vietnam. Greenpeace moved into Asia starting with an office in Japan in 1989 and then in China in 1997. Greenpeace Southeast Asia was officially launched in 2000 and offices were set up in Thailand and the Philippines. Greenpeace is focusing its efforts on biological diversity conservation and climate change.[48] The International Rivers Network has been a key proponent of regional cooperation for protection of the Mekong Basin.[49] It helped set up the Rivers Watch East and Southeast Asia, which now links about 25 groups in East and Southeast Asia that are working to prevent projects that are destructive to river ecosystems.[50] The Woodrow Wilson International Center's Environmental Change and Security Project's China Environment Forum has worked actively to help NGOs in China, Taiwan, and Hong Kong to develop stronger networks through their Initiative on Cross-Straits Environmental Cooperation.[51] In Yunnan province the International Fund for Animal Welfare (China) is working with local communities to protect endangered species (and in particular, the Asian elephant) from extinction due to development, human encroachment into wildlife areas, and poaching.[52] The fund's efforts are of interest to the provincial government of Yunnan as well as to Beijing as it aids the state in fulfilling its obligations under the Convention on International Trade in Endangered Species (CITES) and at the same time encourages conservation, which will be critical if ecotourism is to take off in the region.

The international NGO community has played a very significant role in capacity-building efforts in the region. This is not to say that their efforts are always accepted by local NGOs, which sometimes complain of a type of neocolonialism by wealthy Western NGOs with their own goals and priorities that are not always in tune with local needs and perspectives or which may hire too many of their own researchers rather than have local staff undertake the work. Governments in the region also have the ability to prevent international NGOs from obtaining permission to establish offices if they prove to be too radical. Nevertheless, on the whole, the international NGO community has played a very important role as a catalyst for greater local and regional environmental protection activities and their presence has generally been accepted and welcomed.

International environmental agreements and regional environmental cooperation

Significantly, participation in international environmental agreements among East Asian countries is relatively high. As of February 2005, all ASEAN countries had ratified the Montreal Protocol on Substances that Deplete the Ozone Layer, only Singapore and Brunei had not ratified the Kyoto Protocol to the Framework Convention on Climate Change, and only Brunei had not joined the Convention on Biological Diversity. China, Japan, Mongolia, South Korea, and Russia have also all ratified these agreements.[53] North Korea has become a party to the Biodiversity Convention and the Montreal Protocol but is not a signatory to the Kyoto Protocol.

As a result of these international environmental agreements various regional programmes for the elimination of ozone-depleting substances, climate change impact studies and greenhouse gas mitigation, and biodiversity conservation have sprung up in the region. Some of the programmes are outgrowths of the agreements themselves. Others are at the initiative of international environmental groups, the international scientific community, or regional economic bodies. Still others are at the initiative of local groups and institutions that are eager to improve regional environmental, health, and safety conditions.

Global climate change

A good example of regional programme development can be seen in the case of climate change. East Asia's large populations and relatively rapid economic development have combined to make the region a major contributor of greenhouse gases. China is already the world's second largest producer of greenhouse gases and, if economic development continues apace, then sometime in the next few decades China will surpass the United States as the world's largest emitter. Russia is now the world's third largest source of greenhouse gas, and over the course of the 1990s India moved up to take fourth position, surpassing Japan, which now ranks fifth. South Korea is the world's tenth largest energy-consuming nation. This means that four of the world's top ten greenhouse gas-emitting nations are in Asia, and then five if Russia is included. Moreover, in many Asian states emissions are rapidly increasing. Between 1980 and 2000, South Korea's energy-related carbon dioxide emissions increased by 231.4 per cent (compared with 22.5 per cent during this same time frame for the United States).[54] This means that as nations gear up to begin thinking about what happens after the Kyoto Protocol's first commitment period of 2012 ends, Asia will be a major focus of attention.

The climate change negotiations have led to a variety of transnational initiatives in East Asia. Some are focused on improving scientific understanding of climate change impacts and building scientific capacity in the region. The Global Change Impacts Center for Southeast Asia, a core project of the International Geosphere–Biosphere Programme (IGBP) – itself an outgrowth of the international climate change negotiations – for instance, set up an Impacts Center Southeast Asia (ICSEA) in 1995. The idea behind ICSEA is that it is important to foster local scientific capacity related to climate change impacts and to enhance regional scientific cooperation related to the impacts of land use and climate change on terrestrial ecosystems. The centre is based in the Southeast Asian Center for Tropical Biology, one of ten regional institutions created through Southeast Asian inter-ministerial cooperation for education, in Indonesia.[55] Similarly, IGBP, the International Human Dimensions Programme on global environmental change, and the World Climate Research Programme sponsor a non-profit organisation, SysTem for Analysis, Research, and Training (START), to establish regional networks of scientists that can study the regional impacts of environmental change and provide advice to policy-makers. A Southeast Asian START regional centre was set up in Bangkok, Thailand.[56]

Stratospheric ozone depletion

Another area where cooperation has emerged in response to a global environmental accord is in relation to the phase out of ozone-depleting chemicals. As a result of the earlier phasing out of ozone-depleting chemicals under the terms of the Montreal Protocol and its amendments in the industrialised states, developing

Asia has become the region using the largest amount of such chemicals. The Montreal Protocol established different phase out schedules for industrialised and developing countries and required that industrialised states assist developing states in transitioning from using the harmful chemicals through a multilateral fund established under the GEF. In addition, numerous bi- and trilateral initiatives were begun. The Ministry of Economy, Trade and Industry and the Japan Industrial Conference for Ozone Layer Protection, for example, have worked together with the United States Environmental Protection Agency to hold workshops and training programmes in Thailand, Vietnam, China, Malaysia, and Indonesia on technical issues related to the phasing out of ozone-depleting chemicals.[57] UNEP has created a regional network of ozone officers, the Southeast Asia and the Pacific Network, to facilitate information exchange related to implementation of the Montreal Protocol. Funded by the government of Sweden, the network has worked on raising public awareness of the need to phase out ozone-depleting chemicals and safe disposal methods.

Trade in endangered species

A third area that can be taken as an example of where a global environmental agreement has stimulated greater regional action is in relation to CITES. The 13th meeting of the Conference of the Parties to CITES was held in Bangkok, Thailand, in autumn 2004. As a sign of growing concern about the deteriorating state of tropical forests, countries in Southeast Asia agreed to have Ramin, a tropical hardwood, listed on CITES Appendix II, the first such listing of a commercial timber species in Asia. The Appendix II listing will require the strengthening of international trade controls on this threatened timber species. ASEAN also released a statement on CITES at the meeting. This called for the development of a regional action plan for enhanced law enforcement, scientific research, and trade monitoring. TRAFFIC Southeast Asia, an NGO, played an important role in pushing for this agreement.[58]

The 2004 Indian Ocean tsunami

The many developments described above suggest that East Asia is ripe for greater multilateral environmental cooperation. The importance of this confronted the region in a particularly dramatic and harsh way on the morning of 26 December 2004 when an earthquake measuring 9.0 on the Richter scale struck off the coast of Sumatra, Indonesia. The earthquake and subsequent aftershocks sent tsunami waves travelling at 500–800 kilometres (approx. 300–500 miles) per hour across the Indian Ocean. Tsunami waves that were estimated to be between 10 and 15 metres (30 and 50 feet) in height crashed onto coastal shorelines.

Initial estimates were that hundreds had died. By the time the true scale of the tsunami was realised, the death toll had climbed into the hundreds of thousands. The tsunami caused death and destruction in at least 11 countries as far apart as Southeast Asia and Africa. As of 22 February 2005, official death tolls collated from government and health official statistics stood at 169,752, with another 127,294 missing, most of whom are presumed to be dead.[59]

The figures are daunting and the scale of the destruction difficult to comprehend. International aid agencies and voluntary groups struggled to coordinate their efforts and provide sufficient food relief and clean water to survivors in an effort to prevent a second humanitarian disaster from malnutrition, dehydration, and disease. By mid-February 2005, the UN had coordinated food relief to over 1.2 million people and fresh water to 500,000. It also estimated that US$5.5 billion had been spent in humanitarian assistance.[60] On their tour of the region, former US presidents Bill Clinton and George Bush suggested that at least another US$4 billion in reconstruction aid would be needed.[61]

Not only did the tsunami cause widespread death and destruction, but also it resulted in many serious environmental challenges. It left behind huge amounts of waste and debris. It caused coastal erosion and destroyed farmland. It destroyed industries working with hazardous materials. It contaminated groundwater supplies. Environmentally destructive coastal development was a contributing factor both in the high death toll and in the destruction of coastal towns and villages. In many areas that were most severely affected by the tsunami, coastal areas had been cleared of forests either for farming purposes or to develop resorts and other buildings.[62] The widespread destruction of mangrove swamps and coral reefs for shrimp and fish farms, to clear land for farming, and to develop resorts and coastal communities throughout much of Southeast Asia has removed natural buffer zones that protect coastlines from the full strength of the ocean. In areas where mangrove swamps remained, there were fewer deaths.[63] Tellingly, the Indonesian government has announced plans to replant 30,000 hectares with mangrove trees along the coast of Sumatra to serve as a buffer against future tsunamis.[64] The tsunami also prompted a discussion within ASEAN regarding the importance of promoting sustainable coastal development.

Overcoming obstacles to deeper environmental cooperation

East Asia has been moving towards greater regional environmental cooperation. Especially since the early 1990s, in both Southeast Asia and Northeast Asia, a wide variety of environmental networks and cooperative programmes have emerged. There are, however, still many obstacles to deeper and more effective multilateral environmental cooperation. Some of the obstacles are issues that the international community can more easily assist East Asian states in addressing. These include areas such as improving basic environmental information to provide the basis for the development of sound policies, strengthening local environmental expertise through training programmes and participation in joint projects, transfer of environmental technologies that are suitable to the development level of recipients, and enhancing environmental monitoring capacities through the sharing of experience, technology, and know-how. Also important is the provision of substantial financial assistance to aid in the development of environmental capacity (human, infrastructural, and technological) at the local, national, and regional levels.

More challenging, but, ultimately, very important, will be addressing the deepest barriers that exist to more effective regional environmental protection. One of these is to convince the states of East Asia that giving up a degree of sovereignty in order to develop regional environmental agreements may be necessary in order to tackle the most serious of the pollution problems facing the region. Without such commitment, environmental protection will remain dependent upon the goodwill of member states participating in voluntary cooperative projects and programmes. Another is to convince governments of the region of the importance of precautionary approaches to environmental protection at the regional level. Pollution has been viewed as an unpleasant, but largely unavoidable, component of development. If East Asia is to avoid a more serious degradation of the environment, then states in the region must be willing to initiate programmes and formulate agreements that will prevent resource depletion, pollution, and destruction of natural areas before they occur. Otherwise, they risk pollution and other environmental problems becoming so bad that reversing trends will become extremely difficult or even impossible. Yet another is to convince governments of the importance of integrating environmental protection goals into energy, transport, housing, health, security, and other policy areas. Otherwise, environmental protection risks remaining a secondary goal and even the most ambitious of cooperative environmental protection projects can be rendered almost meaningless by trade or development policies that are formulated with no consideration of their environmental implications.

Conclusion

The range of transboundary environmental issues that is adversely affecting the quality of life in East Asia and raising concerns about long-term sustainability is large. Over-fishing, marine pollution, environmentally destructive coastal development, and energy transport and development are threatening the long-term health of seas throughout Asia, including the Sea of Bengal, the South China Sea, the Yellow Sea, and the Sea of Okhotsk. Tropical deforestation and loss of biodiversity are progressing at such rapid rates throughout much of Asia that many species have become extinct in recent years and biodiversity is seriously threatened. Loss of biodiversity has not only long-term ecological consequences, but also economic, social, and health implications. International environmental problems, such as global warming, stratospheric ozone depletion, acid rain, the transport and disposal of hazardous wastes, food safety and disease, and the management of toxic chemicals are also issues that are demanding that the governments of East Asia work more closely together.

Southeast Asia began its regional environmental cooperation earlier than Northeast Asia and has done somewhat more to internationalise that coopera- tion. ASEAN began to include environmental matters in its regional programmes in the late 1970s and to formulate international environmental objectives in the 1980s. There is no institution comparable with ASEAN in Northeast Asia and, as a result, Northeast Asia has far less experience with regional cooperation in any domain. Northeast Asia is at least a decade behind ASEAN in pursuing regional approaches to solving environmental problems. There are signs, however, that politicians in Northeast Asia are starting to take environmental protection more seriously and are more open than they were in the past to regional environmental protection. Northeast Asia has the potential to catch up rapidly with Southeast Asia in terms of regional environmental cooperation, if it chooses to do so. This is the case, in part, because Southeast Asia has not moved very quickly in the last quarter of a century to institution- alise cooperation and thus, despite a longer history with working together on environmental matters, actual programmes and policies remain relatively few in number. It is also because of the strong pollution control capacities of Japan and increasingly Korea, which means that regional leadership potential exists should the climate for joint problem solving improve.

When compared with the situation of Europe, the extent of regional environ- mental cooperation within and between Southeast and Northeast Asia is still very limited. There are numerous factors that have inhibited deeper cooperation. Historical animosities continue to problematise interstate relations. There is considerable distrust within the region and there are few states that can lay claim to having warm relations with their neighbours. There are, moreover, far larger differences in the level of wealth and environmental capacity of states in East Asia than is the case in Europe and this means that states come to the negotiating table with different needs, priorities, and abilities to solve problems. There are only a handful of entities with fairly extensive pollution-control abilities and financial resources in East Asia (Japan, Singapore, Hong Kong, and Korea). Moreover, while there are growing demands for pollution control from the increasingly large middle classes in Malaysia, Thailand, and even China, pollu- tion problems are still severe in these countries and developmental concerns continue to outweigh environmental ones. The remainder of the region (including much of China) is very poor and has very limited experience with environmental controls. This means that the same kinds of problems that plague North–South environmental cooperation exist within both Southeast and Northeast Asia. The concerns of the richest nations of the region often are not shared by the devel- oping states and there is always the big question of how environmental control efforts are to be paid for.

It is also the case that there is limited enthusiasm for the establishment of legally binding international environmental agreements in either Southeast or

Northeast Asia. This stems from both an unwillingness to pool sovereignty in regional institutions and the different legal and political traditions of states in the region. As a result, there has been little effort to harmonise environmental standards or establish commonly agreed emissions limits among states, although there have been some small steps taken in this direction in Southeast Asia. Rather, in both regions, there is a preference for looser forms of cooperation as in the form of jointly developed environmental goals, action plans, and projects.

Despite all of these difficulties, pressures on regional leaders to take cooperation to a deeper level are growing. The time when environmental problems could be ignored is in the past. Recent disasters and health-related events, including the 2004 Indian Ocean tsunami, the record flooding caused by Typhoon Olga in October 2004 that killed dozens in South Korea, the Philippines, and Vietnam, the SARS scare of 2002–3, the recurring avian influenza virus, the increasingly severe red tides affecting regional seas, the alarming rise in HIV/AIDS infections in the region, the Indonesian forest fires in 1997–8 that left a blanket of debilitating haze across a large swath of Southeast Asia, and the 1997 Nadhodka oil spill that threatened Japan's coastal shorelines, all suggest that greater cooperation in disaster prevention and response and transnational health and environmental problems is critical for the region.

As the condition of regional ecological systems deteriorates and transboundary pollution problems become increasingly severe, the states of East Asia are being forced to work together more closely on pollution control and prevention and in responding to natural calamities. In the future, it can be expected that regional environmental agreements will become more common and that regional bodies will be established to address particular environmental and natural resource problems. While it may be many years before either region is ready to establish a large number of legally binding international environmental agreements, other forms of cooperation are likely to become more common, including joint nature conservation and pollution clean-up projects, information exchange networks, and regional environmental centres. Greater regionalism will also be fostered through participation in global environmental agreements.

In the coming decade, Southeast Asia, in particular, is likely to move in the direction of greater harmonisation of environmental laws, the establishment of cooperative monitoring and research programmes, the setting up of regional environmental organisations, and the introduction of regional environmental agreements. Indeed, Southeast Asia's future economic competitiveness is likely to depend on how well the countries of the region integrate sustainable development concepts into their national policies and programmes and work together to address transboundary and common pool resource problems.

Compared with the smaller economies of Southeast Asia, regional integration will be more difficult in Northeast Asia. This is, to a large part, a reflection of the competition and distrust that still exist among the major economies of the region and their very different economic levels. Nevertheless, even in Northeast Asia, there are many signs that regional cooperation on pollution control, nature conservation, and natural disaster response will deepen. Furthermore, the links between the states of Northeast Asia and ASEAN are rapidly strengthening as economic interdependence progresses; regional scientific, academic, and NGO networks expand; and the transboundary implications of environmental degradation, viral infections, and natural disasters are more fully realised.

This is not to imply that regional environmental cooperation in East Asia will follow the same path as that experienced in Europe. As Breslin also noted in Chapter 2, the situations of Europe and East Asia are quite different. There is greater overall wealth in Europe, smaller differences in the economic levels of states in the region (even when the enlarged European Union is taken into account), a more developed academic, scientific, and technological infrastructure, and arguably more cultural and political similarity. East Asia is characterised by substantial diversity in terms of religion, economic level, political system type, language, and education. Harmonisation and integration have not been easy in the European context, and expansion to the east is placing great strains on European institutions and testing the ability of developing a European identity. Efforts to harmonise environmental standards, forge international environmental agreements, and ensure compliance with those agreements will surely be even more difficult in both Southeast and Northeast Asia than has been the case in Europe. On the other hand, East Asian states have the benefit of being late-comers to regional integration and, thus, can learn from the successes and failures of the European Union, the North American Free Trade Agreement, and global environmental agreements.

Notes

1   World Bank Group, 'Dramatic Decline in Global Poverty, But Progress Uneven', 23 April 2004, *World Development Indicators*, Washington, DC: World Bank Group. Online. Available: http://worldbank.org.
2   There are a growing number of books on regional environmental security and regional environmental cooperation in East Asia. See, for example, Miranda Schreurs and Dennis Pirages, *Ecological Security in Northeast Asia*, Seoul: Yonsei University Press, 1998; Alan Dupont, *East Asia Imperiled: Transnational Challenges to Security*, Cambridge: Cambridge University Press, 2001; Paul Harris (ed.), *International Environmental Cooperation: Politics and Diplomacy in Pacific Asia*, Boulder, CO: University Press of Colorado, 2003; Ramesh Thakur and Edward Newman (eds), *Broadening Asia's Security Discourse and Agenda: Political, Social, and Environmental Perspectives*, Tokyo: United Nations University Press, 2004; P. G. Harris (ed.), *Confronting Environmental Change in East and Southeast Asia: Eco-Politics, Foreign Policy and Sustainable Development*, Tokyo: United Nations University Press, 2005; I. Hyun and M. A. Schreurs (eds), *The Environmental Dimension of Asian Security: Conflict and Cooperation over Pollution, Energy and Natural Resources*, Washington, DC: United States Institute of Peace Press, forthcoming.
3   Discussion with Yong Ren of the State Environmental Protection Agency, in Beijing, China, 19 June 2005.
4   Geohive: Global Statistics, 11 July 2005. Online. Available: http:www.geohive.com.
5   'China's Car Sales up 15% in 2004 After Nearly Doubling in 2003', *The Detroit News: Autos Insider*, 14 January 2005. Online. Available: http://www.detnews.com/2005/autosinsider/0501/14/-060176.htm.

6 'Acid Rain Causes Annual Economic Loss of 110 billion yuan in China', *China Daily (Xinhua)*, 10 October 2003. Online. Available: http://www2.chinadaily.com.cn/en/doc/2003-10/10/content_270868.htm. Similar figures were provided in meetings with Chinese environmental experts and State Environmental Protection Agency officials held in Beijing in June 2005.

7 Miranda Schreurs, 'Regional Security and Cooperation in the Protection of Marine Environments in Northeast Asia', in Hyun and Schreurs (eds) *The Environmental Dimension of Asian Security*, forthcoming.

8 See In-taek Hyun and Samuel Kim, 'The Environment-Security Nexus in Northeast Asia', in Hyun and Schreurs (eds) *The Environmental Dimension of Asian Security*, forthcoming.

9 Rainforest web. Online. Available: http://www.rainforestweb.org/Rainforest_Regions/Asia/Indonesia/.

10 A hotspot is defined as a region where there are at least 1,500 endemic species of vascular plants (that is, more than 0.5 per cent of the world's total) but where at least 70 per cent of original habitat has been lost. Russell A. Mittermeier, Patricio Robler Gil, Michael Hoffman, John Pilgrim, Thomas Brooks, Cristina Goettsch Mittermeier, John Lanoreux, Gustavo A.B. da Fonseca, Harrison Ford (foreword), and Peter Seligmann (preface), *Hotspots Revisited: Earth's Richest and Most Endangered Terrestrial Ecoregions*, Washington, DC: Conservation International, 2005. Online. Available: http://www.biodiversityhotspots.org/xp/Hotspots/hotspotsScience/hotspots_revisited.xml.

11 The author spent January 2005 in Vietnam and visited various environmental groups working in the Mekong River Delta.

12 The author had the opportunity to visit the Kunming Institute of Zoology in Yunnan, China, in January 2005 and was shown their extensive collection of preserved animal species and pelts (some from animals threatened with extinction), including some that were acquired after being confiscated by the police from poachers.

13 See, for example, Mario Rautner, Martom Hardiono, and Raymond Alfred, 'Borneo: Treasure Island at Risk', Frankfurt am Main: WWF Germany, June 2005. Online. Available: http://www.panda.org/downloads/forests/treasureislandatrisk.pdf.

14 See 'Indonesia-Singapore Environment Partnership (ISEP) and the Indonesia-Singapore Joint Working Group on the Environment (ISWG)', Ministry of the Environment and Water Resources, Singapore. Online. Available: http://app.env.gov.sg/view.asp?cid = 154&pid = 118&nid = 123&id = SAS462.

15 Ministry of the Environment, Singapore and State Environmental Protection Agency, China, 'Signing of the Memorandum of Understanding on the Environment between the People's Republic of China's State Environmental Protection Agency and the Republic of Singapore's Ministry of the Environment', 24 May 2004. Online. Available: http://app.env.gov.sg/press.asp?id = CDS1276.

16 'Manila Declaration on the ASEAN Environment', Manila, 30 April 1981. Online. Available: http://www.asean.sec.org/6077.htm.

17 'ASEAN Declaration on Heritage Parks and Reserves', Bangkok, Thailand, 29 November 1984. Online. Available: http://www.aseansec.org/6078.htm.

18 'Jakarta Resolution on Sustainable Development', Jakarta, 30 October 1987. Online. Available: http://www.aseansec.org/6081.htm.

19 'Agreement on Conservation of Nature and Natural Resources', Kuala Lumpur, 9 July 1985. Online. Available: http://www.aseansec.org/6080.htm. See also Lorraine Elliott, 'ASEAN and Environmental Cooperation', *The Pacific Review*, 2003, vol. 16, no.1, pp. 38.

20 Elliott, 'ASEAN and Environmental Cooperation', 2003, pp. 40–1.

21 *News Release, Ninth ASEAN Ministerial Meeting on the Environment*, Yangon: 17–18 December 2003. Online. Available: http://www.aseansec.org/15520.htm.

22 Regional Centre for Biodiversity Conservation. 23 February 2005. Online. Available : http://www.arcbc.org/default.asp.
23 *Joint Statement of the Ninth Informal ASEAN Ministerial Meeting on the Environment*, Makati City, 28 September 2005. Online. Available: http://www.aseansec.org/17776.htm.
24 Association of Southeast Asian Nations, 'Press Release'. Online. Available: http://www.aseansec.org/13402.htm.
25 'Joint Press Statement on the Eighth Informal ASEAN Ministerial Meeting on the Environment and the 3rd ASEAN+3 Environment Ministers Meeting', Singapore, 13–14 October 2004. Online. Available: http://www.aseansec.org/16481.htm.
26 National Institute for Environmental Research, 'Report of the First Meeting of the National Focal Points', ENR/MTG/NEACEDT/RE, 14–16 February 2001, North East Asian Centre for Environmental Data and Training. Online. Available: http://www.nier.go.kr/nierdepart/board/bbs/bview.php?sm = &p_headid = 12&p_seq = 1&p = 1. See also NEASPEC: http://www.neaspec.org/.
27 *Tripartite Environment Ministers Meeting, Joint Communiqué of the Sixth Tripartite Environment Ministers Meeting among Korea, China and Japan*, Tokyo, 4–5 December 2004. Online. Available: http://eng.me.go.kr/user/global/bilateral/3_bilateral.html?msel = c3#.
28 See ECOASIA. Online. Available: http://www.ecoasia.org/.
29 See A. Brettell, 'Security, Energy and the Environment: The Atmospheric Link', in Hyun and Schreurs (eds) *The Environmental Dimension of Asian Security*, forthcoming.
30 The author was taken on a tour through Kita Kyushu and its many environmental recycling, pollution control, and energy efficiency projects and introduced to Kita Kyushu's environmental cooperation programmes by Professor Hidefumi Imura. For more information on Kita Kyushu's environmental initiatives and its international cooperation see: http://www.iges.or.jp/kitakyushu/main_outline_background.htm and http://www.kanmon.biz/kitakyushu/en/project/project03.html.
31 United Nations Economic and Social Commission for Asia and the Pacific, Human Settlements, 'Issue Paper on: Urban Environment Management in Asia and the Pacific'. Online. Available: http://www.unescap.org/huset/hangzhou/paper/urban_paper.htm.
32 RAPIDC International Co-operation, 'Air Pollution in Megacities'. Online. Available: http://www.york.ac.uk/inst/sei/rapidc2/apma.html.
33 Southeast Asia Urban Environmental Management Applications Project. Online. Available: http://www.sea-uema.ait.ac.th/jar.htm.
34 See Sulan Chen, 'Induced and Instrumental Cooperation: Potential Legitimation and Confidence Building in the Environmental Politics of the South China Sea', Ph.D. dissertation, University of Maryland, 2005.
35 United Nations Environment Programme, Global Environment Facility, and UNEP/GEF South China Sea Project, 'Review of Regional and Subregional Agreements and Soft Laws on Marine Environment in South China Sea', 19 April 2004, UNEP/GEF/SCS/RTF-L.2/7. My thanks to Sulan Chen for providing me with this report and for her intellectual contributions to thinking about regional cooperation in the case of the South China Sea, the topic of her dissertation.
36 UNEP/NOWPAP/POMRAC/FPM 1/4, 11 March 2003.
37 There is an expanding literature on environmental movements, civil society, and NGOs in East Asia. This includes Arne Kalland and Gerard Persoon (eds), *Environmental Movements in Asia*, London: RoutledgeCurzon, 1999; Yok-shiu Lee and Alvin So (eds), *Asia's Environmental Movements: Comparative Perspectives*, Armonk, NY: East Gate Books, 1999; Keiko Hirata, *Civil Society in Japan: The Growing Role of NGOs in Tokyo's Aid and Development Policy*, New York: Palgrave Macmillan, 2002; Kim Reimann, 'Building Networks from the Outside In: International Movements, Japanese NGOs, and the Kyoto Climate Conference', *Mobilization*, 2003, vol. 6, no. 1, pp. 69–82; Esook Yoon, Shin-wah Lee, and Fengshui Wu, 'The State and Nongovernmental

Organizations in Northeast Asia's Environmental Security', in Hyun and Schreurs (eds) *The Environmental Dimension of Asian Security*, forthcoming; Fengshui Wu, 'Double-mobilization: Transnational Advocacy Networks for China's Environment and Public Health', Ph.D. dissertation, University of Maryland, 2005.

38 In China there have been various cases of individuals being imprisoned for speaking out against the Three Gorges Dam. Examples include Dai Qing, who spent 10 months in prison before going into exile in the United States; and He Kechang, Jian Qingshan, Ran Chongxin, and Wen Dingchun who were imprisoned after complaining to Beijing that local officials had embezzled funds intended for their resettlement because of the Three Gorges Dam construction project. See *Amnesty International Urgent Action*, 23 April 2001. There has also been repression of HIV/AIDS activism. For example, gynaecologist Gao Yaojie, who helped raise national and international awareness about the spread of HIV/AIDS in Henan province in China among peasants who had had blood transfusions or had sold plasma at local blood banks, was put under investigation herself by the local cadre and prevented from attending a ceremony in the United States where she was to receive an award from the Global Health Council for her work. See Business Week Online, 8 July 2002, 'Gao Yaojie: Aids Activist, China'. Online. Available: http://www.businessweek.com/magazine/content/02-27/b3790611.htm. Now, however, the Chinese government boasts of her accomplishments. An example of this is Y. Wang, 'Gao Yaojie: A Crusader for AIDS Prevention', *China Pictorial*, 4 February 2005. Online. Available: http://www.china-pictorial.com/chpic/htdocs/English/content/200502/3-1.htm.

39 Joshua Gordon makes this point in relation to environmental NGOs in Indonesia in his article, 'NGOs, the Environment and Political Pluralism in New Order Indonesia', *Explorations in Southeast Asian Studies: A Journal of the Southeast Asian Studies Student Association*, 1998, vol. 2, no. 2. Online. Available: http://www.hawaii.edu/cseas/pubs/explore/v2/gordon.html. A similar argument is made in relation to Cambodia and Vietnam in Sunil Subhanrao Pednekar, 'NGOs and Natural Resource Management in Southeast Asia', *TDRI Quarterly Newsletter*, September 1995, vol. 10, no. 3. Online. Available: http://www.gdrc.org/ngo/thai-ngo.html.

40 Statement on Cooperation for the Sustainable Development of the Mekong River Basin, 4 April 1995. Online. Available: http://www.hartford-hwp.com/archives/54/205.html. For a good article on China's role in the damming of the Mekong River see Katri Makkonen, 'Mekong Cooperation: The Linkages between Poverty, Environment, and Transboundary Water Management in Southwest China's Yunnan Province'. Online. Available: http://www.helsinki.fi/nacs/finland2005/papers/makkonen.pdf.

41 R. Litzinger, 'Damming the Angry River', *China Review*, November 2004, no. 30. Online. Available: http://www.gbcc.org.uk/30article3.htm.

42 'Monks and Nuns in Southeast Asia Pledge to Save their Forests', *ARC Alliance of Religions and Conservation News and Resources*, 16 June 2004. Online. Available: http://www.arcworld.org/news.asp?pageID = 57.

43 'China Environmental NGO Activists Visited Korea to Understand the Korean Environment Movement', Green Korea, 30 November 2000. Online. Available: http://www.greenkorea.org.

44 'Asia for Animals Conference in Singapore', 22–24 June 2005. Online. Available: http://www.acres.org.sg/asiaforanimals/. The author spoke with Li Zhang, Director of the International Fund for Animal Welfare, China, in Beijing on 19 June 2005 immediately prior to his departure for this conference.

45 Waste Not Asia, 'Report: First Asian Anti-Incineration Alliance Meeting'. Online. Available: http://www.no-burn.org/regional/pdf/wna2000report.pdf.

46 The author visited IFAW and CITES staff in Yunnan, China, and CARE and UNDP staff in Vietnam as part of a study abroad course on Women, Environment and

Development in China and Vietnam that she co-led with Lois Vietri of the University of Maryland during January 2005.

47 For more information, see WWF Indochina. Online. Available: http://www. wwfindochina.org.

48 Online. Available : http://www.greenpeacesoutheastasia.org/en/seaabout.html.

49 SSee International Rivers Network's Southeast Asia campaign information. Online. Available: http://www.irn.org/programs/seasia/.

50 See *Rivers Watch East and Southeast Asia*. Online. Available: http://www.rwesa.org/.

51 See Jennifer Turner and Fengshui Wu, 'Green NGO and Environmental Journalist Forum, 9–10 April 2001, Hong Kong Conference Report'. Online. Available: http://wwics.si.edu/topics/pubs/cgreen-en-1.pdf. The author has had frequent discussions with both co-authors on this subject.

52 The author met IFAW China staff in Kunming, Yunnan, in January 2005.

53 For the status of ratification of these conventions, see United Nations Environment Programme, Ozone Secretariat, Status of Ratification. Online. Available: http://www.unep.org/ozone/Treaties_and_Ratification/2C_ratification.asp. Also see United Nations Framework Convention on Climate Change, Kyoto Protocol, status of ratification. Online. Available: unfccc.int/essential_background/kyoto_protocol/status_of_ratification/items/2613.php. United Nations Environment Programme, 'Parties to the Convention on Biological Diversity', *Secretariat of the Convention on Biological Diversity*. Online. Available: http://www.biodiv.org/world/parties.asp.

54 United States General Accounting Office, 28 October 2003, 'Climate Change Trends in Greenhouse Gas Emissions and Emissions Intensity in the United States and Other High-Emitting Nations', GAO-04-416R.

55 See Impacts Center Southeast Asia. Online. Available: http://www.icsea.biotrop.org/about.htm.

56 See SysTem for Analysis, Research, and Training. Online. Available: http://www.start.org/.

57 For more information on these workshops, see Japan Industrial Conference for Ozone Layer Protection. Online. Available: http://www.jicop.org/english/cooper_e.html.

58 Traffic International. Online. Available: http://www.traffic.org/news/combat.html.

59 CNN, 'Tsunami Death Toll', 20 February 2005. Online. Available: http://www.cnn.com/2004/WORLD/asiapcf/12/28/tsunamideaths.

60 'United Nations Coordinates International Response to Tsunami', United Nations Foundation, 14 February 2005. Online. Available: http://www.unfoundation.org/files/pdf/2005/UNroleintsunamirelief.pdf.

61 'Clinton, Bush Tour Tsunami Damage', CBS News, 19 February 2005. Online. Available: http://www.cbsnews.com/stories/2004/12/26/world/main663057.shtml.

62 United Nations Environment Programme, Press Release IHA/1055, UNEP/283, UNEP Post-Tsunami Assessment Finds Environmental Impacts in Maldives. Online. Available: http://www.un.org/News/Press/docs/2005/iha1055.doc.htm.

63 Nirmal Ghosh, 'Destroyed Mangroves Could Have Saved Lives', *The Straits Times, Singapore*, 8 January 2005. Online. Available: http://www.ecologyasia.com/news-archives/2005/jan-05/st_050108_1.htm.

64 Andrew Quinn, 'Indonesia to Replant Mangroves in Tsunami Defense', Reuters, 18 January 2005. Online. Available: http://www.forestsandtradeasia.org/posting/Indonesia/English/287.

11 Regionalism and community building in East Asia

Challenges and opportunities[1]

Aileen San Pablo-Baviera

Introduction

If one were to rely on the dominant literature on the theory and practice of regional integration, and then look at what is commonly known about the geographic zone referred to as East Asia (Southeast Asia and Northeast Asia), there would be much reason to discount the feasibility of an East Asian community ever becoming a reality. The diversity among the countries of the region – in terms of culture and worldview, political–legal systems, levels of economic and technological development, asymmetry in size and in power attributes, degrees of political maturity and stability, among other factors – militate against the development of a common or collective East Asian identity. Furthermore, mutual suspicion and occasional hostilities still characterise relations among countries of the region, most importantly between its two great powers – Japan and China. East Asia also continues to be a region of sharp divisions harking back to the Cold War, with unresolved conflicts across the Taiwan Straits and on the Korean peninsula, as well as potential flashpoints arising from the territorial, maritime, and resource disputes among various countries in the region.

There are, on the other hand, a number of commonalities among the countries and peoples of East Asia that might strengthen the argument for a prospective East Asian community. One source lists them as the following: 'the experience of warfare, "Asian values", common institutions, a distinctive brand of capitalism, deeper economic integration', and even some common perspectives on relations with other countries.[2] Whether or not these commonalities are enough to underpin full integration remains a question. It appears, however, that rather than regionalism being built from the ground up and as a consequence of internal unities and complementarities, in East Asia regionalism has apparently emerged largely as a reaction to external forces, including influences of the international political economy and of the policies of great powers.[3]

There are several ongoing and overlapping initiatives at regional cooperation involving countries of the East Asian region. The Association of Southeast Asian Nations (ASEAN) has been in existence since 1967, although only since 1999 has it had its full membership of all 10 Southeast Asian countries. Only in October 2003 did ASEAN outline its intentions to move from 'intergovernmentalism' towards 'integration', which is articulated in the Bali Concord II as becoming a Security Community, an Economic Community, and a Socio-Cultural Community.[4]

Even as ASEAN tries to speed up its own integration, it has found itself at the centre of other broader regional cooperation initiatives. Most prominent of these are the Asia-Pacific Economic Cooperation Forum (APEC) and the security-oriented ASEAN Regional Forum (ARF), both of which include major players from outside the East Asian region, such as the United States. The Asia– Europe Meeting (ASEM) and the Forum for East Asia and Latin America Cooperation (FEALAC), meanwhile, are trans-regional dialogue mechanisms also involving East Asian countries.

More faithfully adhering to the geographic 'footprint' of East Asia is the ASEAN+3 dialogue mechanism, involving the 10 member countries of ASEAN and the Northeast Asian countries of China, Japan, and South Korea. When first bruited about in 1990 by Malaysian Prime Minister Mahathir Mohamad as the proposal to establish an East Asian Economic Group, the vision of an East Asian community consisting of Southeast Asia and Northeast Asia was staunchly opposed by the United States and consequently Japan, as well as by some ASEAN countries. However, it now seems to be well on its way to implementation via the ASEAN+3 process. Annual summits of East Asian leaders take place in the form of the ASEAN+1 and the ASEAN+3 dialogues, apart from meetings of ASEAN+3 ministers of foreign affairs, trade, economic affairs, finance, agriculture, labour, tourism, and environment. Some actual cooperative economic and financial ventures among these countries are underway, as highlighted by Hamilton-Hart, Thomas, and Chavez in this volume, catalysed by the 1997 Asian crisis. These include setting up early warning systems for future risks of financial meltdown, currency swap arrangements, financial assistance for infrastructure projects, capacity-building workshops, bilateral free trade arrangements, closer economic partnership agreements, and other such measures.

The 2001 vision document prepared by the East Asian Vision Group outlined a comprehensive array of proposals for cooperation by the ASEAN+3 countries. Many proposals have already begun to be implemented, having obtained the endorsement of the governments.[5] The goals appear to have been set as both short-term (for example, financial coordination and enhanced trade) and strategic (for example, establishing an East Asian Free Trade Area), indicating a growing awareness in the region not only of the present common problems, but of the sense of shared destiny. At the non-official or Track II level, a Network of East Asian Think Tanks composed of policy analysts and practitioners, a Network of East Asian Studies consisting of academics, and an East Asia Forum among high-level officials, business leaders, and scholars have in recent years been engaged in regular meetings trying to put flesh on the concept of an 'East Asian community'. At the offical level, the East Asia Summit that took place in Kuala Lumpur in December 2005 had the ASEAN+3 countries at its core, but – following a long debate on the dangers of exclusivity – these were joined by Australia, New Zealand, and India.

In this concluding chapter, we shall examine why an East Asian community – at present defined geographically as consisting of the ASEAN members, China, Japan, and Korea – may be an idea whose time has come, taking into consideration the rapidly changing global environment. At the same time this chapter will explore the challenges and opportunities that lie ahead of those charged with overseeing this project of regional community building, including its political, security, economic, developmental, and socio-cultural dimensions. Problems and prospects associated with institutionalisation will be addressed. Finally, some conditions for the success or failure of East Asian identity building will be outlined.

The external environment of East Asian community building

The economic impetus

The apparent popularity of the concept of East Asian regionalism today, compared with the past, can in large part be attributed to three sets of economic factors: the emergence of regional economic blocs in North America and Europe; the effects of the 1997 Asian crisis and similar problems arising from globalisation; and the rise of China.

As the formation of the North American Free Trade Agreement (NAFTA) and the European Union (EU) threatened to restrict East Asian access to its traditional markets and sources of foreign capital, East Asian countries perceived it necessary to build similar self-help mechanisms. It was hoped that the region's stronger economies such as Japan and China could play a role in enhancing intra-regional trade and investments, at the same time that they could provide leadership in giving East Asia a stronger voice in global economic affairs. An East Asian community based on the ASEAN+3 was already perceived as a much more attractive regional trade and investment entity in comparison with the ASEAN Free Trade Area. After all, East Asia hosts the fastest growing economies in the world, a factor that has, since the 1990s, led to shifting the centre of gravity of the global economy away from the West and towards the Asia-Pacific.

Much of this growth can be traced to China, which experienced real growth averaging at 10 per cent annually from 1990 to 2000. However, it is also true that each of the three Northeast Asian economies is quite strong compared with most economies in Southeast Asia, and account for much of the growth in intra-Asian and intra-Asia–Pacific trade. There is also more market-led integration and interdependence among the 13 countries of ASEAN+3 than for the ASEAN 10 alone.

The idea of an East Asian community became even more desirable when the 1997 Asian crisis wiped out the accumulated wealth of recent years in a number of East Asian economies, resulting in a widening gap within and among countries of the region and increasing the vulnerability of certain groups to the forces of economic globalisation. Even Japan, its economy in the doldrums for well over a decade, was not spared, and difficult as it may be for Japan to admit, its future economic growth appears to depend on the demand coming from China and the rest of East Asia.

At the time of the crisis, China, Japan, and South Korea were already dialogue partners of ASEAN. The crisis demonstrated how an economic downturn in one country can have spillover effects in neighbouring economies. For example, currency fluctuations in Thailand affected the export competitiveness of neighbouring states that produced similar goods for the same markets.[6] China and Japan were affected to a lesser degree than South Korea and Southeast Asia, but they were also perceived as indirectly helping to cause the crisis, with China being faulted for its 1994 devaluation of the renminbi, and Japan for perhaps helping create overcapacity in the region without opening its markets to exports from neighbouring states.

Japan was the only country capable of infusing massive new capital to help contain the crisis, which it did through the $30 billion New Miyazawa Initiative. Meanwhile, China's cooperation in preventing any further devaluation of the renminbi was seen as a critical factor that led to a speedy recovery for the worst-hit economies. Beijing's offer of financial assistance in the form of grants and loans to Thailand and Indonesia was also much appreciated.

The initial response of the region to the crisis was to expand monetary cooperation and enhance macroeconomic policy coordination, but because the crisis also underscored the unintended effects of economic interdependence, it gave way to proposals for greater regional cooperation in trade and investment.[7] In contrast to the important role that Japan and China played in containing the effects of the crisis, and to the cooperation that East Asian countries demonstrated towards each other in its wake, the solutions prescribed by the IMF were perceived in the region as inappropriate and more interested in furthering the economic reform agenda of the West than in helping the region cope with its problems.

For Southeast Asia, one important consideration behind its interest in the ASEAN+3 arrangement was the need to better confront the anticipated economic challenges as well as the opportunities posed by China's WTO accession. China's accession is expected to impact on Southeast Asia in several ways, both positive and negative: by increasing access to China's domestic markets, increasing imports by China from neighbouring countries, spurring competition with China for third-country markets, and promoting expansion in both foreign direct investment in China and outward investment from China.[8] In addition, it is expected to increase transparency and predictability in Chinese rules and regulations covering foreign economic interests. To ensure that the negative impacts of WTO accession do not outweigh the anticipated mutual benefits for China and Southeast Asia, the two sides decided to enter into a separate China–ASEAN Free Trade Agreement. The agreement provides for establishing a free trade area by 2010, but has an 'early harvest' provision, which allows the least developed countries of Southeast Asia to benefit much earlier from trade opportunities.

Many other proposals for preferential trading arrangements have sprouted in East Asia in the last few years. Singapore has signed or is currently negotiating

FTAs with Japan, Korea, and Taiwan. Korea has proposed the same to Thailand and Japan, while Japan is pursuing an FTA with the Philippines and 'closer economic partnership' with Thailand. ASEAN as a whole is conducting official discussions to this end with China, Japan, and Korea separately, and with all three collectively under the ASEAN+3 framework.[9] While there are still many issues to resolve, and while some of these negotiations may not be successfully concluded in the end, it is an indication that countries are looking to regional economic integration to speed up their respective national growth and development.

The political impetus

A number of external political factors provide an important, if perhaps less clearly articulated, backdrop to the new East Asian regionalism. The end of the Cold War broke down the ideological divisions that used to be major fault lines in both Northeast and Southeast Asia, thus making it possible for Vietnam, Laos, Cambodia, and Myanmar to join ASEAN, and for China, Japan, and South Korea to explore new opportunities for bilateral and trilateral cooperation with each other. While it is true that the Korean conflict and China–Taiwan tensions remain as the unfinished business of the Cold War, they have become largely national questions rather than ideological ones that in the bipolar years could have given rise to more serious conflicts involving rival great powers.

The old system of bilateral alliances created by the Cold War has persisted, at least the so-called 'spokes' around the US 'hub'. However, the role of military alliances has diminished as alternative security mechanisms began to emerge, principally organised around multilateral security dialogues. New arrangements such as the ARF have proven to be more functional in certain ways, particularly when the threats to stability and security arise from transnational causes and are of such a nature that military force is not the best nor even an appropriate solution. Among such 'non-traditional' security threats are environmental crises, transnational crime, international terrorism, pandemic diseases, and the like.

Even great powers such as the United States and China, although unwilling to suffer diminution of their influence and the flexibility to make unilateral decisions, have had to pay some attention to these new regional multilateral arrangements in order to ensure that their policies remain relevant and attuned to regional sentiments, as discussed by Goh and Acharya in this volume. But the ARF has thus far not tried to come up with direct solutions to regional conflicts. Its participants remain divided on their expectations of the Forum, reflecting sharp divisions in their strategic perceptions, with one fault line being that between the East Asian participants who prefer more gradualist processes and the Anglo-American participants who are accustomed to more formal, institutionalised, and results-oriented approaches. This, too, may have contributed to some actors' beginning to prefer smaller, more manageable aggregations of culturally more similar and geographically contiguous members (ASEAN or East Asia) as the focus of their efforts to enhance security.

The emergence of China as a new great power, and, in the view of some, the need to socialise it into more predictable patterns of behaviour, is another driving force for regional political coordination and integration. The economic implications of China's rise for the region have already been referred to. In the political arena, China has emerged from decades of internal preoccupation and, following the logic of its economic interdependence and growing economic clout, is starting to project a more assertive and confident posture on major political and security issues affecting its interests. These include the Taiwan issue, the Korean peninsula question, disputes in the South China Sea and in the East China Sea, the human rights debate with the West, and US–Japan security cooperation, among others.

On the one hand, China is keen to project itself as a responsible great power, ready not only to abide by the rules of international politics, but to participate in defining them. On the other hand, many still consider China a revisionist power, one that remains deeply dissatisfied with the status quo and one that aspires for even greater influence relative to other great powers. The desire to nudge China towards the first scenario – that of the responsible and benign great power – is one persuasive justification for strengthening regional political–security cooperation in the context of ASEAN+3 or an East Asian community. Without multilateral political–security cooperation, China's neighbours will have very little influence over China's strategic policy direction or on the resurgent rivalry between China and Japan for regional status, although it must be said that even with regional-level engagement, small powers can expect to have only incremental and indirect influence on great powers.

It may also be argued that the current initiative for East Asian regionalism would not have been possible were it not for the role that ASEAN plays. ASEAN's relative economic success, its non-confrontational norms of interstate behaviour, its foreign policy posture of independence and neutrality, and its own successes in promoting subregional coordination and cooperation, have lent it some credibility and acceptability as a 'driving force' for new regionalism in the eyes of its neighbours and dialogue partners. ASEAN is also well placed to engage other countries in dialogue over regional security, especially as new concepts and approaches to security consistent with ASEAN's own perspectives began to gain ground – for example, comprehensive security, common security, inclusiveness, consensus building, and regional solutions to regional problems.

Even the events of 11 September 2001, demonstrating the ferocious ability of the invisible enemy – international terrorism – to strike at the heart of the world's foremost military power, may have aided the cause of East Asian regionalism in several ways.

First of all, with global attention turning to terrorism as the latest and gravest threat to world security, the countries of East Asia and many others throughout the world closed ranks to build their counter-terrorist defences, separately and collectively, especially under strong pressure from the United States. Other security issues in East Asia, including intra-regional disputes, seemed to recede in the background, albeit temporarily.

Second, by making clear that it was digging in for a long-drawn-out battle against international terrorism, the United States may have sent the signal to China's wary neighbours that they will have to manage the rise of China without active US help, thus pushing them on to the path of even closer engagement with China. China, fighting its home-grown Muslim separatists from Xinjiang, seized the opportunity after 9/11 to redefine itself as an ally in the US fight against terrorism, rather than the emerging threat that it was touted to be prior to 9/11, especially in Washington's opinion circles.

Third, the George W. Bush administration increasingly turned unilateralist in its efforts to fight terrorism, threatening 'regime change' and 'pre-emption' on sovereign states where it deemed necessary. This rankled many in East Asia, including China and ASEAN, where opposition to foreign intervention and adherence to non-interference in internal affairs have been long-cherished values. Finally, as the Bush government became perceived as anti-Muslim, many peoples in East Asian states that had large Muslim populations found themselves becoming alienated and more distrustful of US and, by extension, Western intentions.

To what extent this last set of factors may have caused the option of regionalism to be more attractive is arguable, but certainly even close allies of the United States in the region became increasingly uncomfortable with Washington's propensity to act unilaterally and its willingness to wage war on states without feeling compelled to seek international legitimacy, as had happened over Iraq. Unless Washington recovers the moral high ground and its own credibility as a responsible leader of the international community, states may feel that they would do better to invest in developing regional arrangements for solutions to their security problems.

Challenges and opportunities of community building in East Asia

Despite these economic and political conditions that may have encouraged the countries of East Asia to look more towards each other, the project of building a community is fraught with many challenges and obstacles. It is the objective in this section to identify some of these challenges, as well as to highlight opportunities to move towards successful integration in the region. The assumption, based on the 2001 report of the East Asian Vision Group titled 'Towards an East Asian Community: Region of Peace, Prosperity and Progress' and the 1999 Joint Statement of the ASEAN+3, is that the envisioned community will work not only towards common economic and functional goals, but towards political and security cooperation as well.

The political–security dimension

The most serious political obstacle to long-term cooperation among the East Asian countries is no doubt the on-again off-again power play between the United States and China. The United States remains indecisive as to whether to look at China as a strategic partner or a strategic competitor, a situation which is expected to remain in the short to medium term, for reasons that both governments may have little control over.[10] An East Asian integration effort that excludes the United States may, in Washington's eyes, be suspected as merely giving China opportunities to promote its domination of the region. The fact is that most countries of East Asia – including China – prioritise their relations with the United States ahead of relations with any other country in the region. For some – such as US allies Japan, Korea, and the Philippines – this has translated into security dependence on the United States in real as well as psychological terms, leading to a vulnerability to US pressure. Should the situation arise where competition and conflict decisively take centre stage in China–US relations, many governments in East Asia will be faced with pressure to disengage from China. Such a scenario would spell the failure of regionalism. Thus, it is necessary for the ASEAN+3 group collectively to ensure that the East Asian community-building process does not become an arena for China–US strategic competition. How this can be done remains a mystery at this point in time.

The incipient rivalry between Japan and China can just as easily destroy the community-building project from within. They are the two biggest economies and have the two most sophisticated military forces of the region (notwithstanding constraints on Japan from its pacifist constitution). It is important for Beijing and Tokyo to be willing to tolerate the other playing a major role, for as long as their actions are consistent with the region's common interests. Efforts by one to undermine the other can only slow down the process of cooperation, and diminish their credibility as leading agents of progress for East Asia. Each of them must extend mutual assurances to the other that they will not try to dominate the agenda of East Asian cooperation. If one of them does, the other is bound to try to foil the attempt, and the entire region may end up becoming preoccupied with the intramurals of the two powers rather than with the business at hand. For this reason, it is crucial that ASEAN be prepared to stay at the helm and serve as the driving force for the vision of an East Asian community, and to do so in a manner whereby both China and Japan are able to play constructive, non-threatening, and mutually reinforcing roles that focus on common regional aspirations.

A third challenge is the relative lack of experience in security dialogue and cooperation among the three Northeast Asian countries, especially in comparison with ASEAN. The potential for military conflict remains high in their subregion, and thus far there has been little room for solutions based on cooperative security or common security frameworks. Whether the issue is the Taiwan Straits conflict, the nuclearisation of North Korea, or Korean unification, it is great power interests that dictate the pace and direction of conflict resolution.

By and large, the scenarios still tend to be zero-sum rather than win–win solutions, with the role of the United States often overshadowing those of the regional stakeholders themselves. Thus, the ASEAN+3 processes should continue to encourage subregional security dialogue among China, Japan, and Korea to take place.

Right now, subregional cooperation and dialogue in East Asia is asymmetrical. While the ASEAN countries conduct themselves collectively in relation to the Northeast Asian dialogue partners, China, Japan, and Korea have no coordinated agenda for dialogue with ASEAN. This may be changing, however. A first ever trilateral summit of the leaders of China, Japan, and Korea took place in Manila in 1999 on the sidelines of the ASEAN+3 meeting. Since then, the leaders have met regularly. These trilateral meetings will certainly not be enough immediately to prevent or ease the tensions that periodically surface among the three, but as an additional channel for dialogue, particularly one connected to the external process of ASEAN dialogue relations, it allows the parties occasionally to step back from their historical and contemporary bilateral grievances and to focus on shared interests.

One challenge is that there are sharp differences between the countries of Northeast Asia and Southeast Asia in the manner they define threats to security, in their strategic cultures and perspectives, and in the patterns of security interactions among them. One cannot help but wonder if a strong basis of unity might exist or eventually develop among them that will result in agreement on a common security framework or approach. For instance, can ASEAN norms and practices of non-confrontation, consultation, consensus building, gradualism, and informality – perhaps appropriate to the types of interstate problems confronting ASEAN – serve the security interests of China, Japan, and Korea as well as they appear to have served Southeast Asia? Or will the more hard-nosed realism of Northeast Asia – forged in a history of war, invasion, Cold War competition, and the backdrop of nuclear threat – perhaps rub off on ASEAN instead? From today's vantage point, it is ASEAN's norms and practices, rather than those in Northeast Asia, which have been more successful in moderating interstate tensions and promoting mutually beneficial cooperation among countries of the region, and can thus hopefully provide some lessons for China, Japan, and Korea in managing their relations.

For the immediate to medium term, the strong emphasis that many countries in East Asia place on sovereignty, territorial integrity, and non-interference in internal affairs also threatens their unity. In any effort at regionalism, it is presumed that some sovereignty over certain affairs will have to be relinquished in favour of the collective will or in exchange for considerable benefits for the individual state concerned. In the course of regional consultations, however, it is to be expected that sovereignty will continue to be invoked now and then, perhaps to seek exemption from multilateral obligations or to block consensus or to defect from an agreement, all in the name of the national interest.

While smaller countries often have more reason to be jealous and zealous about sovereignty, it is actually the more powerful states that have the capacity to assert sovereignty in full measure and with far more serious impact. The same is true for territorial integrity. China is the country of East Asia perceived to be the most assertive in issues of territorial rights and jurisdictional claims, particularly in its maritime border facing Korea, Japan, and Southeast Asia, and over Taiwan and the South China Sea islands. It can play a crucial role in demonstrating readiness to set aside disputes in the interests of regionalism; if China can set the example, it becomes more likely that others will follow suit.

On the other side of the challenges mentioned here are opportunities, windows for pursuing cooperation that may help East Asia attain the stable peace that has eluded it for so long. The future of East Asia hinges very much on Japan's economic recovery, political resiliency of a democratic South Korea, improved relations between Seoul and Pyongyang, and the readiness of China and Japan to embark on more constructive relations with each other. Each of these requires an external constituency that will support and encourage these actors through the difficult tasks ahead. ASEAN can provide such encouragement in an ASEAN+3 or East Asian cooperation framework, but first of all Southeast Asia must improve its understanding of Northeast Asian issues and problems.

The project of East Asian community building can also convince the countries of Northeast Asia to have a more abiding interest in Southeast Asian countries, not only as pawns in balance of power games or as expansion areas for markets and influence, but as common stakeholders in regional as well as global peace and development. While intra-Northeast Asian unity and cooperation is very important and immediate as noted above, ultimately it is Northeast Asia–Southeast Asia integration that will help secure the future of the East Asian community. Non-traditional security issues have been identified where immediate cooperation involving all East Asian countries might be pursued. Specifically, these are combating transnational crime, maritime piracy, trafficking of persons and illegal substances, controlling the spread of infectious diseases, and taking joint action against terrorism.[11] In the processes of pursuing multilateral coordination and cooperation in these activities, the parties can gradually build mutual confidence, enhance sensitivity to each other's concerns, and develop habits of consultation and consensus building that will serve them well in addressing more difficult bilateral problems.

The United States is no longer opposing the East Asian initiative, although it remains concerned about the possibility of an East Asian grouping that might turn exclusivist, despite ASEAN+3's current avowed posture of 'open regionalism'.[12] This may indicate Washington's confidence that its strong bilateral ties with certain countries and its active economic and military presence in the region will ensure its continued primacy. Perhaps of greater interest to the United States is how China might try to make use of its economic, financial, and functional linkages with Southeast Asia to expand its political influence and undermine those of Japan and the United States.

Economic, social, and development dimensions

If there is one reason to believe that the ASEAN+3 and its vision of an East Asian community might lead to more successful regional economic cooperation than APEC or possibly more hopeful regional political–security cooperation than the ARF, it is because, rather than being purely utilitarian, the ASEAN+3 – as Goh and Acharya also noted in their chapter – is identity oriented. The East Asian Vision Group report goes beyond the emphasis on taking advantage of economic complementarities. It discusses articulating an East Asian voice in international affairs. The report acknowledges that economic cooperation cannot be undertaken independently of improving the regional security situation nor independently of addressing the long-term problems of social justice and human development. This interrelation of economic, social, political, and security issues requires broader frameworks of cooperation, and such broad frameworks imply long-term commitments to a common vision. Such a commitment to a common vision cannot yet be presumed to exist in East Asia and will have to be negotiated for many years to come among the ASEAN+3 countries, but the premise is that the emerging sense of regional identity will facilitate agreement on such a vision and support the process of further integration.

It is the economic aspect of community building that seems to have the most clarity at this time, and thus is expected to lead the way for other areas of coopera-tive action. The strategic economic vision that the ASEAN+3 process has articulated is the creation of an Asian Economic Community, which means: expanding currency swap arrangements under the Chiang Mai Initiative, setting up regional exchange rate regimes, strengthening information sharing on trade and investments or setting up an Asian Monetary Fund as a lender of last resort, in the short term. Over the long term it means becoming a single market, building an East Asian Free Trade Area by consolidating existing bilateral and multilateral FTAs (including AFTA), and establishing a common currency or monetary union.[13]

With the trauma of the Asian crisis not too far behind them, and inspired by the market-led integration or regionalisation that has already taken place, the ASEAN+3 countries may indeed be looking forward to the benefits of this type of economic integration, but there are some big and small challenges as well. One fundamental concern is that the collective agenda of liberalisation will force certain members to undertake structural reforms in their economies which may cause pain for domestic interests, as elaborated by Hamilton-Hart. While there are 13 countries involved in East Asian community building (for the moment), key decisions about economic and financial issues are really made by only a few, and not always with the proper consultative processes undertaken with domestic stakeholders. One may expect domestic resistance to arise after agreements have been concluded, rather than being taken into account beforehand.

Some countries may also wish to make precise use of regional frameworks to push ahead with otherwise domestically unpopular structural reforms. It is easier to address internal opposition when one can argue that regional and international regimes are being established, and that to survive and maintain an edge the economies have no option but to subject themselves to said regimes. This may be said to be true for Japan, where strong agricultural lobbies have long stalled market liberalisation, and for China, where Communist Party conservatives still maintain reservations about the rapid pace of China's integration with the global capitalist economy.

The diversity in economic structures creates challenges of its own. Much of economic regionalisation in East Asia is driven by very active private sector players. However, in some of the less developed countries, such private industries as may exist have not yet reached the level of organisation that enable them to assert any corporate influence on official policy.

Such diversity in the levels of economic development among the countries of East Asia, while being a source of complementarities, can also result in problems. Between the two extremes of Japan, on the one hand, and Laos, on the other, is a whole range of differing degrees of affluence and poverty, power and powerlessness. Comparing across the region, more efforts have to be directed to human resource development, capacity building, and strengthening of infrastructure in the less developed countries such as Cambodia, Laos, Vietnam, and Myanmar if the gap is to be narrowed and if regionalism, as Chavez has argued, is to benefit all rather than just a few. Social investment in education, health, and basic social services will have to increase before any blueprint for economic growth can be considered sustainable. Indeed, the East Asian Study Group report identified poverty alleviation, comprehensive human resources development, and healthcare as among the priority short-term measures for cooperation. While these remain primary responsibilities of the states themselves, placing them on the regional agenda means a shared commitment to address them together.

The technological gap among East Asians should also be addressed. The digital divide between some countries, for instance Korea and Myanmar, will impede bilateral cooperation such that the more advanced economies may prefer to deal only with other advanced economies in the expectation of better and faster returns. On another point, while technology transfer is desirable and has also been included in the EASG report's immediate measures for implementation, attention should be given to ensuring that such technology transfer is appropriate to the needs and conditions (economic, social as well as cultural) of the recipient country.

Overcoming differences among social and political systems will be a true challenge, and this is perhaps where the EAVG and the EASG reports are indeed visionary and can be truly path breaking. Again, a whole range of systems thrive in the region, from what has sometimes been considered ultra-democratic Philippines to authoritarian Vietnam and praetorian Myanmar. The nature of governance in these countries will be important factors in the process of community building, a process which may start out as utilitarian in purpose but ultimately has to be underpinned by common basic norms and values. The development of common norms will not happen overnight but it is rather encouraging that at this early stage, the need for agreement on certain norms is acknowledged in the documents outlining the vision of an East Asian community.

Inasmuch as ASEAN has moved to become a 'community of caring societies', the ASEAN+3 through the EAVG and EASG recommendations have also acknowledged the need for more human security-centred, more participative, and more consultative approaches to regional development. The EAVG and EASG ventured to give NGOs a role in the (perhaps long-term) future, in the context of strengthening state–civil society partnerships in tackling social and environmental problems,[14] even knowing that there are countries in the region where civil society is virtually non-existent as of yet.

Issues of institutionalisation

At this juncture, issues of institutionalisation loom large on the agenda of East Asian cooperation. An East Asian community cannot remain amorphous, that is without structure or form. And no vision – no matter how progressive – can be so inspiring that it can move governments, enterprises, and citizens to take actions autonomously transcending national borders without first having to establish the mechanisms and procedures through which policy coordination and information exchanges can take place and become regularised. Thus the question of institutionalisation of an East Asian community is of fundamental concern.

There are a number of unanswered questions that will have to be addressed through time. First, how will East Asian community building, currently consisting of the countries of ASEAN, China, Japan, and Korea, relate to existing regional cooperation initiatives such as APEC, ARF, ASEM, or ASEAN itself? At present, ASEAN plays a central role in many of the key processes, and some of the proposals for East Asian cooperation actually are expanded versions of the successful experiences of ASEAN. But if East Asian cooperation on many of these functional and economic matters were to get off the ground, then ASEAN itself would likely be of reduced relevance even to its own members. If the Southeast Asian states wish to see ASEAN survive as a separate institution because they expect it still to play a strategic role in the future – perhaps as a hedge against failure of the East Asia concept – then measures to secure ASEAN must be set in place even while earnest efforts to transform the ASEAN+3 into the East Asia Community (with a capital 'C') are undertaken.

ASEAN thus becomes saddled with the simultaneous burdens of continuing to intensify its own integration in Southeast Asia (not to mention subregional initiatives among a smaller number of its members), shepherding the ASEAN+3 process towards gradually evolving into the East Asian Community, 'driving' the

ARF process towards establishing more stable and predictable security regimes in its immediate neighbourhood, and participating actively in achieving APEC's mission of trade liberalisation and facilitation in the Asia–Pacific. These different levels of regional cooperation are committed to the same vision broadly defined as peace and prosperity (in Southeast Asia/East Asia/Asia–Pacific) and may have their distinctive added value or contributions to make. However, with their overlapping memberships and some similar programme thrusts (for example, cooperation against terrorism and transnational crime), it is not unlikely that over time – if and when the states become engaged in less dialogue and more action – they may evolve into duplicating and eventually competing arrangements, resulting in inefficient use of resources and unnecessary dispersion of efforts.

Another issue in institutionalisation is the extent to which the East Asian community-building project should be managed as an ASEAN+3 effort, instead of a 3+ASEAN concept. The ASEAN+3 framework seems to presume that ASEAN takes the lead, that the main locus of concern is the ASEAN region, and that the '+3' countries are there to help the ASEAN countries in whatever way they can, albeit driven by their shared interests with ASEAN. From an economic perspective, some would look at this situation as rather like the tail wagging the dog, what with the dynamic economies of Northeast Asia being in a much better position to take the lead. Recent events demonstrate that China has been taking much of the initiative in hastening its own integration with ASEAN.

The question of who leads, however, has been answered not from economic considerations but from realpolitik ones. Only ASEAN can drive the process for a number of reasons. First, only ASEAN is acceptable to all other parties. As stated earlier, neither Beijing nor Tokyo will allow the other to take the leadership role, and South Korea has yet to establish itself as a major stakeholder in Southeast Asia. Second, while China, Japan, and South Korea are the stronger economies, Northeast Asia as a whole is less stable than the Southeast Asian region, due to the flashpoints in the Korean peninsula and Taiwan Strait, as well as difficult Chinese–Japanese and Korean–Japanese relations.

If the driving force behind East Asian community building were from Northeast Asia, any outbreak of armed conflict there would for certain condemn the community-building project to the dustbin of history, whereas if ASEAN were to lead and conflict occur involving Northeast Asian countries, it might still be able to salvage regionalism by temporarily reverting to separate dialogues with the antagonists, if necessary, and playing the role of an interlocutor, if not mediator. Third, and perhaps most importantly, it is ASEAN which has developed the norms and achieved familiarity with the behavioural patterns required of regionalism and multilateralism, including consultation, accommodation, harmonisation of interests, self-restraint, gradualism, and inclusiveness. ASEAN moreover is not a military organisation. In contrast, Japan and South Korea perhaps by necessity tend to rely on their respective bilateral military alliances with the United States, while China to some extent still demonstrates xenophobia and tends to have a zero-sum attitude towards its security.

Some would point to a third institutional option, neither ASEAN+3 nor 3+ASEAN, but eventually an East Asian 13. The major implication of this is that ASEAN ceases to be a bloc within East Asia, and that the 10 Southeast Asian countries come to the table without need for prior coordination among them, but rather each representing only their national constituencies. Indeed, the vision of an East Asian Community presumes a fully integrated region, not merely a mechanism for coordination by two or more separate subregional enti-ties. However, there are also problems with the scenario of an East Asian 13.

First, following decades of existence and institutionalisation, ASEAN cannot simply be done away with, nor its programmes simply expanded to include the Northeast Asian countries, which may have totally different priorities from those of ASEAN in the first place. Second, the newer members of ASEAN may feel that they have yet to enjoy the anticipated fruits of their socialisation into ASEAN and yet still another layer of regionalism is emerging with ASEAN+3, bringing new challenges and pressures that they may feel unprepared to address. Third, for the Southeast Asian states to approach China, Japan, and South Korea as individual nation states rather than with the corporate identity of ASEAN may diminish their influence and attraction, especially for the less devel-oped states.

Over the long term, membership in the East Asian Community could conceivably become open to other regional states – for example, East Timor, North Korea, Mongolia, perhaps even Taiwan – but this is currently not on the agenda. Yet, already the issue of who should be part of an East Asian commu-nity-building project is causing a stir, in connection with preparations for the East Asian Summit to be held in Kuala Lumpur in December 2005.

The convening of the East Asian Summit was originally one of the proposals of the East Asia Vision Group, but was expected to evolve after a period of holding lower-level dialogues and developing dense interactions among bureaucrats, a process which would by then have led to a clearer understanding of the roadmap to community. The East Asian Study Group endorsed the recommendation as a long-term measure to be implemented. However, contrary to expectations, the EAS will be held much earlier, and as of this writing, participation has expanded such that, apart from the ASEAN+3 countries, expected to join the meeting are Australia, New Zealand, and India. Japan has also been quietly lobbying for some kind of participation by the United States, stretching the definition of East Asia beyond geography. The question that arises, however, is that if the EAS were to involve much more than the ASEAN+3 countries, would it still be linked to the ASEAN+3-driven East Asian community-building project, or would it be yet another parallel effort? What could an 'expanded East Asia' contribute that is not already being taken up in APEC and the ARF? Will participation by the United States and other non-Asian parties not undermine the original purpose and detract from the original value envisioned by the ASEAN+3 framers?

Yet another challenge to the institutionalisation of an East Asian community is the need to ensure that the regionalisation of the market and policy coordination by the states be accompanied by successful and substantive interactions among civil society sectors and organisations across the region, whatever the character of said civil society may be in particular countries. This way, regional community building avoids becoming the elitist project that ASEAN tended to be during its early decades, and anchors itself on more solid support through a process of 'regionalism from below'. One difficulty here is that many organised civil society groups in the region have banded around the common cause of opposition to globalisation and liberalisation, something that puts them at odds with many governments in the region, the diversity of which Curley described in her discussion of regional civil society. Only if regional cooperation involving state actors and market forces can demonstrate its utility in mediating and cushioning the effects of unchecked globalisation, even while turning the forces of globalisation to the region's advantage, will such a type of complementary grassroots regionalism emerge in East Asia.

East Asian identity building

Ultimately, community building is all about building a common regional identity. In this aspect, too, East Asia finds itself challenged. The diversity of cultures and historical experiences across the region renders the issue of a regional identity quite problematic. Some countries, notably the young, post-colonial, multi-ethnic states of Southeast Asia, have relatively weak national identities. Large sections of the population accord primary identification and loyalty to their ethno-linguistic group, religious community, social class, or other subnational collective rather than to the nation state, in some cases resulting in separatist, communal, or other types of social conflict. In such divided societies, even the construction of national – much less East Asian – identity is considered work in progress. This may result in difficulty in generating domestic policy consensus on the key issues that states must face at the regional level – one important requirement for regional cooperation.

At the opposite end are the more homogeneous societies of China, Japan, and South Korea – where peoples may well have a surplus of national pride, underpinned by strong cultural identities. National pride and strong cultural identity can equally get in the way of regional cooperation, such as when they translate into a fierce attachment to independence and persistent remembrance of historical grievances against neighbours, as in the case of China–Japan and Korea–Japan relations. Building a regional community and a regional identity based on newly defined common goals while trying to overcome historical divisions and antagonisms will certainly be a long-term challenge.

Countries in the region are also undergoing internal transformations that are bound to affect the level of commitment by their elites to regional cooperation. These include the economic, technological, and social revolutions underway in China; democratisation growth pains for Indonesia, the Philippines, Korea, and Thailand; the transition from centrally planned to market-oriented economies in

Vietnam and China; political development issues in Cambodia, Laos, and Myanmar; elite succession and policy reform in Japan, Singapore, Malaysia, and Brunei, and so on. For some, but not necessarily all, these will imply a degree of preoccupation with domestic concerns, reducing attention and commitment to regional issues. Most notably, since the fall of Suharto in 1998, Indonesia has been unable to exercise the leadership it formerly enjoyed over the ASEAN region in terms of shepherding community-building initiatives; while the Arroyo government in the Philippines finds itself hard pressed to justify regionalist/globalist policies in the face of growing popular dissatisfaction over government corruption and ineptness. Against this backdrop there is bound to be a lack of champions and interlocutors among the region's key figures for the more conscious efforts at East Asian identity building, as perhaps compared with ASEAN's early years of community building.

While East Asian regionalism, as argued earlier, may have strong political and economic impetus, the question of building a regional identity must also rely on social and cultural affinities. In this regard, the Confucian-influenced societies of China, Japan, Korea, and Vietnam may have much more in common with each other than with other Southeast Asian countries. The less obvious commonalities across the East Asian region have yet to be unearthed, for which reason groups such as the East Asia Forum and the Network of East Asia Studies are keen to engage in collaborative research projects and regular discussions and dialogues. Of particular interest is a proposal to write a history of East Asia from the perspective of the region's own scholars.

The key to building an East Asian socio-cultural community is in the active linkages that have yet to be built among scholars, writers, civil society organisations, non-governmental organisations, youth, professionals from different walks of life, artists, and others. Rather than merely looking back to the past, the task of building a regional identity involves crafting a common destiny based on common aspirations, thus the crucial role of the youth, the producers of knowledge, and other meaning-makers in society.

With this long list of potential pitfalls, trouble spots and requisite conditions for the building of a successful East Asian Community, it is easy to be sceptical, if not outright cynical, about its future prospects. As the history of European integration as well as the experiences of ASEAN show, regional community building is not for the easily disheartened, but for visionaries and strategists, namely those who are prepared to move forward steadfastly, particularly who choose – as an old Chinese expression goes – *to stand high and to look far*. But the real strength of the peoples of East Asia, which may yet be the key to successful regionalism, is not their possession of such a vision, but rather their pragmatism and their patience in pursuing it.

Notes

1 This chapter draws in part from a rapporteur's report presented by the author at the China–ASEAN Research Institute's Roundtable on 'Regionalism and Community Building in East Asia', organised by the University of Hong Kong's Centre for Asian Studies in October 2002.

2   Richard Stubbs, 'ASEAN+3: Emerging East Asian Regionalism?', *Asian Survey*, 2002, vol. 42, no. 3, pp. 440–55.

3   Mark Beeson, 'ASEAN+3 and the Rise of Reactionary Regionalism', *Contemporary Southeast Asia*, August 2003, vol. 25, no. 2, pp. 251–68.

4   The ASEAN Economic Community seeks to transform ASEAN into a single market and production base, characterised by the free movement of goods, services, investment, and capital by 2020. The elimination of tariff and non-tariff barriers is expected to enhance economic efficiency, productivity, and competitiveness in the region, even while the region remains open and outward looking towards other economic partners and stays committed to the multilateral trading system. The Security Community is described as a comprehensive framework for political and security cooperation, including providing mechanisms to resolve conflicts among member states and giving more emphasis to 'non-traditional security issues' such as terrorism. It is also thus far negatively defined as 'neither a military bloc nor a political union'. Meanwhile, the goal of a Social Cultural Community is the embodiment of the region's efforts to nurture more socially progressive and 'caring societies', putting a human face on what has been roundly criticised in the past as an elitist, state-centred, or even authoritarian, project. This is according to Sundram Pushpanathan, ASEAN's head of external relations, as quoted in *Asia Times*, 'ASEAN to adopt three-pronged charter to speed up integration', 2 October 2003.

5   The Vision document was drawn up at the unofficial 'Track II' level by a committee known as the East Asian Vision Group (EAVG), composed of 26 representatives from the 13 ASEAN+3 countries. The ASEAN+3 governments then appointed an East Asian Study Group (EASG) as the official mechanism to study the EAVG report. EASG in turn endorsed major recommendations of the EAVG while classifying them into short-term and long-term packages for cooperation.

6   Mari Pangestu and Sudarshan Gooptu, 'New Regionalism: Options for East Asia', in Kathie Krumm and Homi Kharas (eds) *East Asia Integrates: A Trade Policy Agenda for Shared Growth*, Washington, DC: World Bank and Oxford University Press, 2004, p. 40.

7   Ibid.

8   Elena Ianchovichina, Sethaput Suriwart-Narueput, and Min Zhao, 'Regional Impact of China's Accession to the WTO', in Krumm and Kharas (eds) *East Asia Integrates*, p. 22.

9   Pangestu and Gooptu, p. 42.

10 In an earlier article I argued that China, for as long as it continues to be led by a Communist Party, represents to the United States the unfinished business of the Cold War, and the one thing that makes the triumph of liberal democracy incomplete. Moreover, following the collapse of the Soviet Union, China remains the only credible justification for US military preponderance in the world, the one thing that Washington will not readily relinquish. See Aileen Baviera, 'The China Factor in US Alliances in East Asia and the Pacific', *Australian Journal of International Affairs*, July 2003, vol. 57, no. 2, pp. 339–52.

11 Policy Recommendations Paper, 'Towards an East Asian Community' by the Network of East Asian Think Tanks (NEAT), submitted to the ASEAN+3 Summit, Vientiane, 29–30 November 2004.

12 EAVG Report.

13 Policy Recommendations Paper, 'Towards an East Asian Community'.

14 EASG Report Executive Summary.

Appendix

Current status of regional cooperative regimes in Northeast Asia, East Asia and the Asia–Pacific

Region	Cooperation regime	Level	Participating countries (observer states)	Characteristics	Process
Northeast Asia	Northeast Asia Cooperation Dialogue (NEACD)	Track II	ROK, DPRK, US, Japan, PRC, Russia	Dialogue for the promotion of regional security, military transparency and confidence building Delegations composed of foreign and defence ministers, military officials and academics (in their individual capacity)	1993 La Jolla 1994 Tokyo 1995 Podmoskovie, Russia 1996 Beijing 1996 Seoul 1997 Harriman, New York 1997 Tokyo 1998 Moscow 1999 Beijing 2000 Seoul 2001 Honolulu 2002 Tokyo 2002 Moscow 2003 Qingdao 2004 Washington, DC 2005 Seoul
Northeast Asia	Limited nuclear-weapons-free zone for Northeast Asia	Track II	ROK, US, Japan, PRC, Russia, Mongolia (Finland, France, Argentina)	Assessment of regional nuclear threats Participation at the semi-governmental level	1995 Preparatory Meeting in Atlanta 1996 Buenos Aires 1996 Bordeaux 1997 Moscow 1998 Helsinki 1999 Tokyo 2000 Beijing 2001 Seoul 2002 Ulaanbaatar 2004 Jeju Island

Region	Cooperation regime	Level	Participating countries (observer states)	Characteristics	Process
East Asia	Association of Southeast Asian Nations (ASEAN)	Track I	Malaysia, Thailand, Indonesia, Singapore, Philippines, Vietnam, Laos, Myanmar, Brunei, Cambodia (Papua New Guinea)	Annual Summit meeting aimed to foster cooperation and mutual assistance among members	1967 Bangkok (1st A SEAN Ministerial Meeting) 1976 Bali (1st ASEAN Summit) 1977 Kuala Lumpur (2nd ASEAN Summit) 1987 Manila (3rd ASEAN Summit) 1992 Singapore (4th ASEAN Summit) 1995 Bangkok (5th ASEAN Summit) 1996 Jakarta (1st Informal Summit) 1997 Kuala Lumpur (2nd Informal Summit) 1998 Hanoi (6th ASEAN Summit) 1999 Manila (3rd Informal Summit) 2000 Singapore (4th Informal Summit) 2001 Bandar Seri Begawan (7th ASEAN Summit) 2002 Phnom Penh (8th ASEAN Summit) 2003 Bali (9th ASEAN Summit) 2004 Vientiane (10th ASEAN Summit) 2005 Kuala Lumpur (11th ASEAN Summit)

Cooperation regime	Level	Participating countries (observer states)	Characteristics	Process
ASEAN+3	Track I	ASEAN + ROK, PRC, Japan	Expanded from ASEAN since 1997	1997–2004 See ASEAN
ASEAN Regional Forum (ARF)	Track I, Track II	ROK, DPRK, US, Japan, PRC, Russia, Australia, Canada, Malaysia, New Zealand, Thailand, Brunei, Myanmar, Indonesia, Singapore, Laos, Vietnam, Philippines, Cambodia, Mongolia, India, Pakistan, EU, Papua New Guinea, East Timor	Informal multilateral dialogue of 25 members that seeks to address security issues in the Asia–Pacific region	1994 Bangkok 1995 Brunei 1996 Jakarta 1997 Subangjaya 1998 Manila 1999 Singapore 2000 Bangkok 2001 Hanoi 2002 Bandar Seri Begawan 2003 Phnom Penh 2004 Jakarta 2005 Vientiane

Region	Cooperation regime	Level	Participating countries (observer states)	Characteristics	Process
East Asia	East Asian Vision Group (EAVG)	Track II	ASEAN+3	Drafted a report on moving towards building an East Asian community. Report included recommendations on how to promote economic, political, environmental, social, cultural, educational cooperation in the long term	1998 First proposed at the ASEAN+3 Summit in Hanoi 1999 EAVG launched 2001 Submitted the final report at the ASEAN+3 Summit in Bandar Seri Begawan
East Asia	East Asian Study Group (EASG)	Track I	ASEAN+3	Drafted report on how to implement EAVG recommendations at the governmental level	2000 First proposed at the ASEAN+3 Summit in Singapore 2001 EASG launched 2002 Final report submitted at the ASEAN+3 Summit in Phnom Penh

Region	Cooperation regime	Level	Participating countries (observer states)	Characteristics	Process
Asia–Pacific	Asia–Pacific Economic Cooperation (APEC)	Track I	Australia, Brunei, Canada, Chile, PRC, Hong Kong, Japan, Indonesia, ROK, Malaysia, Mexico, New Zealand, Peru, Papua New Guinea, Philippines, Singapore, Chinese Taipei, Thailand, Vietnam, Russia, US	Intergovernmental forum for facilitating economic growth, cooperation, trade and investment in the Asia–Pacific region. No treaty obligations required of its participants. Decisions made within APEC are reached by consensus	1989 Canberra 1990 Singapore 1991 Seoul 1992 Bangkok 1993 Blake Island 1994 Bogor 1995 Osaka 1996 Manila 1997 Vancouver 1998 Kuala Lumpur 1999 Auckland 2000 Bandar Seri Begawan 2001 Shanghai 2002 Los Cabos 2003 Bangkok 2004 Santiago 2005 Busan
Asia–Pacific	Council for Security Cooperation in the Asia–Pacific (CSCAP)	Track II	ROK, DPRK, US, Japan, China, Russia, Australia, Canada, New Zealand, Malaysia, Thailand, Indonesia, Singapore, Philippines, Vietnam, Mongolia, Brunei, Cambodia, Papua New Guinea, India, EU	Discussion and research on various security issues in the region, led by strategic studies institutes from 21 countries in the Asia–Pacific region	1993 Lombok (Adoption of Charter) Since June 1994, annually held in Kuala Lumpur

Region	Cooperation regime	Level	Participating countries (observer states)	Characteristics	Process
Asia–Pacific	Asia Security Conference (ASC)	Track II	ROK, US, Japan, PRC, Russia, UK, France, Australia, Thailand, Indonesia, Cambodia, Mongolia, Philippines, Brunei, Malaysia, Myanmar, Singapore, East Timor, India, New Zealand	Non-governmental high-level defence management conference hosted by the IISS	Since 2002, annually held in Singapore
Asia	Conference on Interaction and Confidence-Building Measures in Asia (CICA)	Track I	PRC, Afghanistan, Russia, Azerbaijan, Uzbekistan, Iran, Israel, Egypt, India, Palestine, Tajikistan, Kazakhstan, Kyrgyzstan, Turkey, Mongolia, Pakistan (ROK, US, Japan, Ukraine, Indonesia, Vietnam, Thailand, Malaysia)	Intergovernmental multilateral security cooperation regime created with the aim to promote confidence building and prevent conflict among countries in the Central Asian region	1993 1st Experts Meeting 1993 2nd Experts Meeting 1994 Senior Officials Meeting 1996 Deputy Foreign Ministers Meeting 1997 Special Working Group Meeting 1997 Deputy Foreign Ministers Meeting 1999 Foreign Ministers Meeting (formally launched) 2000 Preparatory Meeting 2002 1st Summit Meeting 2004 Foreign Ministers Meeting

Region	Cooperation regime	Level	Participating countries (observer states)	Characteristics	Process
Asia	Shanghai Cooperation Organisation (SCO)	Track I	PRC, Russia, Kazakhstan, Tajikistan, Kyrgyzstan, Uzbekistan	Established with the aim to counter terrorist, separatist, and fundamentalist activities in Central Asia	2002 Established as a result of an agreement by the heads of state in St Petersburg 2004 SCO Secretariat established
Asia–Europe	Asia–Europe Meeting (ASEM)	Track II	25 EU member states, EU Commission, ASEAN+3 member states	Promote mutual recognition and build a partnership between the two regions, which would reflect the new global context of the 1990s and the perspectives of the new century	1996 Bangkok (ASEM I) 1998 London (ASEM II) 2000 Seoul (ASEM III) 2002 Copenhagen (ASEM IV) 2004 Hanoi (ASEM V)

Region	Cooperation regime	Level	Participating countries (observer states)	Characteristics	Process
Asia–Latin America	Forum for East Asia Latin America Cooperation (FEALAC)	Track I	Australia, Brunei, Cambodia, China, Indonesia, Japan, Korea, Laos, Malaysia, Myanmar, New Zealand, Philippines, Singapore, Thailand, Vietnam, Argentina, Bolivia, Brazil, Colombia, Costa Rica, Cuba, Chile, Ecuador, Mexico, El Salvador, Panama, Paraguay, Peru, Uruguay Venezuela, Guatemala, Nicaragua	Ministerial meeting between the two regions to establish a closer working relationship and to promote further collaboration in key areas of education and science and technology	2001 Santiago 2004 Manila

Cooperation regime proposals that have never been realised:

1 All-Asian Security Forum, May 1985, Former Soviet General Secretary Mikhail Gorbachev.

2 ASEAN-PMC (Post-Ministerial Conference), July 1990, Former Australian Foreign Minister Gareth Evans.

3 North Pacific Cooperative Security Dialogue, July 1991, Former Canadian Foreign Minister Cecil Clarke.

4 Proposals that are currently being pursued:

5 Northeast Asian Security Dialogue (NEASD), May 1994, Korean proposal at the ARF-SOM (still being pursued).

Bibliography

'Abdullah: China Can Help ASEAN to Rally', *New Straits Times*, Kuala Lumpur, 29 July 1998.

Abdullah, Saiful Azhar, 'New Sense of Confidence to Meet Economic Problems in the Region', *New Straits Times*, 18 December 1997.

Acharya, Amitav, 'ASEAN and Conditional Engagement', in James Shinn (ed.) *Weaving the Net: Conditional Engagement with China*, New York: Council on Foreign Relations, 1996, pp. 220–48.

Acharya, Amitav, 'A Concert of Asia?', *Survival*, Autumn 1999, vol. 41, no. 3, pp. 84–101.

Acharya, Amitav, 'Containment, Engagement, or Counter-Dominance: Malaysia's Response to the Rise of Chinese Power', in Alastair Johnston and Robert Ross (eds) *Engaging China: The Management of an Emerging Power*, London: Routledge, 1999, pp. 129–51.

Acharya, Amitav, *Constructing a Security Community in Southeast Asia: ASEAN and the Problem of Regional Order*, London: Routledge, 2001.

Acharya, Amitav, *Regionalism and Multilateralism: Essays on Cooperative Security in the Asia Pacific*, Singapore: Eastern Universities Press, 2003.

Acharya, Amitav, 'Seeking Security: The East Asian Way', *The Straits Times*, 30 December 2004.

Achieving the APEC Vision. Second Report of the Eminent Persons Group, Singapore: APEC Secretariat, August 1994.

'Acid Rain Causes Annual Economic Loss of 110 billion yuan in China', *China Daily (Xinhua)*, 10 October 2003. Online. Available: http://www2.chinadaily.com.cn/en/doc/2003-10/10/content_270868.htm.

Adler, Emanuel, 'Imagined (Security) Communities: Cognitive Regions in International Relations', *Millennium*, 1997, vol. 26, no. 2, pp. 249–77.

Adler, Emanuel and Michael Barnett (eds), *Security Communities*, Cambridge: Cambridge University Press, 1998.

'AEM approves recommendations of HLTF to formalise AEC', *Financial Times Information*, 2 September 2003.

'Agreement on Conservation of Nature and Natural Resources', Kuala Lumpur, 9 July 1985. Online. Available: http://www.aseansec.org/6080.htm.

Akamatsu, Kaname, 'A Historical Pattern of Economic Growth in Developing Countries', *The Developing Economies*, 1962, Preliminary Issue No. 1, pp. 3–25.

Alagappa, Muthiah (ed.), *Civil Society and Political Change in Asia: Expanding and Contracting Democratic Space*, Stanford, CA: Stanford University Press, 2004.

Amin, Ash, 'Regions Unbound: Towards a New Politics and Place', *Geografiska Annaler B*, 2004, vol. 86, no. 1, pp. 31–42.

'Amnesty International Issues Appeal for Three Gorges Dam Protestors', 23 April 2001, Online. Available: http://www.threegorgesprobe.org/tgp/index.cfm?DSP = context&ContentID=2014.

Amyx, Jennifer, 'Japan and the Evolution of Regional Financial Arrangements in East Asia', in Ellis Krause and T. J. Pempel (eds) *Beyond Bilateralism: US-Japan Relations in the New Asia-Pacific*, Stanford, CA: Stanford University Press, 2004, pp. 198–218.

'APEC Ministers to Focus on Stability and Reputation', Agence France Press, 2000.

Areddy, James, 'Miyazawa Suggests Asia Adopt Tricurrency Link', *The Asian Wall Street Journal*, 18 January 1999, p. 3.

Ariff, Mohamed, 'Trade, Investment and Interdependence', in Simon Tay, Jesus Estanislao and Hadi Soesastro (eds) *Reinventing ASEAN*, Singapore: Institute of Southeast Asian Studies, 2001, pp. 45–66.

'ASEAN Accelerates Integration of Priority Sectors', *ASEAN Secretariat Media Release*, Vientiane, 29 November 2004.

'ASEAN, Australia, New Zealand to further cooperation projects, FTA negotiations', *Xinhua*, 26 September 2005.

'ASEAN-China to Implement First Phase of FTA on 1 July', *Malaysian National News Agency*, 7 June 2005.

'ASEAN Declaration on Heritage Parks and Reserves', Bangkok, 29 November 1984. Online. Available: http://www.aseansec.org/6078.htm.

'ASEAN Drops Bid to Invite China, Japan, Korea to Phuket', *Japan Economic Newswire*, 10 April 1995.

'ASEAN Free Trade Area Council Meeting Ends in Phnom Penh', *BBC Monitoring*, 22 September 2003.

'ASEAN, India delay FTA target until January 2007', *Japan Economic Newswire*, 26 September 2005.

ASEAN: Narrowing the Development Gap, Jakarta: ASEAN Secretariat, May 2005.

'ASEAN Regional Forum: Powell, North Korea's Peak Hold Brief Talks', *The Nation*, Bangkok, 2 August 2002.

'ASEAN Sec-General Thanks Malaysia's Effort to Organise AMCA Meetings', *Financial Times Information*, 14 October 2003.

'ASEAN Seeks Completion of FTA Talks with S. Korea by 2007', *Asia Pulse*, 6 September 2004.

'ASEAN to Adopt Three-pronged Charter to Speed Up Integration', 2 October 2003.

'ASEAN to Make Final Decision on New Membership May 31', *Japan Economic Newswire*, 7 April 1997.

'ASEAN to Set Up Human Resource Development Committee', *Financial Times Information*, 14 October 2003.

Asia 2002 Yearbook, Hong Kong Far Eastern Economic Review, 2002.

'Asian Central Banks to Work Together on Monetary Policy', *The Straits Times*, 26 February 2005.

'Asian Central Banks Unveil Details of Second Asian Bond Fund', *Channel News Asia*, 12 May 2005.

Asian Development Bank, *Subregional Cooperation Strategy and Programme Status Report: Southeast Asia*, 2002. Online. Available: http://www.adb.org/Documents/CSPs/SERD/reg_in225_02.pdf.

Asian Development Bank, *Asian Development Outlook 2004*, Manila: Asian Development Bank, 2004.

Asian Development Bank, *Asian Development Outlook 2005*, Manila: Asian Development Bank, 2005.

Asian Development Bank, 'Chiang Mai Initiative (CMI): Current Status and Future Directions', *Public statement*, 12 May 2004. Online. Available: http://aric.adb.org.

'Asian Officials Agree to Forex Stability Panel', *Global News Wire – Asia Africa Intelligence Wire*, 8 March 2005.

Australian Department of Foreign Affairs and Trade, *In the National Interest*, Canberra: Australian Government Printing Service, 1997.

Baguioro, Luz, 'Manila Pushes for an Asian Currency', *The Straits Times*, 8 January 1999.

Baker, James, 'America in Asia: Emerging Architecture for a Pacific Community', *Foreign Affairs*, 1991/92, vol. 70, no. 5, pp. 1–18.

Baker, James, *The Politics of Diplomacy: Revolution, War & Peace, 1989–1992*, New York: G.P. Putnam's Sons, 1995.

Balassa, Bela, *The Theory of Economic Integration*, London: Allen and Unwin, 1961.

Battistella, Graziano, 'Unauthorized migrants as global workers in ASEAN', Paper presented at the IUSSP Regional Population Conference on Southeast Asia's Population in a Changing Asian Context, Chulalongkorn University, Thailand, 10–12 June 2002.

Baviera, Aileen, 'The China Factor in US Alliances in East Asia and the Pacific', *Australian Journal of International Affairs*, July 2003, vol. 57, no. 2, pp. 339–52.

Beeson, Mark, 'ASEAN+3 and the Rise of Reactionary Regionalism', *Contemporary Southeast Asia*, August 2003, vol. 25, no. 2, pp. 251–68.

Beeson, Mark, 'Sovereignty Under Siege: Globalisation and the State in Southeast Asia', *Third World Quarterly*, 2003, vol. 24, no. 2, pp. 357–74.

Bello, Walden, 'East Asia's Future: Strategic Economic Cooperation or Marginalization?', 1 October 2002. Online. Available: http://www.focusweb.org.

Bergsten, Fred and Yung Chul Park, 'Toward Creating a Regional Monetary Arrangement in East Asia', *ADB Institute Research Paper Series No. 50*, December 2002.

Bernard, Mitchell and John Ravenhill, 'Beyond Product Cycles and Flying Geese: Regionalization, Hierarchy, and the Industrialization of East Asia', *World Politics*, 1995, vol. 47, no. 2, pp. 171–209.

Blair, Dennis and John Hanley, 'From Wheels to Webs: Reconstructing Asia-Pacific Security Arrangements', *The Washington Quarterly*, 2001, vol. 21, no. 1, pp. 7–17.

Bøås, Morten, Marianne Marchand and Timothy Shaw, 'Special Issue: New Regionalisms in the New Millennium', *Third World Quarterly*, 1999, vol. 20, no. 5, pp. 897–1070.

Bowles, Paul, 'ASEAN, AFTA and the "New Regionalism"', *Pacific Affairs*, 1997, vol. 70, no. 2, pp. 219–34.

Brash, Donald, 'The Pros and Cons of a Currency Union – A Reserve Bank Perspective', Speech, 22 May 2000.

Breslin, Shaun, 'Decentralisation, Globalisation and China's Partial Engagement with the Global Economy', *New Political Economy*, 2000, vol. 5, no. 2, pp. 205–26.

Breslin, Shaun and Glenn Hook (eds), *Microregionalism and World Order*, Basingstoke: Palgrave, 2002.

Brettell, Anna (forthcoming) 'Security, Energy and the Environment: The Atmospheric Link', in In-taek Hyun and Miranda Schreurs (eds) *The Environmental Dimension of Asian Security: Conflict and Cooperation over Pollution, Energy and Natural Resources*, Washington, DC: United States Institute of Peace Press.

Bull, Benedicte, '"New Regionalism" in Central America', *Third World Quarterly*, 1999, vol. 20, no. 5, pp. 957–70.

Buzan, Barry, *People, State and Fear*, London: Harvester, 1983.

Buzan, Barry and Ole Wæver, *Regions and Powers: The Structure of International Security*, Cambridge: Cambridge University Press, 2003.

Caballero-Anthony, Mely, 'Non-state Regional Governance Mechanism for Economic Security: The Case of the ASEAN People's Assembly', *The Pacific Review*, 2004, vol. 17, no. 4, pp. 567–85.

Caballero-Anthony, Mely, 'Revising Human Security in Southeast Asia', *Asian Perspective*, 2004, vol. 28, no. 3, pp. 155–89.

Caballero-Anthony, Mely, *Regional Security in Southeast Asia: Beyond the ASEAN Way*, Singapore: Institute of Southeast Asian Studies, 2005.

Calleya, Stephen, *Navigating Regional Dynamics in the Post-Cold War World*, Aldershot: Dartmouth, 1997.

Calvo, Guillermo and Carmen Reinhart, 'Fear of Floating', *Quarterly Journal of Economics*, 2002, vol. 117, no. 2, pp. 379–408.

Capie, David, 'Power, Threats and Identity: Rethinking Institutional Dynamics in the Pacific, 1945–2000', Ph.D. Thesis, York University, Toronto, 2001.

Capie, David and Paul Evans (eds), *The Asia-Pacific Security Lexicon*, Singapore: Institute of South East Asian Studies, 2002.

Castells, Manuel, *The Rise of the Network Society: The Information Age: Economy, Society, and Culture, Volume 1*, Oxford: Blackwell, 1996.

Cha, Victor, *Alignment Despite Antagonism: The US-Korea-Japan Security Triangle*, Stanford, CA: Stanford University Press, 1999.

Chan, Norman, 'Governor's Statement', Address to the Thirty-fourth Asian Development Bank Annual Meeting, Honolulu, 9–11 May 2001. Online. Available: http://www.info.gov.hk/hkma/speeches/speechs/norman/20010510e.htm.

Charrier, Philip, 'ASEAN's Inheritance: the Regionalization of Southeast Asia, 1941–61', *The Pacific Review*, 2001, vol. 14, no. 3, pp. 313–38.

Chavez, Jenina, 'Economic Integration in the ASEAN: In Need of Another Miracle', *Asian Exchange*, 1998, vol. 13, no. 2, pp. 7–41.

Chavez, Jenina, 'From Flying Geese to Cog and Wheel: Some Issues on Sub-regional Economic Zones', *Asian Exchange*, 1998, vol. 14, no. 1, pp. 9–32.

Chavez, Jenina, 'Co-opting Cooperation: The Asian Development Bank and Sub-regional Economic Zones', in *Creating Poverty: The ADB in Asia*, Bangkok: Focus on the Global South, 2000, pp. 23–9.

Chellam, Raju, 'Singapore, Indonesia Sign Accord on Phone Testing', *The Business Times*, 22 April 2004.

Chen, Jie, 'Burgeoning Transnationalism of Taiwan's Social Movement NGOs', *Journal of Contemporary China*, 2001, vol. 10, no. 29, pp. 613–44.

Chen, Sulan, 'Induced and Instrumental Cooperation: Potential Legitimation and Confidence Building in the Environmental Politics of the South China Sea', Ph.D. dissertation, University of Maryland, 2005.

Chia Siow Yue and Wendy Dobson, 'Harnessing Diversity', in Wendy Dobson and Chia Siow Yue (eds) *Multinationals and East Asian Integration*, Singapore: Institute of Southeast Asian Studies, 1997. Online. Available: http://www.web.cdri.ca/es/ev-68168-201-1-DO_TOPIC.html.

'China, ASEAN Agree to End Tariffs', *The China Daily*, 26 October 2004.

'China, ASEAN to Expand Cultural Cooperation', *Xinhua*, 3 August 2005.

'China's Car Sales up 15% in 2004 After Nearly Doubling in 2003', *The Detroit News: Autos Insider*, 14 January 2005. Online. Available: http://www.detnews.com/2005/autosinsider/0501/14/-060176.htm.

'China Environmental NGO Activists Visited Korea to Understand the Korean Environment Movement', *Green Korea*, 30 November 2000. Online. Available: http://www.greenkorea.org.

'China, Indonesia Sign Swap Pact Up To 2bn dollars', *BBC Worldwide Monitoring*, 17 October 2005.

'China Says Its Ocean Gas Project not Issue for Talks with Japan', *Japan Economic Newswire*, 29 September 2005.

'China Wary of US-ASEAN Anti-Terrorism Pact', Agence France Presse, 30 July 2002.

Christensen, Thomas, 'China, the US-Japan Alliance, and the Security Dilemma in East Asia', *International Security*, 1999, vol. 23, no. 4, pp. 49–80.

Christoffersen, Gaye, 'The Role of East Asia in Sino-American Relations', *Asian Survey*, May/June 2002, vol. 42, no. 3, pp. 369–96.

'Clinton, Bush Tour Tsunami Damage', 19 February 2005. Online. Available: http://www.cbsnews.com/stories/2004/12/26/world/main663057.shtml.

Cocks, Peter, 'Towards a Marxist Theory of European Integration', *International Organization*, 1980, vol. 34, no. 1, pp. 1–40.

Colás, Alejandro, *International Civil Society*, Cambridge: Polity, 2002.

Conflict Research Consortium, University of Colorado, 'Collective Security', International Online Training Program on Intractable Conflict. Online. Available: http://www.colorado.edu/conflict/peace/treatment/collsec.htm.

Cossa, Ralph, 'Asian Multilateralism: Dialogue on Track II', *JFQ Forum*, 1995. Online. Available: http://www.dtic.mil/doctrine/jel/jfq_pubs/jfq1007.pdf.

Cossa, Ralph, 'A Chance to Patch Up the US-Japan Alliance', *International Herald Tribune*, 22 September 1998.

Cossa, Ralph, 'Bilateralism, Multilateralism, and the Search for Security in East Asia', Paper presented at Conference on 'Multilateralism, Bilateralism and the Search for Asian Security', St Antony's College, Oxford, May 2000.

Council on Foreign Relations, *The United States and Southeast Asia: A Policy Agenda for the New Administration*, Report of An Independent Task Force, New York: Council on Foreign Relations, 2001.

Cox, Robert, 'Civil Society at the Turn of the Millennium: Prospects for an Alternative', *Review of International Studies*, 1999, vol. 25, no. 1, pp. 3–28.

Cox, Robert with Timothy Sinclair, *Approaches to World Order*, Cambridge: Cambridge University Press, 1996.

Cronin, Patrick and Emily Metzgar, 'ASEAN and Regional Security', *Strategic Forum*, October 1996, no. 85. Online. Available: http://www.ndu.edu/inss/strforum/SF_85/forum85.html.

Curley, Melissa, 'NGOs in China: The Role of International Organizations and South-South Cooperation', *Asian Perspective*, 2002, vol. 26, no. 4, pp. 171–200.

de Brouwer, Gordon, 'Does a Formal Common-Basket Peg in East Asia Make Economic Sense?', in Gordon de Brouwer (ed.) *Financial Markets and Policies in East Asia*, London: Routledge, 2002, pp. 286–314.

Dent, Christopher, 'ASEM and the "Cinderella Complex" of EU-East Asia Economic Relations', *Pacific Affairs*, 2001, vol. 74, no. 1, pp. 25–52.

Dibb, Paul, 'Will America's Alliances in the Asia-Pacific Region Endure?', *Working Paper No. 345*, Canberra: Strategic and Defence Studies Centre, May 2000.

Dieter, Heribert and Richard Higgott, 'Exploring Alternative Theories of Economic Regionalism: From Trade to Finance in Asian Co-operation?', *Review of International Political Economy*, 2003, vol. 10, no. 3, pp. 430–54.

Dobson, Wendy, 'East Asian Integration: Synergies Between Firm Strategies and Government Policies', in Wendy Dobson and Chia Siow Yue (eds) *Multinationals and East Asian Integration*, Singapore: Institute of Southeast Asian Studies, 1997. Online. Available: http://www.web.idrc.ca/es/ev-68133-201-1-DO_TOPIC.html.

Dollah, Siti Rahil, 'China Calls for E. Asian-ASEAN Finance Dialogue', *Japan Economic Newswire*, 16 December 1998.

Donnan, Shawn and Andrew Ward, 'China, Japan and Korea to Widen Co-operation', *Financial Times*, 7 October 2003.

Dupont, Alan, *East Asia Imperilled: Transnational Challenges to Security*, Cambridge: Cambridge University Press, 2001.

'East Asia Market Proposal to be Talked at ASEAN Summit', *Japan Economic Newswire*, 24 January 1991.

'East Asian Nations to Scrutinize Short-Term Capital Flows', *Jiji Press Ticker Service*, 18 March 1999.

'Economic Bloc', *Nihon Keizai Shimbun*, 22 June 1991.

Edwards, Michael, *Future Positive – International Co-operation in the Twenty-first Century* (revised edn), London: Earthscan, 2004.

Eichengreen, Barry, *European Monetary Unification: Theory, Practice and Analysis*, Cambridge, MA: MIT Press, 1997.

Eichengreen, Barry and Tamim Bayoumi, 'Is Asia an Optimum Currency Area? Can it Become One? Regional, Global and Historical Perspectives on Asian Monetary Relations', in Stefan Collignon, Jean Pisani-Ferry and Yung Chul Park (eds) *Exchange Rate Policies in Emerging Asian Countries*, London: Routledge, 1999, pp. 347–66.

Elliott, Lorraine, 'ASEAN and Environmental Cooperation', *The Pacific Review*, 2003, vol. 16, no. 1, pp. 29–52.

Emmers, Ralf, 'The Influence of the Balance of Power Factor within the ASEAN Regional Forum', *Contemporary Southeast Asia*, August 2001, vol. 23, no. 2, pp. 275–91.

Engardio, Peter and Dexter, Roberts 'The China Price', *Business Week* (Asian edn), 6 December 2004, pp. 48–58.

Evans, Gareth, 'What Asia Needs is a Europe-Style CSCA', *International Herald Tribune*, 27 July 1990.

Evans, Gareth and Bruce Grant, *Australia's Foreign Relations in the World of the 1990s*, Melbourne: Melbourne University Press, 1992.

Evans, Paul, *Asia's New Regionalism: Implications for Canada*, Asia Pacific Foundation of Canada, 2003.

Fawcett, Louise and Andrew Hurrell (eds), *Regionalism in World Politics: Regional Organization and International Order*, Oxford: Oxford University Press, 1996.

Finnemore, Martha and Kathryn Sikkink, 'International Norm Dynamics and Political Change', *International Organization*, 1998, vol. 52, no. 4, pp. 887–917.

Foreign Press Center, Japan, 'Prospects for an East Asian Summit are Both Optimistic and Cautious', 3 December 2004. Online. Available: http://www.fpcj/e/shiryo/jb/0455.htm.

Francis, David, *The Politics of Economic Regionalism: Sierra Leone in ECOWAS*, Aldershot: Ashgate, 2001.

Friedberg, Aaron, 'Ripe for Rivalry: Prospects for Peace in a Multipolar Asia', *International Security*, 1993/4, vol. 18, no. 3, pp. 5–53

Frieden, Jeffry, 'Invested Interests: The Politics of National Economic Policies in a World of Global Finance', *International Organization*, 1991, vol. 45, no. 4, pp. 425–51.

Fukazawa, Junichi, 'First Round of FTA Talks with ASEAN Reveals Snags', *Yomiuri Shimbun*, 17 February 2004.

Fukushima, Akiko, *Multilateral Confidence Building Measures in Northeast Asia: Receding or Emerging?*. Online. Available: http://www.stimson.org/japan/pdf/fukushima.pdf.

Funabashi, Yoichi, *Asia Pacific Fusion: Japan's Role in APEC*, Washington, DC: Institute for International Economics, 1995.

Gabel, Matthew, 'Divided Opinion, Common Currency: The Political Economy of Public Support for EMU', in Barry Eichengreen and Jeffry Frieden (eds) *The Political Economy of European Monetary Unification*, Boulder, CO: Westview, 2001, pp. 49–76.

Gamble, Andrew and Anthony Payne (eds), *Regionalism and World Order*, Basingstoke: Macmillan, 1996.

'Gao Yaojie: Aids Activist, China', *Business Week Online*, 8 July 2002. Online. Available: http://www.businessweek.com/magazine/content/02-27/b3790611.htm.

Garnaut, Ross, 'Introduction – APEC ideas and reality', in Ippei Yamazawa, *Asia Pacific Economic Cooperation (APEC). Challenges and Tasks for the Twenty-first Century*, Pacific Trade and Development Conference Series, London: Routledge, 2000, pp. 1–18.

Gaylican, Christine, 'RP to Revive Early Harvest Program Talks with China', *Philippine Daily Inquirer*, 19 April 2004.

George, Cherian, 'Call for Regions to Hold Top-level Forum', *The Straits Times*, 15 October 1994.

Ghosh, Nirmal, 'Destroyed Mangroves Could Have Saved Lives', *The Straits Times, Singapore*, 8 January 2005. Online. Available: http://www.ecologyasia.com/news-archives/2005/jan-05/st_050108_1.htm.

Ghosh, Nirmal, 'Manila Supports PM Goh's Europe-Asia Summit Idea', *The Straits Times*, 17 February 1995.

Gilpin, Robert, *The Political Economy of International Relations*, Princeton, NJ: Princeton University Press, 1987.

Glasius, Marlies, David Lewis and Hakan Seckinelgin, *Exploring Civil Society – Political and Cultural Contexts*, London: Routledge, 2004.

Goh, Chok Tong, Keynote address to US-ASEAN Business Council annual dinner, Washington, DC, reprinted in *The Straits Times*, Singapore, 15 June 2001.

Goh, Evelyn, 'Hegemonic Constraints: The Implications of September 11 for American Power', *Australian Journal of International Affairs*, 2003, vol. 57, no. 1, pp. 77–97.

Goh, Gillian, '"The ASEAN Way": Non-Intervention and ASEAN's Role in Conflict Management', *Stanford Journal of East Asian Affairs*, 2003, vol. 3, no. 1, pp. 113–18.

Gordon, Joshua, 'NGOs, the Environment and Political Pluralism in New Order Indonesia', *Explorations in Southeast Asian Studies: A Journal of the Southeast Asian Studies Student Association*, Fall 1998, vol. 2, no. 2. Online. Available: http://www.hawaii.edu/cseas/pubs/explore/v2/gordon.html.

Gourevitch, Peter, 'Squaring the Circle: The Domestic Sources of International Cooperation', *International Organization*, 1996, vol. 50, no. 2, pp. 349–73.

Grant, J. Andrew and Fredrik Söderbaum (eds), *The New Regionalism in Africa*, Aldershot: Ashgate, 2003.

Grugel, Jean, 'New Regionalism and Modes of Governance – Comparing US and EU Strategies in Latin America', *European Journal of International Relations*, 2004, vol. 10, no. 4, pp. 603–26.

Grugel, Jean and Wil Hout, 'ASEAN, AFTA and the "New Regionalism"', in Jean Grugel and Wil Hout (eds) *Regionalism Across the North South Divide*, London: Routledge, 1998, pp. 169–77.

Gurtov, Mel, *Pacific Asia? Prospects for Security and Cooperation in East Asia*, Lanham, MD: Rowman & Littlefield, 2002.

Hamilton-Hart, Natasha, 'Co-operation on Money and Finance: How Important? How Likely?', *Third World Quarterly*, 2003, vol. 24, no. 2, pp. 283–97.

Hamilton-Hart, Natasha, 'Capital Flows and Financial Markets in Asia: National, Regional, or Global?', in Ellis Krause and T. J. Pempel (eds) *Beyond Bilateralism: US-Japan Relations in the New Asia-Pacific*, Stanford, CA: Stanford University Press, 2004, pp. 133–53.

'Hard Day for Thailand's Foreign Exchange, Stock Markets', *Xinhua*, 15 May 1997.

Harris, Paul (ed.), *International Environmental Cooperation: Politics and Diplomacy in Pacific Asia*, Boulder, CO: University Press of Colorado, 2003.

Harris, Paul (ed.), *Confronting Environmental Change in East and Southeast Asia: Eco-Politics, Foreign Policy and Sustainable Development*, Tokyo: United Nations University Press, 2005.

Haryati, Abdul Karim, 'BIMP-EAGA still Vital for Sabah's Domestic Mart', *Malaysia Economic News*, 20 June 2001.

'Hashimoto Gives Up EAEC Meeting: Official', *Jiji Press Ticker Service*, 6 April 1995.

Hashimoto, Ryutaro, *Reforms for the New Era of Japan and ASEAN: For a Broader and Deeper Partnership*, 14 January 1997. Online. Available: http://www.mofa.go.jp/region/asia-paci/asean/pmv9701/policy.html.

Hassan, Mohamed and Thangam Ramnath (eds), *Conceptualising Asia-Pacific Security*, Kuala Lumpur: ISIS Malaysia, 1996.

Hatakeyama, Noboru, 'FTA Movements in the Asia Pacific Region', *Journal of Japanese Trade & Industry*, 1 May 2004.

He, Baogang, 'Transnational Civil Society and the National Identity Question in East Asia', *Global Governance*, 2004, vol. 10, no. 2, pp. 227–46.

Henning, Randolph, *East Asian Financial Cooperation*, Washington, DC: Institute for International Economics, 2002.

Henning, Randolph, 'The Complex Political Economy of Cooperation and Integration', in Gordon de Brouwer and Wang Yunjong (eds) *Financial Governance in East Asia: Policy Dialogue, Surveillance and Cooperation*, London: RoutledgeCurzon, 2004, pp. 83–100.

Henson, Bertha, 'PM: Time to Forge Europe-E. Asia Link', *The Straits Times*, 20 October 1994.

Hentz, James and Morten Bøås, *New and Critical Security and Regionalism Beyond the Nation State*, Aldershot: Ashgate, 2003.

Heron, Tony, *The New Political Economy of United States-Caribbean Relations: The Apparel Industry and the Politics of NAFTA Parity*, Aldershot: Ashgate, 2004.

Hettne, Bjorn and Frederik Söderbaum, 'Theorising the Rise of Regionness', *New Political Economy*, 2000, vol. 5, no. 3, pp. 457–73.

Hettne, Björn, András Inotai and Osvaldo Sunkel (eds), *Globalism and the New Regionalism*, New York: St Martin's Press, 1999.

Hettne, Björn, András Inotai and Osvaldo Sunkel (eds), *National Perspectives on the New Regionalism in the North*, Basingstoke: Macmillan, 2000.

Hettne, Björn, András Inotai and Osvaldo Sunkel (eds), *National Perspectives on the New Regionalism in the South*, Basingstoke: Macmillan, 2000.

Hettne, Björn, András Inotai and Osvaldo Sunkel (eds), *National Perspectives on the New Regionalism in the Third World*, Basingstoke: Macmillan, 2000.

Hettne, Björn, András Inotai and Osvaldo Sunkel (eds), *The New Regionalism and the Future of Security and Development*, Basingstoke: Palgrave, 2000.

Hettne, Björn, András Inotai and Osvaldo Sunkel (eds), *Comparing Regionalisms: Implications for Global Development*, Basingstoke: Palgrave, 2001.

Hew, Denis and Hadi Soesastro, 'Realizing the ASEAN Economic Community by 2020: ISEAS and ASEAN-ISIS Approaches', *ASEAN Economic Bulletin*, 2003, vol. 20, no. 3, pp. 292–6.

Higgott, Richard, 'The Asian Economic Crisis: A Study in the Politics of Resentment', *New Political Economy*, 1998, vol. 3, no. 3, pp. 333–56.

Higgott, Richard, 'The International Political Economy of Regionalism: Europe and Asia Compared', in William Coleman and Geoffrey Underhill (eds) *Regionalism and Global Economic Integration: Europe, Asia, and the Americas*, London: Routledge, 1998, pp. 42–67.

Hirata, Keiko, *Civil Society in Japan: The Growing Role of NGOs in Tokyo's Aid and Development Policy*, New York: Palgrave Macmillan, 2002.

Hirono, Ryokichi (ed.), *Regional Co-operation in Asia*, Asian Development Experience, Singapore: Institute of Southeast Asian Studies, 2003, vol. 3.

Hiwatari, Nobuhiro, 'Embedded Policy Preferences and the Formation of International Arrangements after the Asian Financial Crisis', *The Pacific Review*, 2003, vol. 16, no. 3, pp. 331–59.

Hook, Glenn and Ian Kearns (eds), *Subregionalism and World Order*, Basingstoke: Macmillan, 1999.

Howell, Jude, 'Making Civil Society from the Outside – Challenges for Donors', *The European Journal of Development Research*, 2000, vol. 12, no. 1, pp. 3–22.

Howell, Jude and Jenny Pearce, *Civil Society and Development – A Critical Exploration*, Boulder, CO: Lynne Rienner, 2002.

Hughes, Christopher, 'Japanese Policy and the East Asian Currency Crisis: Abject Defeat or Quiet Victory?', *Review of International Political Economy*, 2000, vol. 7, no. 2, pp. 219–53.

Hughes, Christopher, 'Tumen River Area Development Programme (TRADP): Frustrated Microregionalism as a Microcosm of Political Rivalries', in Shaun Breslin and Glenn Hook (eds) *Microregionalism and World Order*, Basingstoke: Palgrave, 2002, pp. 115–43.

Huisken, Ron, 'Civilizing the Anarchical Society: Multilateral Security Processes in the Asia-Pacific', *Contemporary Southeast Asia*, August 2002, vol. 24, no. 2, pp. 187–202.

Hund, Markus, 'ASEAN+3: Towards a New Age of Pan-East Asian Regionalism? A Skeptic's Appraisal', *The Pacific Review*, 2003, vol. 16, no. 3, pp. 383–417.

Hurrell, Andrew, 'Explaining the Resurgence of Regionalism in World Politics', *Review of International Studies*, 1995, vol. 21, no. 4, pp. 331–58.

Hyun, In-taek and Samuel Kim (forthcoming) 'The Environment-Security Nexus in Northeast Asia', in In-taek Hyun and Miranda Schreurs (eds) *The Environmental Dimension of Asian Security: Conflict and Cooperation over Pollution, Energy and Natural Resources*, Washington, DC: United States Institute of Peace Press.

Hyun, In-taek and Miranda Schreurs (eds) (forthcoming) *The Environmental Dimension of Asian Security: Conflict and Cooperation over Pollution, Energy and Natural Resources*, Washington, DC: United States Institute of Peace Press.

Ianchovichina, Elena, Sethaput Suriwart-Narueput and Min Zhao, 'Regional Impact of China's Accession to the WTO', in Kathie Krumm and Homi Kharas (eds) *East Asia Integrates: A Trade Policy Agenda for Shared Growth*, Washington, DC: World Bank and Oxford University Press, 2004, pp. 21–38.

Ikenberry, John, *After Victory: Institutions, Strategic Restraint, and the Rebuilding of Order after Major Wars*, Princeton, NJ: Princeton University Press, 2001.

Ilagan-Bian, Joji, 'Crisscrossing Mindanao', *Philippine Daily Inquirer*, 18 March 2002.

Ilagan-Bian, Joji, 'Eight Years On', *Philippine Daily Inquirer*, 1 July 2002.

'Indon-Japan Currency Swap Deal Doubles to US$6b', *Business Times Singapore*, 1 September 2005.

Information on the BIMP-EAGA. Online. Available: http://www.medco.gov.ph/medcoweb/bimpeaga.asp.

Institute on Global Conflict and Cooperation, 'The Northeast Asia Cooperation Dialogue', 1993. Online. Available: http://www-igcc.ucsd.edu/regions/northeast_asia/neacd/neacddefault.php.

Institute on Global Conflict and Cooperation, 'Track Two Diplomacy in Northeast Asia: Debrief from the Recent Meetings of the NEACD and US-DPRK Dialogue', IGCC Policy Seminar, 27 April 2004, UC Washington Center. Online. Available: http://www-igcc.ucsd.edu/NEACDpolicyseminar.php.

International Games Archives, 'BIMP-EAGA Games'. Online. Available: http://www.internationalgames.net/bimpeage.htm.

International Monetary Fund, *World Economic Outlook September 2002*, Washington, DC, 2002.

International Monetary Fund, *World Economic Outlook April 2005*, Washington, DC, 2005.

International Red Cross and Red Crescent Societies, *World Disasters Report 2001*, Bloomfield, CT: Kumarian Press, 2001.

Irvine, David, 'Making Haste Less Slowly: ASEAN from 1975', in Alison Broinowski (ed.) *Understanding ASEAN*, London: Macmillan, 1982, pp. 37–69.

Irvine, Roger, 'The Formative Years of ASEAN: 1967–75', in Alison Broinowski (ed.) *Understanding ASEAN*, London: Macmillan, 1982, pp. 8–36.

Ito, Takatoshi, 'A Case for a Coordinated Basket for Asian Countries', Paper prepared for the report of the study group on Exchange Rate Regimes for Asia, Kobe Research Project, 2002. Online. Available: http://www.mof.go.jp/jouhou/kokkin/tyousa/kobe_e.htm.

'Jakarta Resolution on Sustainable Development', Jakarta, 30 October 1987. Online. Available: http://www.aseansec.org/6081.htm.

'Japan, ASEAN kick off first round of formal FTA negotiations', *Japan Economic Newswire*, 12 April 2005.

'Japan Calls for Malaysia to Scrap Tariff on Farm Exports', *Japan Economic Newswire*, 21 July 2004.

'Japan may Halt FTA Talks with S. Korea for Ones with Other Nations', *Asia Pulse*, 25 February 2004.

'Japan Pushing for FTAs to Shore Up Presence in Asia', *Japan Economic Newswire*, 17 September 2004.

'Japan to Propose Letting Qualified Filipino Nurses Work Indefinitely', *Japan Economic Newswire*, 25 October 2004.

'Japan to Skip Proto-EAEC Meet, inviting SE Asia Anger', *Japan Economic Newswire*, 10 April 1995.

Jayasuriya, Kanishka (ed.), *Governing the Asia Pacific: Beyond the 'New Regionalism'*, Basingstoke: Palgrave, 2004.

Jayasuriya, Kanishka and Andrew Rosser, 'Economic Crisis and the Political Economy of Economic Liberalisation in South-East Asia', in Gary Rodan, Kevin Hewison and Richard Robison (eds) *The Political Economy of South-East Asia: Conflicts, Crises and Change* (2nd edn), Melbourne: Oxford University Press, 2001, pp. 233–58.

Jervis, Robert, 'Security Regimes', *International Organization*, 1982, vol. 36, no. 2, pp. 357–78.

Johnston, Alastair, 'Is China a Status Quo Power?', *International Security*, 2003, vol. 27, no. 4, pp. 5–56.

'Joint Japan-China study to examine FTA impact', *The Daily Yomiuri*, 19 October 2004.

Jomo, K. S. (ed.), *Southeast Asian Paper Tigers? From Miracle to Debacle and Beyond*, New York: Routledge, 2003.

Kalland, Arne and Gerard Persoon (eds), *Environmental Movements in Asia*, London: RoutledgeCurzon, 1999.

Kasahara, Shigehisa, 'The Flying Geese Paradigm: A Critical Study of its Applications to East Asian Regional Development', *UNCTAD Discussion Papers No. 169*, April 2004.

Kassim, Yang Razali, 'ASEAN and the Hashimoto Doctrine', *Business Times*, 15 January 1997.

Katzenstein, Peter, 'Regionalism in Comparative Perspective', *Cooperation and Conflict*, 1996, vol. 31, no. 2, pp. 123–60.

Katzenstein, Peter, 'Introduction: Asian Regionalism in Comparative Perspective', in Peter Katzenstein and Takashi Shiraishi (eds) *Network Power: Japan and Asia*, Ithaca, NY: Cornell University Press, 1997, pp. 1–46.

Katzenstein, Peter, 'Regionalism in Asia', in Shaun Breslin, Christopher Hughes, Nicola Phillips and Ben Rosamond (eds) *New Regionalisms in the Global Political Economy: Theories and Cases*, London: Routledge, 2002, pp. 104–18.

Katzenstein, Peter and Nobuo Okawara, 'Japan, Asian-Pacific Security, and the Case for Analytical Eclecticism', *International Security*, 2001/2, vol. 26, no. 3, pp. 153–85.

Katzenstein, Peter, Robert Keohane and Stephen Krasner, 'International Organization and the Study of World Politics', *International Organization*, 1998, vol. 52, no. 4, pp. 645–85.

Kaur, Karamit, '3-nation Open Skies Agreement on Cargo', *The Straits Times*, 26 February 2004.

Kazmin, Amy, 'Singapore and Thailand Seek Bilateral Deals', *Financial Times*, 8 October 2003.

Keck, Margaret and Kathryn Sikkink, *Activists Beyond Borders – Advocacy Networks in International Politics*, Ithaca, NY: Cornell University Press, 1998.

Kelly, James, 'US Policy in East Asia and the Pacific: Challenges and Priorities', Testimony before the Subcommittee on East Asia and the Pacific, House Committee on International Relations, 12 June 2001.

Kelly, James, 'US-East Asia-Pacific Relations', Statement before the Subcommittee on East Asia and the Pacific, House International Relations Committee, 14 February 2002.

Keohane, Robert, *After Hegemony: Cooperation and Discord in the World Political Economy*, Princeton, NJ: Princeton University Press, 1984.

Kerkvliet, Ben, Russell Heng and David Koh, *Getting Organized in Vietnam – Moving in and Around the Socialist State*, Singapore: Institute of Southeast Asian Studies, 2003.

Khosa, Meshack and Yvonne Muthien, *Regionalism in the New South Africa*, Aldershot: Ashgate, 1998.

Kikuta, Masanori, 'US Opposed Plan to Form New Asian Economic Group', *Japan Economic Newswire*, 5 March 1991.

Kilby, Christopher, 'Sovereignty and NGOs', in Kendall Stiles (ed.) *Global Institutions and Local Empowerment – Competing Theoretical Perspectives*, Basingstoke: Macmillan, 2000, pp. 48–64.

Kim, Chang Jin and Lee Jong-Wha, 'Exchange Rate Regimes and Monetary Independence in East Asia', Paper prepared for a conference on 'Linkages in East Asia: Implications for Currency Regimes and Policy Dialogue', Joint Australia–Japan

Research Project on Future Financial Arrangements in East Asia, Seoul, 23–24 September 2002.

Kim, Samuel, 'Northeast Asia in the Local-Regional-Global Nexus: Multiple Challenges and Contending Explanations', in Samuel Kim (ed.) *The International Relations of Northeast Asia*, Lanham, MD: Rowman & Littlefield, 2004, pp. 3–65.

Kin, Kwan Weng, 'From "Japan passing" to "Japan bashing"?', *The Straits Times*, 19 November 1998.

Kirshner, Jonathan, 'Disinflation, Structural Change, and Distribution', *Review of Radical Political Economics*, 1998, vol. 30, no. 1, pp. 53–89.

Klintworth, Gary, *Vietnam's Intervention in Cambodia in International Law*, Canberra: Australian Government Printing Service, 1989.

Koizumi, Junichiro, *Japan and ASEAN in East Asia – A Sincere and Open Partnership*, 14 January 2002. Online. Available: http://www.mofa.go.jp/region/asia-paci/pmv0201/speech.html.

Kojima, Kiyoshi, 'The "Flying Geese" Model of Asian Economic Development: Origin, Theoretical Extensions and Regional Policy Implications', *Journal of Asian Economics*, 2000, vol. 11, no. 4, pp. 375–401.

Korhonen, Pekka, 'The Theory of the Flying Geese Pattern of Development and its Interpretations', *Journal of Peace Research*, 1994, vol. 31, no. 1, pp. 93–108.

Kuroda, Haruhiko and Masahiro Kawai, 'Strengthening Regional Financial Cooperation in East Asia', in Gordon de Brouwer and Wang Yunjong (eds) *Financial Governance in East Asia: Policy Dialogue, Surveillance and Cooperation*, London: RoutledgeCurzon, 2004, pp. 136–66.

Kwan, C. H., 'A yen bloc in Asia', *Journal of the Asia Pacific Economy*, 1996, vol. 1, no. 1, pp. 1–21.

Kwan, C. H., *Yen Bloc: Toward Economic Integration in Asia*, Washington, DC: Brookings Institution Press, 2001.

Lagon, Mark, 'The Illusions of Collective Security', *The National Interest*, Summer 1995, vol. 40, pp. 50–55.

Landsberg, Martin and Paul Burkett, 'Contradictions of Capitalist Industrialization in East Asia: A Critique of "Flying Geese" Theories of Development', *Economic Geography*, 1998, vol. 74, no. 2, pp. 87–110.

Laursen, Finn (ed.), *Comparative Regional Integration: Theoretical Perspectives*, Aldershot: Ashgate, 2003.

Lawan, Thanadsillapakul, *Open Regionalism and Deeper Integration: The Implementation of ASEAN Investment Area (AIA) and ASEAN Free Trade Area (AFTA)*, Thailand: Institute of International Business and Economic Law Studies, 2000.

Lawrence, Robert, *Regionalism, Multilateralism and Deeper Integration*, Washington, DC: The Brookings Institution, 1996.

Lee, Siew Hua, 'Thailand Agrees to Hold First Europe-Asia Summit', *The Straits Times*, 10 March 1995.

Lee, Yok-shiu and Alvin So (eds), *Asia's Environmental Movements: Comparative Perspectives*, Armonk, NY: M.E. Sharpe, 1999.

Leifer, Michael, 'The ASEAN Regional Forum', *Adelphi Paper No. 302*, London: Oxford University Press, 1996.

Lejot, Paul, Douglas Arner, Liu Qiao, Mylene Chan and Marshall Mays, 'Asia's Debt Capital Markets Appraisal & Agenda for Policy Reform', *HKIEBS Working Paper No. 1072*, Hong Kong, September 2003.

Lim, Linda Y.C., 'Free Market Fancies: Hong Kong, Singapore, and the Asian Financial Crisis', in T. J. Pempel (ed.) *The Politics of the Asian Economic Crisis*, Ithaca, NY: Cornell University Press, 1999, pp. 101–15.

Lincoln, Edward, *East Asian Economic Regionalism*, Washington, DC: The Brookings Institution, 2004.

'Li Peng is Supportive of East Asia Market Idea', *Japan Economic Newswire*, 13 December 1990.

Litzinger, Ralph, 'Damming the Angry River', *China Review No. 30*, November 2004. Online. Available: http://www.gbcc.org.uk/30article3.htm.

Low, Linda, 'Multilateralism, Regionalism, Bilateral and Crossregional Free Trade Arrangements: All Paved with Good Intentions for ASEAN', *Asia Economic Journal*, 2003, vol. 17, no. 1, pp. 65–86.

MacIntyre, Andrew, *The Power of Institutions: Political Architecture and Governance*, Ithaca, NY: Cornell University Press, 2003.

MacLean, Sandra, Fahimul Quadir and Timothy Shaw (eds), *Crises of Governance in Asia and Africa*, Aldershot: Ashgate, 2001.

MacLeod, Gordon, 'New Regionalism Reconsidered: Globalization and the Remaking of Political Economic Space', *International Journal of Urban and Regional Research*, 2001, vol. 25, no. 4, pp. 804–29.

MacNamara, Kathleen, *The Currency of Ideas: Monetary Politics in the European Union*, Ithaca, NY: Cornell University Press, 1998.

'Mahathir Hints at Japan-ASEAN Summit before G-7 Talks', *Japan Economic Newswire*, 27 March 1997.

Makkonen, Katri, 'Mekong Cooperation: The Linkages between Poverty, Environment, and Transboundary Water Management in Southwest China's Yunnan Province'. Online. Available: http://www.helsinki.fi/nacs/finland2005/papers/makkonen.pdf.

'Malaysia to Initiate East Asian Trade Bloc', *Japan Economic Newswire*, 10 December 1990.

'Manila Declaration on the ASEAN Environment', Manila, 30 April 1981. Online. Available: http://www.asean.sec.org/6077.htm.

Manoli, Panagiota, 'The Formation of Black Sea Economic Cooperation: A Case of Subregionalism', Ph.D. Thesis, University of Warwick, 2003.

Manor, James, 'Civil Society under Different Types of Governments', Online paper, Civil Society and Governance Programme, Institute of Development Studies. Available: http://www.ids.ac.uk/civsoc/PolicyBriefs/policy10.doc.

Mansfield, Edward and Helen Milner (eds), *The Political Economy of Regionalism*, New York: Columbia University Press, 1997.

Mansfield, Edward and Helen Milner, 'The New Wave of Regionalism', *International Organization*, 1999, vol. 53, no. 3, pp. 589–627.

Marozzi, Justin, 'ASEAN Single Currency Mooted', *Financial Times*, 25 July 1998.

Masuyama, Seiichi, 'The Role of Japan's Direct Investment in Restoring East Asia's Dynamism: Focus on ASEAN', in Seiichi Masuyama, Donna Vandenbrink and Chia Siow Yue (eds) *Restoring East Asia's Dynamism*, Singapore: Institute of Southeast Asian Studies, 2000, pp. 213–58.

Mattli, Walter, *The Logic of Regional Integration: Europe and Beyond*, Cambridge: Cambridge University Press, 1999.

McGowan, B., 'Trade Bloc not Endorsed', *Courier Mail*, 18 March 1991.

McKinnon, Ronald, 'Euroland and East Asia in a Dollar-Based International Monetary System: Mundell Revisited', in Guillermo Calvo, Rudi Dornbusch and Maurice Obstfeld (eds) *Money, Capital Mobility and Trade: Essays in Honor of Robert A. Mundell*, Cambridge, MA: MIT Press, 2001, pp. 413–29.

Midford, Paul, 'Japan's Leadership Role in East Asian Security Multilateralism: The Nakayama Proposal and the Logic of Reassurance', *The Pacific Review*, 2000, vol. 13, no. 3, pp. 367–97.

Milintachinda, Piamsak, Mario Artaza and David Parsons, *APEC 2003 Outcomes and Outlook for 2004: What it Means for the Region*, Singapore: Institute of Southeast Asian Studies, 2004.

Milner, Anthony and Deborah Johnson, 'The Idea of Asia', in John Ingleson (ed.) *Regionalism, Subregionalism and APEC*, Melbourne: Monash Asia Institute, 1997, pp. 1–19.

Milner, Helen, 'International Theories of Cooperation among Nations: Strengths and Weaknesses', *World Politics*, 1992, vol. 44, no. 3, pp. 466–94.

Mittelman, James, 'Rethinking the "New Regionalism" in the Context of Globalization', *Global Governance*, 1996, vol. 2, no. 2, pp. 189–214.

Mittelman, James (ed.), *The Globalization Syndrome: Transformation and Resistance*, Princeton, NJ: Princeton University Press, 2000.

Mittermeier, Russell, Patricio Gil, Michael Hoffman, John Pilgrim, Thomas Brooks, Cristina Mittermeier, John Lamoreux, Gustavo de Fonseca, Harrison Ford (Foreword) and Peter Seligmann (Preface), *Hotspots Revisited: Earth's Richest and Most Endangered Terrestrial Ecoregions*, Washington, DC: Conservation International, 2005. Online. Available: http://www.biodiversityhotspots.org/xp/Hotspots/hotspotsScience/hotspots_revisited.xml.

'Monks and Nuns in Southeast Asia Pledge to Save their Forests', *ARC Alliance of Religions and Conservation News and Resources*, 16 June 2004. Online. Available: http://www.arcworld.org/news.asp?pageID = 57.

Montaperto, Ronald, 'Smoothing the Wrinkles', in *Comparative Connections (An E-Journal on East Asian Bilateral Relations)*, Second Quarter 2004. Online. Available: http://www.csis.org/pacfor/cc/0402Qchina_asean.html.

Moravcsik, Andrew, *The Choice for Europe: Social Purpose and State Power from Messina to Maastricht*, Ithaca, NY: Cornell University Press, 1998.

Munakata, Naoko, 'Whither East Asian Economic Integration?', *RIETI Discussion Paper Series*, June 2002. Online. Available: http://www.rieti.go.jp/en/publications/dp/02e007.pdf.

Muni, Sukh Deo, *China's Strategic Engagement with the New ASEAN: An Exploratory Study of China's Post-Cold War Political, Strategic and Economic Relations with Myanmar, Laos, Cambodia and Vietnam*, Monograph No. 2, Singapore: Institute of Defence and Strategic Studies, 2002.

Narine, Shaun, 'ASEAN and the Idea of an "Asian Monetary Fund": Institutional Uncertainty in the Asia Pacific', in Andrew Tan and Kenneth Boutin (eds) *Non-Traditional Security Issues in Southeast Asia*, Singapore: Institute of Defence and Strategic Studies, 2001, pp. 227–56.

Narine, Shaun, *Explaining ASEAN: Regionalism in Southeast Asia*, Boulder, CO: Lynne Rienner, 2002.

National Institute for Environmental Research, 'Report of the First Meeting of the National Focal Points', North East Asian Centre for Environmental Data and Training, 14–16 February 2001. Online. Available: http://www.nier.go.kr/nierdepart/board/bbs/bview.php?sm=&p_headid=12&p_seq=1&p=1.

Ngiam, Kee Jin, 'The Future of Financial Cooperation in East Asia', *The Journal of East Asian Affairs*, Spring/Summer 2003, vol. XVII, no. 1, pp. 121–47.

Ngoo, Irene, 'Many keen on Asia-Europe summit', *The Straits Times*, 3 May 1995.

Ngoo, Irene and Song Tan Kin, 'Japan wants NZ, Aussies in Asia-EU Summit', *The Straits Times*, 25 July 1995.

Nishihara, Masashi, 'The Role of the Japan-US Alliance for Northeast Asian Security', *Japan Close-up*, September 1996, p. 7.

'N. Korea and US Spar at ASEAN Forum', *Financial Times*, London, 26 July 2001.

Ohmae, Kenichi, *The End of the Nation State: The Rise of Regional Economies*, New York: Free Press, 1996.

Ohno, Kenichi, 'Exchange Rate Management in Developing Asia: Reassessment of the Pre-crisis Soft Dollar Zone', Asian Development Bank Institute Paper, Japan: Tokyo, 1999.

Oman, Charles, 'Globalization, Regionalization, and Inequality', in Andrew Hurrell and Ngaire Woods (eds) *Inequality, Globalization and World Politics*, Oxford: Oxford University Press, 1999, pp. 36–65.

Othman, Zulkifli, 'Australia, NZ Fail to Get Meet Invitation', *Business Times*, 1 August 1995.

Pangestu, Mari and Sudarshan Gooptu, 'New Regionalism: Options for East Asia', in Kathie Krumm and Homi Kharas (eds) *East Asia Integrates: A Trade Policy Agenda for Shared Growth*, Washington, DC: World Bank and Oxford University Press, 2004, pp. 39–58.

Pednekar, Sunil, 'NGOs and Natural Resource Management in Southeast Asia', *TDRI Quarterly Newsletter*, September 1995, vol. 10, no. 3. Online. Available: http://www.gdrc.org/ngo/thai-ngo.html.

Pelagidis, Theodore and Harry Papasotiriou, 'Globalization or Regionalism? States, Markets, and the Structure of International Trade', *Review of International Studies*, 2002, vol. 28, no. 3, pp. 519–35.

Perkmann, Markus and Sum Ngai-Ling (eds), *Globalization, Regionalization and Cross-Border Regions*, Basingstoke: Palgrave, 2002.

'Philippine, S. Korean Central Banks Ink bilateral Swap Deal', *Asia Pulse*. 18 October 2005.

'Philippines, Singapore Settle Petrochem Tariff Dispute', *AFX News Limited*, 9 September 2003.

Phillips, Nicola, 'Regionalist Governance in the New Political Economy of Development: "Relaunching" Mercosur', *Third World Quarterly*, 2001, vol. 22, no. 4, pp. 565–83.

Phillips, Nicola, 'Governance after Financial Crisis: South American Perspectives on the Reformulation of Regionalism', in Shaun Breslin, Christopher Hughes, Nicola Phillips and Ben Rosamond (eds) *New Regionalisms in the Global Political Economy: Theories and Cases*, London: Routledge, 2002, pp. 66–81.

Phillips, Nicola, *The Southern Cone Model: The Political Economy of Regional Capitalist Development in Latin America*, London: Routledge, 2004.

Pillsbury, Michael, 'The Future of the ARF: An American Perspective', in Khoo How San (ed.) *The Future of the ARF*, Singapore: Institute of Defence and Strategic Studies, 1999, pp. 133–51.

Powell, Colin, Roundtable with ASEAN Journalists, Washington, DC, 25 July 2002. Online. Available: http://www.state.gov/secretary/rm/2002/12207.htm.

Preventive Diplomacy: Charting A Course for the ASEAN Regional Forum, CSCAP CSBM International Working Group Report, Pacific Forum CSIS, July 2002. Online. Available: http://www.csis.org/pacfor/issues/3-02.htm.

Quinn, Andrew, 'Indonesia to Replant Mangroves in Tsunami Defense', Reuters, 18 January 2005. Online. Available: http://www.forestsandtradeasia.org/posting/Indonesia/English/287.

Rajan, Ramkishen, 'Examining the Case for an Asian Monetary Fund', *Visiting Researcher Series No. 3*, Singapore: Institute of Southeast Asian Studies, February 2000.

Rajan, Ramkishen, 'Examining the Case for Currency Basket Regimes for Southeast Asia', *Visiting Researcher Series No. 1*, Singapore: Institute of Southeast Asian Studies, January 2000.

Rajan, Ramkishen, 'Financial and Macroeconomic Co-operation in ASEAN: Issues and Policy Initiatives', in Mya Than (ed.) *ASEAN Beyond the Crisis: Challenges and Initiatives*, Singapore: Institute of Southeast Asian Studies, 2001, pp. 126–47.

Rajaretnam, M., 'Principles in Crisis: The Need for New Directions', in Kao Kim Hourn (ed.) *ASEAN's Non-Interference Policy: Principles under Pressure?*, London: ASEAN Academic Press, 2000, pp. 37–50.

Ramakrishna, Kumar, '9/11, American Praetorian Unilateralism, and the Impact on State-Society Relations in Southeast Asia', *Working Paper No. 26*, Singapore: Institute of Defence and Strategic Studies, June 2002.

Ramkisken, Rajan, 'Examining the Case for an Asian Monetary Fund', *Working Paper No. 3*, Singapore: Institute of Southeast Asian Studies, 2000.

RAPIDC International Co-operation, *Air Pollution in Megacities*. Online. Available: http://www.york.ac.uk/inst/sei/rapidc2/apma.html.

Rautner, Mario, Martin Hardiono and Raymond Alfred, 'Borneo: Treasure Island at Risk', WWF Germany, June 2005. Online. Available: http://www.panda.org/downloads/forests/treasureislandatrisk.pdf.

Ravenhill, John, *APEC and the Construction of Pacific Rim Regionalism*, Cambridge: Cambridge University Press, 2001.

Ravenhill, John, 'The New Bilateralism in the Asia Pacific', *Third World Quarterly*, 2003, vol. 24, no. 2, pp. 299–317.

Rawley, Anthony, 'Asian Bond Fund Set for Launch', *The Business Times Singapore*, 2 June 2003.

'Recommendations of the High-Level Task Force on ASEAN Economic Integration', 7 October 2003. Online. Available: http://www.aseansec.org/hltf.htm.

Regional Centre for Biodiversity Conservation, 23 February 2005. Online. Available: http://www.arcbc.org/default.asp.

Reifer, Thomas, 'Geopolitics, Globalization and Alternative Regionalisms: Possibilities for Global Peace, Democracy and Social Justice', Paper presented at the ASEM4People Conference in Copenhagen, Denmark, 19–23 September 2002.

Reimann, Kim, 'Building Networks from the Outside In: International Movements, Japanese NGOs, and the Kyoto Climate Conference', *Mobilization*, 2003, vol. 6, no. 1, pp. 69–82.

Robles, Alfredo, *The Political Economy of Interregional Relations: ASEAN and the EU*, Aldershot: Ashgate, 2004.

Rodan, Gary, Kevin Hewison and Richard Robison (eds), *The Political Economy of South-East Asia: Conflicts, Crises and Change* (2nd edn), Melbourne: Oxford University Press, 2001.

Rosamond, Ben, *Theories of European Integration*, Basingstoke: Macmillan, 2000.

Rosecrance, Richard and Peter Schott, 'Concerts and Regional Intervention', in David Lake and Patrick Morgan (eds) *Regional Orders: Building Security in a New World*, Pennsylvania State University Press, 1997, pp. 140–64.

Ross, Robert, 'The Geography of the Peace: East Asia in the Twenty-first Century', *International Security*, Spring 1999, vol. 23, no. 4, pp. 81–118.

Roth, Stanley, *Remarks at Closing Plenary Session of the World Economic Forum*, Hong Kong, 15 October 1997.

Rowley, Anthony, 'Moves To Bolster Regional Currency Swap Arrangement', *Business Times Singapore*, 5 May 2005.

Rozman, Gilbert, 'Flawed Regionalism: Reconceptualizing Northeast Asia in the 1990s', *The Pacific Review*, 1998, vol. 11, no. 1, pp. 1–27.

Rozman, Gilbert, *Northeast Asia's Stunted Regionalism: Bilateral Distrust in the Shadow of Globalization*, New York: Cambridge University Press, 2004.

Rozman, Gilbert, 'Russian Foreign Policy in Northeast Asia', in Samuel Kim (ed.) *The International Relations of Northeast Asia*, Lanham, MD: Rowman & Littlefield, 2004, pp. 201–24.

Saich, Tony, 'Negotiating the State: The Development of Social Organizations in China', *China Quarterly*, March 2000, no. 161, pp. 124–41.

Sakakibara, Eisuke, *Nihon to sekai ga furueta hi* [The Days Japan and the World were Shaken], Tokyo: Chuokoronshinsha, 2000.

Salvatore, Dominick, 'Protectionism and World Welfare: Introduction', in Dominick Salvatore (ed.) *Protectionism and World Welfare*, Cambridge: Cambridge University Press, 1993, pp. 1–17.

Sandhu Kernial Singh *et al.* (eds), *The ASEAN Reader*, Singapore: Institute of Southeast Asian Studies, 1992.

Sato, Koichi, 'EAEC koso to ASEAN+3 hikoshiki shunokaigi' [EAEC idea and ASEAN+3 informal leaders meeting], *Toa No. 404*, February 2001, p. 64.

Sato, Koichi, *ASEAN Rejime: ASEAN niokeru kaigi gaiko no hatten to kadai* [ASEAN Regime: Development of and challenges for conference diplomacy of ASEAN], Tokyo: Keiso shobo, 2003, pp. 84–103.

Schak, David and Wayne Hudson (eds), *Civil Society in Asia*, Aldershot: Ashgate, 2003.

'Scholars question benefits of FTA between S. Korea, China, Japan', *Asia Pulse*, 13 September 2004.

Schreurs, Miranda (forthcoming) 'Regional Security and Cooperation in the Protection of Marine Environments in Northeast Asia' in In-taek Hyun and Miranda Schreurs (eds) *The Environmental Dimension of Asian Security: Conflict and Cooperation over Pollution, Energy and Natural Resources*, Washington, DC: United States Institute of Peace Press.

Schreurs, Miranda and Dennis Pirages, *Ecological Security in Northeast Asia*, Seoul: Yonsei University Press, 1998.

Schulz, Michael, Fredrik Söderbaum and Joakim Ojendal (eds), *Regionalization in a Globalizing World*, London: Zed, 2001.

Scott, Allen and Michael Storper, 'Regions, Globalization, Development', *Regional Studies*, 2003, vol. 37, nos 6 and 7, pp. 579–93.

Scott, James, 'European and North American Contexts for Cross-border Regionalism', *Regional Studies: The Journal of the Regional Studies Association*, 1999, vol. 33, no. 7, pp. 605–17.

Segal, Gerald, 'North-East Asia: Common Security or à la carte?', *International Affairs*, 1991, vol. 67, no. 4, pp. 755–67.

Severino, Rodolfo, 'Towards an ASEAN Security Community', *Trends in Southeast Asia Series No. 8*, Singapore: Institute of Southeast Asian Studies, February 2004.

Shaw, Tim, 'New Regionalisms in Africa in the New Millennium: Comparative Perspectives on Renaissance, Realisms and/or Regressions', *New Political Economy*, 2000, vol. 5, no. 3, pp. 399–414.

Shigetomi, Shinichi (ed.), *The State and NGOs – Perspectives from Asia*, Singapore: Institute of Southeast Asian Studies, 2002.

Shin, Kwanho and Wang Yunjong, 'Monetary Integration Ahead of Trade Integration in East Asia', Paper prepared for 'Linkages in East Asia: Implications for Currency Regimes and Policy Dialogue conference', Seoul, 23–24 September 2002.

Shin-wha Lee, 'South Korea's Strategy for Inter-Korean Relations and Regional Security Cooperation', in See Seng Tan and Amitav Acharya (eds) *Asia-Pacific Security Cooperation: National Interests and Regional Order*, London: M.E. Sharpe, 2004, pp. 106–26.

Shorrock, Tim, 'Asia Shifting Towards Economic Regionalism', *Inter-Press Service*, 28 June 2004.

Siddique, Sharon and Sree Kumar (eds), *The Second ASEAN Reader*, Singapore: Institute of Southeast Asian Studies, 2003.

Simon, Sheldon, 'The ASEAN Regional Forum Views the Councils for Security Cooperation in the Asia Pacific: How Track II Assists Track I', *NBR Analysis*, July 2002, vol. 13, no. 4, pp. 5–23.

'Singapore, China to Launch FTA Talks in November', *Japan Economic Newswire*, 14 May 2004.

'Six-Party Talks Process: Now and Beyond', *Yonhap News*, 24 November 2004.

'S. Korea, ASEAN Hold First Meeting to Discuss Free Trade Pact', *Asia Pulse*, 21 February 2005.

'S. Korea, ASEAN Start FTA Study Talks', *Asia Pulse*, 8 March 2004.

'S. Korea, ASEAN to Discuss Trade Framework Agreement this WK', *Asia Pulse*, 7 June 2005.

'S. Korea, Singapore Conclude FTA', *Xinhua*, 29 November 2004.

Smart, Alan, 'The Emergence of Local Capitalisms in China: Overseas Chinese Investment and Pattern of Development', in Li Si-Ming and Tang Wing-Shing (eds) *China's Regions, Polity, & Economy: A Study of Spatial Transformation in the Post-Reform Era*, Hong Kong: University of Hong Kong Press, 2000, pp. 65–96.

'S.M. Lee, Kissinger Rap US Policy Towards China', *The Straits Times Weekly Edition*, Singapore, 20 November 1993, p. 5.

Söderbaum, Fredrik, *The Political Economy of Regionalism: The Case of Southern Africa*, Basingstoke: Palgrave, 2004.

Söderbaum, Fredrik and Timothy Shaw (eds), *Theories of New Regionalism: A Palgrave Reader*, Basingstoke: Palgrave, 2003.

Söderbaum, Fredrik and Ian Taylor (eds), *Regionalism and Uneven Development in Southern Africa: The Case of the Maputo Development Corridor*, Aldershot: Ashgate, 2003.

Soesastro, Hadi, 'East Asia Economic Cooperation: In Search of an Institutional Identity', Paper presented at the 14th Asia-Pacific Roundtable, Kuala Lumpur, June 2000.

Soesastro, Hadi, 'ASEAN in 2030: The Long View', in Simon Tay, Jesus Estanislao and Hadi Soesastro (eds) *Reinventing ASEAN*, Singapore: Institute of Southeast Asian Studies, 2003, pp. 273–310.

Soh, Felix, Susan Sim and Ho Wah Foon, 'Hashimoto Doctrine Seen as Move to Engage ASEAN as Equal Partner', *The Straits Times*, 22 January 1997.

Solidum, Estrella, *The Politics of ASEAN: An Introduction to Southeast Asian Regionalism*, Singapore: Eastern Universities Press, 2003.

Solingen, Etel, 'Economic Liberalization, Political Coalitions, and Emerging Regional Order', in David Lake and Patrick Morgan (eds) *Regional Orders: Building Security in a New World*, University Park, PA: Pennsylvania State University Press, 1997.

Solingen, Etel, *Regional Orders at Century's Dawn: Global and Domestic Influences on Grand Strategy*, Princeton, NJ: Princeton University Press, 1998.

Solingen, Etel, 'ASEAN, *Quo Vadis*? Domestic Coalitions and Regional Cooperation', *Contemporary Southeast Asia*, 1999, vol. 21, no. 1, pp. 30–54.

Sopiee, Noordin, 'East Asian Dream and What it Means', *New Strait Times*, 19 January 1991.

'South Korea, ASEAN Reach Draft Framework Free Trade Agreement', *BBC Monitoring Asia Pacific – Political*, 21 April 2005.

'South Korea Hopes to Sign FTA with ASEAN Late 2005', *Global News Wire – Asia Africa Intelligence Wire*, 10 June 2005.

Stiglitz, Joseph, 'The Post Washington Consensus Consensus', Columbia University Initiative for Policy Dialogue Working Paper, 2004.

Stiles, Kendall (ed.), *Global Institutions and Local Empowerment. Competing Theoretical Perspectives*, Basingstoke: Macmillian Press, 2000.

Stokhof, Wim and Paul Van Der Velde (eds), *Asian-European Perspectives: Developing the ASEM Process*, Richmond: Curzon Press, 2001.

Stubbs, Richard, 'ASEAN+3: Emerging East Asian Regionalism?', *Asian Survey*, 2002, vol. 42, no. 3, pp. 440–55.

'Summit between ASEAN, Japan, China, S. Korea Proposed', *Japan Economic Newswire*, 20 February 1997.

Sun Ge, 'How Does Asia Mean? (Part 1)', *Inter-Asia Cultural Studies*, 2000, vol. 1, no. 1, pp. 13–47.

Sun, Yuting, 'China Opposes Japanese Leaders' Visits to Yasukuni Shrine', *Zhongguo Xinwen She News Agency*, 29 September 2005.

Surin Pitsuwan, 'Currency Turmoil in Asia: The Strategic Impact', Remarks made at the Asia Pacific Roundtable, Kuala Lumpur, 1 June 1998.

Tan, Ricardo, Filologo Pante and George Abonyi, 'Economic Cooperation in the Greater Mekong Subregion', in Kiichiro Fukasaku (ed.) *Regional Co-operation and Integration in Asia*, Paris: OECD, 1995.

'Tariff Among ASEAN Countries Reduced Sharply', *Xinhua*, July 2001, p. 27.

Tay, Simon, Jesus Estanislao and Hadi Soesastro (eds), *Reinventing ASEAN*, Singapore: Institute of Southeast Asian Studies, 2001.

Tecson, Gwendolyn, 'Confronting Regionalism in Asia: A View from the Philippines', in Ryokichi Hirono (ed.) *Regional Co-operation in Asia*, ASEAN Development Experience, Singapore: Institute of Southeast Asian Studies, 2003, vol. 3, pp. 73–91.

Tellis, Ashley and Michael Wills, 'Strategic Asia by the Numbers', in Ashley Tellis and Michael Wills (eds) *Strategic Asia 2004–05: Confronting Terrorism in the Pursuit of Power*, Seattle and Washington, DC: The National Bureau of Asian Research, 2004, pp. 495–511.

Teo, Poh Keng, '"Hashimoto Doctrine" takes Japan Step Closer to ASEAN', *The Nikkei Weekly*, 20 January 1997.

Terada, Takashi, 'Directional Leadership in Institution-building: Japan's Approaches to ASEAN in the Establishment of PECC and APEC', *The Pacific Review*, 2001, vol. 14, no. 2, pp. 195–220.

Teresa, Maria, 'E. Asian Economic and Security Forum Pushed', *Japan Economic Newswire*, 8 October 1999.

Termsak, Chalermpalanupap, 'ASEAN+3: An ASEAN Perspective', in James Chin and Nicholas Thomas (eds) *China and ASEAN: Changing Political and Strategic Ties*, Hong Kong: Centre of Asian Studies, 2005, pp. 19–38.

Thakur, Ramesh and Edward Newman (eds), *Broadening Asia's Security Discourse and Agenda: Political, Social, and Environmental Perspectives*, Tokyo: United Nations University Press, 2004.

'Thanks, but No Thanks for Taipei's APEC Plan', *The China Post*, 28 November 1997.

Thant, Myo Min Tang and Hiroshi Kakazu (eds), *Growth Triangles in Asia: A New Approach to Regional Economic Cooperation*, Oxford: Oxford University Press, 1994.

'The Concepts of Comprehensive Security and Cooperative Security', *CSCAP Memorandum No. 3.* Online. Available: http://www.cscap.org/publications.htm.

Thomas, Nick, 'ASEAN+3: C/community Building in East Asia', *Journal of International and Asia Studies*, 2001, vol. 8, no. 2, pp. 1–19.

Thomas, Nick, 'Building an East Asian Community: Origins, Structure, and Limits', *Asian Perspective*, 2002, vol. 26, no. 4, pp. 83–112.

'Trilateral Cooperation on FTA, Energy Urged', *The Korea Times*, 23 October 2004.

Tow, William, *Asia-Pacific Strategic Relations: Seeking Convergent Security*, Cambridge: Cambridge University Press, 2001.

'Tsunami Death Toll', CNN, 20 February 2005. Online. Available: http://www.cnn.com /2004/WORLD/asiapcf/12/28/tsunamideaths.

Turner, Jennifer and Wu Fengshui, 'Green NGO and Environmental Journalist Forum, Hong Kong Conference Report', 9–10 April 2001. Online. Available: http://wwics.si.edu/ topics/pubs/cgreen-en-1.pdf.

Ullman, Richard, 'Redefining Security', *International Security*, 1983, vol. 8, no. 1, pp. 129–53.

'US to Boost Asia Ties Through APEC, Regional Forum', *The Straits Times*, 21 July 1994.

Uvin, Peter, 'From Local Organisations to Global Governance: The Role of NGOs in International Relations', in Kendall Stiles (ed.) *Global Institutions and Local Empowerment – Competing Theoretical Perspectives*, Basingstoke: Macmillan, 2000, pp. 9–29.

Väyrynen, Raimo, 'Regionalism: Old and New', *International Studies Review*, 2003, vol. 5, no. 1, pp. 25–52.

'Vietnam Invites 3 State Leaders to ASEAN Hanoi Summit', *Japan Economic Newswire*, 3 August 1998.

Virabongsa, Ramangkura, 'Japan must introduce an Asian Currency', *Japan Echo*, 26 June 1999.

Warleigh, Alex, 'In Defence of Intra-disciplinarity: "European Studies", the "New Regionalism", and the Issue of Democratisation', *Cambridge Journal of International Relations*, 2004, vol. 17, no. 2, pp. 301–18.

Wallace, Helen, 'The Institutional Setting: Five Variations on a Theme', in Helen Wallace and William Wallace (eds) *Policy-making in the European Union* (4th edn), Oxford: Oxford University Press, 2000, pp. 3–37.

Wallace, Helen, 'Europeanisation and Globalisation: Complementary or Contradictory Trends?', in Shaun Breslin, Christopher Hughes, Nicola Phillips and Ben Rosamond (eds) *New Regionalisms in the Global Political Economy: Theories and Cases*, London: Routledge, 2002, pp. 137–49.

Walt, Stephen, 'Alliance Formation and the Balance of World Power', *International Security*, Spring 1985, vol. 9, no. 4, pp. 3–43.

Walter, Andrew, *World Power and World Money: The Role of Hegemony and International Monetary Order*, New York: Harvester Wheatsheaf, 1993.

Wang, Yongqiang, 'Gao Yaojie: A Crusader for AIDS Prevention', *China Pictorial*, 4 February 2005. Online. Available: http://www.china-pictorial.com/chpic/htdocs/ English/content/200502/3-1.htm.

Wang, Yunjong, 'Instruments and Techniques for Financial Cooperation', in Gordon de Brouwer and Yunjong Wang (eds) *Financial Governance in East Asia: Policy Dialogue, Surveillance and Cooperation*, London: RoutledgeCurzon, 2004, pp. 189–215.

Watanabe, Kenichiro, Hiroshi Akama and Jun Mifune, 'The Effectiveness of Capital Controls and Monitoring: The Case for the Non-Internationalization of Emerging Market Economies', *EMEAP Discussion Paper*, January 2002.

Weber, Steve, 'Shaping the Postwar Balance of Power: Multilateralism in NATO', in John
    Ruggie (ed.) *Multilateralism Matters: The Theory and Praxis of an Institutional Form*, New
    York: Columbia University Press, 1993, pp. 233–92.
Webber, Douglas, 'Two Funerals and a Wedding? The Ups and Downs of Regionalism in
    East Asia and Asia-Pacific after the Asian Crisis', *The Pacific Review*, 2001, vol. 14, no.
    3, pp. 339–72.
Wei, Kiat Yip, 'Prospects for Closer Economic Integration in East Asia', *Stanford Journal of
    East Asian Affairs*, Spring 2001, vol. 1, pp. 106–11.
Williamson, John, 'The Case for a Common Basket Peg for East Asian Currencies', in
    Stefan Collignon, Jean Pisani-Ferry and Yung Chul Park (eds) *Exchange Rate Policies in
    Emerging Asian Countries*, London: Routledge, 1999, pp. 327–43.
Wu, Fengshui, 'Double-mobilization: Transnational Advocacy Networks for China's Envi-
    ronment and Public Health', Ph.D. dissertation, University of Maryland, 2005.
Yahuda, Michael, *The International Politics of the Asia-Pacific, 1945–1995*, London: Rout-
    ledge, 1996.
Yam, Joseph, 'Asian Monetary Cooperation', Per Jacobsson Lecture, Hong Kong, 21
    September 1997. Online. Available: http://www.info.gov.hk/hkma/eng/speeches/
    speechs/joseph/speech_210997b.htm.
Yamakage, Susumu, *ASEAN pawa: Ajia Taiheiyo no chukaku he* [ASEAN Power: Toward the
    core of Asia Pacific], Tokyo: University of Tokyo Press, 1997.
Yamamoto, Tadashi, 'Summary Report on the Osaka Symposium on Philanthropic
    Development and Cooperation in Asia Pacific', in Tadashi Yamamoto (ed.) *Emerging
    Civil Society in the Asia Pacific Community*, Singapore: Institute of Southeast Asian Studies,
    1995.
Yeo, George, 'Building an ASEAN Economic Community', Speech at the AFTA seminar,
    Jakarta, 31 January 2002. Online. Available: http://www.aseansec.org/13080.htm;
    ASEAN.
Yeo Lay Hwee, 'ASEM: Looking Back, Looking Forward', *Contemporary Southeast Asia*,
    2000, vol. 22, no. 1, pp. 113–44.
Yeoh En-lai, 'Southeast Asian Nations to Set up Environment Fund', Associated Press, 14
    October 2004. Online. Available: http://www.climateark.org/articles/reader.
    asp?linkid=35706.
Yoon, Esook, Shin-wah Lee and Fengshui Wu (forthcoming), 'The State and Nongovern-
    mental Organizations in Northeast Asia's Environmental Security', in In-taek Hyun
    and Miranda Schreurs (eds) *The Environmental Dimension of Asian Security: Conflict and
    Cooperation over Pollution, Energy and Natural Resources*, Washington, DC: United States
    Institute of Peace Press.
Yoon, Y, 'Multilateral Cooperation in Northeast Asia and Inter-Korean Relations', Paper
    presented at the Trilateral International Seminar on 'Peace and Cooperation in North-
    east Asia', Seoul, 13 April 2001.
Zarsky, Lyuba, 'The Domain of Environmental Cooperation in Northeast Asia', Paper
    prepared for the Sixth Annual International Conference, Korea and the Future of
    Northeast Asia: Conflict of Cooperation?, Portland State University, 4–5 May 1995.
    Online.   Available: http://www.nautilus.org/archives/papers/enviro/zarsky_
    domain.html.
Zha, Daojiong, 'Chinese Considerations of "Economic Security"', *Journal of Chinese Polit-
    ical Science*, 1999, vol. 5, no. 1, pp. 69–87.
Zhang, Jun, *Enhanced China-ASEAN Cooperation with the Framework of FEALAC*, China-
    ASEAN Occasional Paper Series, Hong Kong: Centre of Asian Studies, 2004.

Zweig, David, *Internationalizing China: Domestic Interests, Global Linkages*, Ithaca, NY: Cornell University Press, 2002.

Official documents (not otherwise referenced)

'Annex', ASEAN Security Community Plan of Action, Vientiane, 29 November 2004.

APEC Economic Leaders' Declaration of Common Resolve, Bogor, 15 November 1994. Online. Available: http://www.apec.org/apec/leaders——declarations/1994.downloadlinks.0001.LinkURL. Download.ver5.1.9.

ASEAN-People's Republic of China. Online. Available: http://www.aseansec.org/4979.htm.

ASEAN Socio-Cultural Community Plan of Action, Vientiane, 29 November 2004.

Bangkok Summit Declaration of 1995, Bangkok, 14–15 December 1995. Online. Available: http://www.aseansec.org/2081.htm.

Chairman's Press Statement on ASEAN Third Informal Summit, Manila, 28 November 1999.

Chairman's Statement of the Fifth Asia-Europe Meeting, Hanoi, 8–9 October 2004. Online. Available: http://europa.eu.int/comm/external_relations/asem/asem_summits/asem 5/01_chair.pdf.

Chairman's Statement of the First ASEAN + China, Japan, Korea (ASEAN+3) Deputy Finance Ministers and Deputy General Bank Governors Meeting, 18 March 1999.

'Declaration of ASEAN Concord II (Bali Concord II)', Bali, 7 October 2003. Online. Available: http://www.aseansec.org/15160.htm.

Chairperson's Press Statement of the Second Meeting of the ASEAN Ministers Responsible for Culture and Arts (AMCA) and the AMCA Plus Three, Bangkok, 4 August 2005.

East Asian Vision Group, 'Letter of Transmittal', *Towards an East Asian Community: Region of Peace, Prosperity and Progress*, 31 October 2001.

East Asia Vision Group Report, *Towards an East Asian Community: Region of Peace, Prosperity and Progress*, 31 October 2001.

Final Report of the East Asia Study Group, ASEAN+3 Summit, Phnom Penh, 4 November 2002.

For a Better Tomorrow: Asia-Europe Partnership in the Twenty-first Century, Asia–Europe Vision Group Report, 1999.

Forging Closer ASEAN-China Economic Relations in the Twenty-First Century, A Report Submitted by the ASEAN–China Expert Group on Economic Cooperation, October 2001. Online. Available: http://www.aseansec.org/newdata/asean_chi.pdf.

Framework Agreement on Comprehensive Economic Co-operation Between the Association of South East Asian Nations and the People's Republic of China, Phnom Penh, 4 November 2002. Online. Available: http://www.aseansec.org/13196.htm.

Framework Agreement on Comprehensive Economic Cooperation Between the Association of Southeast Asian Nations and the Republic of India, Bali, 8 October 2003.

Framework for Comprehensive Economic Partnership between the Association of Southeast Asian Nations and Japan, Bali, 8 October 2003.

German Bundestag Study Commission (Select Committee), *Globalisation of the World Economy – Challenges and Responses*, 2001. Online. Available:http://www.bundestag.de/gremien/welt/welt_zwischenbericht/zwb003_vorw_einl_engl.pdf.

IHA/1055, UNEP/283, 'UNEP Post-Tsunami Assessment Finds Environmental Impacts in Maldives'. Online. Available: http://www.un.org/News/Press/docs/2005/iha1055.doc.htm.

Introduction to the ASEM Process. Online. Available: http://europa.eu.int/comm/external_relations/asem/asem_process/index_process.htm.

Joint Communiqué of the Sixth Tripartite Environment Ministers Meeting among Korea, China and Japan, Tokyo, 4–5 December 2004. Online. Available: http://eng.me.go.kr/user/global/bilateral/3_bilateral.html?msel = c3#.

Joint Communiqué Twenty-fifth ASEAN Ministerial Meeting, Manila, 21–22 July 1992. Online. Available: http://www.aseansec.org/1167.htm.

Joint Press Release Inaugural Meeting of the ASEAN Investment Area Council, Manila, October 1998.

Joint Press Statement, Korea-Singapore FTA Joint Study Group, 7 October 2003.

Joint Press Statement of the Eighth Informal ASEAN Ministerial Meeting on the Environment and the Third ASEAN+3 Environment Ministers Meeting, Singapore, 13–14 October 2004. Online. Available: http://www.aseansec.org/16481.htm.

Joint Statement of the Ninth Informal ASEAN Ministerial Meeting on the Environment, Makati City, 28 September 2005. Online. Available: http://www.aseansec.org/17776.htm.

Joint Statement on East Asia Cooperation, Manila, 28 November 1999. Online. Available: http://www.aseansec.org/691.htm.

Korean Ministry of National Defense, International Cooperation Division, 'The Concept of Regional Multilateral Security Cooperation'. Online. Available: http://www.mnd.go.kr/cms.jsp?p_id =00505030000000.

Network of East Asian Think Tanks, 'Towards an East Asian Community', Policy recommendations paper, submitted to the ASEAN+3 Summit, Vientiane, 29–30 November 2004.

News Release, Ninth ASEAN Ministerial Meeting on the Environment, Yangon: 17–18 December 2003. Online. Available: http://www.aseansec.org/15520.htm.

Press Release, First ASEAN+3 Environment Ministers Meeting, 21 November 2002. Online. Available: http://www.aseansec.org/13402.htm.

Singapore Declaration of 1992, Singapore, 28 January 1992. Online. Available: http://www.aseansec.org/5120.htm and http://www.aseansec.org/1163.htm.

Statement on Cooperation for the Sustainable Development of the Mekong River Basin, 4 April 1995. Online. Available: http://www.hartford-hwp.com/archives/54/205.html.

The ASEAN Regional Forum: A Concept Paper, Bandar Seri Begawan, August 1995. Online. Available: http://www.aseansec.org/3826.htm.

The Hanoi Declaration, Sixth ASEAN Summit, Hanoi, 16 December 1998.

The Joint Ministerial Statement of the ASEAN+3 Finance Ministers Meeting, Chiang Mai, 6 May 2000.

The Joint Ministerial Statement of the ASEAN+3 Finance Ministers Meeting, Shanghai, 10 May 2002.

The Joint Ministerial Statement of the ASEAN+3 Finance Ministers Meeting, Makati, 7 August 2003.

The Joint Ministerial Statement of the ASEAN+3 Finance Ministers Meeting, 15 May 2004. Online. Available: http://www.aseansec.org.

The Joint Ministerial Statement of the Eighth ASEAN+3 Finance Ministers' Meeting, Istanbul, 4 May 2005.

The Joint Statement of the First ASEAN-India Summit, Phnom Penh, 5 November 2002.

'The Meeting between the ASEAN Heads of State/Government and the Leaders of the People's Republic of China, Japan and the Republic of Korea', *Press Release,* Hanoi, 16 December 1998.

The Twenty-third ASEAN Economic Ministers Meeting, Malaysia, 7–8 October 1991. Online. Available: http://www.aseansec.org/6126.htm.

The Twenty-fifth ASEAN Economic Ministers Meeting, Singapore, 7–8 October 1993. Online. Available: http://www.aseansec.org/6128.htm.

The Vientiane Action Programme (VAP) 2004–2010, Vientiane, November 2004.

United Nations Conference on Trade and Development, *Trade and Development Report 2004*, New York: The United Nations, 2004.

United Nations Conference on Trade and Development, *World Investment Report 2004: The Shift Towards Services*, New York: The United Nations, 2004.

United Nations Economic and Social Commission for Asia and the Pacific, Human Settlements, *Issue Paper on: Urban Environment Management in Asia and the Pacific*. Online. Available: http://www.unescap.org/huset/hangzhou/paper/urban_paper.htm.

United Nations Environment Programme, *Regional Networks of Ozone Officers*. Online. Available: http://www.uneptie/org/ozoneaction/aboutus/networks.asp.

United Nations Environment Programme, *The Status of Pollution Monitoring Regional Activity Centre (POMRAC) of UNEP Action Plan for the Protection, Management and Development of the Marine and Coastal Environment of the Northwest Pacific Region (NOWPAP)*, 11 March 2003. Online. Available: http://www.pomrac.dvo.ru/statpomr.htm.

United Nations Environment Programme, *Ozone Secretariat, Status of Ratification*. Online. Available:http://www.unep.org/ozone/Treaties_and_Ratification/2C_ratification.asp.

United Nations Environment Programme, 'Parties to the Convention on Biological Diversity', Secretariat of the Convention on Biological Diversity. Online. Available: http://www.biodiv.org/world/parties.asp.

United Nations Environment Programme, Press Release IHA/1055, UNEP/283, *Post-Tsunami Assessment Finds Environmental Impacts in Maldives*. Online. Available: http://www.un.org/News/Press/docs/2005/iha1055.doc.htm.

United Nations Environment Programme, Global Environment Facility, and UNEP/GEF South China Sea Project, *Review of Regional and Subregional Agreements and Soft Laws on Marine Environment in South China Sea*, UNEP/GEF/SCS/RTF-L.2/7, 19 April 2004.

United Nations Environmental Scientific Educational and Cultural Organization, 'UNESCO's Director-General Proposes a Tsunami Early Warning System at the World Conference on Disaster Reduction', 25 January 2005. Online. Available: http://www.portal.unesco.org/en/ev.php-URL_ID = 24780&URL_DO_TOPIC& URL_SECTION = 201.html.

United Nations Foundation, *United Nations Coordinates International Response to Tsunami*, 14 February 2005. Online. Available: http://www.unfoundation.org/files/pdf/2005/ UNroleintsunamirelief.pdf.

United Nations Framework Convention on Climate Change, Kyoto Protocol, Status of Ratification. Online. Available: http://www.unfccc.int/essential_background/kyoto_protocol/ status_of_ratification/items/2613.php.

United States Department of Defense, *The United States Security Strategy for the East Asia-Pacific Region*, 1998.

United States Department of Defense, *Quadrennial Defense Review Report*, 30 September 2001. Online. Available: http://www.defenselink.mil/pubs/qdr2001.pdf.

United States Department of State Dispatch, 'The Evolving Security Environment in the Asia-Pacific Region', 4 November 1991, vol. 2, no. 44. Online. Available: http://usembassy.org.nz / about / what / nz _ usrelations / evolve.pdf#search= Department%20of%20Defense,%20East%20Asia%20Strategic%20Initiative%20(EASI).

United States General Accounting Office, 'Climate Change Trends in Greenhouse Gas Emissions and Emissions Intensity in the United States and Other High-Emitting Nations', GAO-04-416R, 28 October 2003.

White House, *National Security Strategy of the United States of America*, September 2002. Online. Available: http://www.whitehouse.gov/nsc/print/nssall.html.

World Bank, *World Development Report*, Oxford: Oxford University Press, various years.

World Bank, 'Dramatic Decline in Global Poverty, But Progress Uneven', *World Development Indicators*, Washington, DC: World Bank Group, 23 April 2004. Online. Available: http://worldbank.org.

World Bank, 'East Asia and Pacific', *The World Bank Annual Report 1999*, New York: Oxford University Press.

Separately referenced websites

Asia for Animals Conference, Singapore, 22–24 June 2005. Online. Available: http://www.acres.org.sg/asiaforanimals/*ECOASIA*. Online. Available: http://www.ecoasia.org/.

Geohive: Global Statistics, 11 July 2005. Online. Available: http://www.geohive.com.

Greenpeace Southeast Asia. Online. Available: http://www.greenpeacesoutheastasia.org/en/seaabout.html.

Impacts Center Southeast Asia. Online. Available: http://www.icsea. biotrop.org/about.htm.

International Rivers Network's Southeast Asia. Online. Available: http://www.irn.org/programs/seasia/.

Japan Industrial Conference for Ozone Layer Protection. Online. Available: http://www.jicop.org/english/cooper_e.html.

Kita Kyushu's Environmental Initiatives. Online. Available: http://www.iges.or.jp/kitakyushu/main_outline_background.htm and http://www.kanmon.biz/kitakyushu/en/project/project03.html.

Prime Minister Hashimoto's Summit with ASEAN, 17 December 1997. Online. Available: http://www.mofa.go.jp/mofaj/kaidan/kiroku/s_hashi/arc_97/asean97/kaigi.html.

Rainforest web. Online. Available: http://www.rainforestweb.org/Rainforest_Regions/Asia/Indonesia/.

Rivers Watch East and Southeast Asia. Online. Available: http://www.rwesa.org/.

Southeast Asia Urban Environmental Management Applications Project. Online. Available: http://www.sea-uema.ait.ac.th/jar.htm.

SysTem for Analysis, Research, and Training. Online. Available: http://www.start.org/.

The 1979 Ramon Magsaysay Award for International Understanding. Online. Available: http://www.rmaf.org.ph/Awardees/Biography/BiographyASEAN.htm.

The Asia-Europe Meeting. Online. Available: http://www.mof.go.jp/english/asem.

The Organisation for Security and Cooperation in Europe. Online. Available: http://www.osce.org/.

Traffic International. Online. Available: http://www.traffic.org/news/combat.html.

WWF Indochina. Online. Available: http://www.wwfindochina.org.

Index

For Product Safety Concerns and Information please contact our EU
representative GPSR@taylorandfrancis.com
Taylor & Francis Verlag GmbH, Kaufingerstraße 24, 80331 München, Germany

9 780415 546874